# GHOST IN THE SHELL

## STAND ALONE COMPLEX

### EPISODE 3: IDOLATER

# 003

## Yu Kinutani

Translation by
Andria Cheng

Lettered by
Paige Pumphrey

**KODANSHA COMICS**

*Ghost In the Shell: Stand Alone Complex: Episode 3: Idolater is a work of fiction. Names, characters, places, and incidents are the products of the author's imagination or are used fictitiously. Any resemblance to actual events, locales, or persons, living or dead, is entirely coincidental.*

*A Kodansha Comics Trade Paperback Original*



*Published in the United States by Kodansha Comics, an imprint of Kodansha USA Publishing, LLC, New York.*

*Publication rights for this English edition arranged through Kodansha Ltd., Tokyo.*

*First published in Japan in 2011 by Kodansha Ltd., Tokyo.*

*ISBN 978-1-612-62094-7*

*Printed in the United States of America.*

*www.kodanshacomics.com*

*9 8 7 6 5 4 3 2*

Translator: Andria Cheng
Lettering: Paige Pumphrey

# GHOST IN
# THE SHELL
## STAND ALONE COMPLEX

EPISODE3 : IDOLATE

003

CONTENTS

# #019: Secret Visit

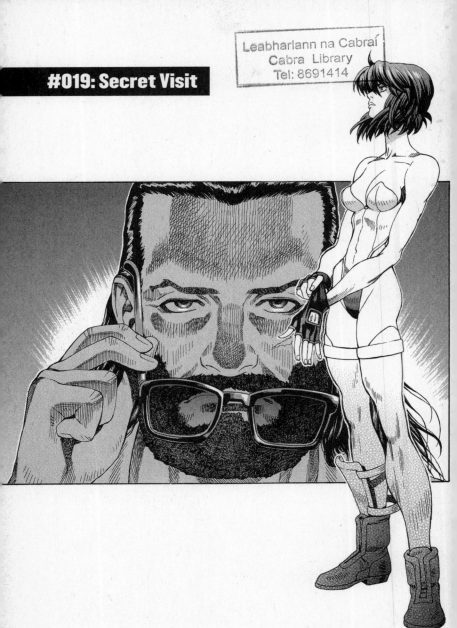

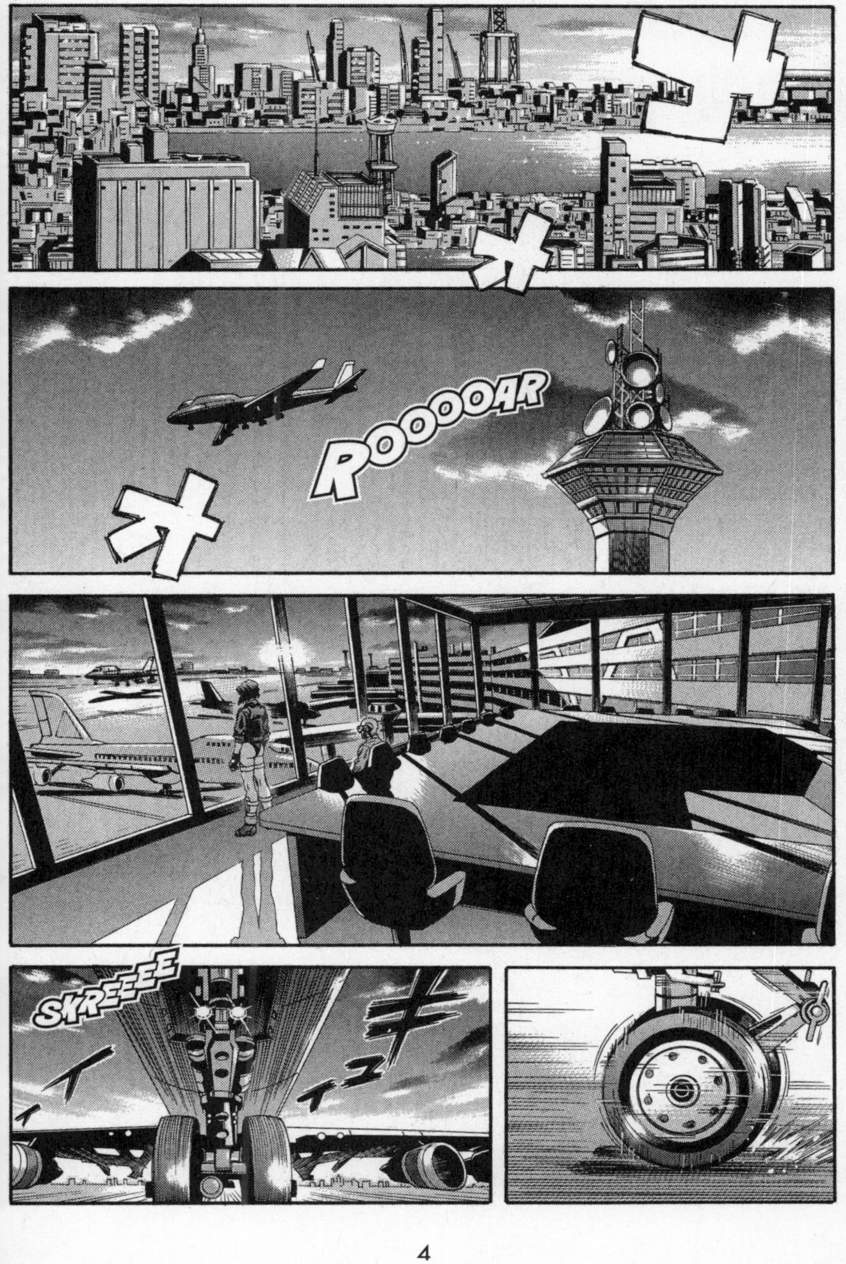
ROOOOAR
SKREEEE

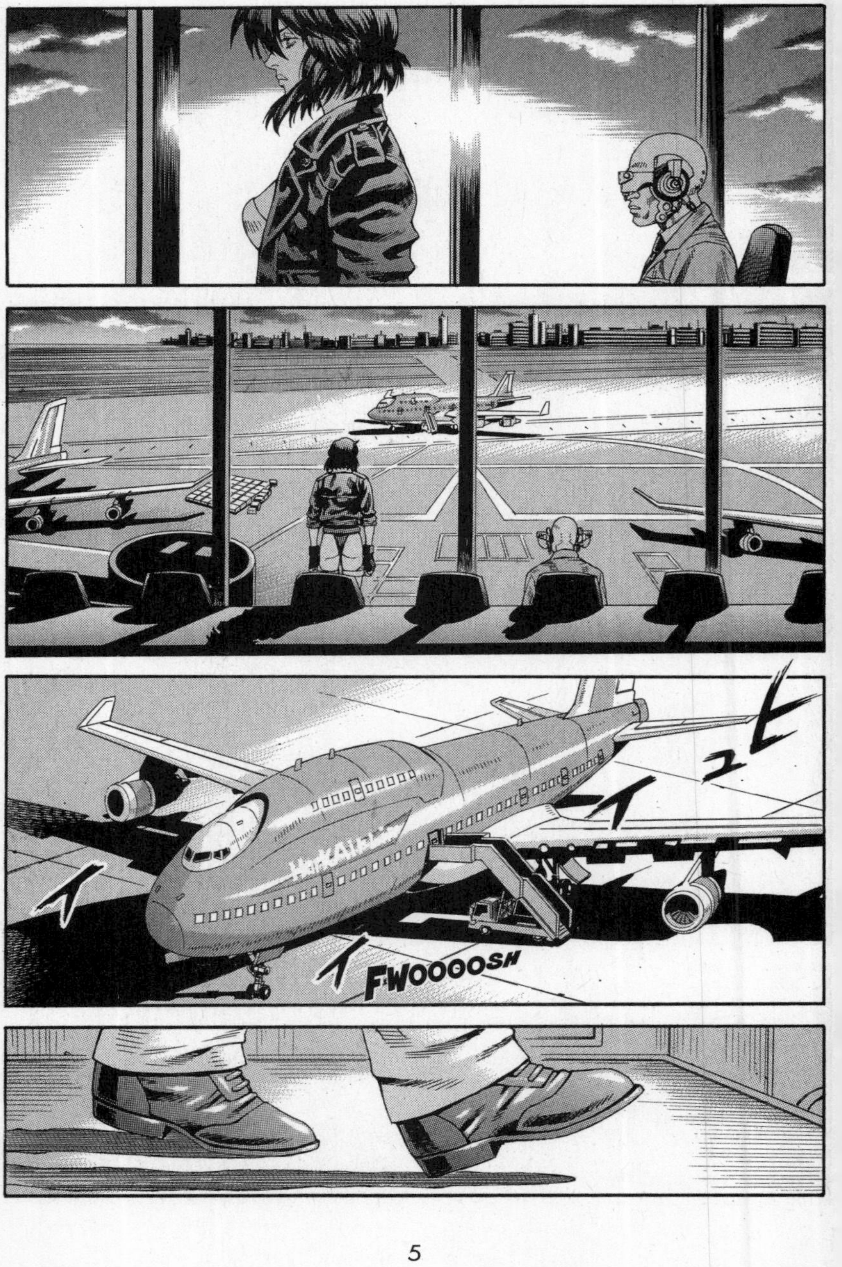
FWOOOOSH

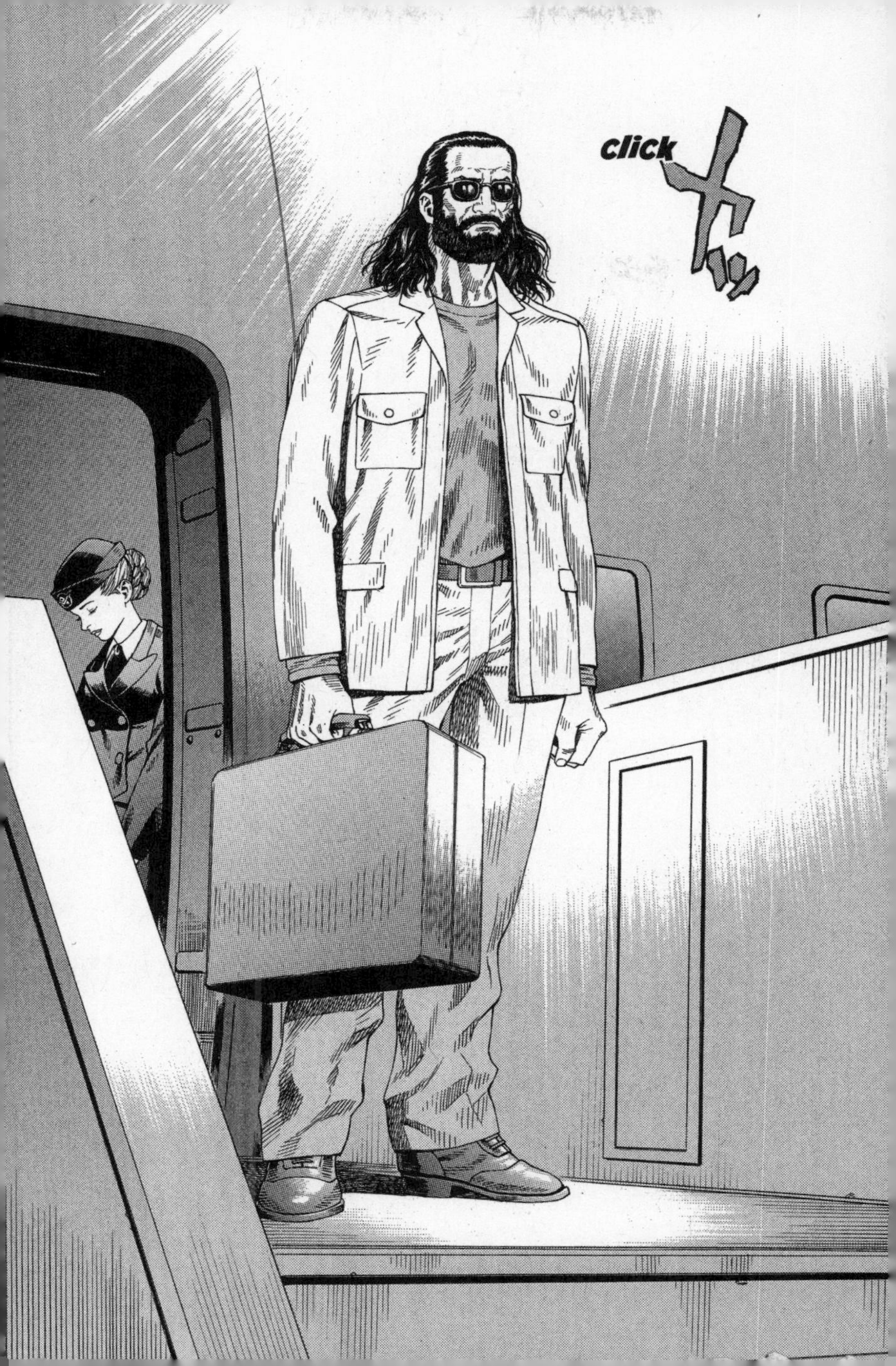
click

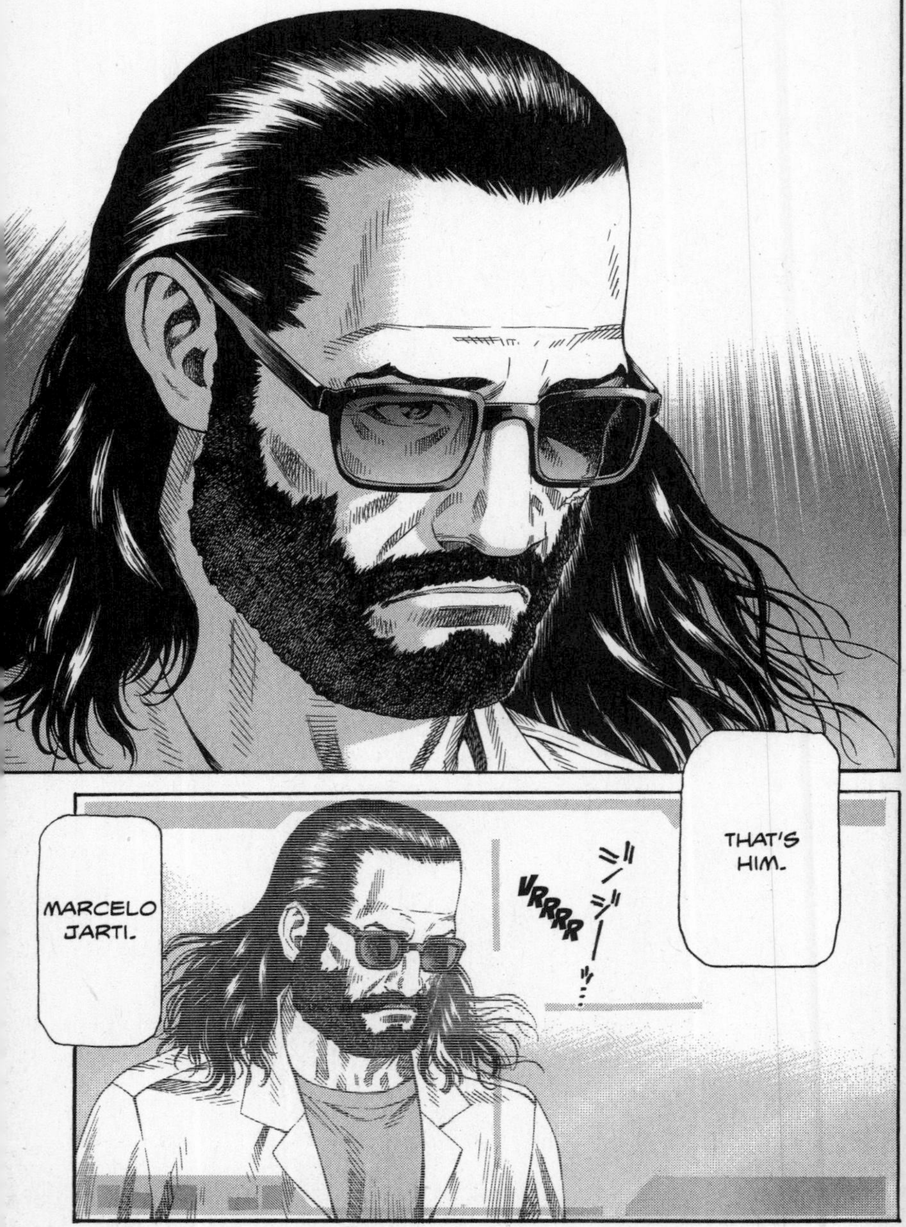
THAT'S HIM.
VRRRR
MARCELO JARTI.

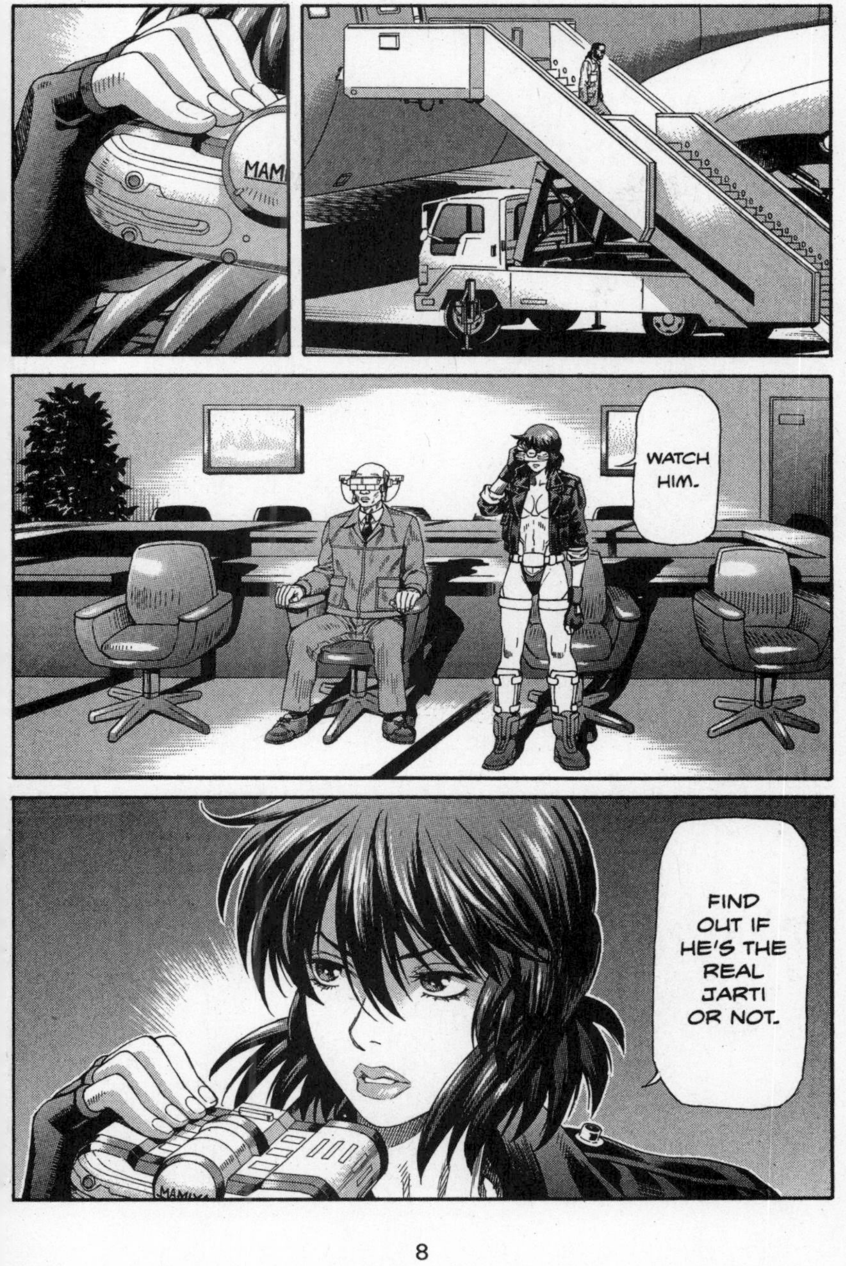
WATCH HIM.
FIND OUT IF HE'S THE REAL JARTI OR NOT.

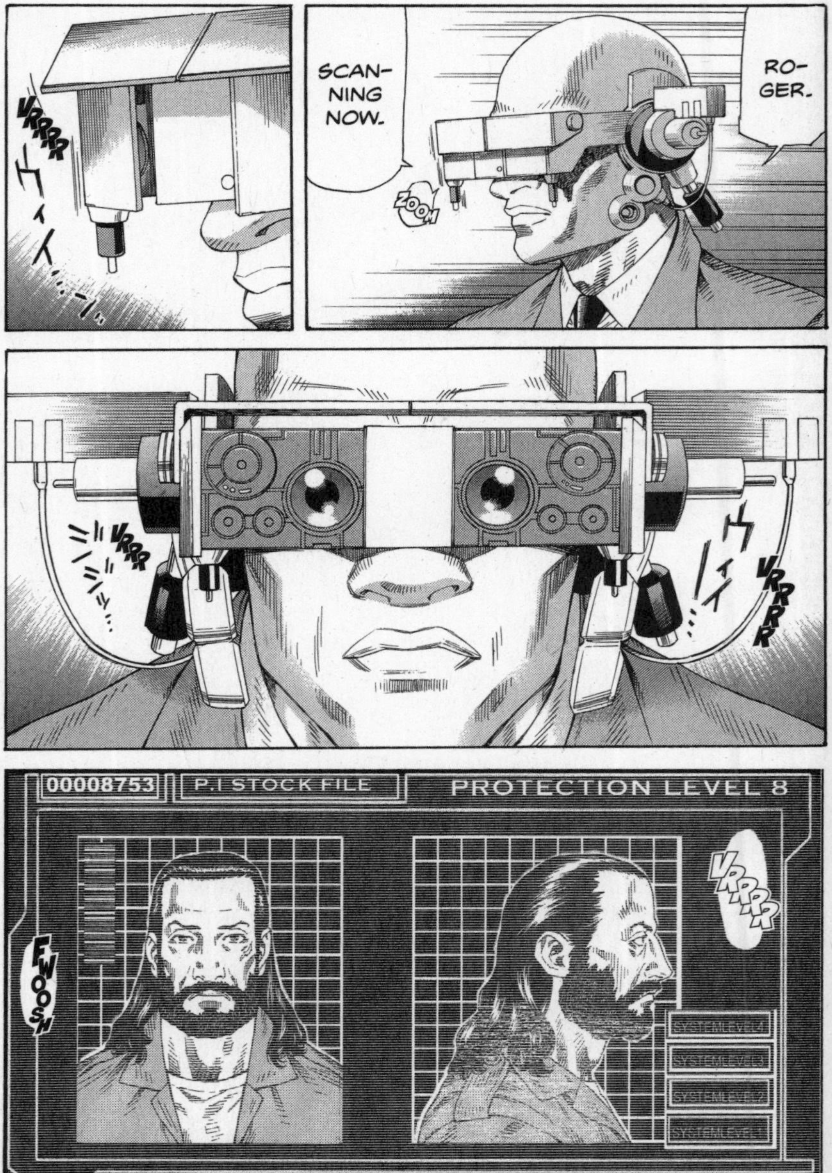
SCAN-NING NOW.
RO-GER.
ZOOM
VRRRR
VRRR
VRRRR
00008753
P.I STOCK FILE
PROTECTION LEVEL 8
VRRRR
FWOOSH
SYSTEMLEVEL4
SYSTEMLEVEL3
SYSTEMLEVEL2
SYSTEMLEVEL1

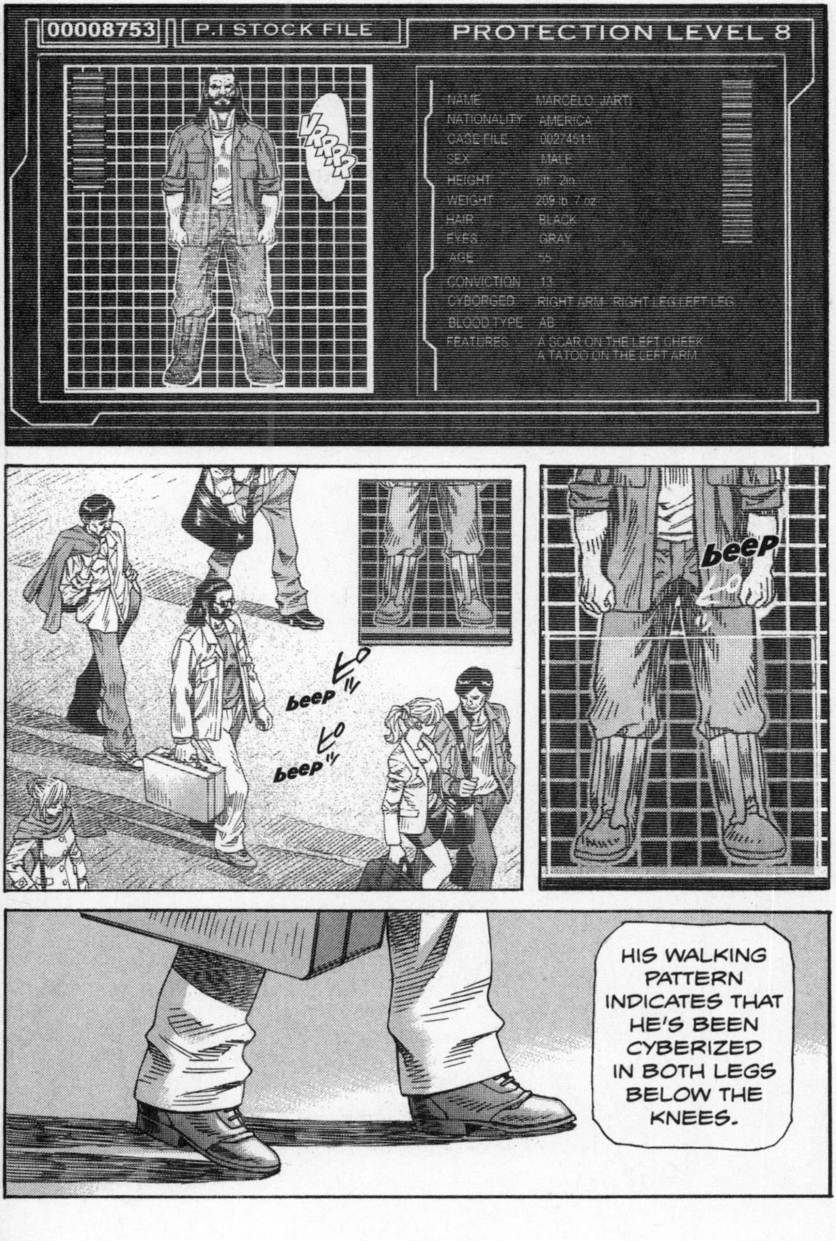
00008753
P.I STOCK FILE
PROTECTION LEVEL 8
VRRRR
NAME MARCELO JARTI
NATIONALITY AMERICA
CASE FILE 00274511
SEX MALE
HEIGHT 5ft 2in
WEIGHT 209 lb 7 oz
HAIR BLACK
EYES GRAY
AGE 55
CONVICTION 13
CYBORGED RIGHT ARM RIGHT LEG LEFT LEG
BLOOD TYPE AB
FEATURES A SCAR ON THE LEFT CHEEK
A TATOO ON THE LEFT ARM
beep
beep
beep
HIS WALKING PATTERN INDICATES THAT HE'S BEEN CYBERIZED IN BOTH LEGS BELOW THE KNEES.

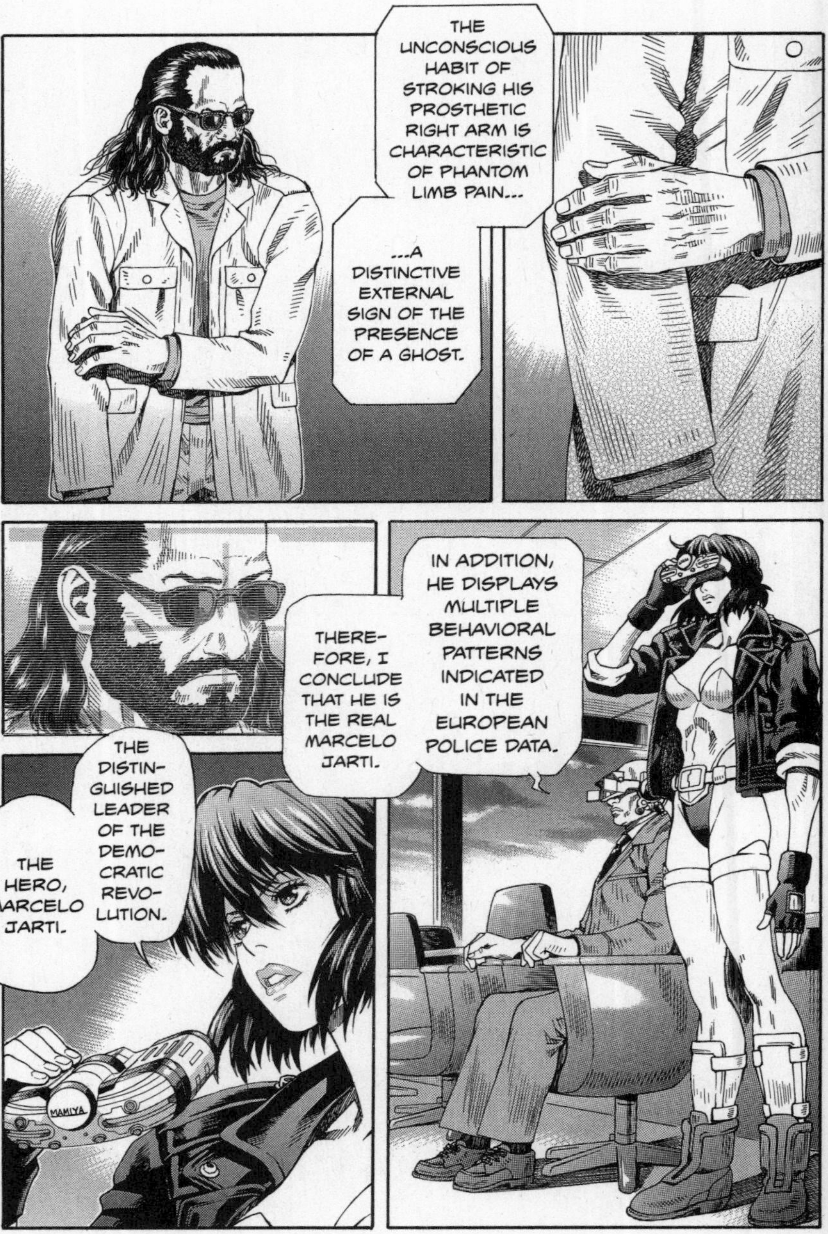

THE UNCONSCIOUS HABIT OF STROKING HIS PROSTHETIC RIGHT ARM IS CHARACTERISTIC OF PHANTOM LIMB PAIN...
...A DISTINCTIVE EXTERNAL SIGN OF THE PRESENCE OF A GHOST.
IN ADDITION, HE DISPLAYS MULTIPLE BEHAVIORAL PATTERNS INDICATED IN THE EUROPEAN POLICE DATA.
THEREFORE, I CONCLUDE THAT HE IS THE REAL MARCELO JARTI.
THE DISTINGUISHED LEADER OF THE DEMOCRATIC REVOLUTION.
THE HERO, MARCELO JARTI.
MAMIYA

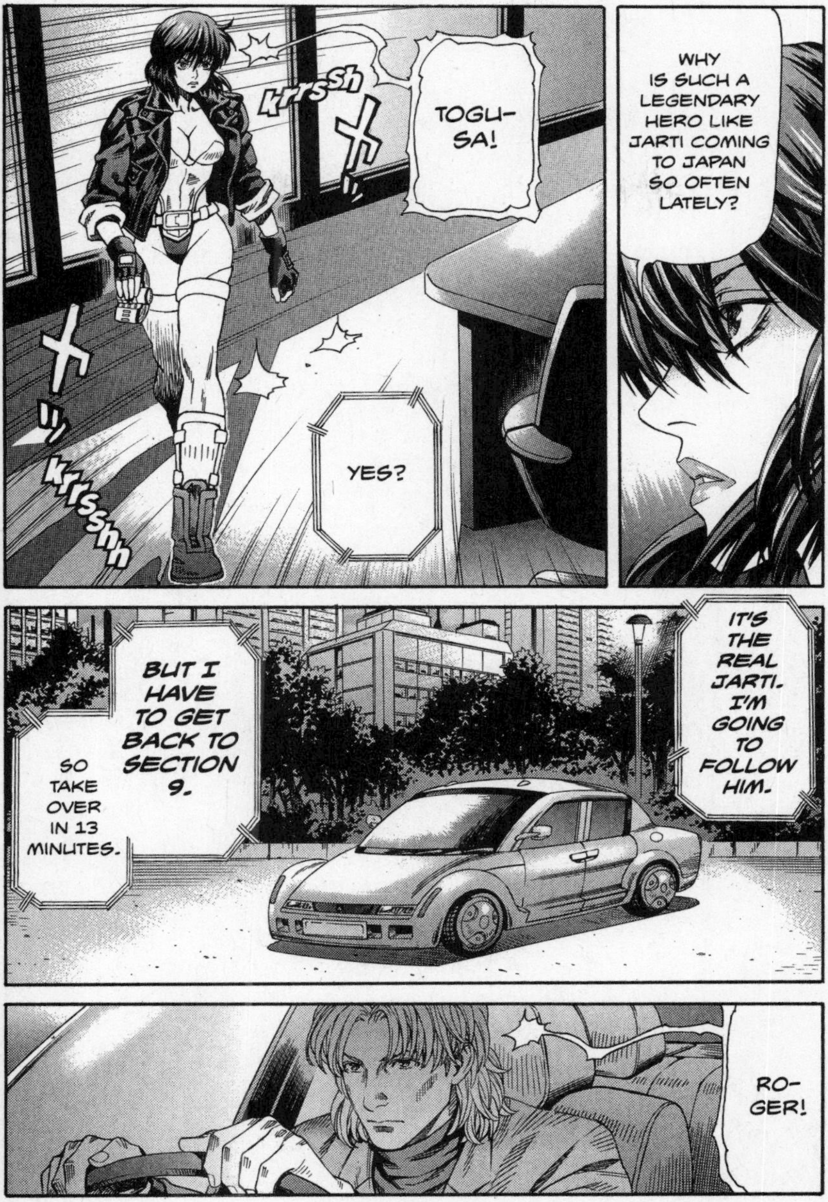
WHY IS SUCH A LEGENDARY HERO LIKE JARTI COMING TO JAPAN SO OFTEN LATELY?
krrsSh
TOGU-SA!
YES?
krrsshn
IT'S THE REAL JARTI. I'M GOING TO FOLLOW HIM.
BUT I HAVE TO GET BACK TO SECTION 9.
SO TAKE OVER IN 13 MINUTES.
RO-GER!

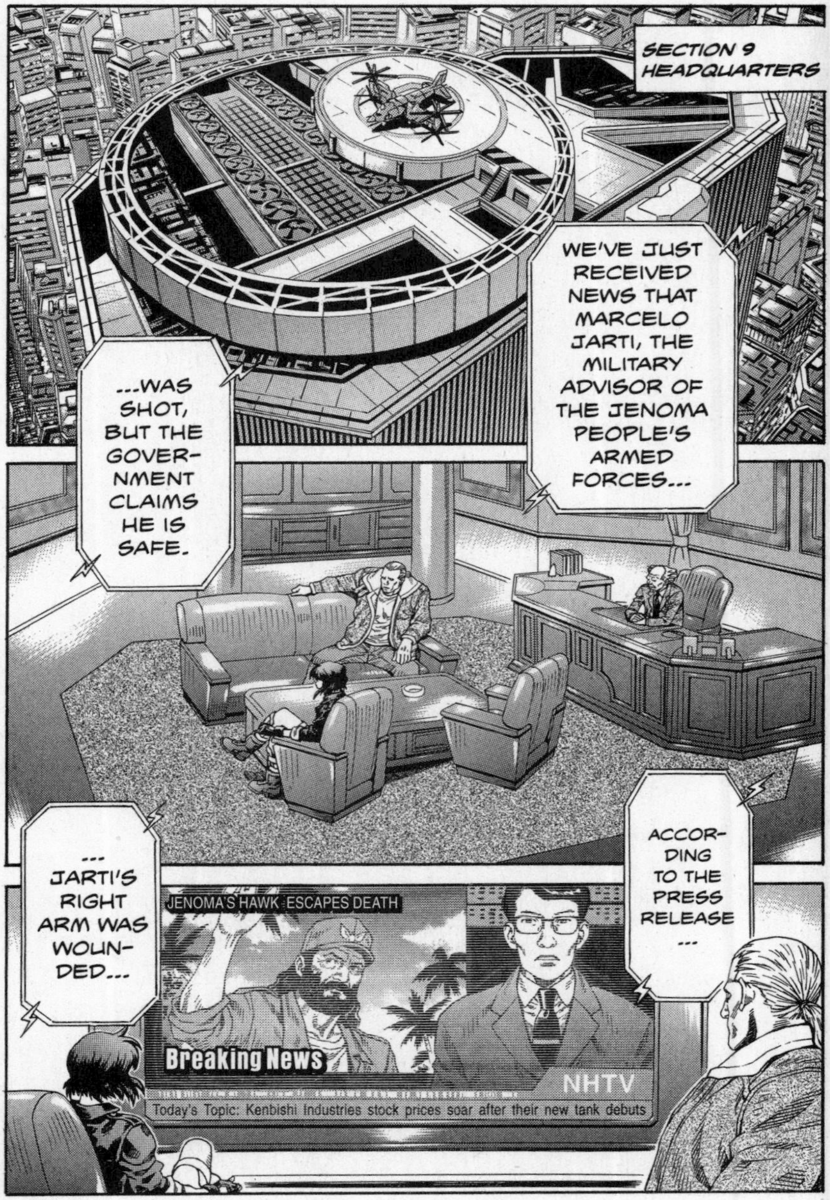
SECTION 9 HEADQUARTERS
WE'VE JUST RECEIVED NEWS THAT MARCELO JARTI, THE MILITARY ADVISOR OF THE JENOMA PEOPLE'S ARMED FORCES...
...WAS SHOT, BUT THE GOVERN-NMENT CLAIMS HE IS SAFE.
ACCOR-DING TO THE PRESS RELEASE...
...JARTI'S RIGHT ARM WAS WOUN-DED...
JENOMA'S HAWK ESCAPES DEATH
Breaking News
NHTV
Today's Topic: Kenbishi Industries stock prices soar after their new tank debuts

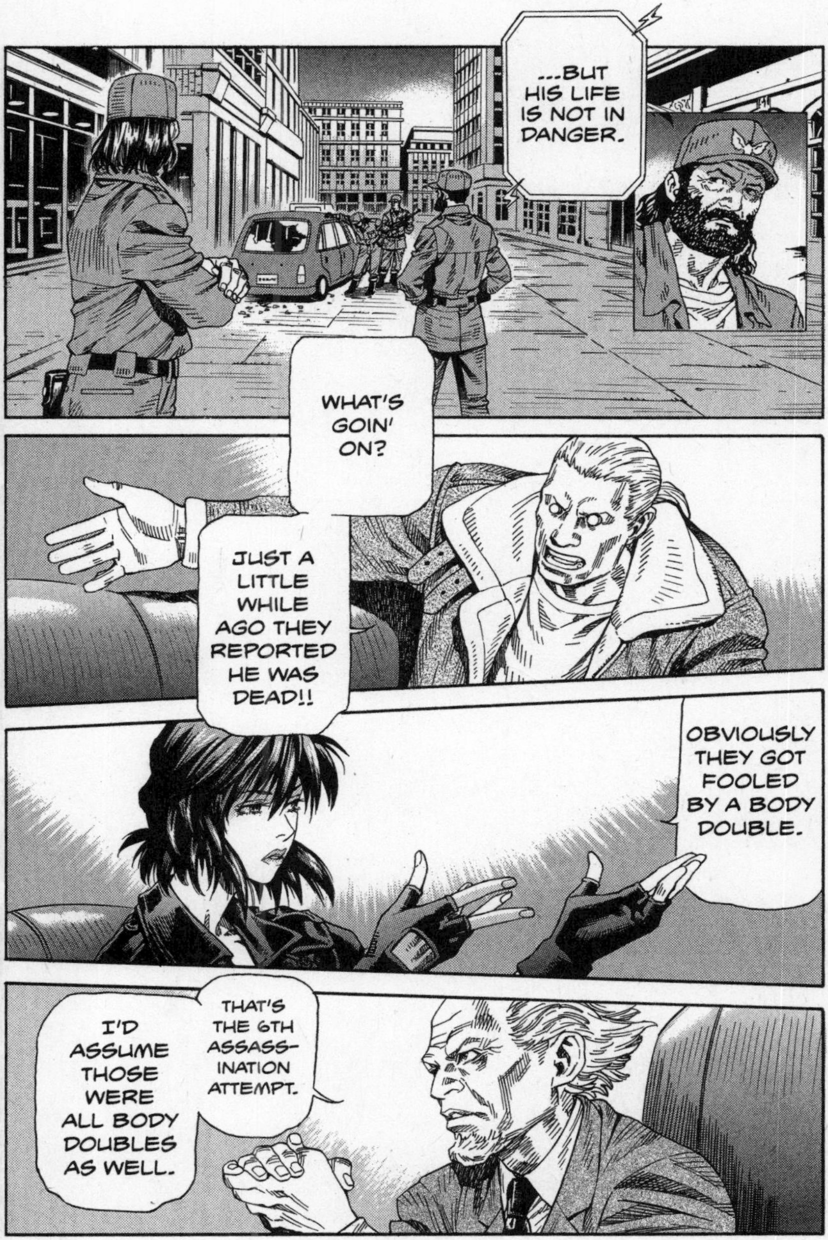
...BUT HIS LIFE IS NOT IN DANGER.
WHAT'S GOIN' ON?
JUST A LITTLE WHILE AGO THEY REPORTED HE WAS DEAD!!
OBVIOUSLY THEY GOT FOOLED BY A BODY DOUBLE.
THAT'S THE 6TH ASSASS-INATION ATTEMPT.
I'D ASSUME THOSE WERE ALL BODY DOUBLES AS WELL.

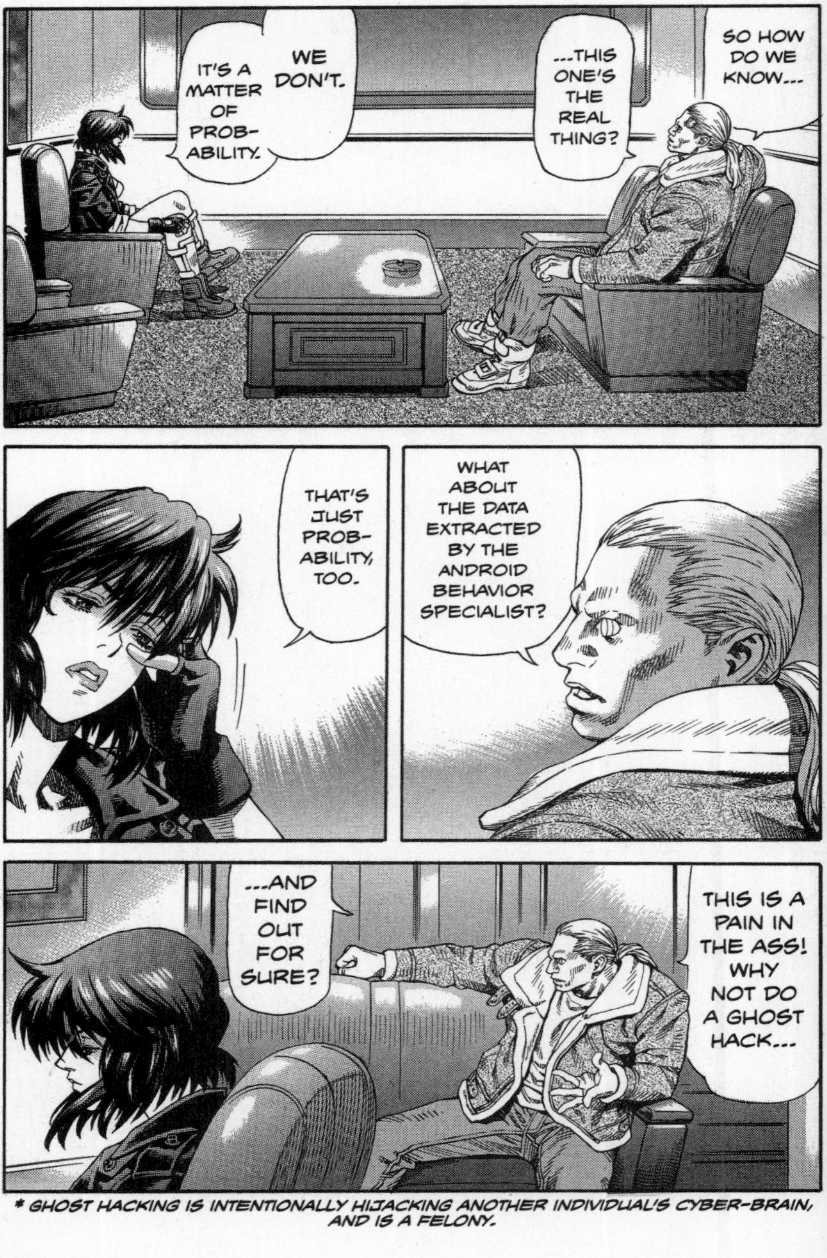
SO HOW DO WE KNOW...
...THIS ONE'S THE REAL THING?
WE DON'T.
IT'S A MATTER OF PROBABILITY.
WHAT ABOUT THE DATA EXTRACTED BY THE ANDROID BEHAVIOR SPECIALIST?
THAT'S JUST PROBABILITY, TOO.
THIS IS A PAIN IN THE ASS! WHY NOT DO A GHOST HACK...
...AND FIND OUT FOR SURE?

* GHOST HACKING IS INTENTIONALLY HIJACKING ANOTHER INDIVIDUAL'S CYBER-BRAIN, AND IS A FELONY.

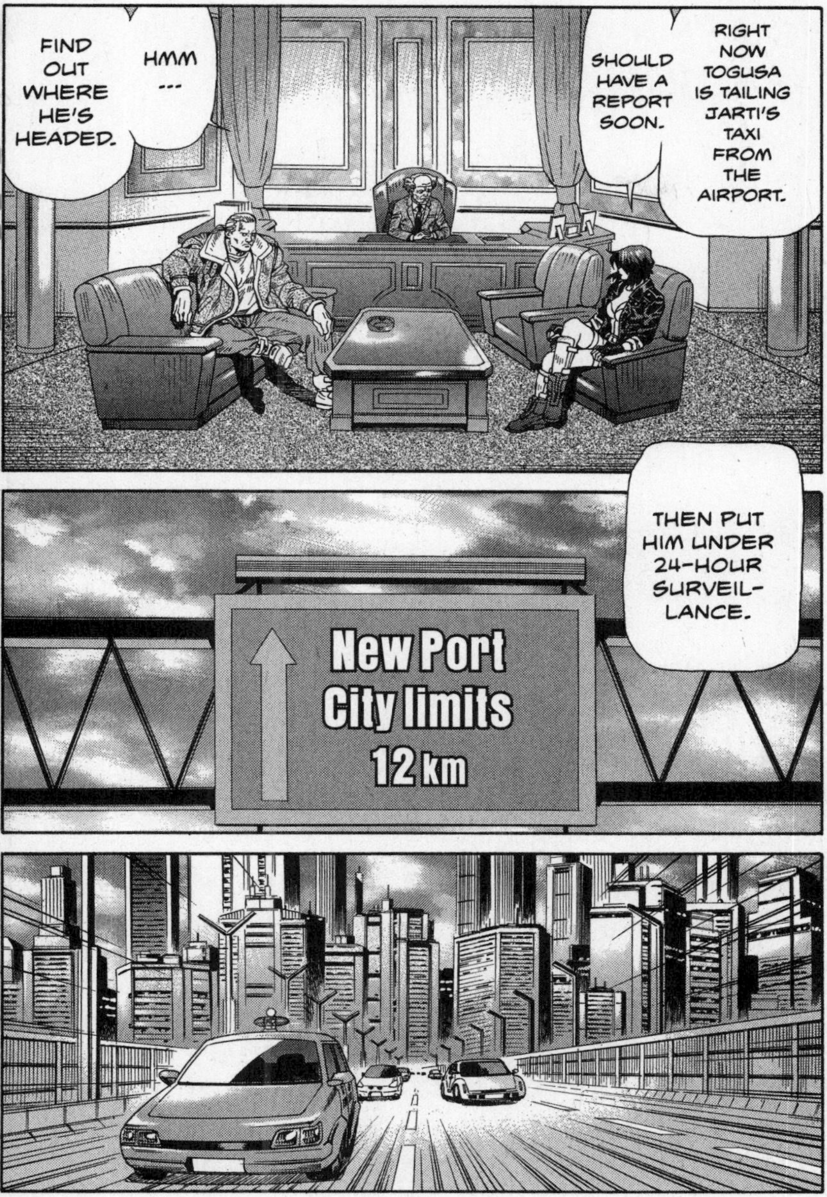
RIGHT NOW TOGUSA IS TAILING JARTI'S TAXI FROM THE AIRPORT.
SHOULD HAVE A REPORT SOON.
HMM ---
FIND OUT WHERE HE'S HEADED.
THEN PUT HIM UNDER 24-HOUR SURVEIL-LANCE.
New Port
City limits
12 km

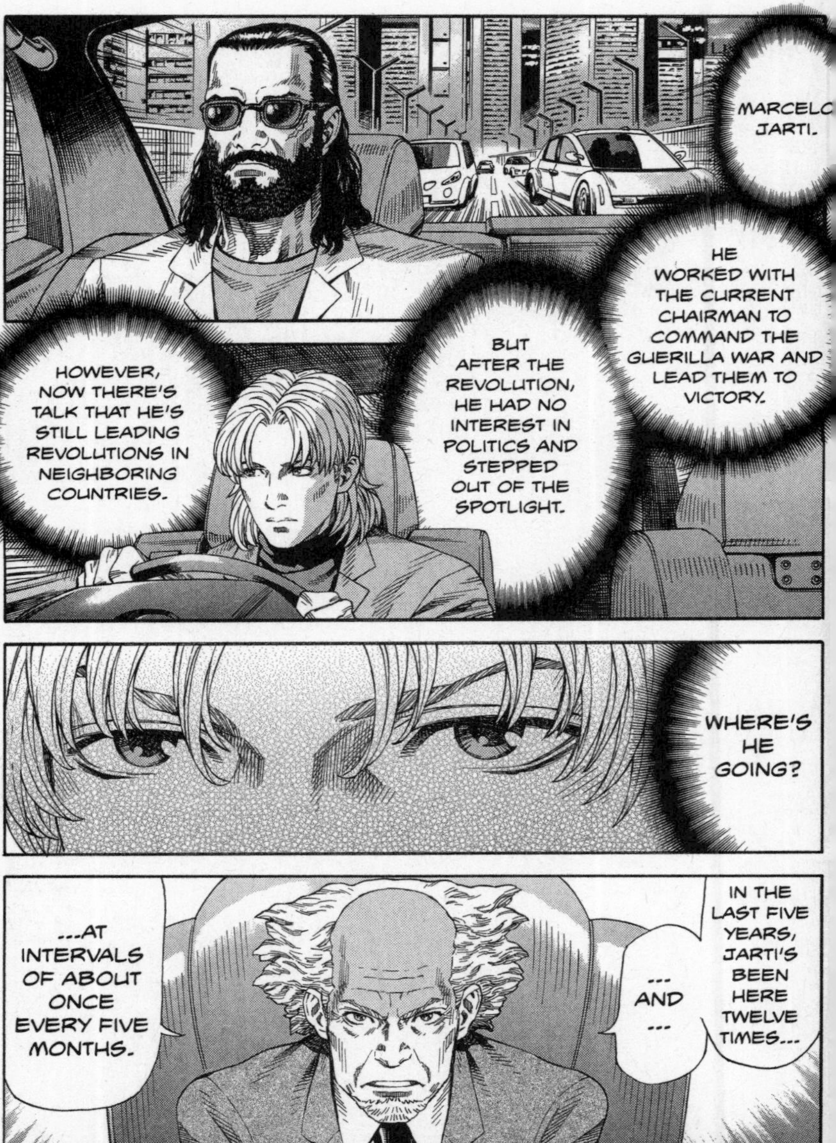
MARCELO JARTI.
HE WORKED WITH THE CURRENT CHAIRMAN TO COMMAND THE GUERILLA WAR AND LEAD THEM TO VICTORY.
BUT AFTER THE REVOLUTION, HE HAD NO INTEREST IN POLITICS AND STEPPED OUT OF THE SPOTLIGHT.
HOWEVER, NOW THERE'S TALK THAT HE'S STILL LEADING REVOLUTIONS IN NEIGHBORING COUNTRIES.
WHERE'S HE GOING?
IN THE LAST FIVE YEARS, JARTI'S BEEN HERE TWELVE TIMES...
...AND...
...AT INTERVALS OF ABOUT ONCE EVERY FIVE MONTHS.

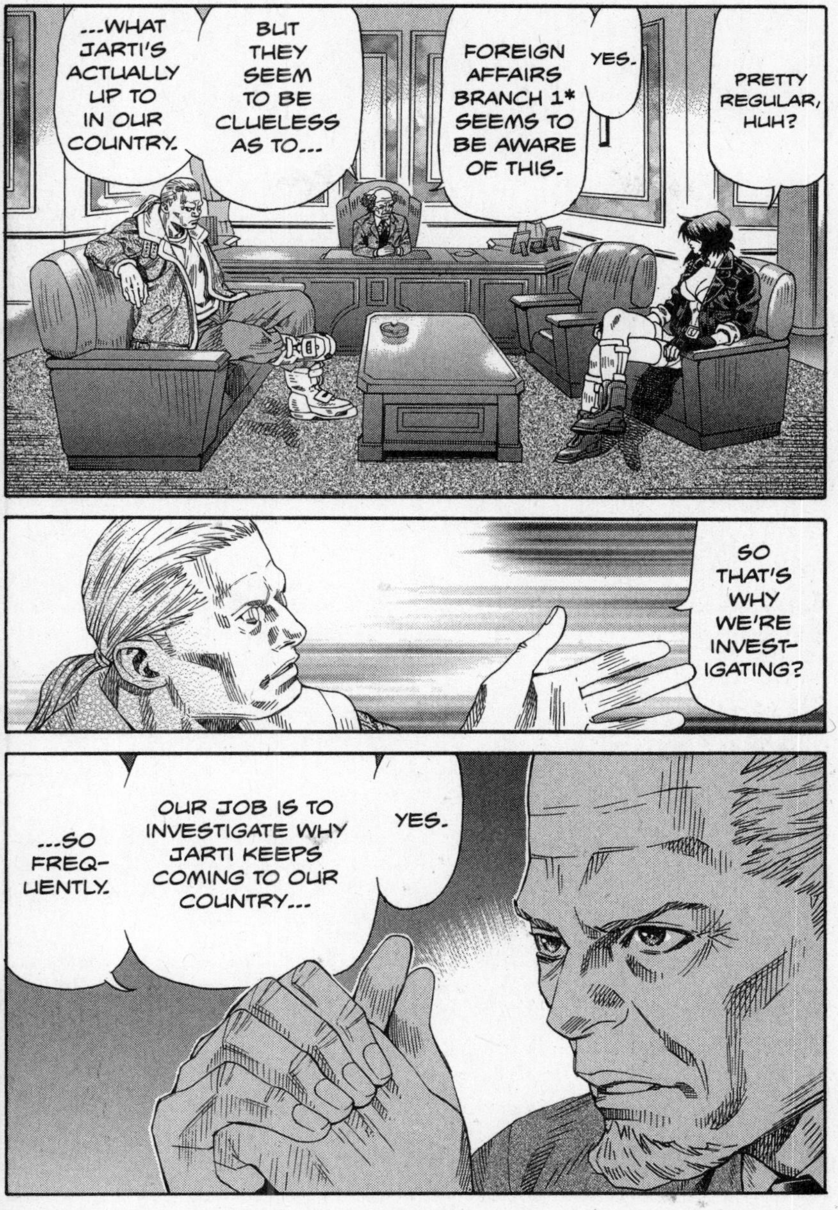
PRETTY REGULAR, HUH?
YES.
FOREIGN AFFAIRS BRANCH 1* SEEMS TO BE AWARE OF THIS.
BUT THEY SEEM TO BE CLUELESS AS TO...
...WHAT JARTI'S ACTUALLY UP TO IN OUR COUNTRY.
SO THAT'S WHY WE'RE INVEST-IGATING?
YES.
OUR JOB IS TO INVESTIGATE WHY JARTI KEEPS COMING TO OUR COUNTRY...
...SO FREQ-UENTLY.

* IN THE SETTING OF THIS WORK, FOREIGN AFFAIRS BRANCH 1 DEALS WITH CRIMES IN COUNTRIES OTHER THAN ASIA; FOREIGN AFFAIRS BRANCH 2 DEALS WITH CRIMES IN ASIAN COUNTRIES.

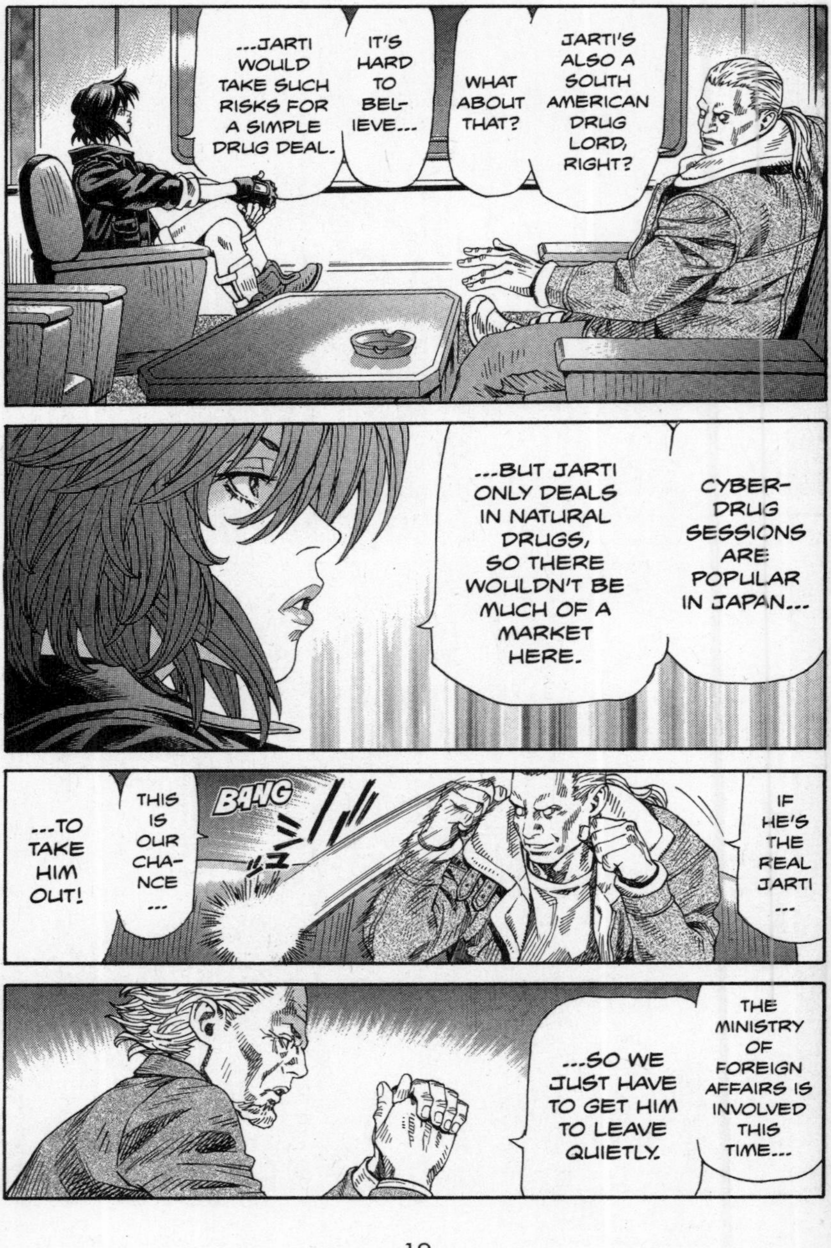
JARTI'S ALSO A SOUTH AMERICAN DRUG LORD, RIGHT?
WHAT ABOUT THAT?
IT'S HARD TO BEL-IEVE...
...JARTI WOULD TAKE SUCH RISKS FOR A SIMPLE DRUG DEAL.
CYBER-DRUG SESSIONS ARE POPULAR IN JAPAN...
...BUT JARTI ONLY DEALS IN NATURAL DRUGS, SO THERE WOULDN'T BE MUCH OF A MARKET HERE.
IF HE'S THE REAL JARTI...
BANG
THIS IS OUR CHA-NCE...
...TO TAKE HIM OUT!
THE MINISTRY OF FOREIGN AFFAIRS IS INVOLVED THIS TIME...
...SO WE JUST HAVE TO GET HIM TO LEAVE QUIETLY.

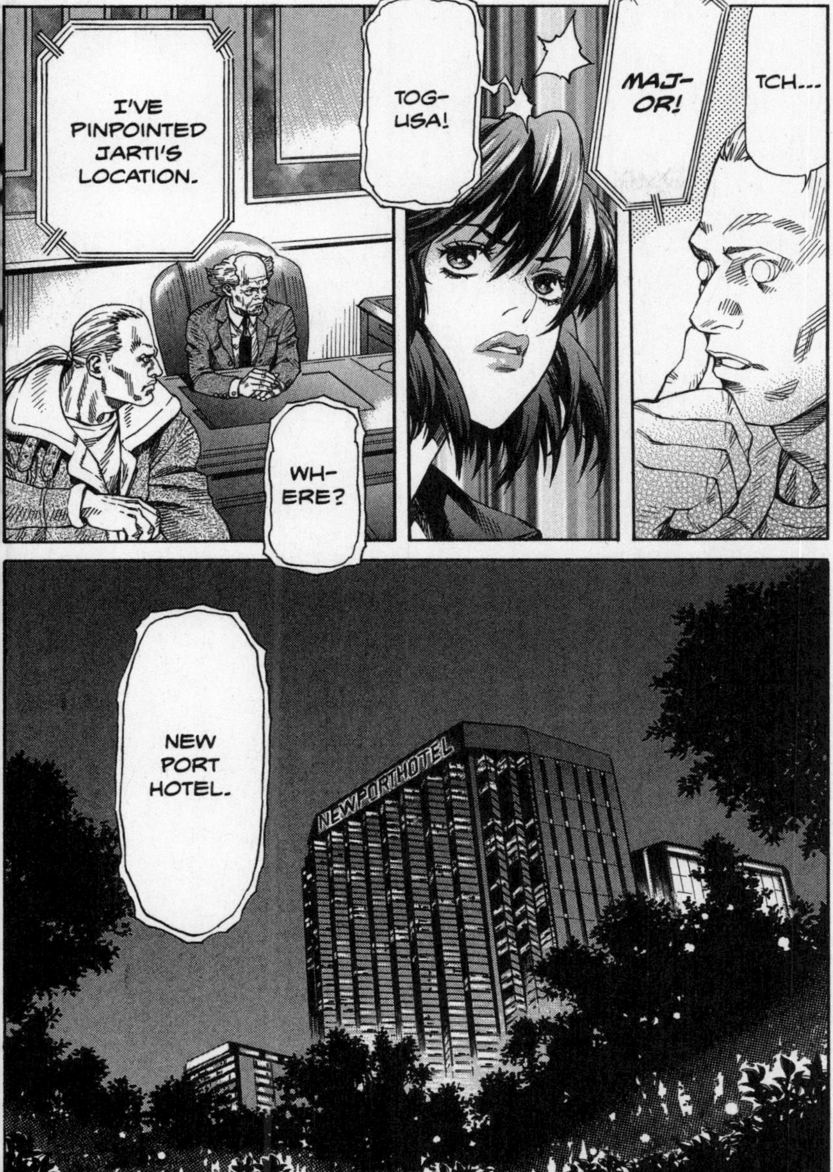
TCH...
MAJ-OR!
TOG-USA!
I'VE PINPOINTED JARTI'S LOCATION.
WH-ERE?
NEW PORT HOTEL.
NEWPORTHOTEL

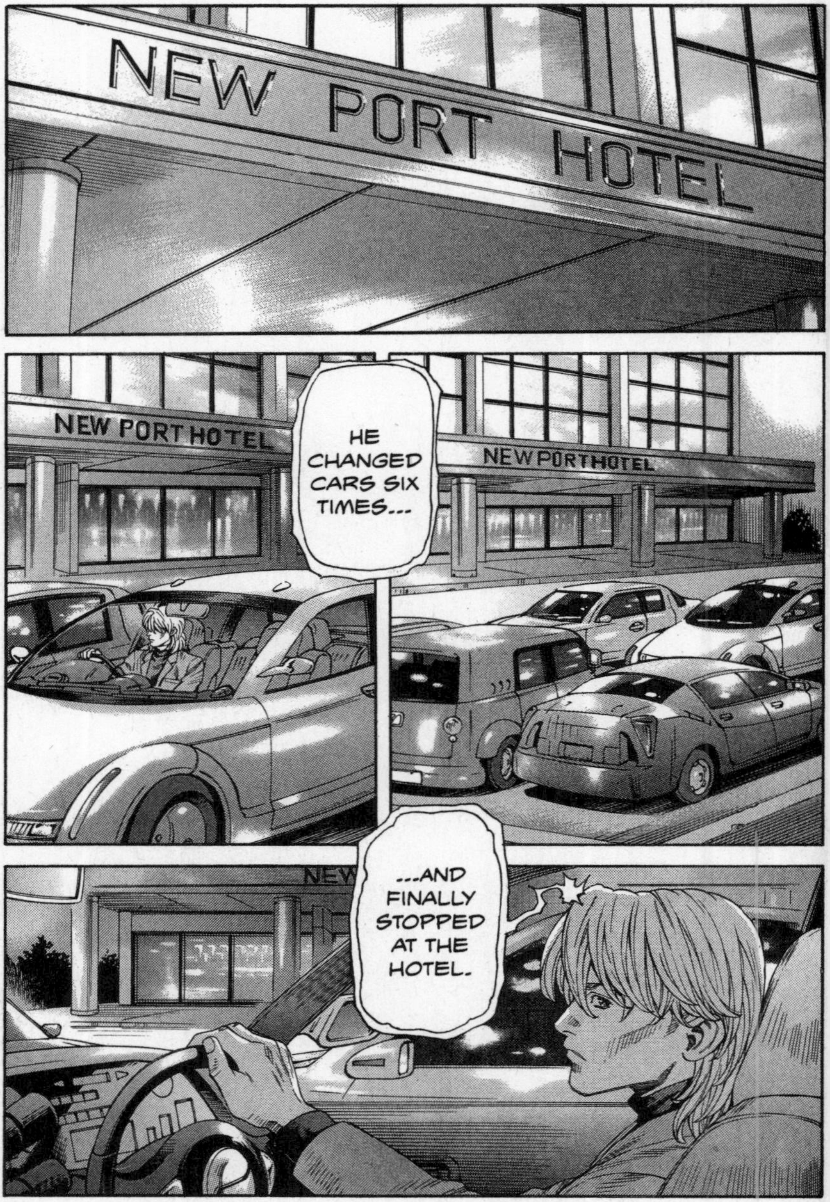
NEW PORT HOTEL
NEW PORT HOTEL
NEWPORTHOTEL
HE CHANGED CARS SIX TIMES...
...AND FINALLY STOPPED AT THE HOTEL.

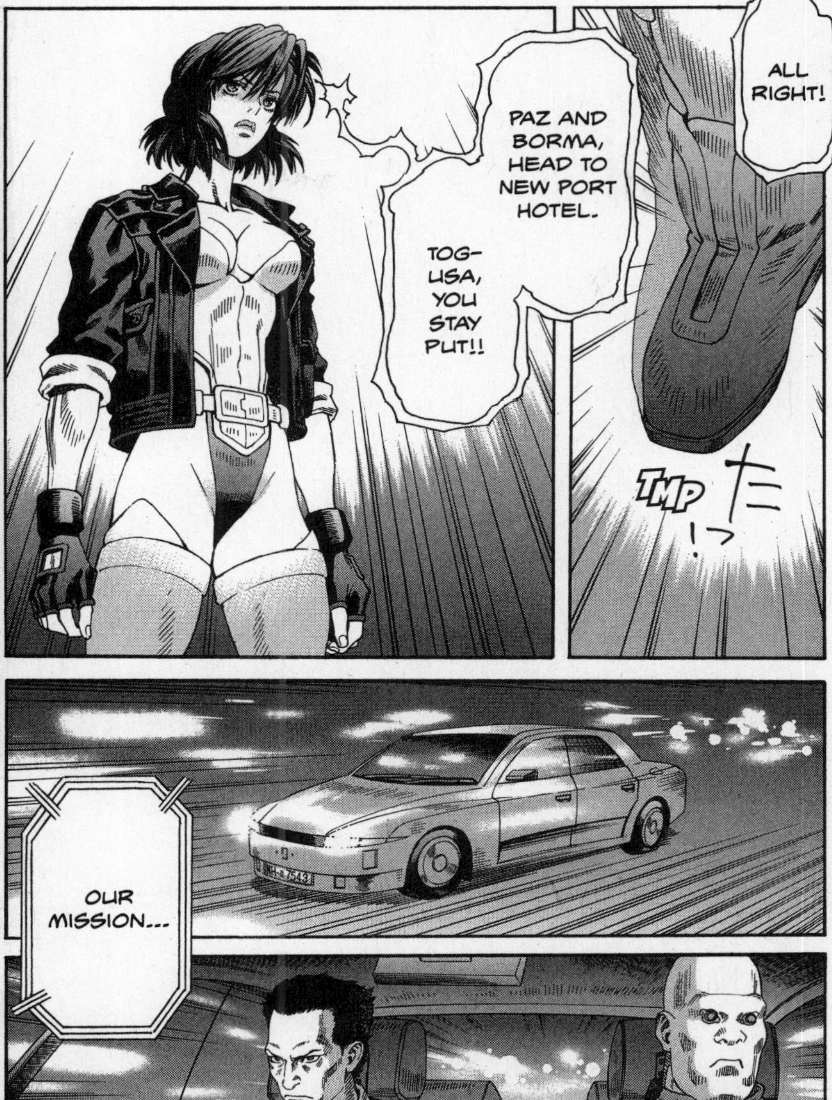
PAZ AND BORMA, HEAD TO NEW PORT HOTEL.
TOG-USA, YOU STAY PUT!!
ALL RIGHT!
TMP
たっ
OUR MISSION...

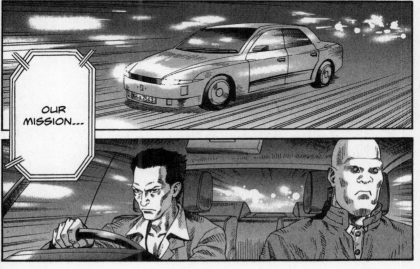

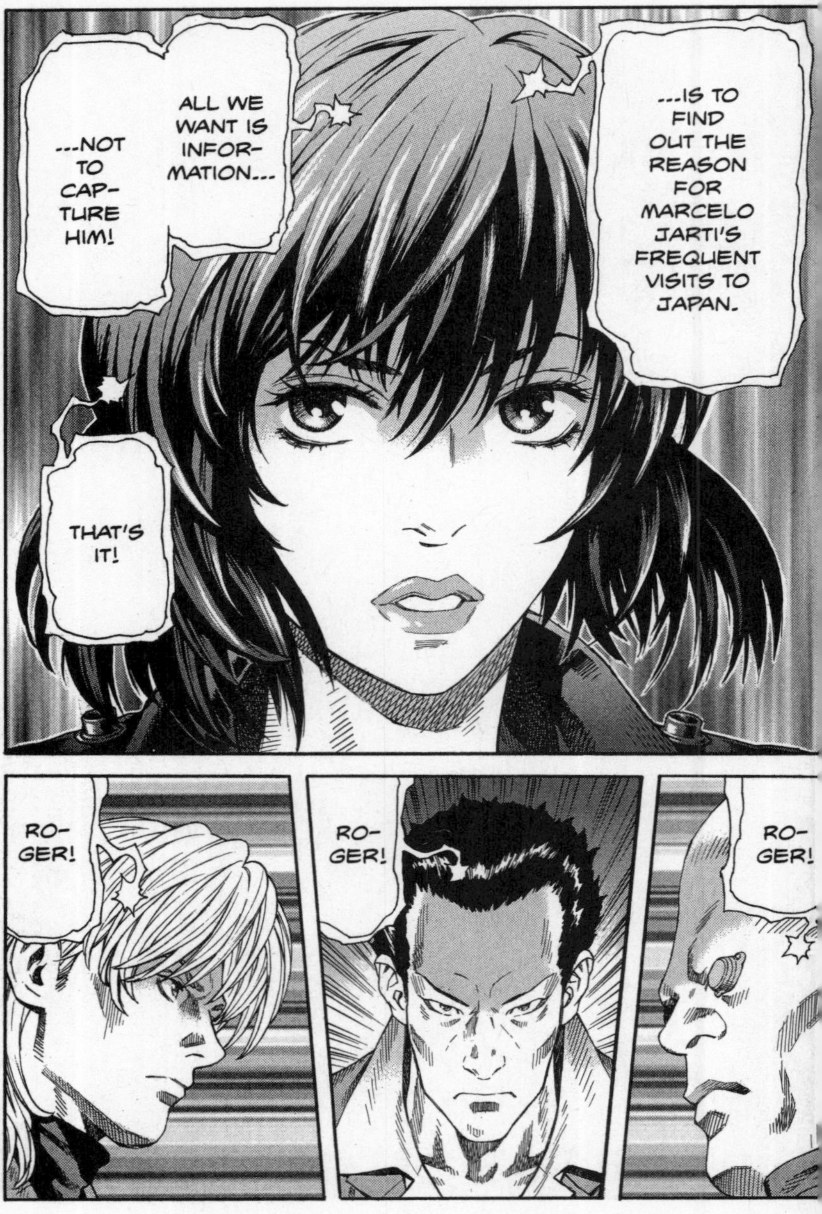
ALL WE WANT IS INFORMATION...
...IS TO FIND OUT THE REASON FOR MARCELO JARTI'S FREQUENT VISITS TO JAPAN.
...NOT TO CAPTURE HIM!
THAT'S IT!
ROGER!
ROGER!
ROGER!

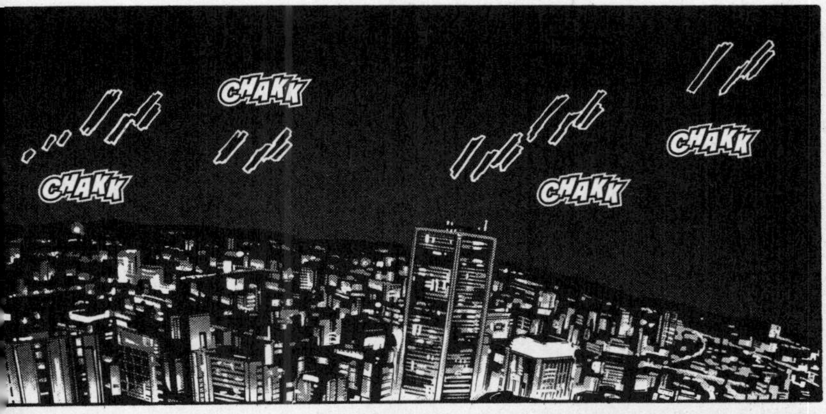
CHAKK
CHAKK
CHAKK
CHAKK
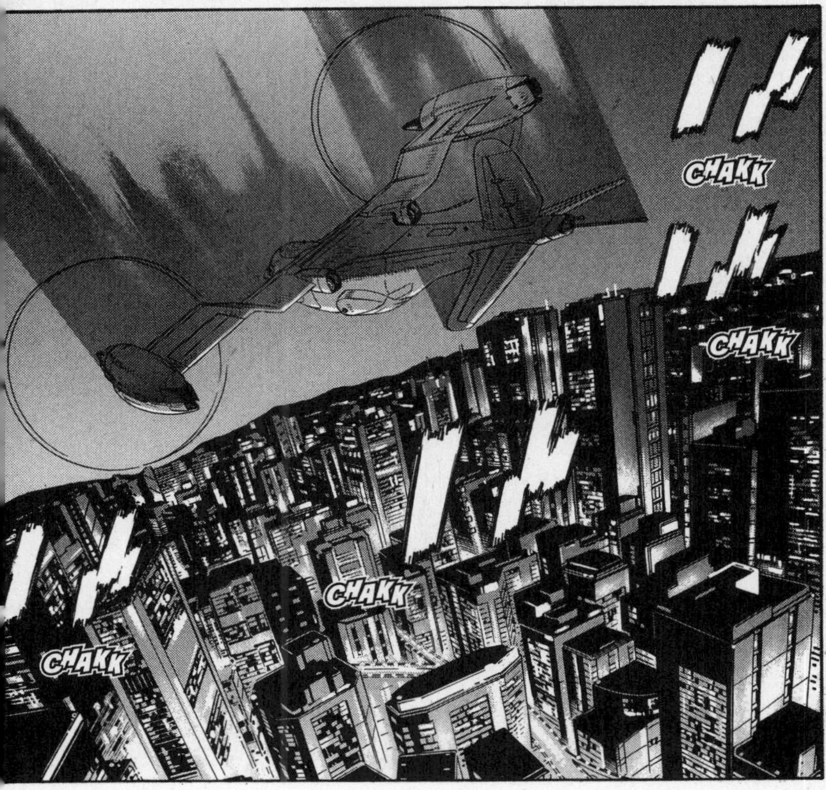
CHAKK
CHAKK
CHAKK
CHAKK

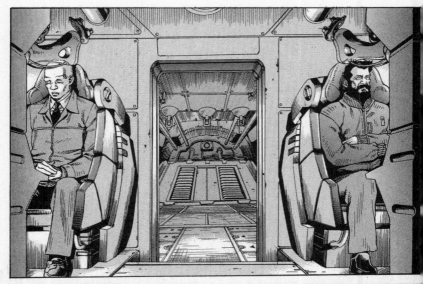

BOR-
MA.

YES?

25

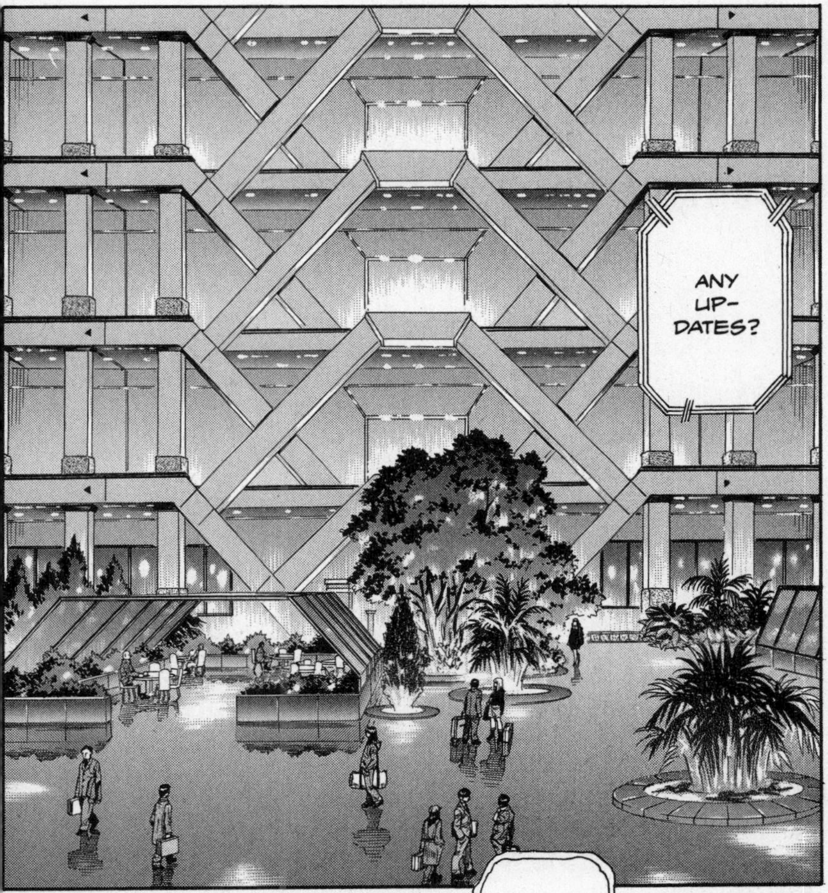
ANY UP-DATES?
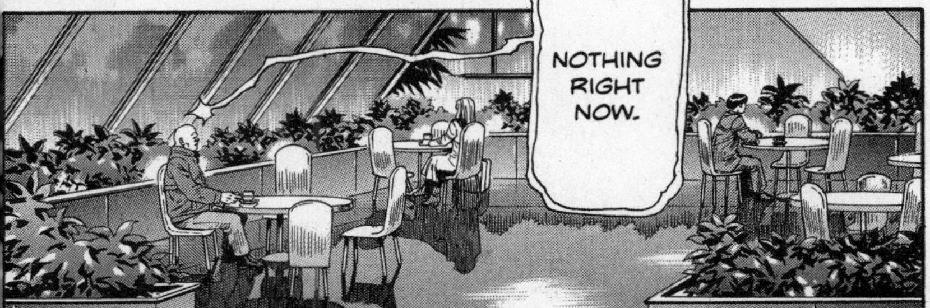
NOTHING RIGHT NOW.

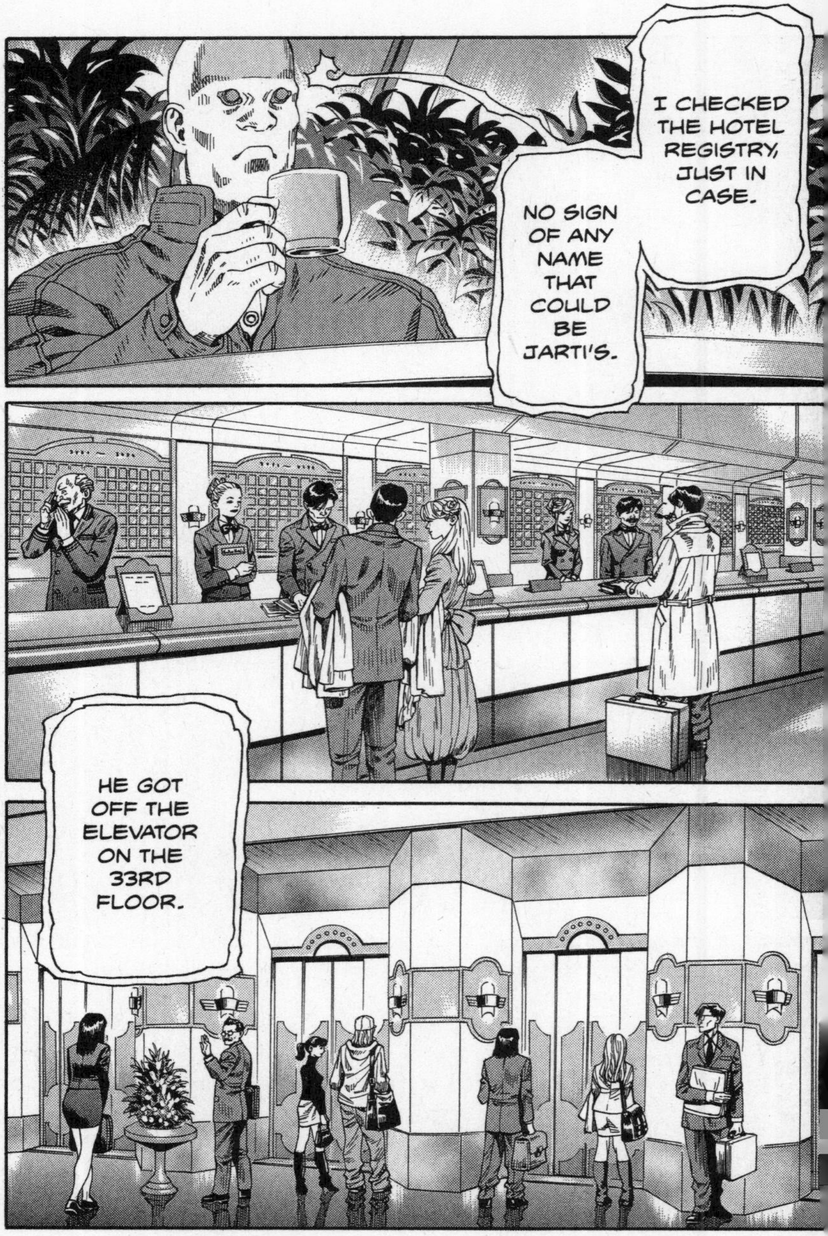
I CHECKED THE HOTEL REGISTRY, JUST IN CASE.
NO SIGN OF ANY NAME THAT COULD BE JARTI'S.
HE GOT OFF THE ELEVATOR ON THE 33RD FLOOR.

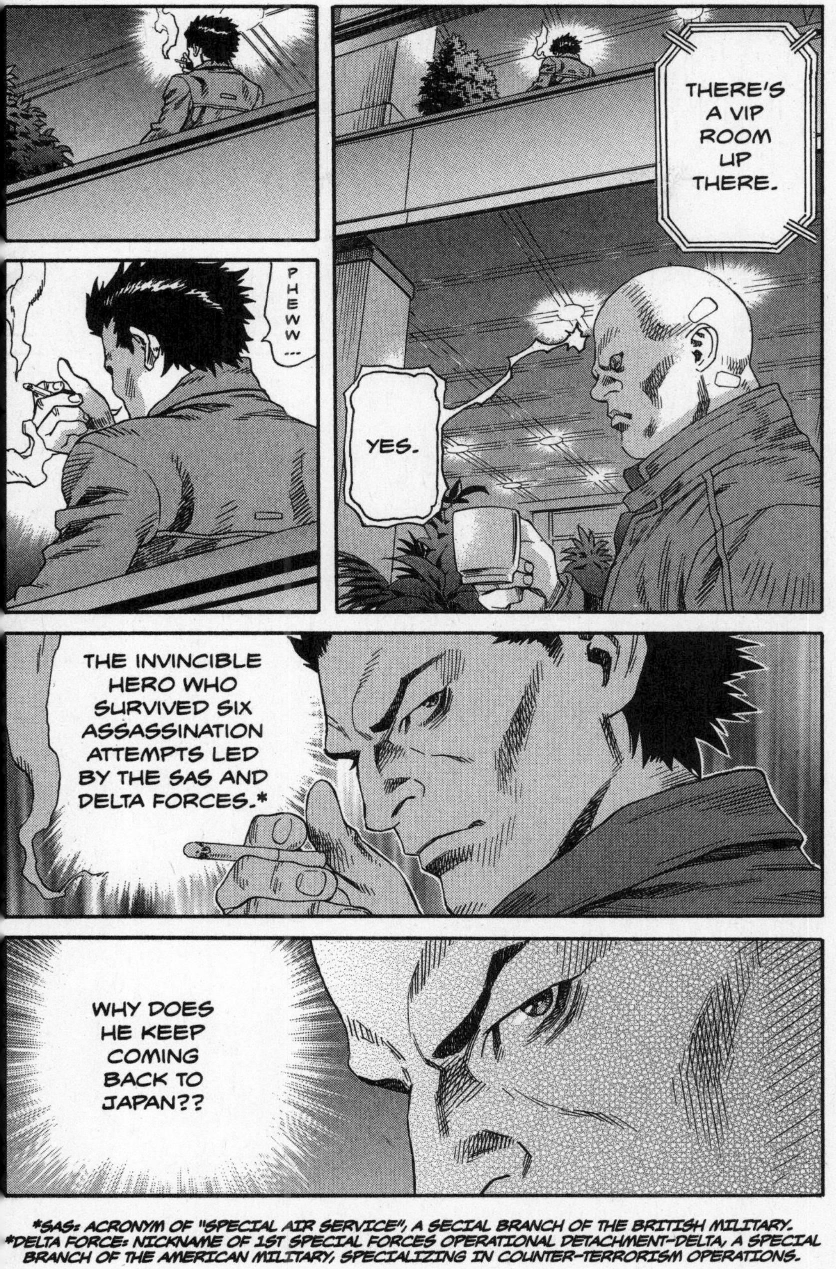
THERE'S A VIP ROOM UP THERE.
YES.
PHEWW...
THE INVINCIBLE HERO WHO SURVIVED SIX ASSASSINATION ATTEMPTS LED BY THE SAS AND DELTA FORCES.*
WHY DOES HE KEEP COMING BACK TO JAPAN??

*SAS: ACRONYM OF "SPECIAL AIR SERVICE", A SECIAL BRANCH OF THE BRITISH MILITARY.
*DELTA FORCE: NICKNAME OF 1ST SPECIAL FORCES OPERATIONAL DETACHMENT-DELTA, A SPECIAL BRANCH OF THE AMERICAN MILITARY, SPECIALIZING IN COUNTER-TERRORISM OPERATIONS.

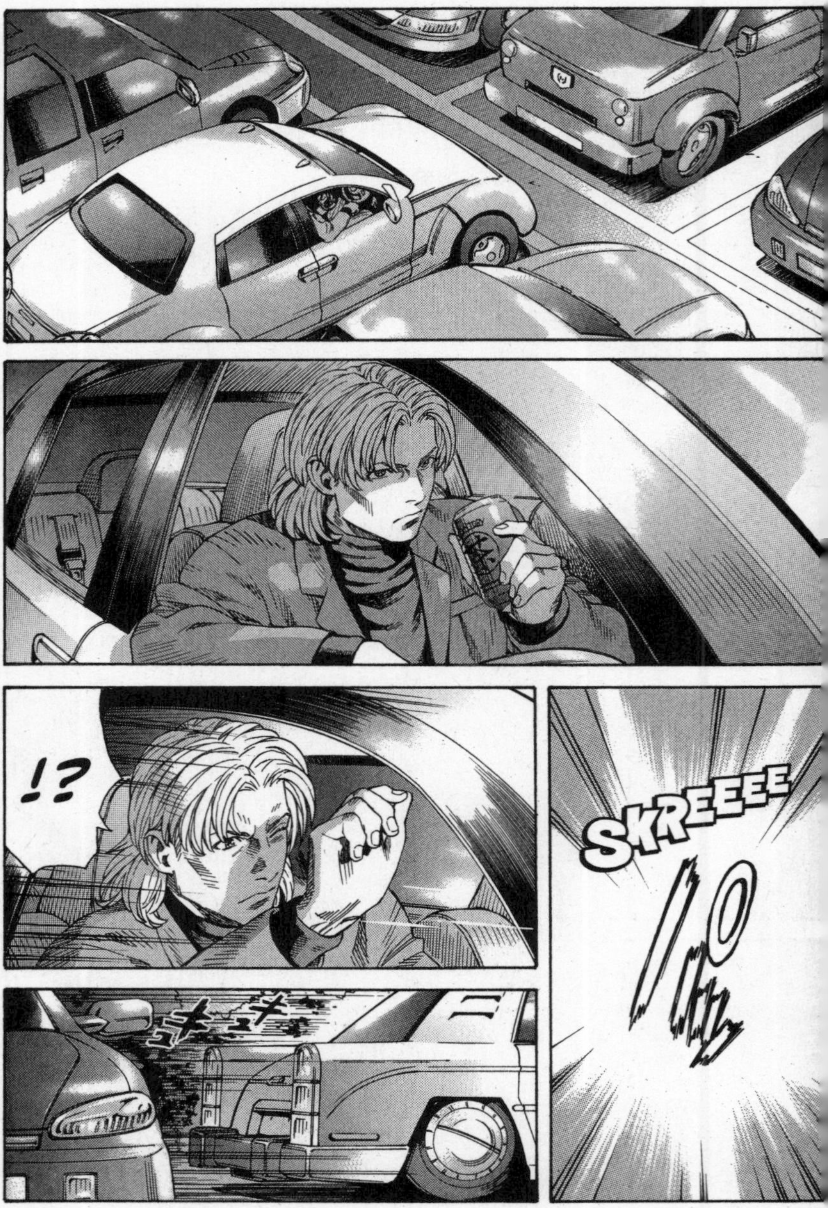
SKREEEE
!?

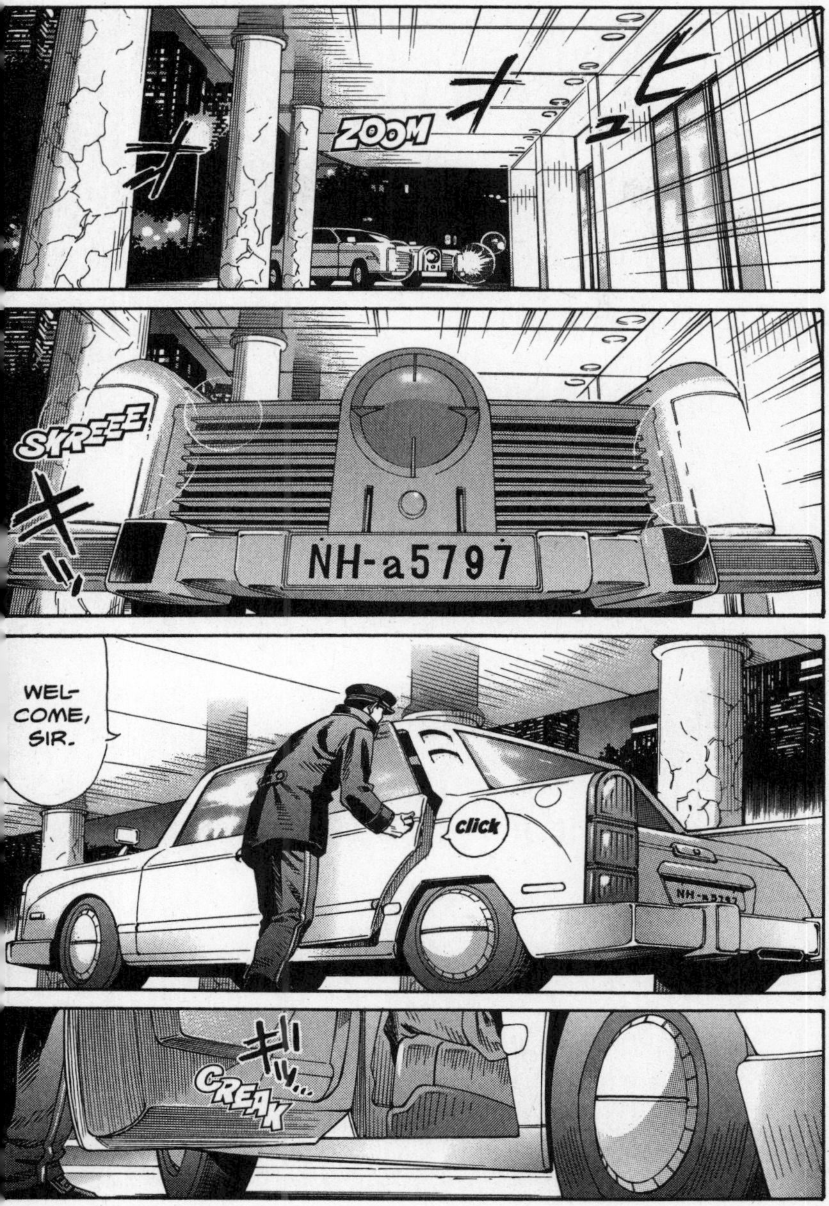
ZOOM
SKREEE
NH-a5797
WEL-
COME,
SIR.
click
CREAK

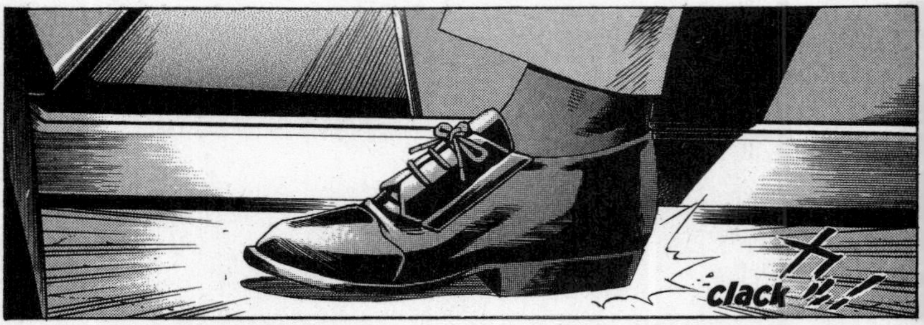
clack
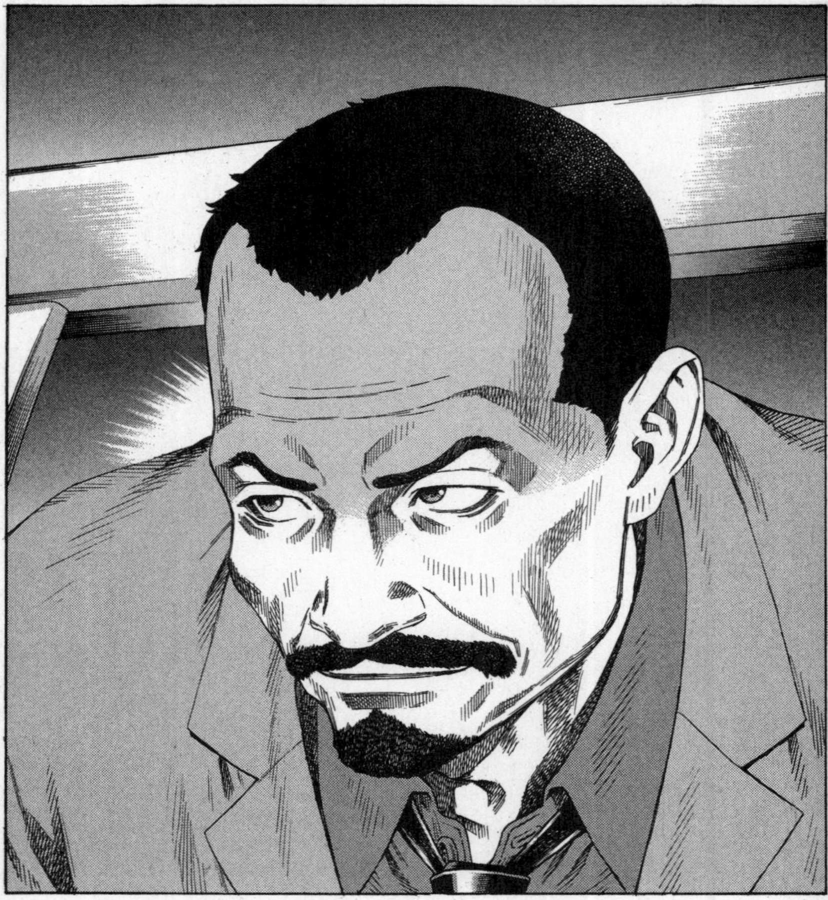

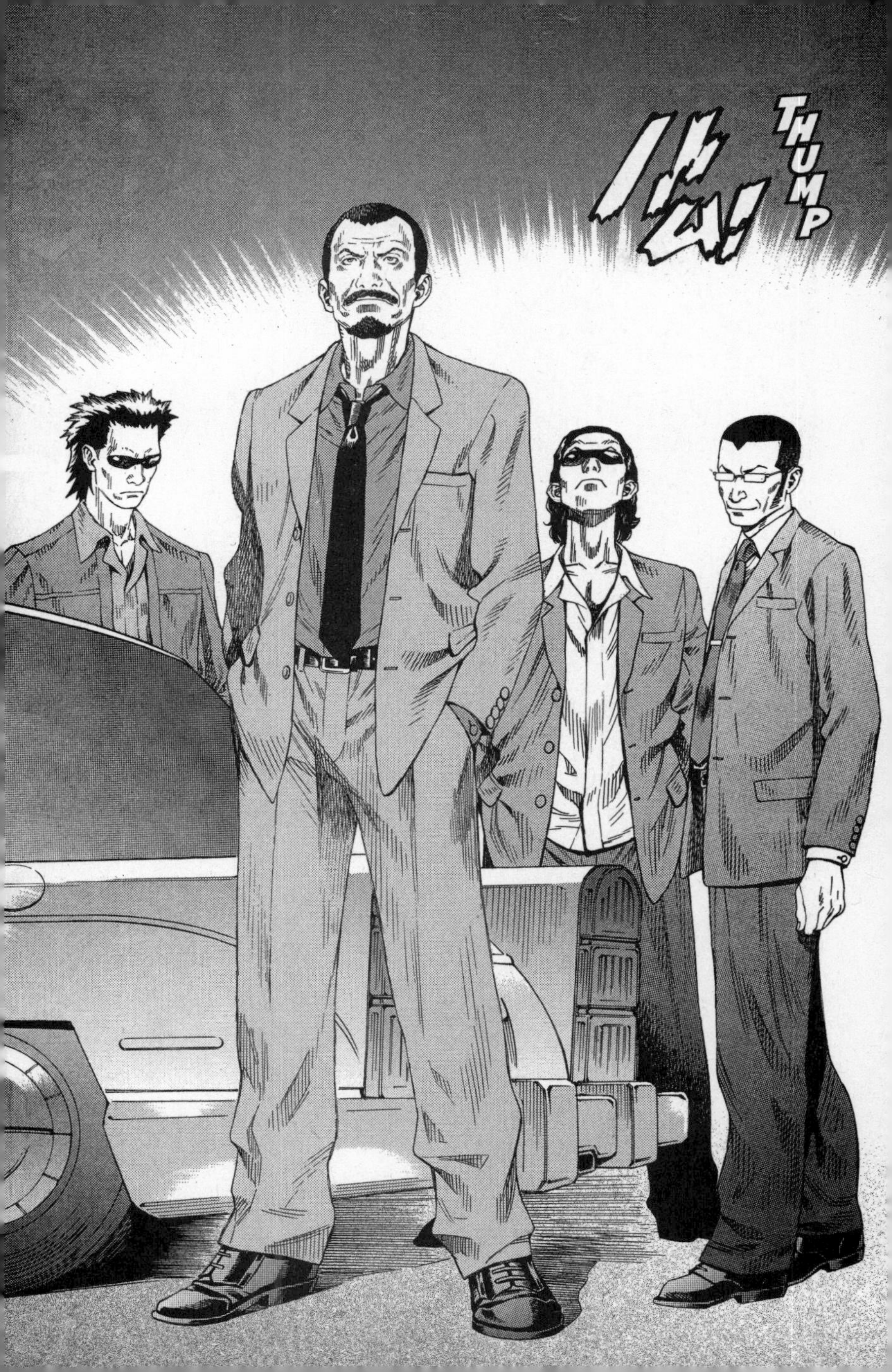
THUMP

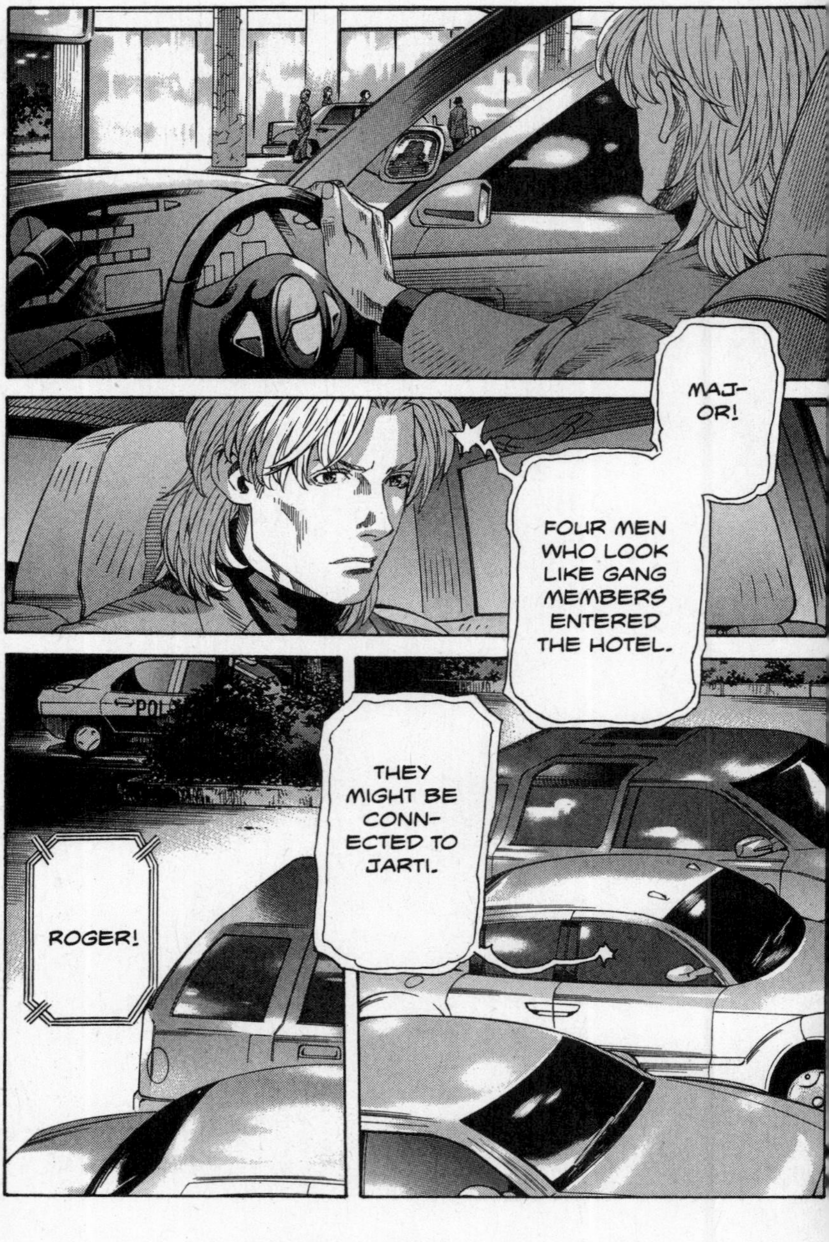
MAJ-
OR!
FOUR MEN WHO LOOK LIKE GANG MEMBERS ENTERED THE HOTEL.
THEY MIGHT BE CONN-ECTED TO JARTI.
ROGER!
POL

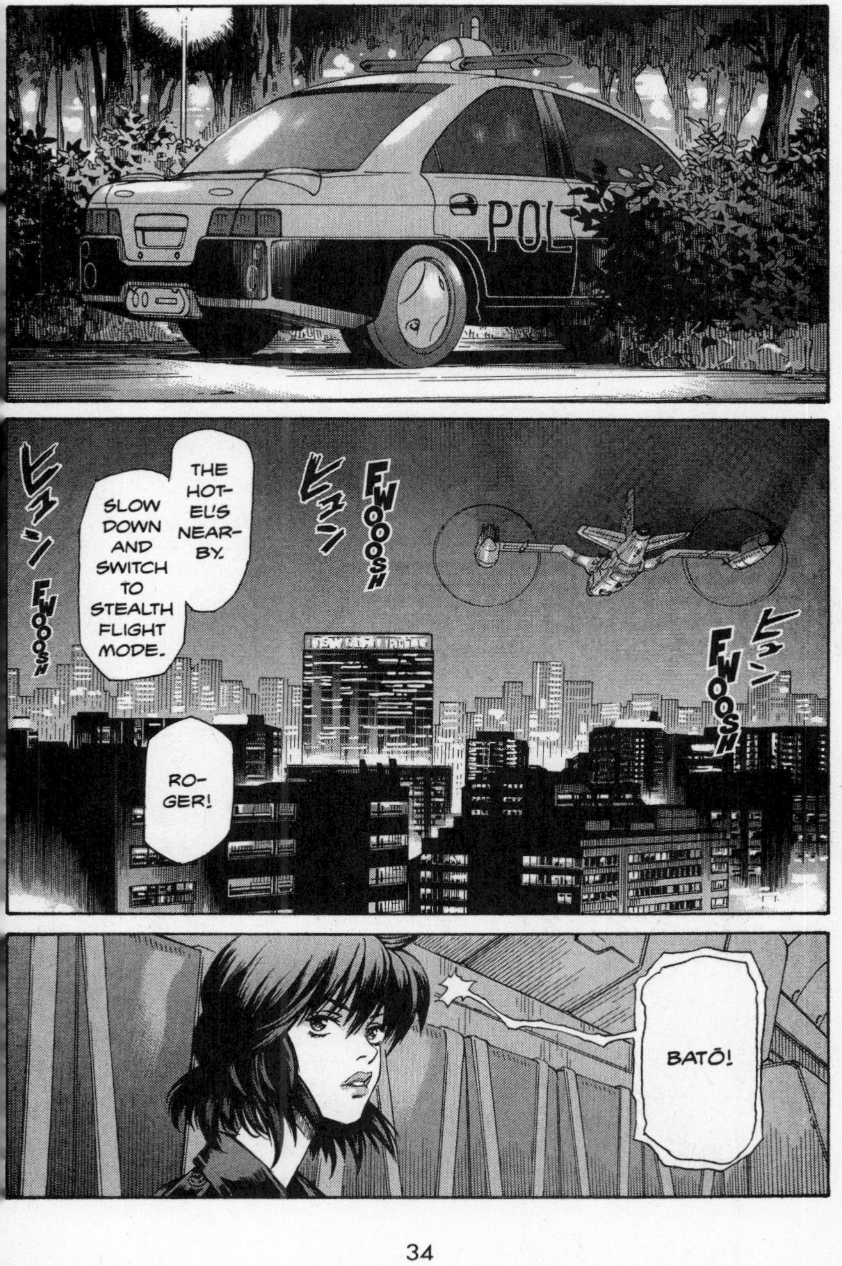
ヒュン
FWOOSH
FWOOOSH
ヒュン
THE HOTEL'S NEARBY.
SLOW DOWN AND SWITCH TO STEALTH FLIGHT MODE.
ヒュン
FWOOOSH
ROGER!
BATŌ!

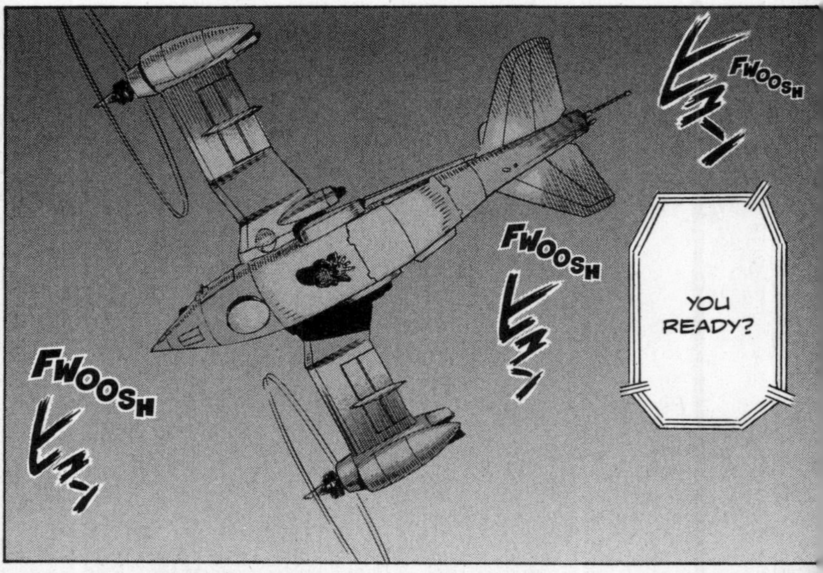
FWOOSH
FWOOSH
FWOOSH
YOU READY?
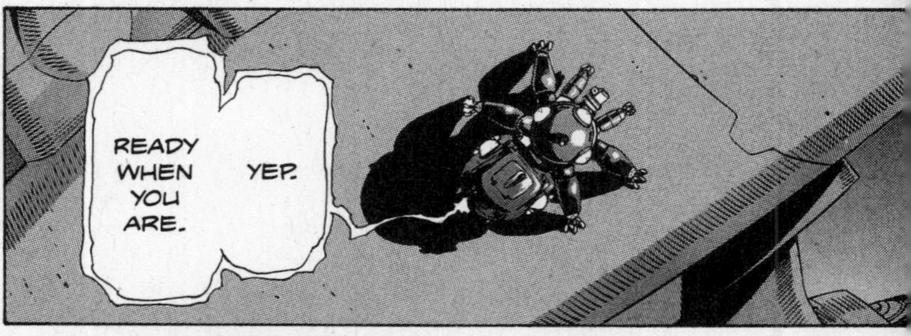
YEP.
READY WHEN YOU ARE.
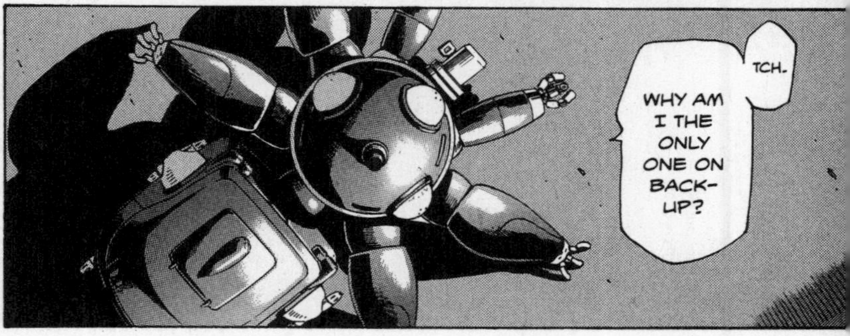
TCH.
WHY AM I THE ONLY ONE ON BACK-UP?

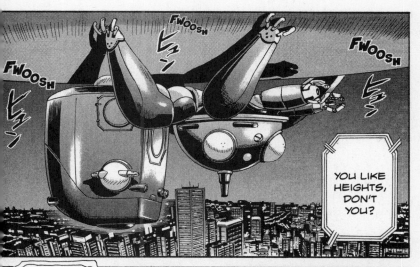

FWOOSH
FWOOSH
FWOOSH
YOU LIKE HEIGHTS, DON'T YOU?
HEH. YEAH, ME AND SMOKE BOTH JUST LOVE HIGH PLACES.
HEH.
NEW PORT HOTEL
FINE! COME DOWN AND STAY POSTED ON THE SIDE OF THE BUILDING!!
GOT IT.

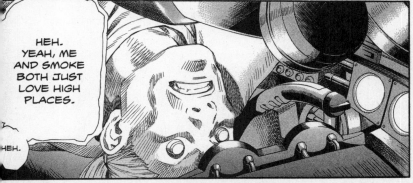

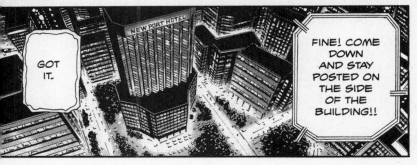

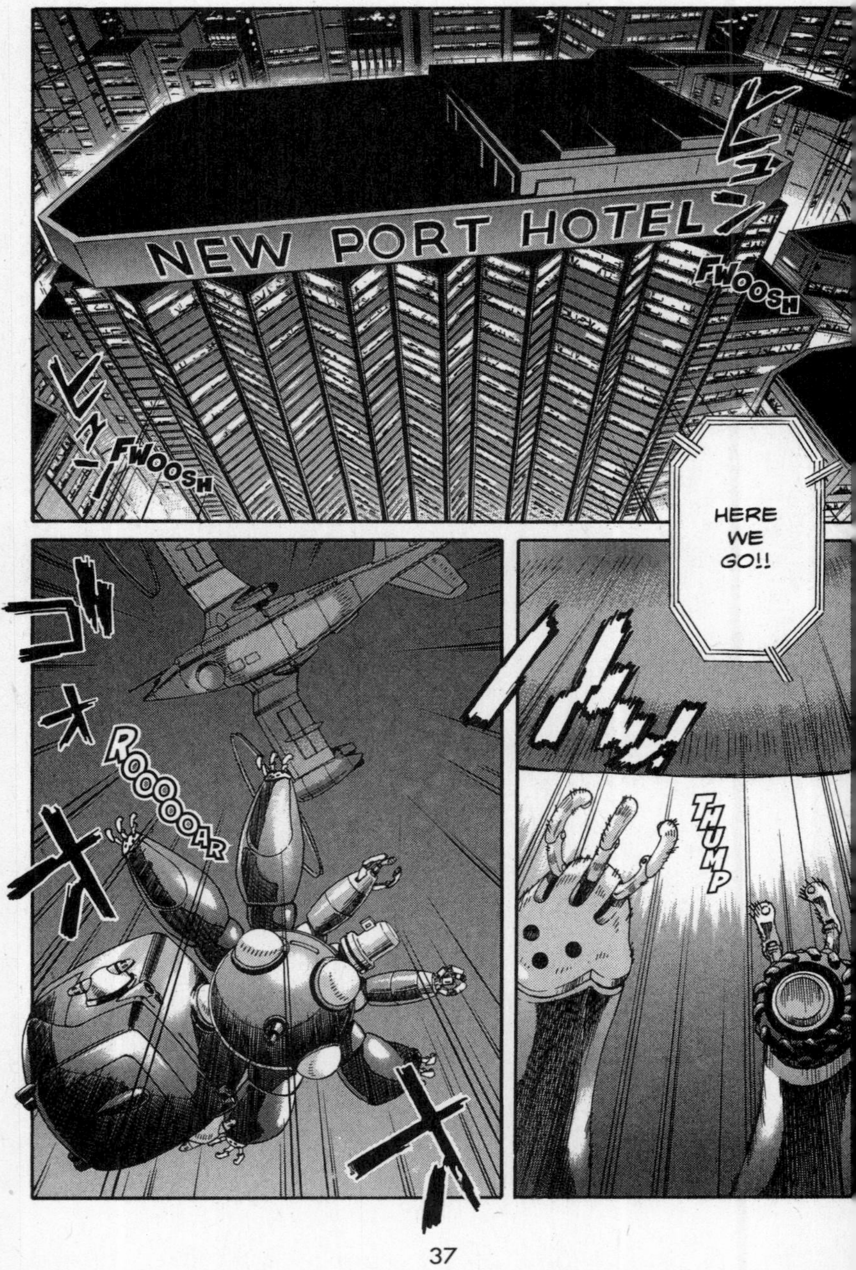
NEW PORT HOTEL
FWOOSH
FWOOSH
HERE WE GO!!
THUMP
ROOOOOAR

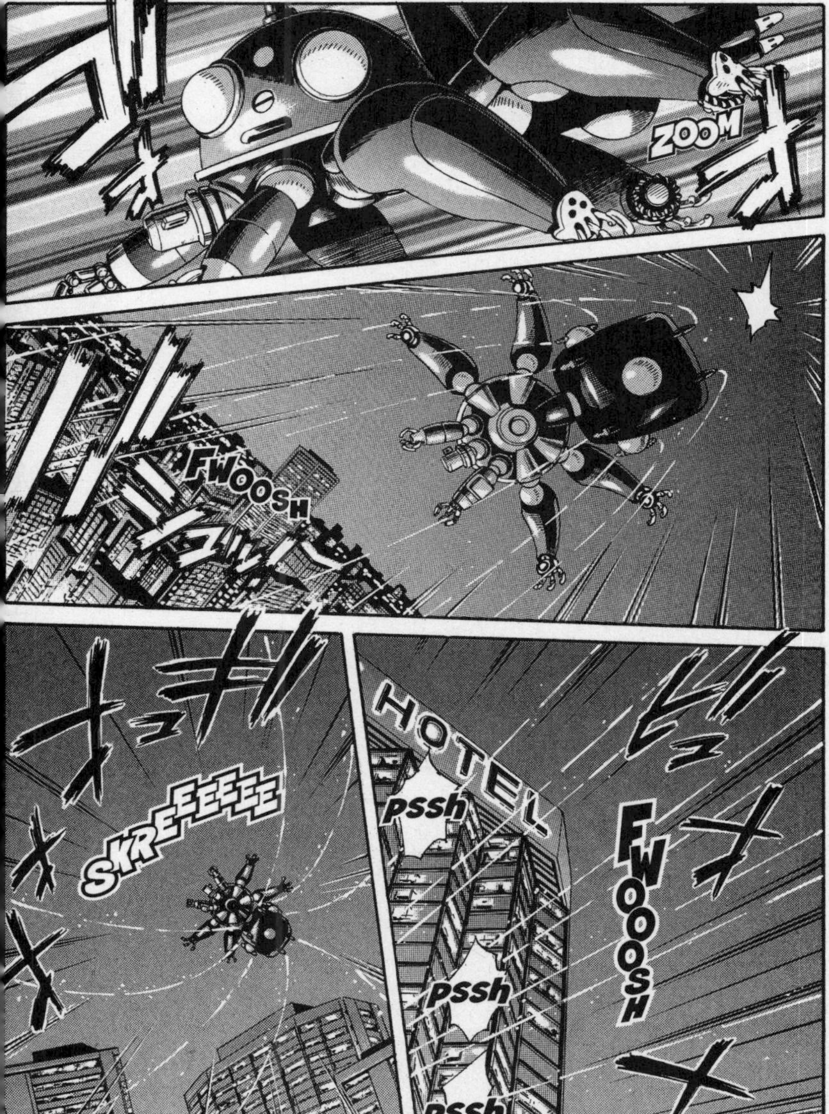
ZOOM
FWOOSH
HOTEL
pssh
pssh
pssh
FWOOOSH
SKREEEEEE

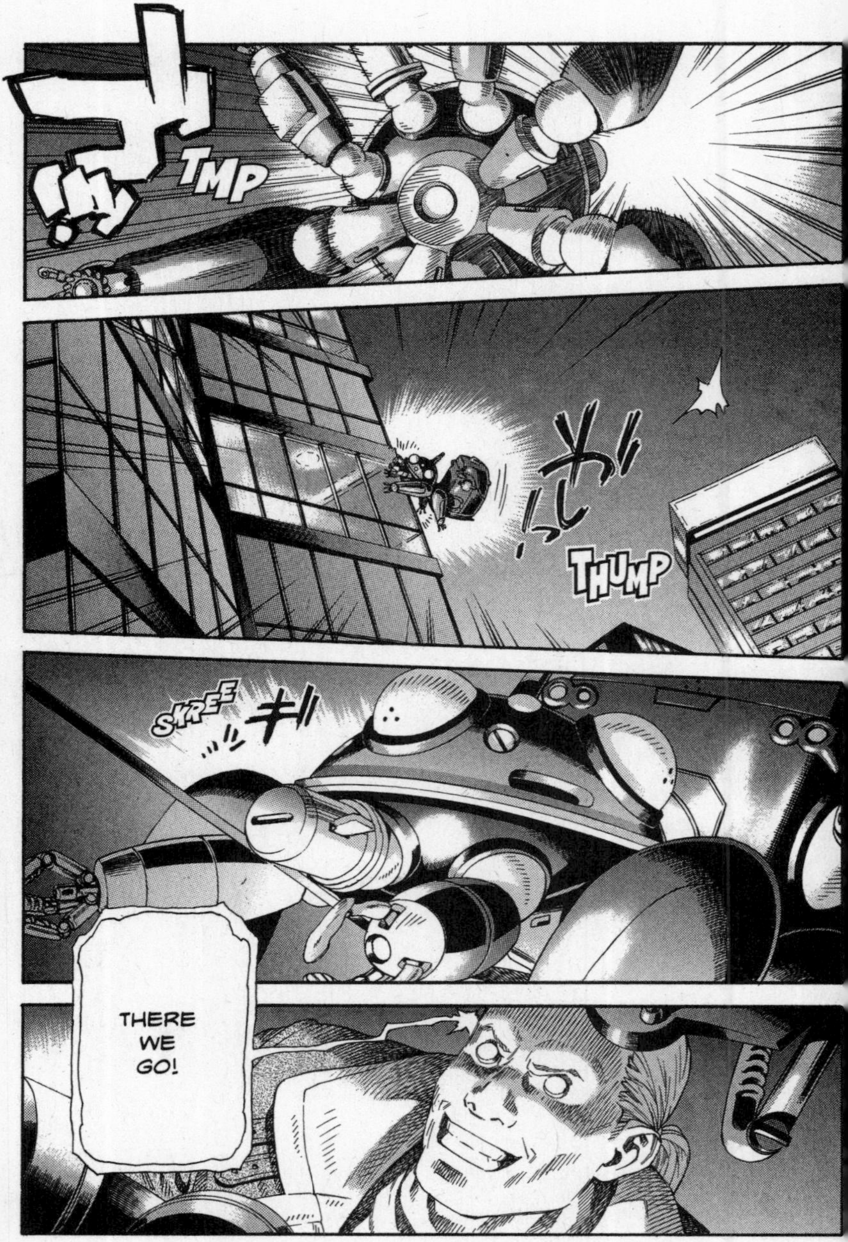
TMP
THUMP
SKREE
THERE WE GO!

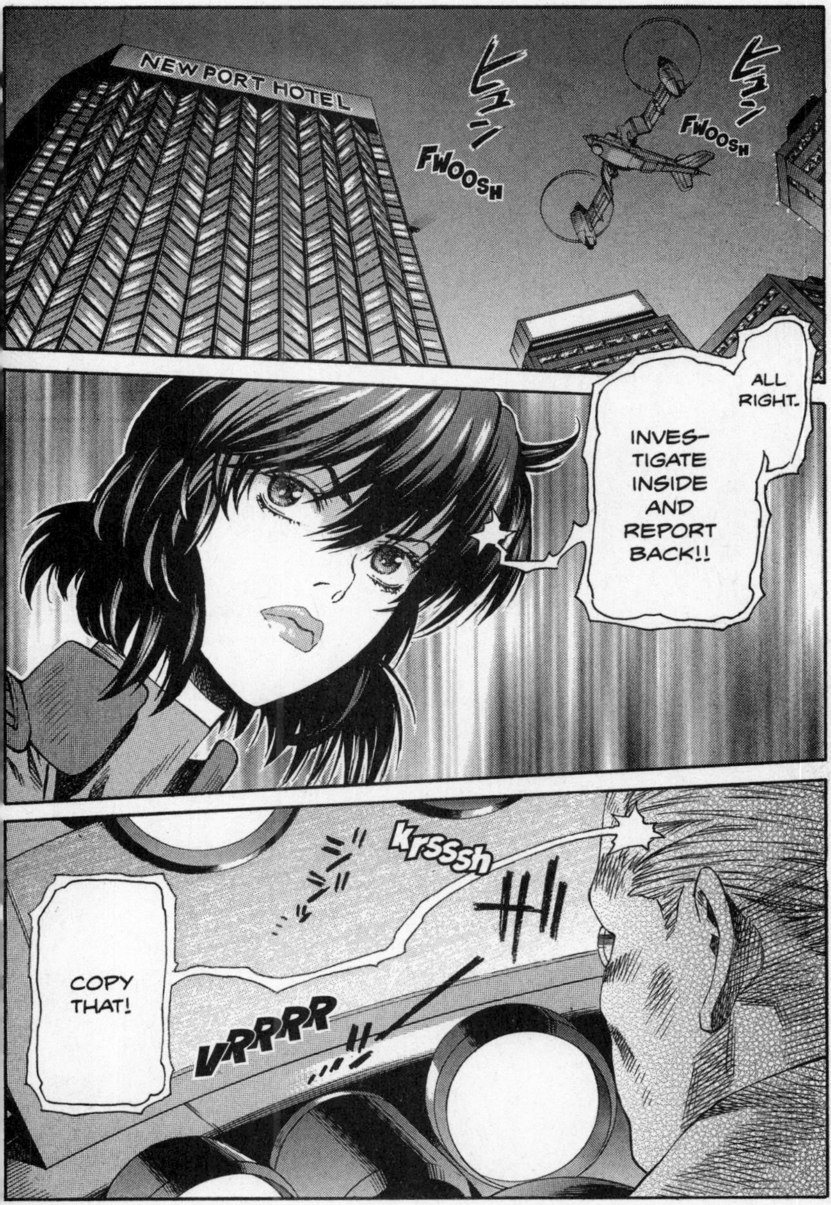
NEW PORT HOTEL
ヒュン
FWOOSH
ヒュン
FWOOSH
ALL RIGHT.
INVES-TIGATE INSIDE AND REPORT BACK!!
krsssh
VRRRR
COPY THAT!

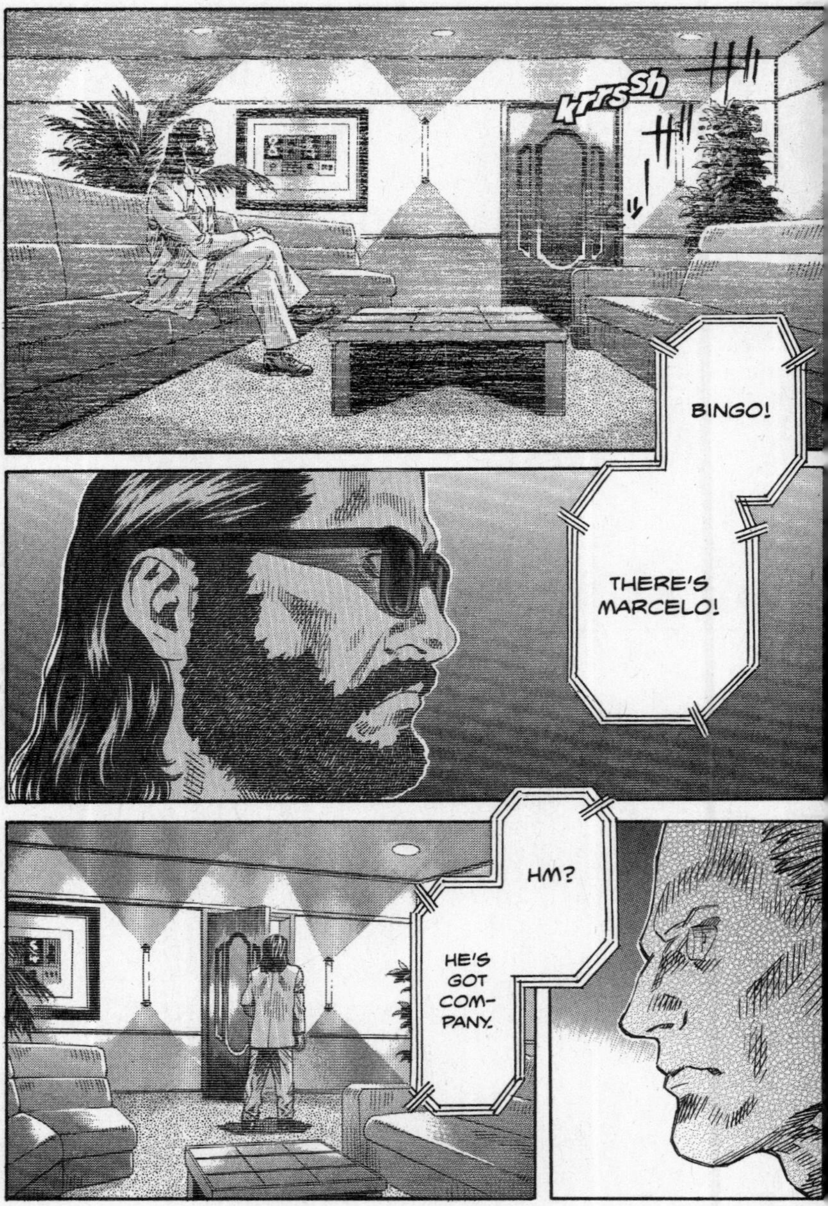
krrssh
BINGO!
THERE'S MARCELO!
HM?
HE'S GOT COM-PANY.

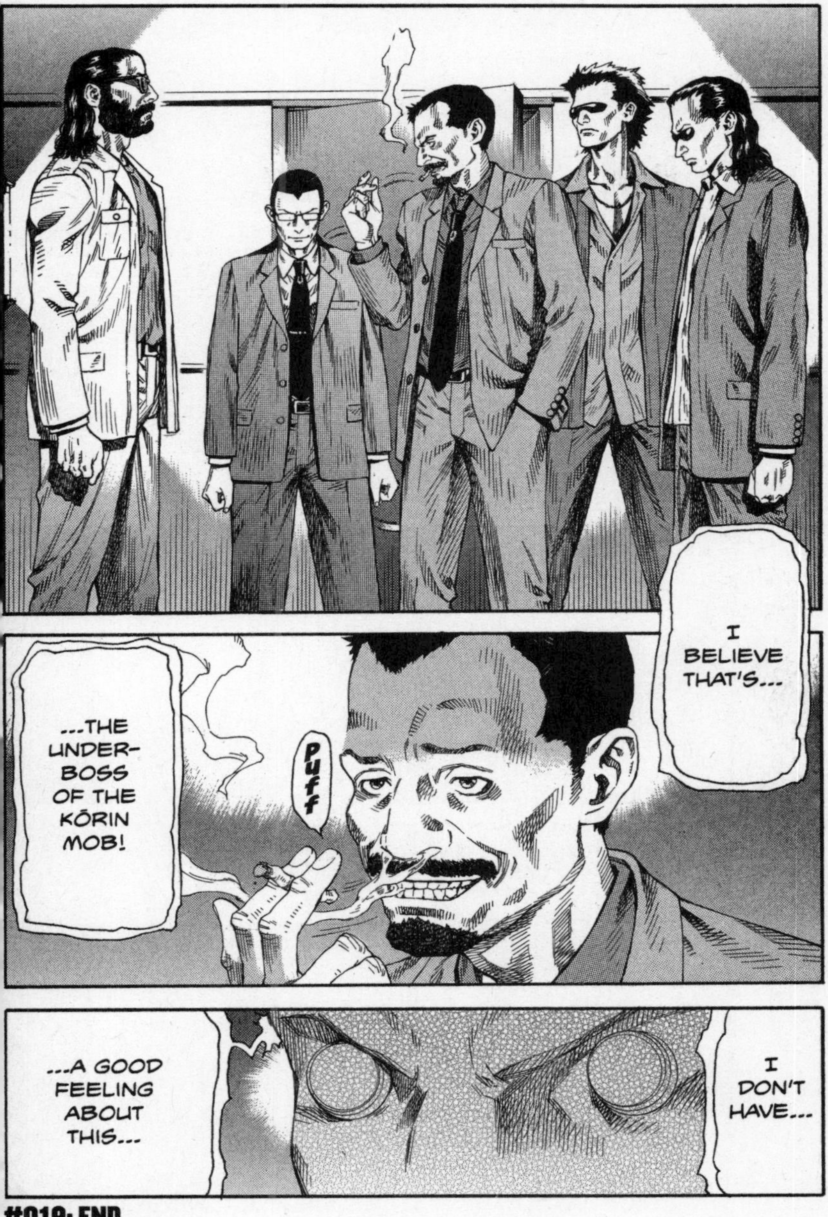
I BELIEVE THAT'S...
Puff
...THE UNDER-BOSS OF THE KŌRIN MOB!
I DON'T HAVE...
...A GOOD FEELING ABOUT THIS...

#019: END

# #020: Secret Meeting

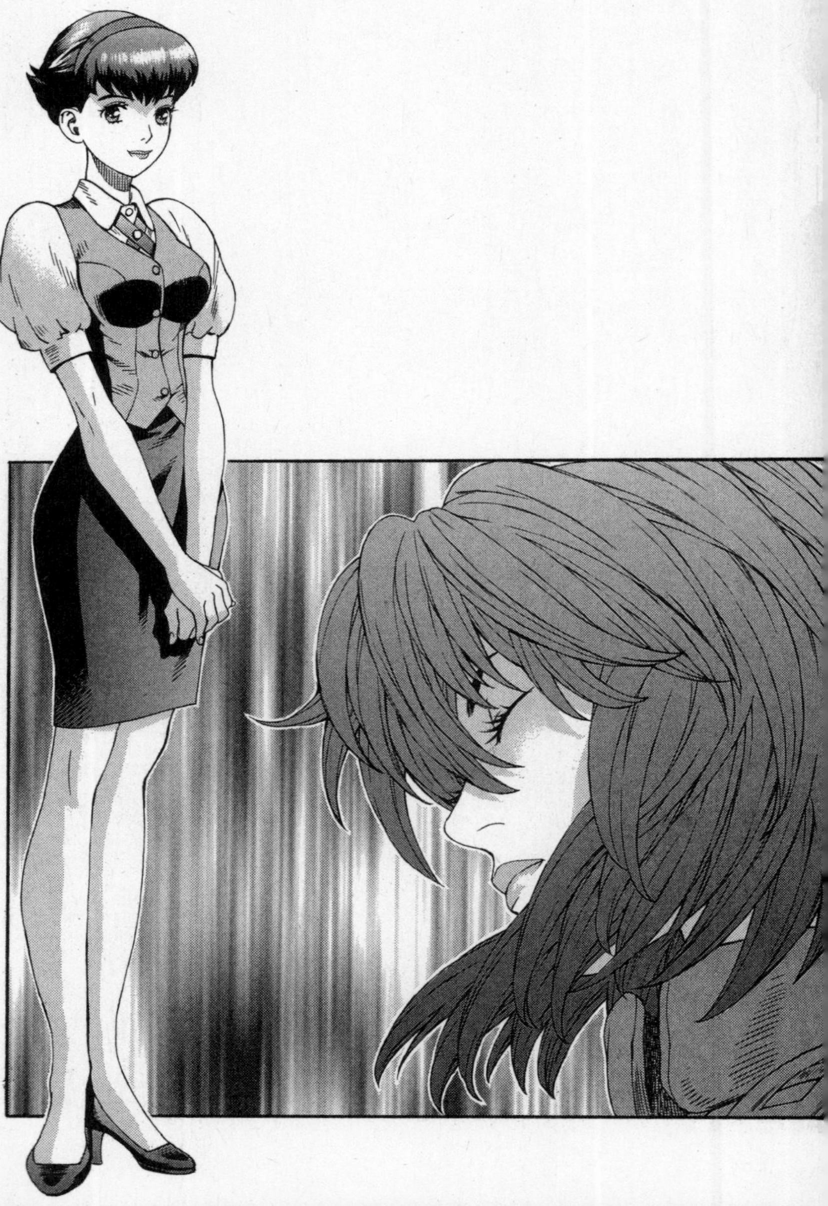

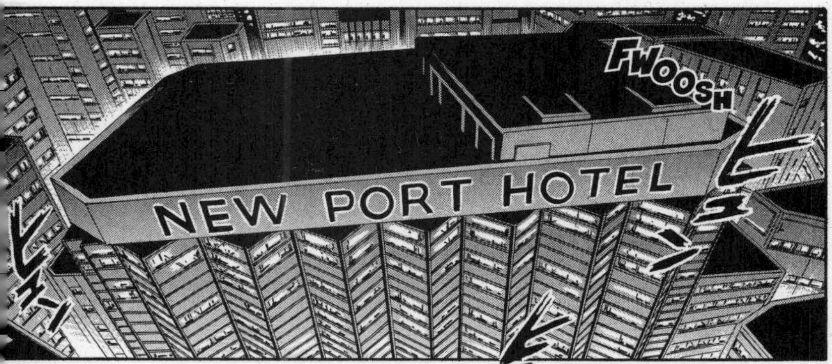
FWOOSH
NEW PORT HOTEL

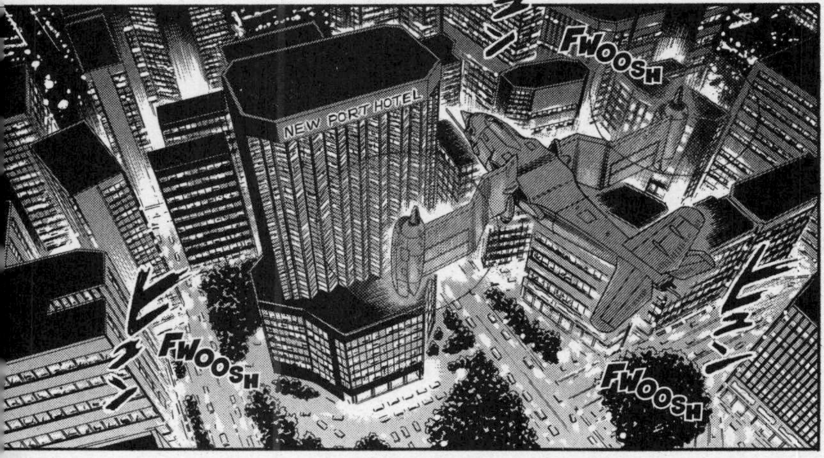
FWOOSH
NEW PORT HOTEL
FWOOSH
FWOOSH

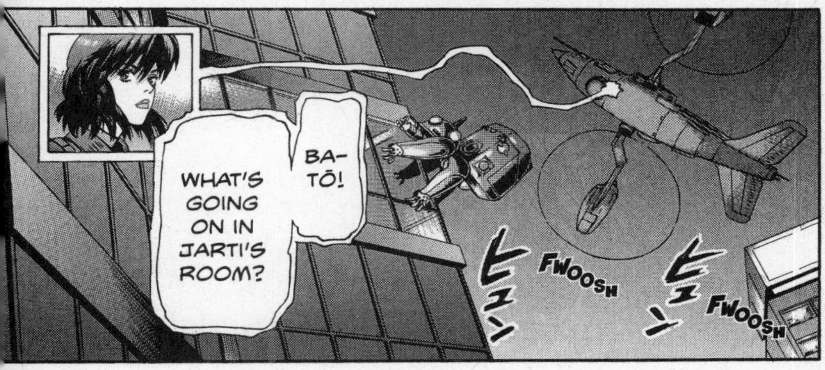
BA-TŌ!
WHAT'S GOING ON IN JARTI'S ROOM?
FWOOSH
FWOOSH

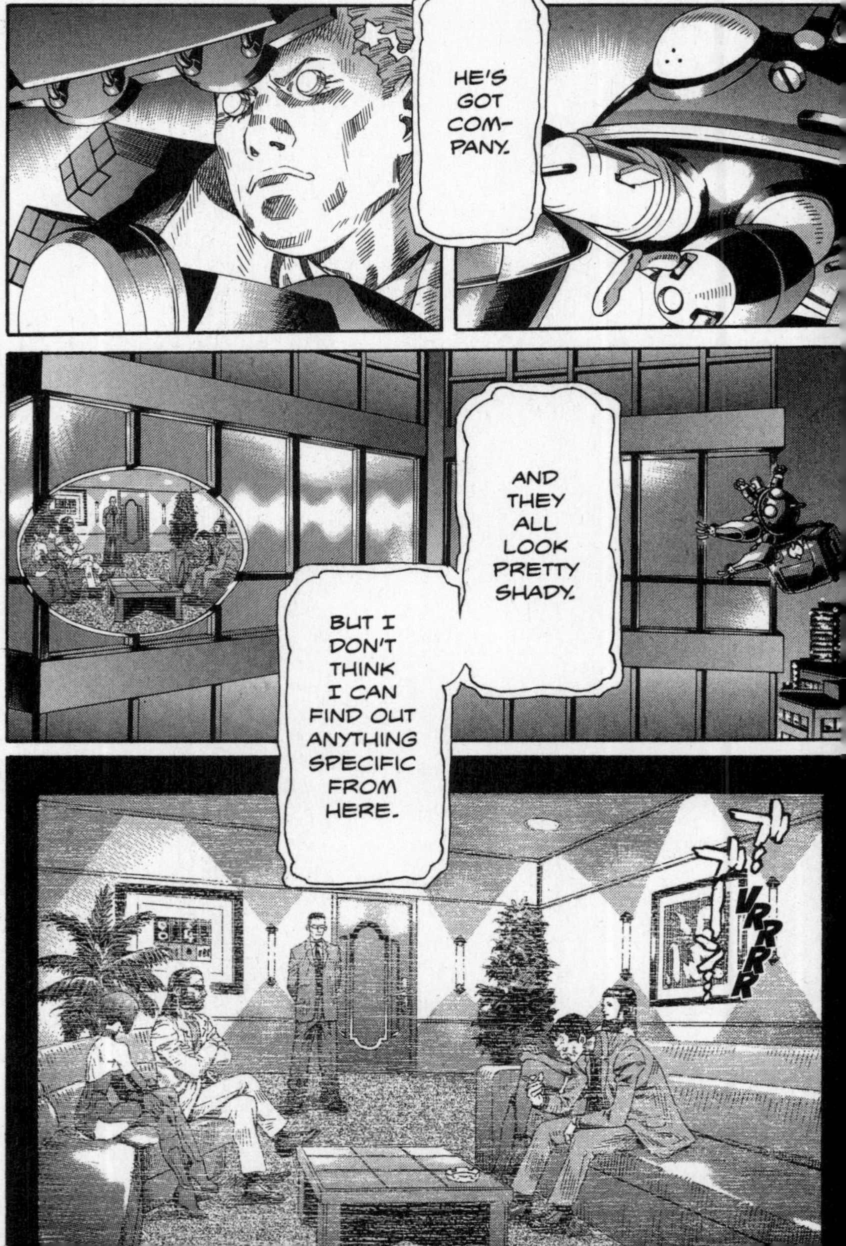
HE'S GOT COM-PANY.
AND THEY ALL LOOK PRETTY SHADY.
BUT I DON'T THINK I CAN FIND OUT ANYTHING SPECIFIC FROM HERE.
VRRRR

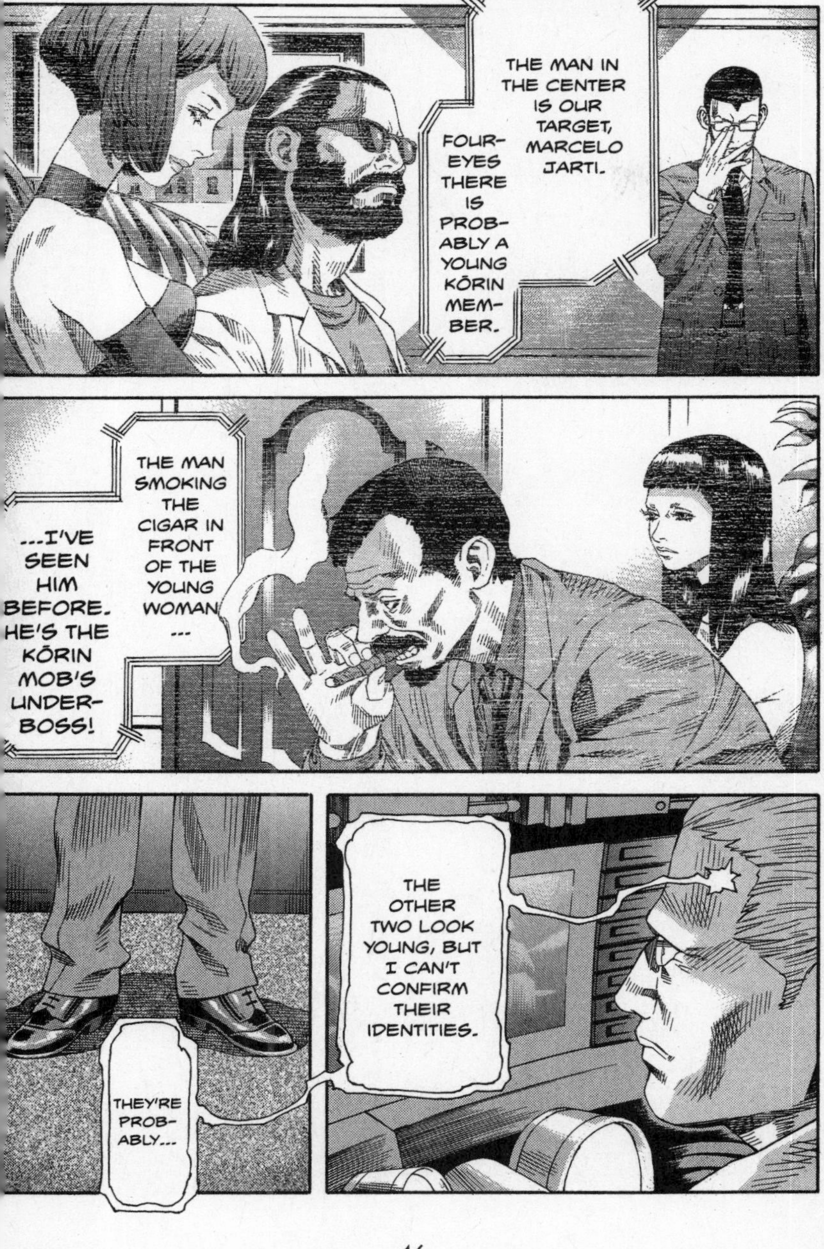
THE MAN IN THE CENTER IS OUR TARGET, MARCELO JARTI.
FOUR-EYES THERE IS PROBABLY A YOUNG KŌRIN MEMBER.
THE MAN SMOKING THE CIGAR IN FRONT OF THE YOUNG WOMAN...
...I'VE SEEN HIM BEFORE. HE'S THE KŌRIN MOB'S UNDERBOSS!
THE OTHER TWO LOOK YOUNG, BUT I CAN'T CONFIRM THEIR IDENTITIES.
THEY'RE PROBABLY...

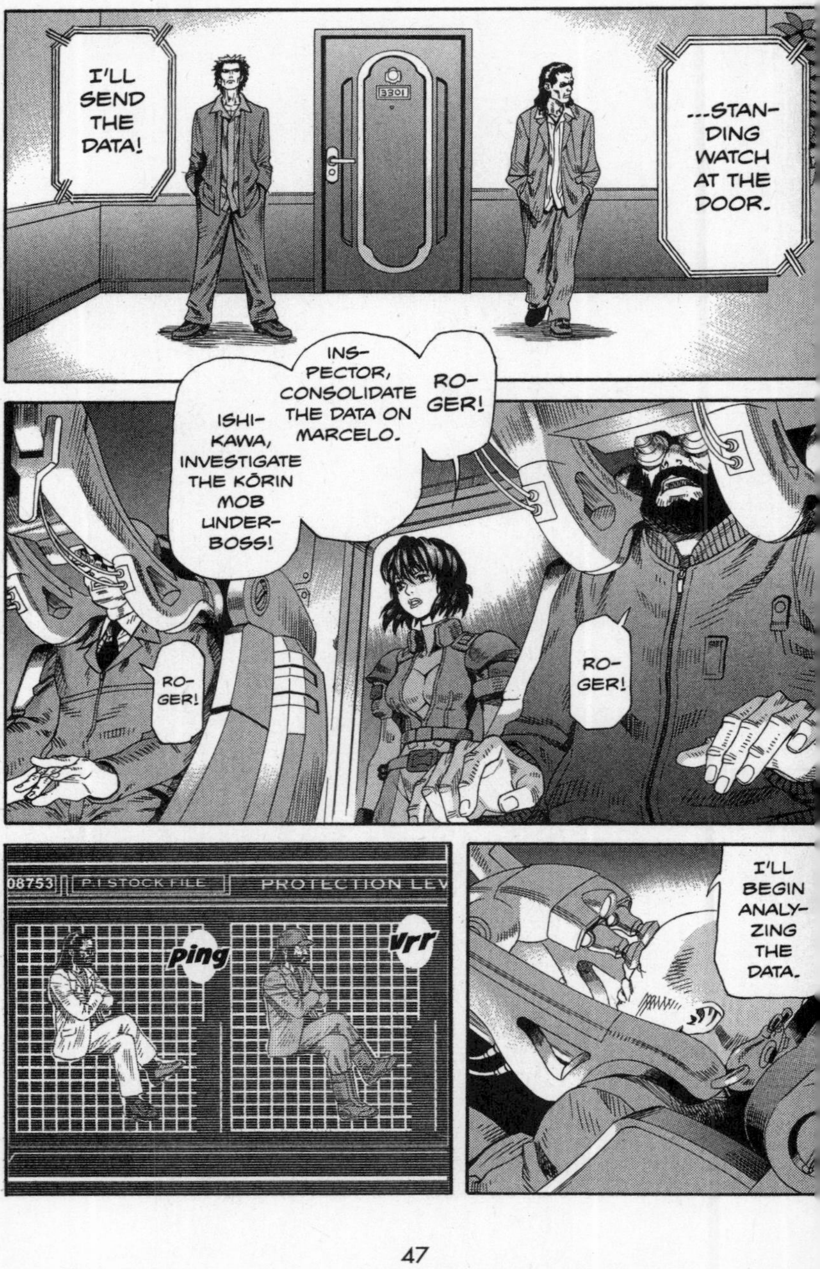
---STAN-DING WATCH AT THE DOOR.
I'LL SEND THE DATA!
INS-PECTOR, CONSOLIDATE THE DATA ON MARCELO.
RO-GER!
ISHI-KAWA, INVESTIGATE THE KŌRIN MOB UNDER-BOSS!
RO-GER!
RO-GER!
I'LL BEGIN ANALY-ZING THE DATA.
08753
P.I STOCK FILE
PROTECTION LEV
ping
vrr

00008753 | P.I STOCK FILE | PROTECTION LEVEL

MATCH

*beep*

IT'S THE REAL ONE.

MAR- CELO JARTI.

*beep*

--- OF THE KŌRIN MOB'S NEW PORT BRANCH.

KANE- KICHI GONDŌ, AN UNDER- BOSS IN CHARGE ---

HERE IT IS!

00008753 | P.I STOCK FILE | PROTECTION LEVEL 8

HE'S PRETTY MUCH THE LYNCHPIN OF THEIR ENTIRE OPERATION.

| NAME | GONDO KANEKICHI |
|---|---|
| NATIONALITY | JAPAN |
| CASEFILE | 98700185 |
| SEX | MALE |
| HEIGHT | 5ft 9in |
| WEIGHT | 147lb |
| HAIR | BLACK |
| EYES | BRAWN |
| AGE | 57 |
| CONVICTION | 34 |
| CYBORGED | NONE |
| BLOOD TYPE | B |
| FEATURES | A BAD FACE |

*beep*

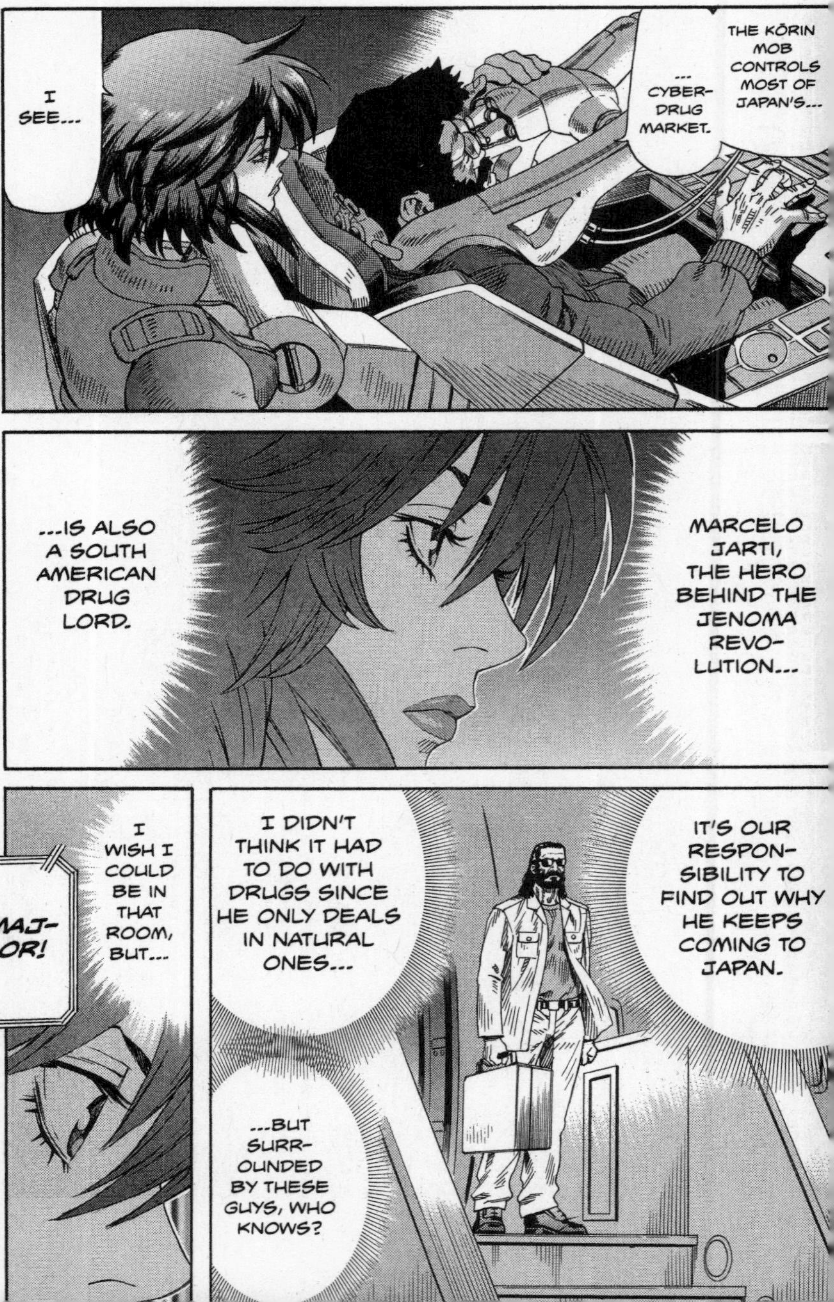
THE KŌRIN MOB CONTROLS MOST OF JAPAN'S...
...CYBER-DRUG MARKET.
I SEE...
MARCELO JARTI, THE HERO BEHIND THE JENOMA REVO-LUTION...
...IS ALSO A SOUTH AMERICAN DRUG LORD.
IT'S OUR RESPON-SIBILITY TO FIND OUT WHY HE KEEPS COMING TO JAPAN.
I DIDN'T THINK IT HAD TO DO WITH DRUGS SINCE HE ONLY DEALS IN NATURAL ONES...
...BUT SURR-OUNDED BY THESE GUYS, WHO KNOWS?
I WISH I COULD BE IN THAT ROOM, BUT...
MAJ-OR!

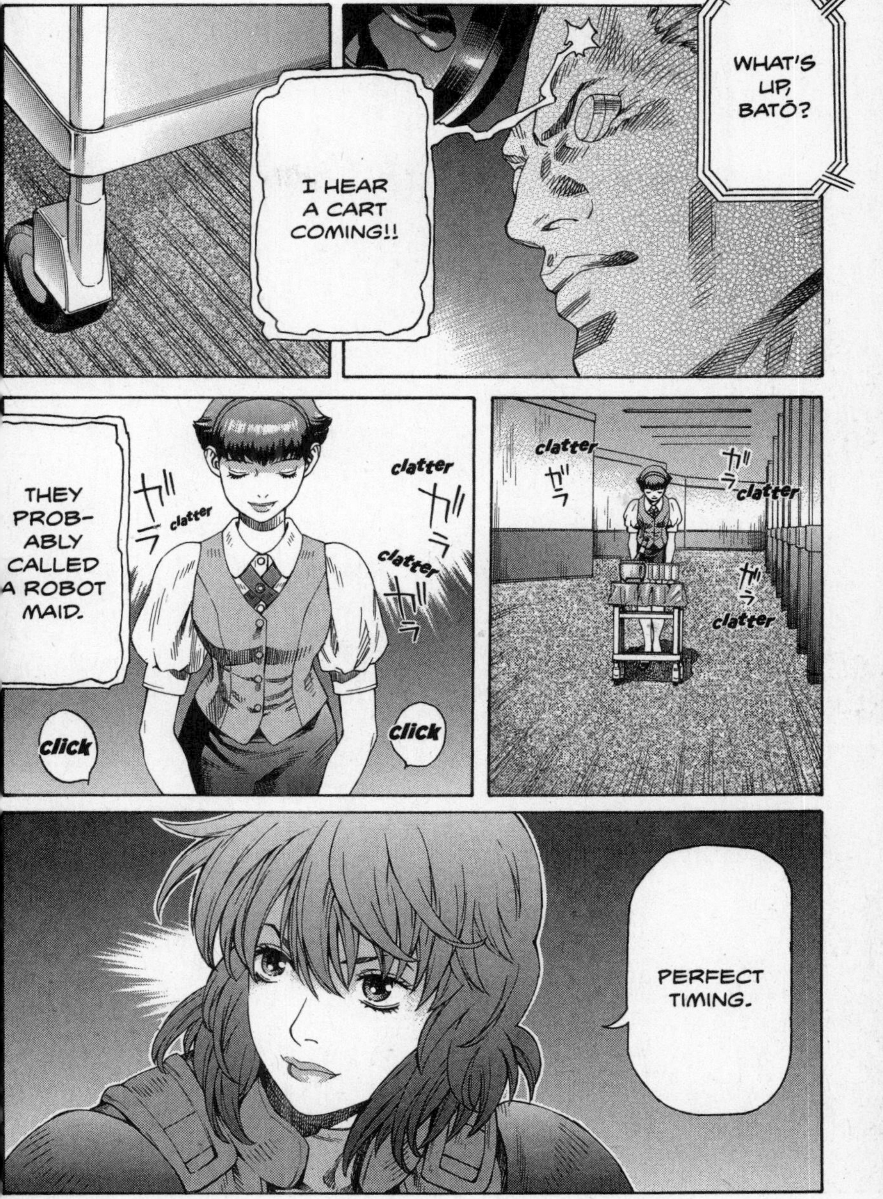
WHAT'S UP, BATŌ?
I HEAR A CART COMING!!
clatter
ガラ
ガラ
clatter
ガラ
clatter
clatter
ガラ
clatter
ガラ
THEY PROBABLY CALLED A ROBOT MAID.
ガラ
clatter
click
click
PERFECT TIMING.

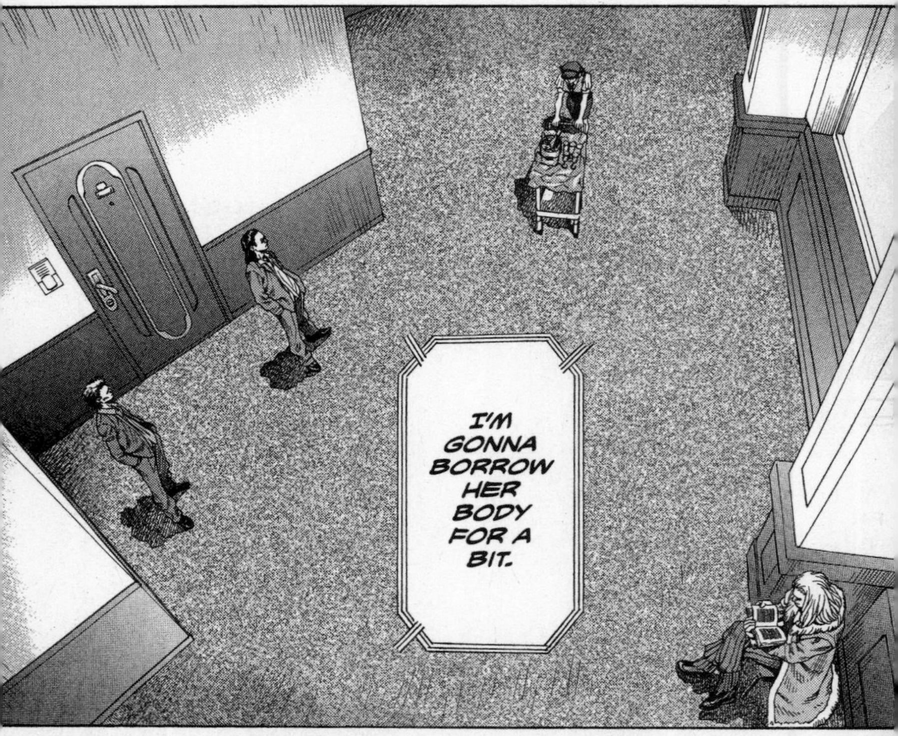
I'M GONNA BORROW HER BODY FOR A BIT.

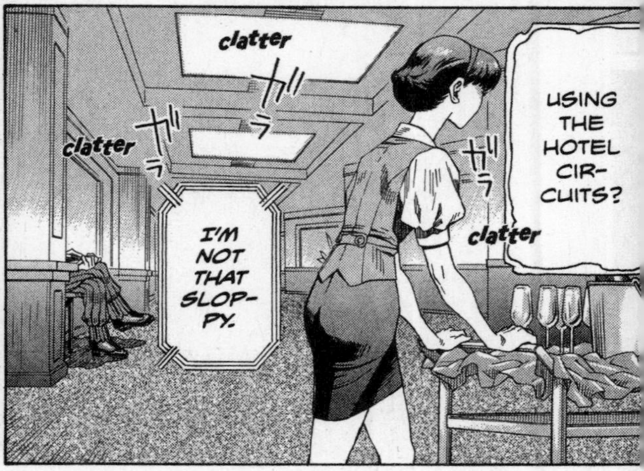
USING THE HOTEL CIR-CUITS?
clatter
clatter
clatter
I'M NOT THAT SLOP-PY.

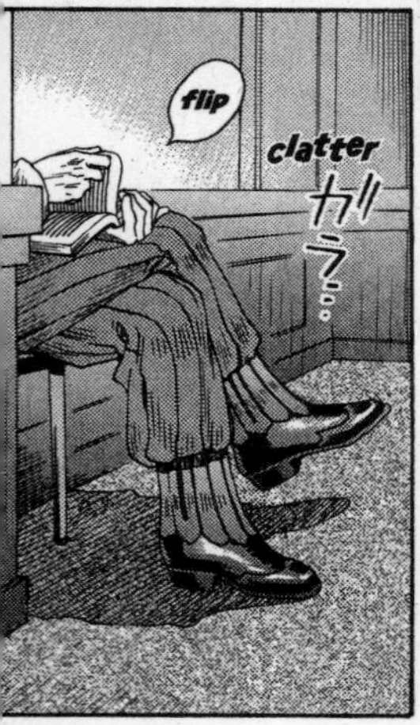
clatter
flip

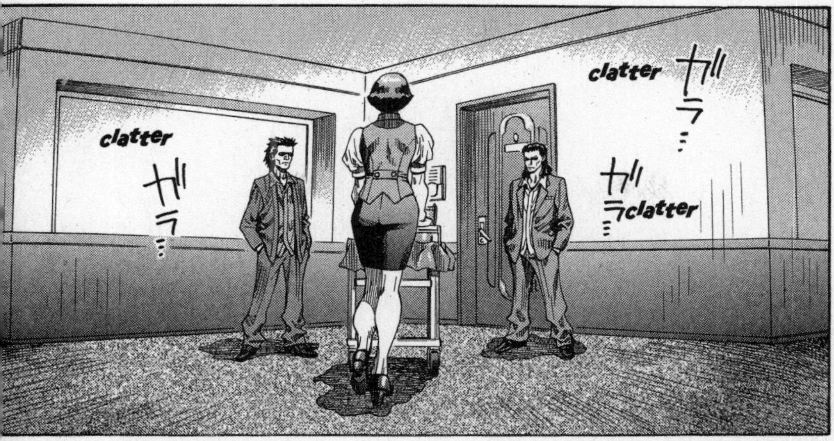
clatter
ガラ…
ガラ
clatter
clatter
ガラ…
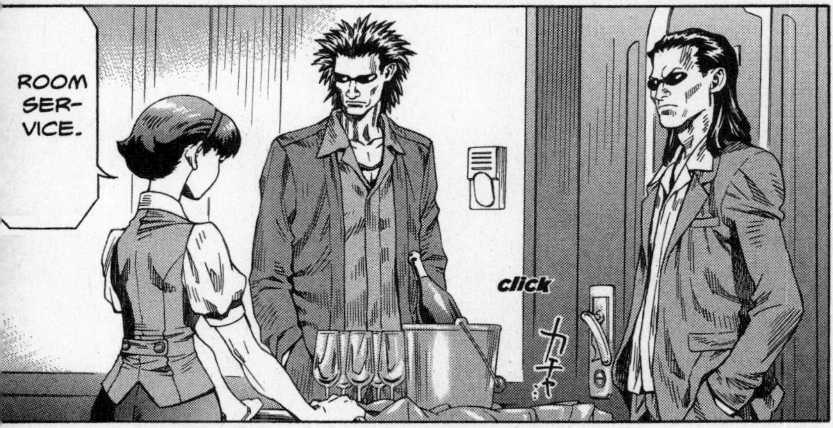
ROOM SER-VICE.
click
カチャ…
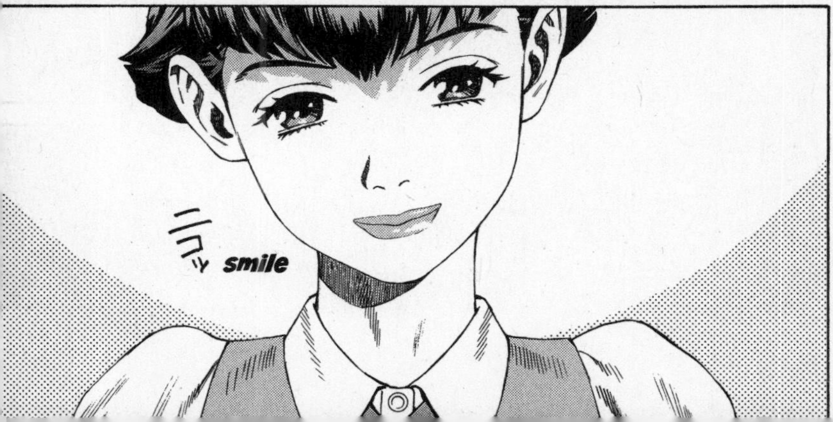
ニコッ
smile

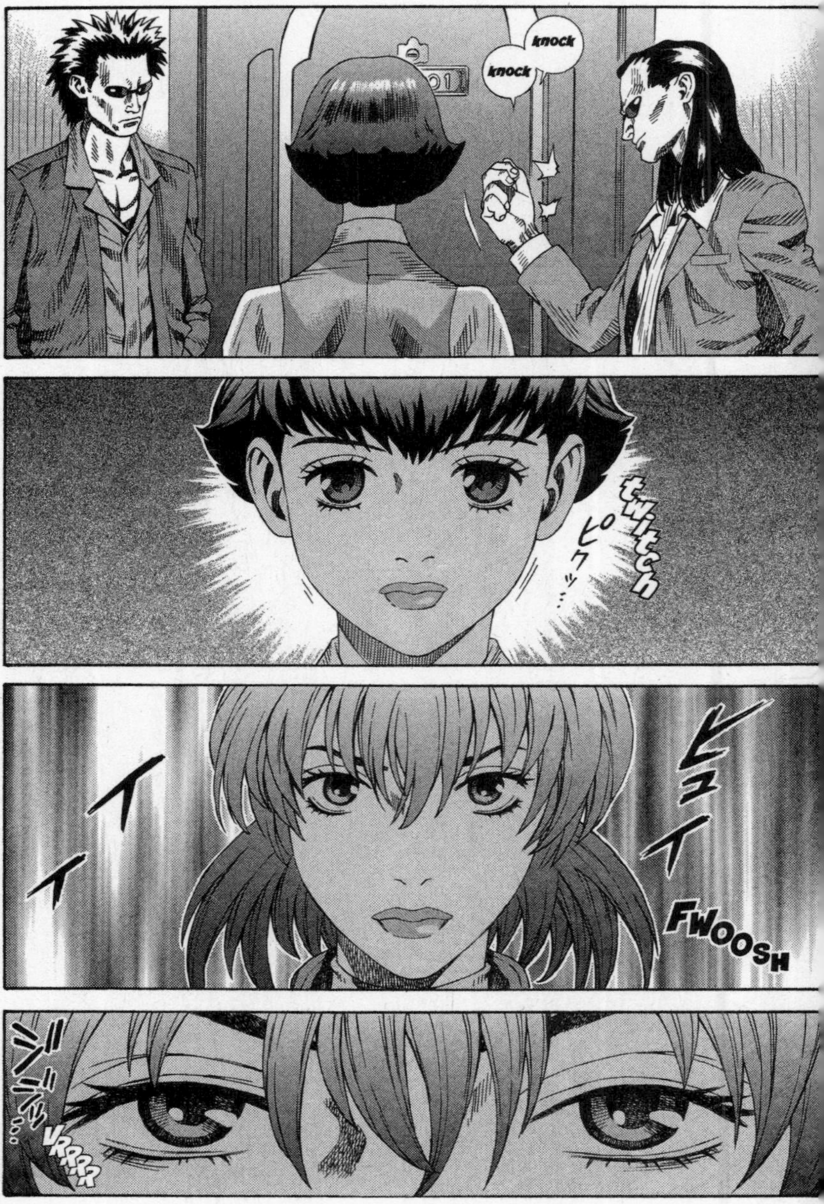
knock
knock
twitch
ピクッ…
FWOOSH
VRRRR

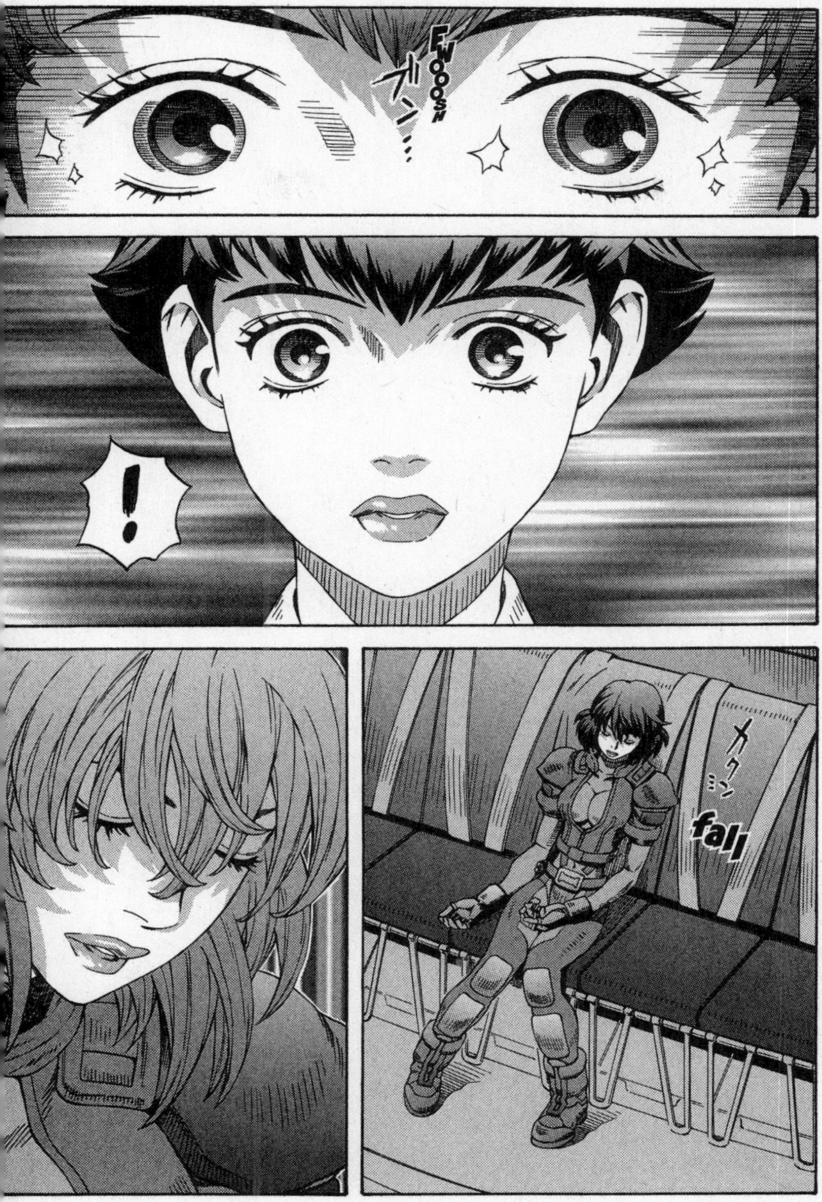
EWOOOSH
ブン…
!
fall

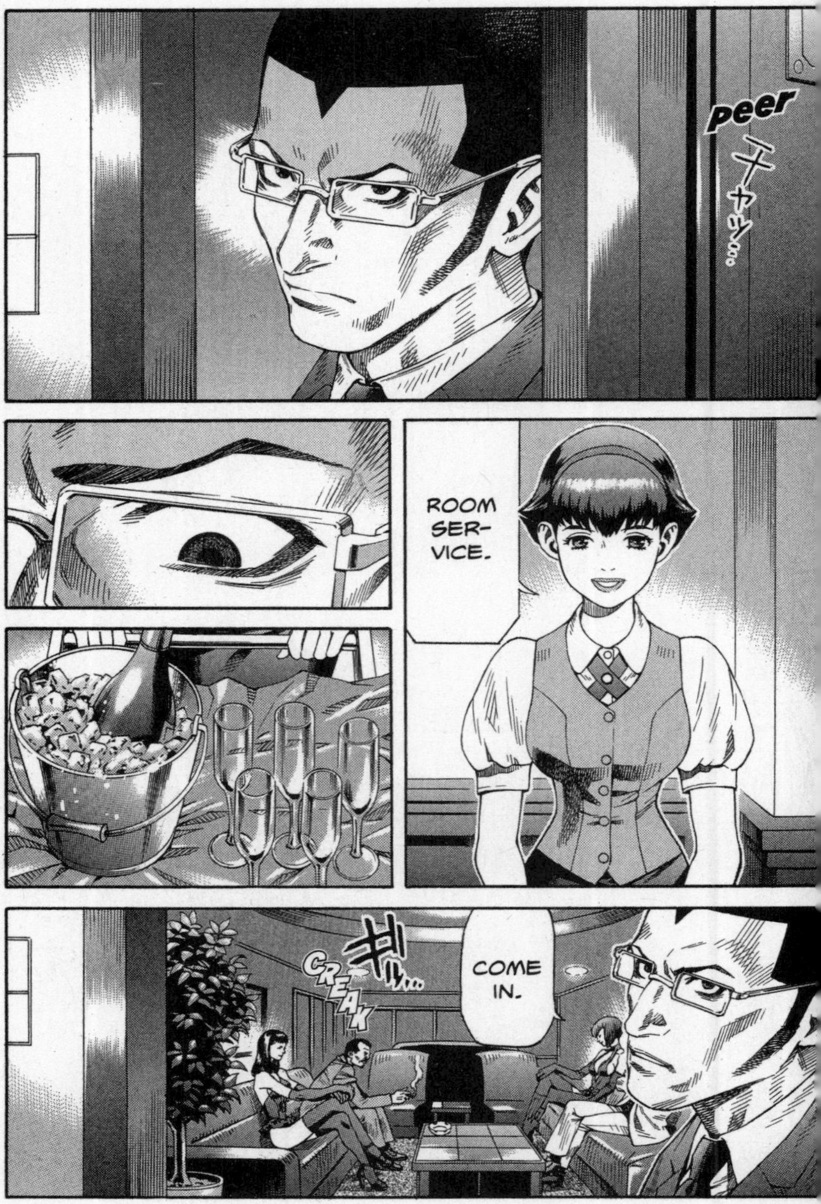
Peer
チャッ…
ROOM SER-VICE.
COME IN.
ギィ…
CREAK

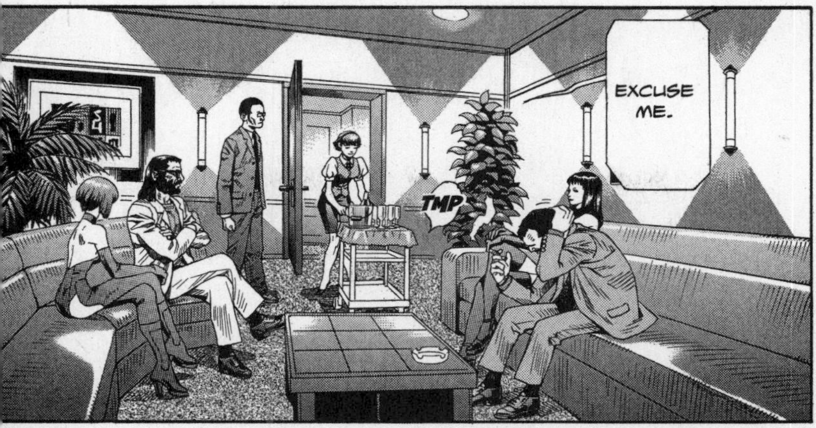
EXCUSE ME.
TMP

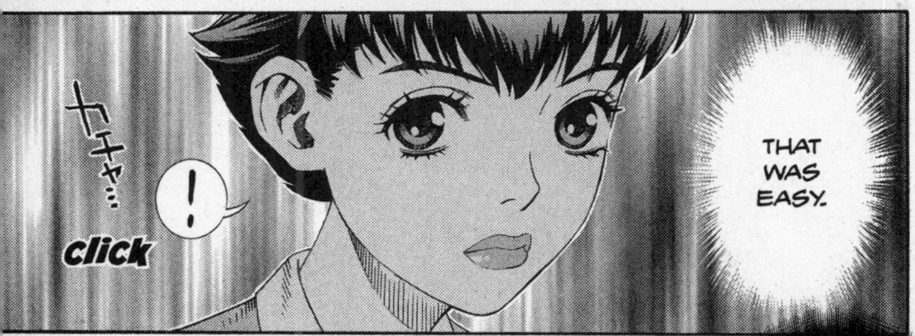
THAT WAS EASY.
!
カチャ…
click

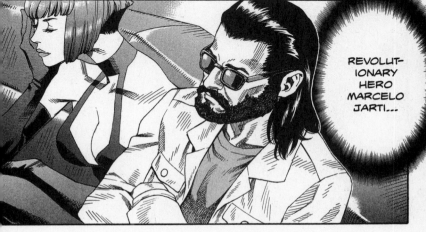

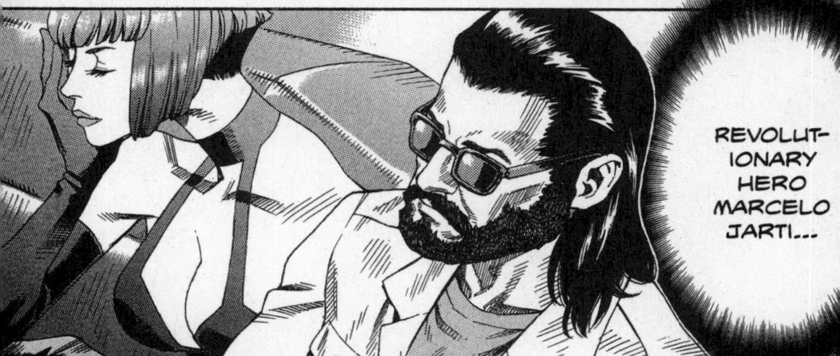
REVOLUTIONARY HERO MARCELO JARTI...

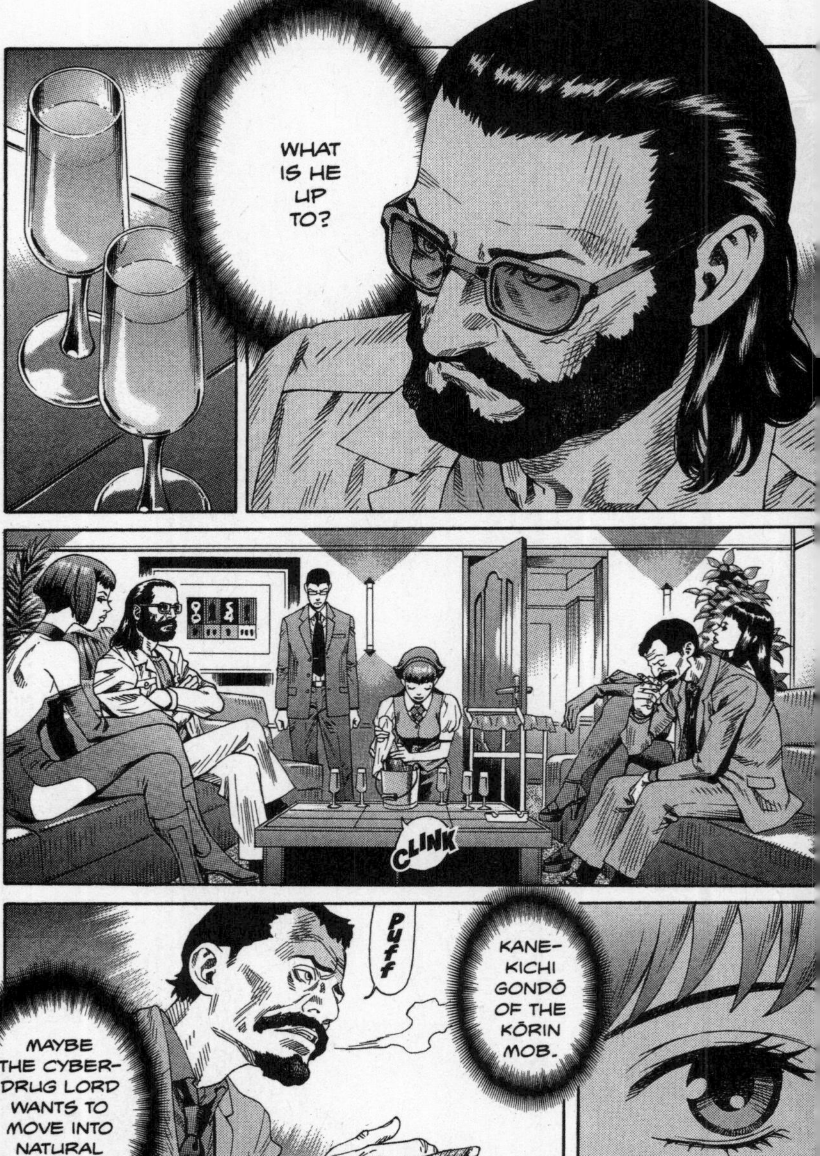
WHAT IS HE UP TO?
CLINK
KANE-KICHI GONDŌ OF THE KŌRIN MOB.
PUFF
MAYBE THE CYBER-DRUG LORD WANTS TO MOVE INTO NATURAL DRUGS, TOO?

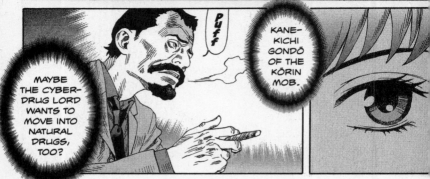

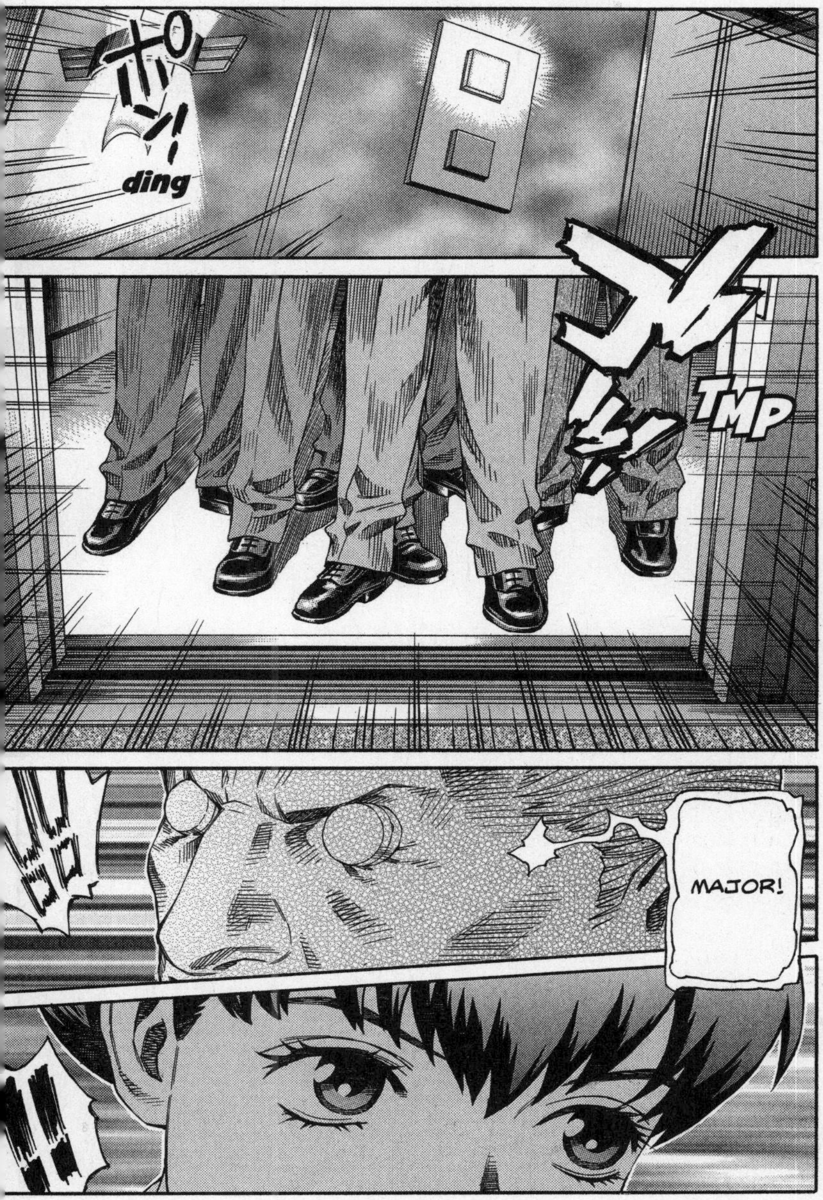
ding
TMP
MAJOR!

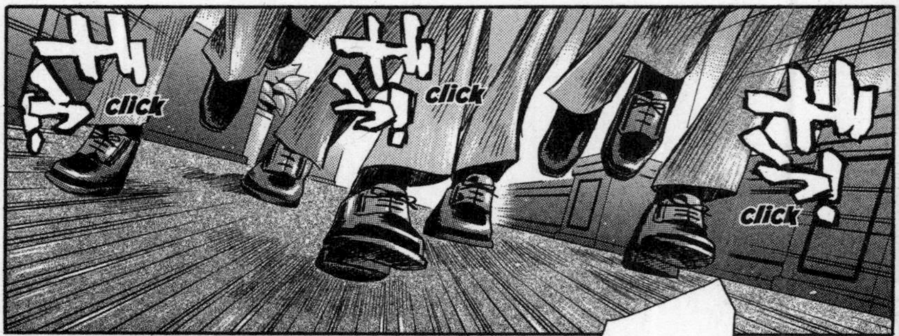
click
click
click

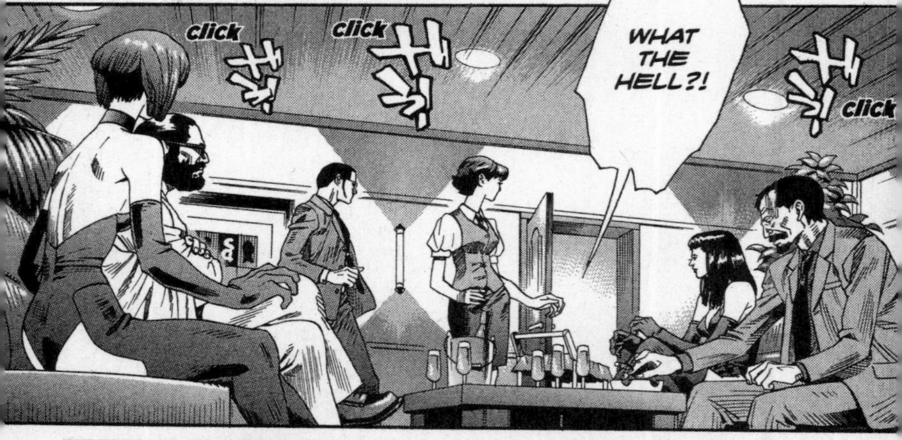
click
WHAT THE HELL?!
click
click

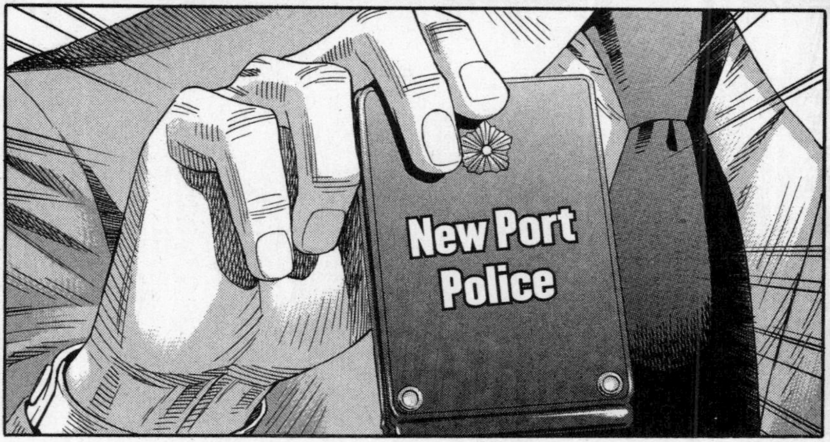
New Port Police

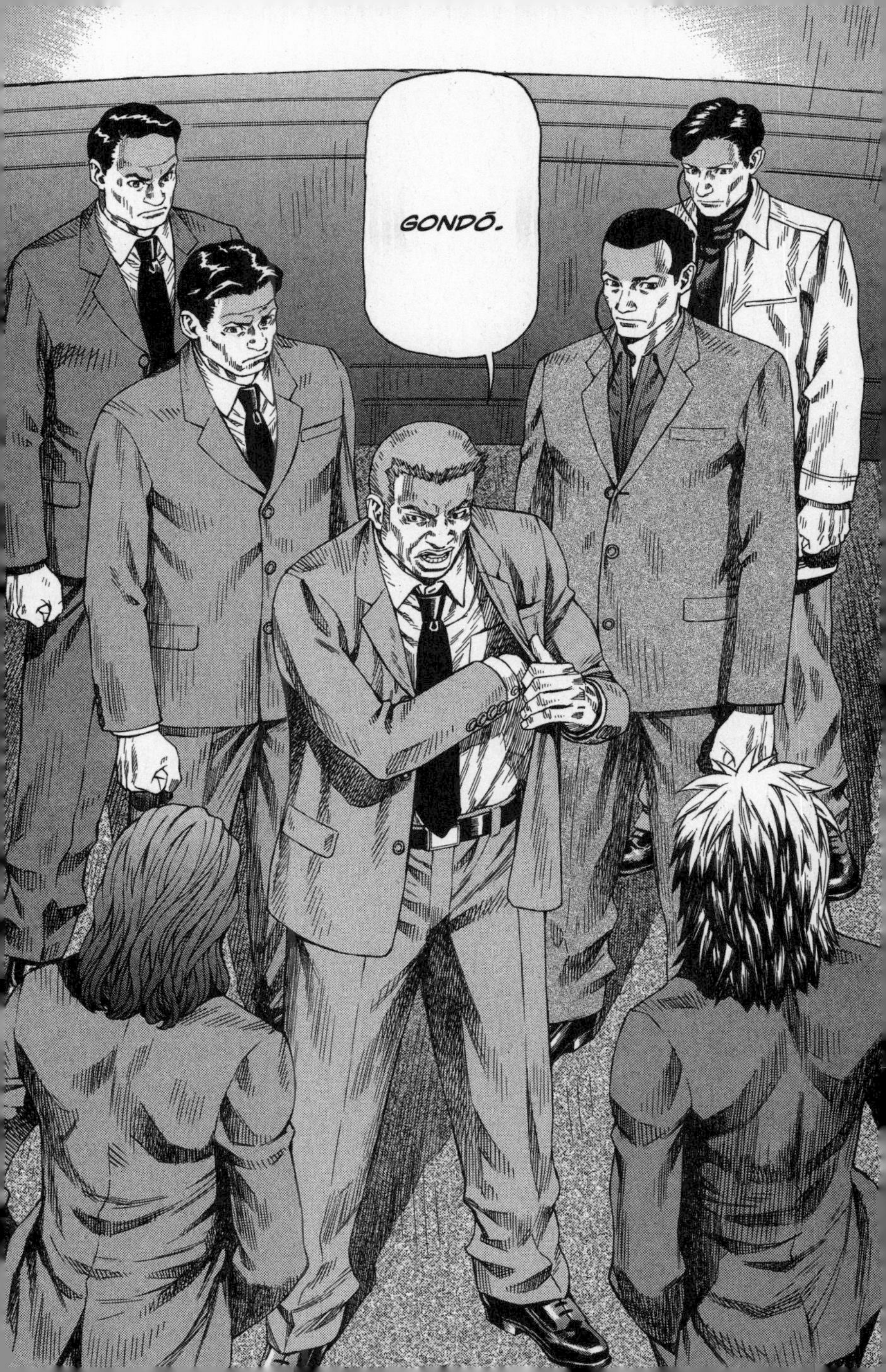
GONDŌ.

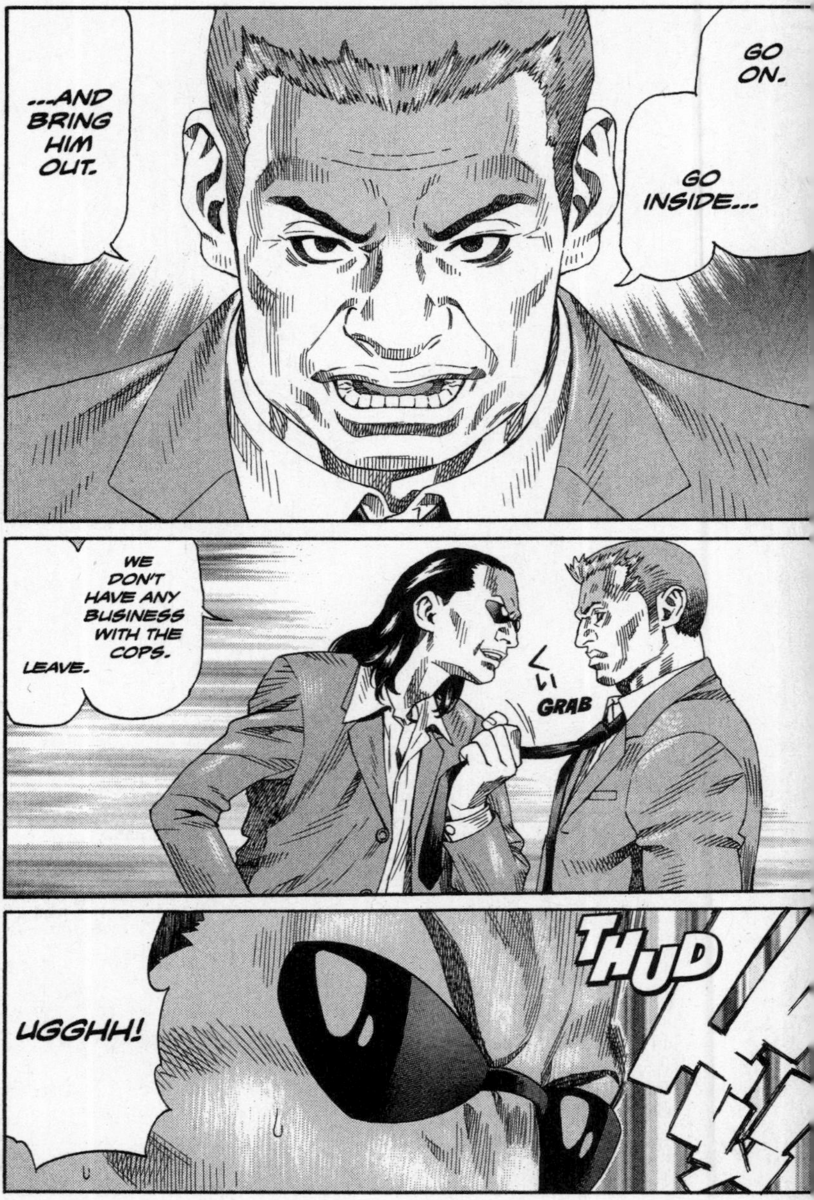
GO ON.
GO INSIDE...
...AND BRING HIM OUT.
WE DON'T HAVE ANY BUSINESS WITH THE COPS. LEAVE.
GRAB
THUD
UGGHH!

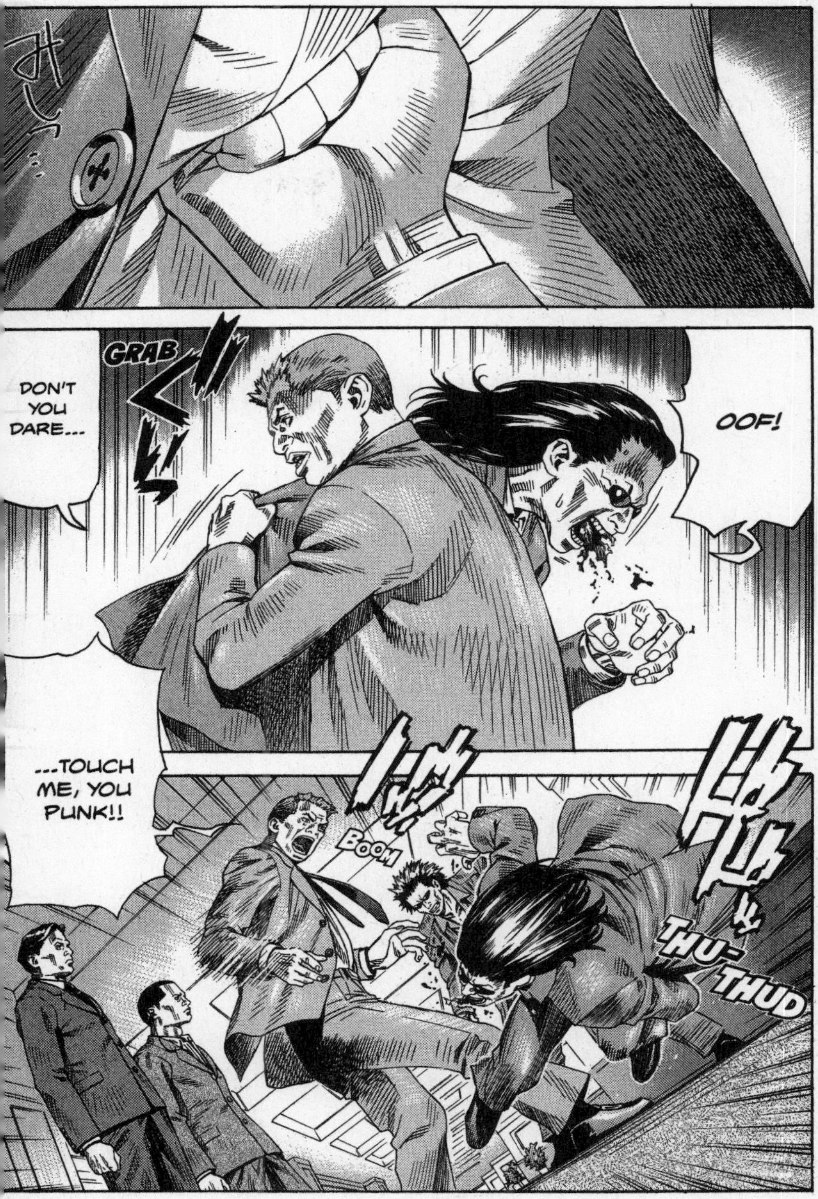
OOF!
GRAB
DON'T YOU DARE...
THU-THUD
BOOM
...TOUCH ME, YOU PUNK!!

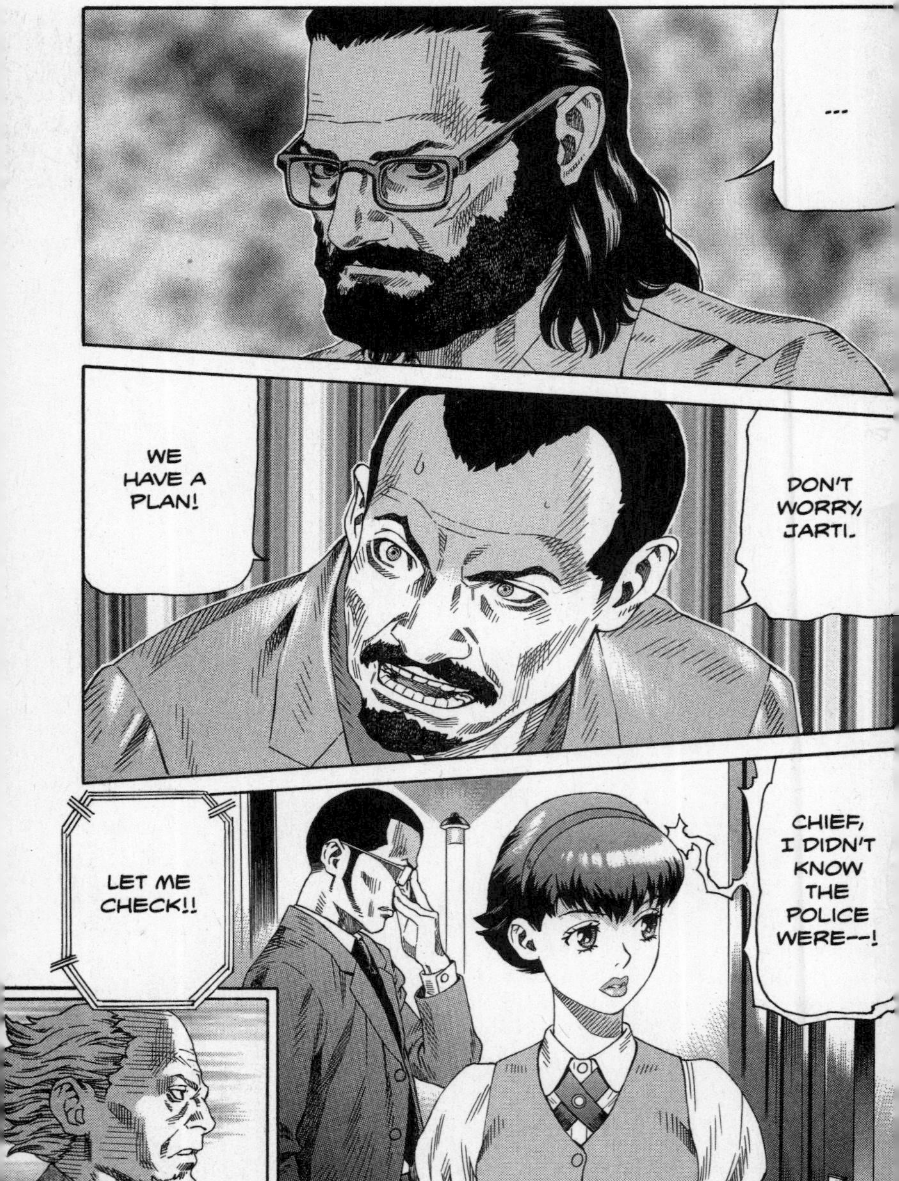
...
DON'T WORRY, JARTI.
WE HAVE A PLAN!
CHIEF, I DIDN'T KNOW THE POLICE WERE--!
LET ME CHECK!!

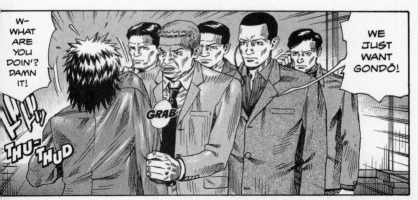

WE JUST WANT GONDŌ!
GRAB
W- WHAT ARE YOU DOIN'? DAMN IT!
THU-THUD
flip
H- HEY! DON'T JUST...
...SIT TH- ERE!
SLAM
TMP

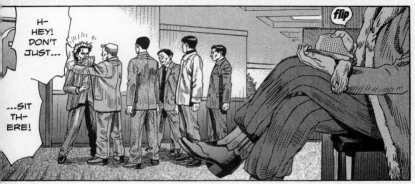

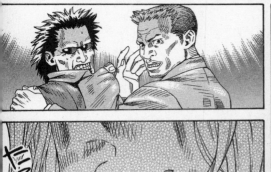

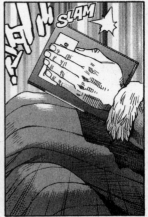

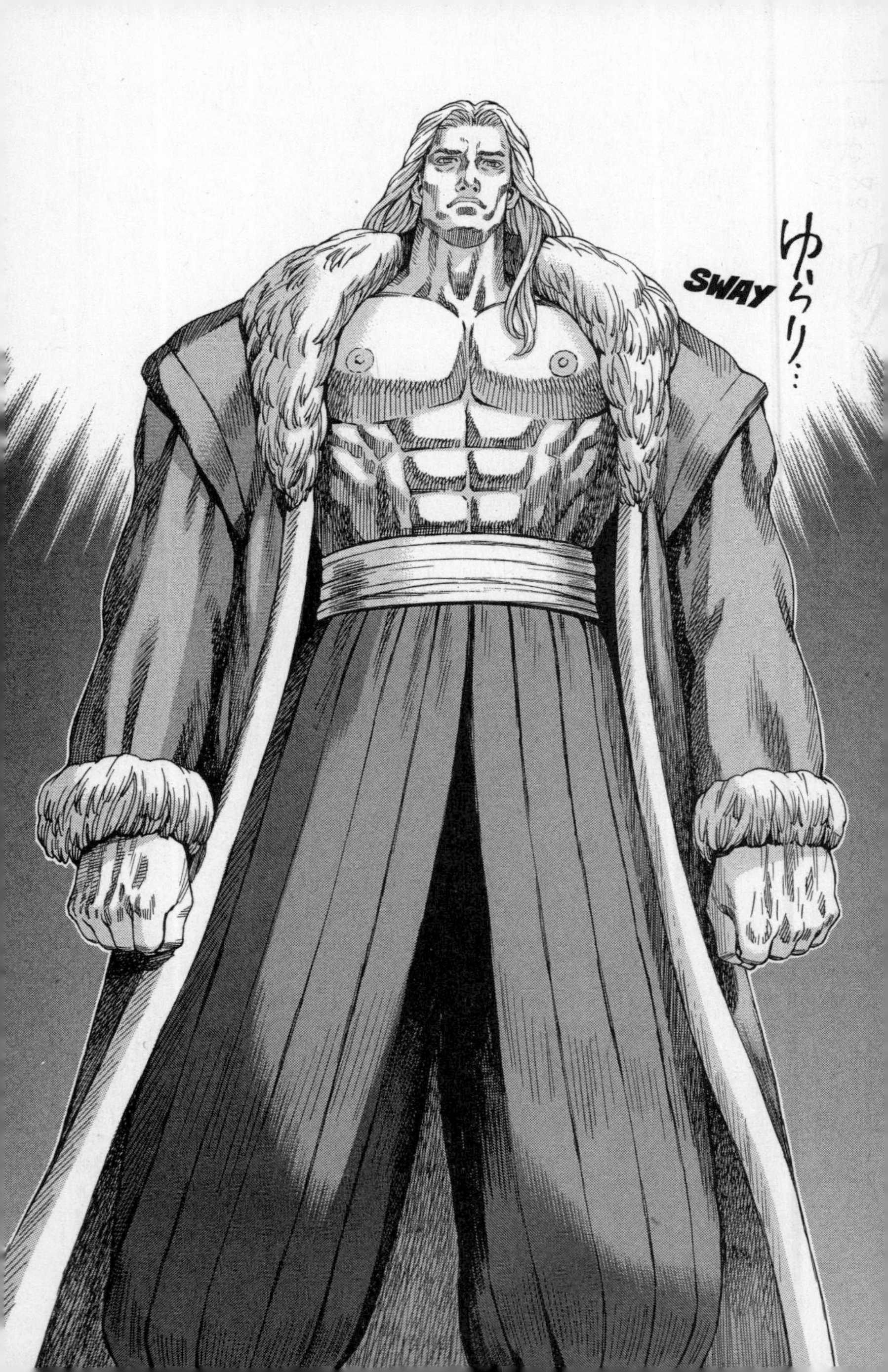
ゆらり…
SWAY

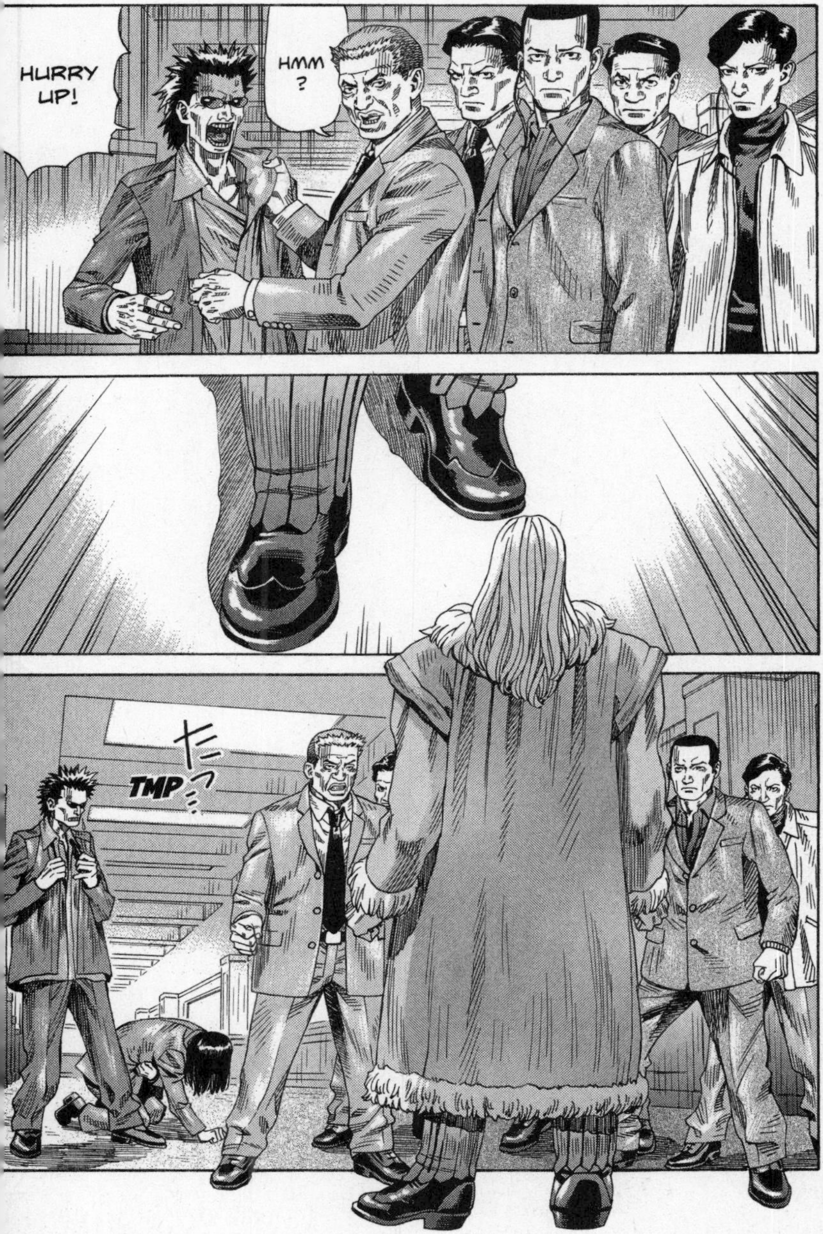
HMM ?
HURRY UP!
TMP

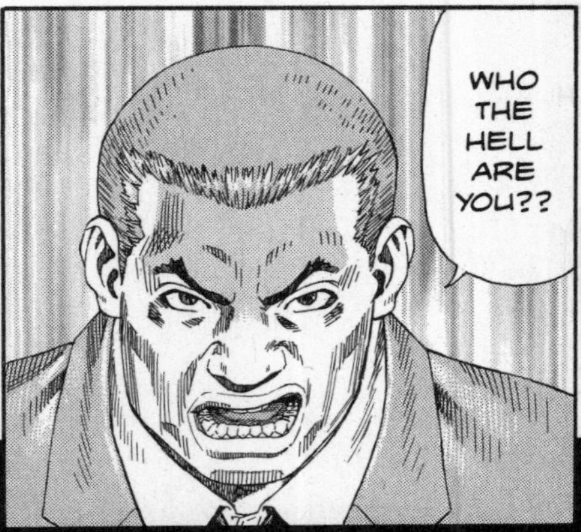
WHO THE HELL ARE YOU??
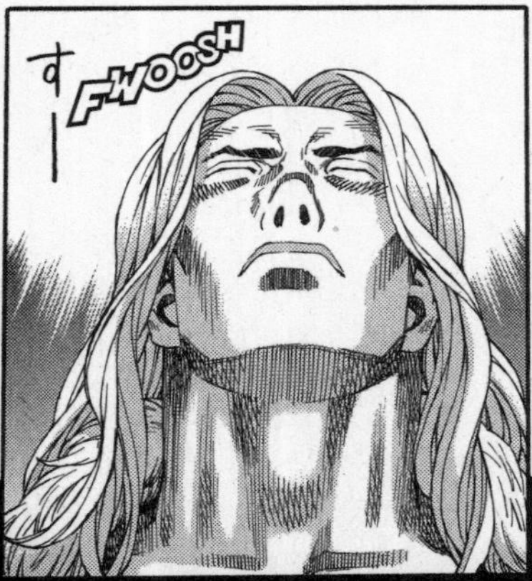
FWOOSH
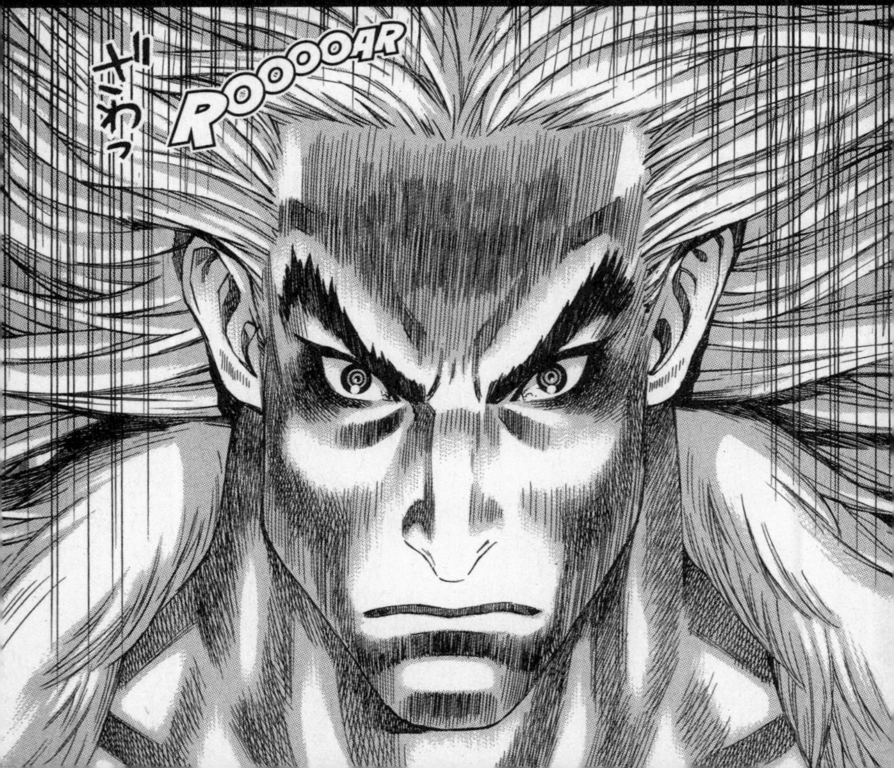
ROOOOOAR

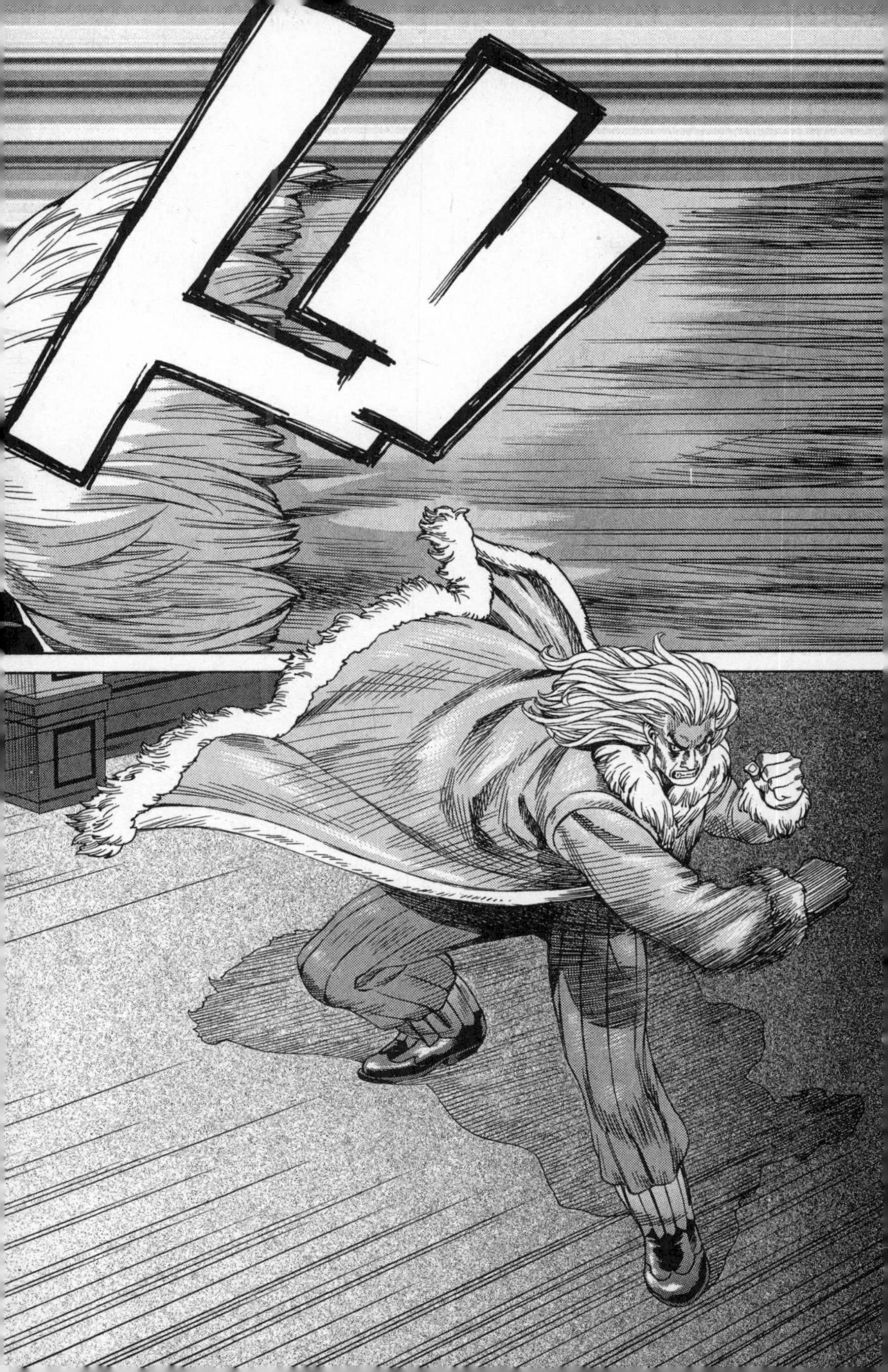

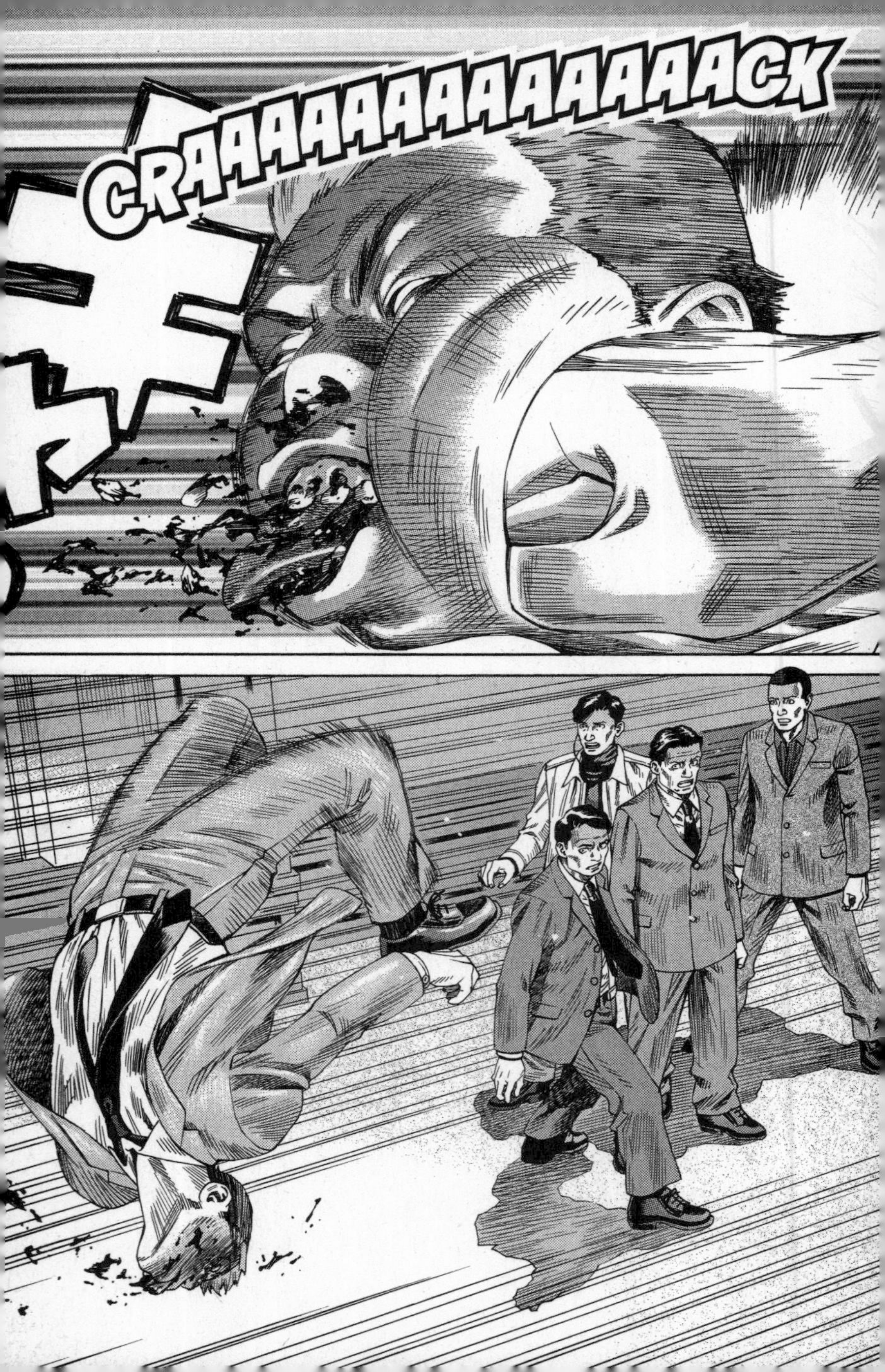
CRAAAAAAAAAAAAACK

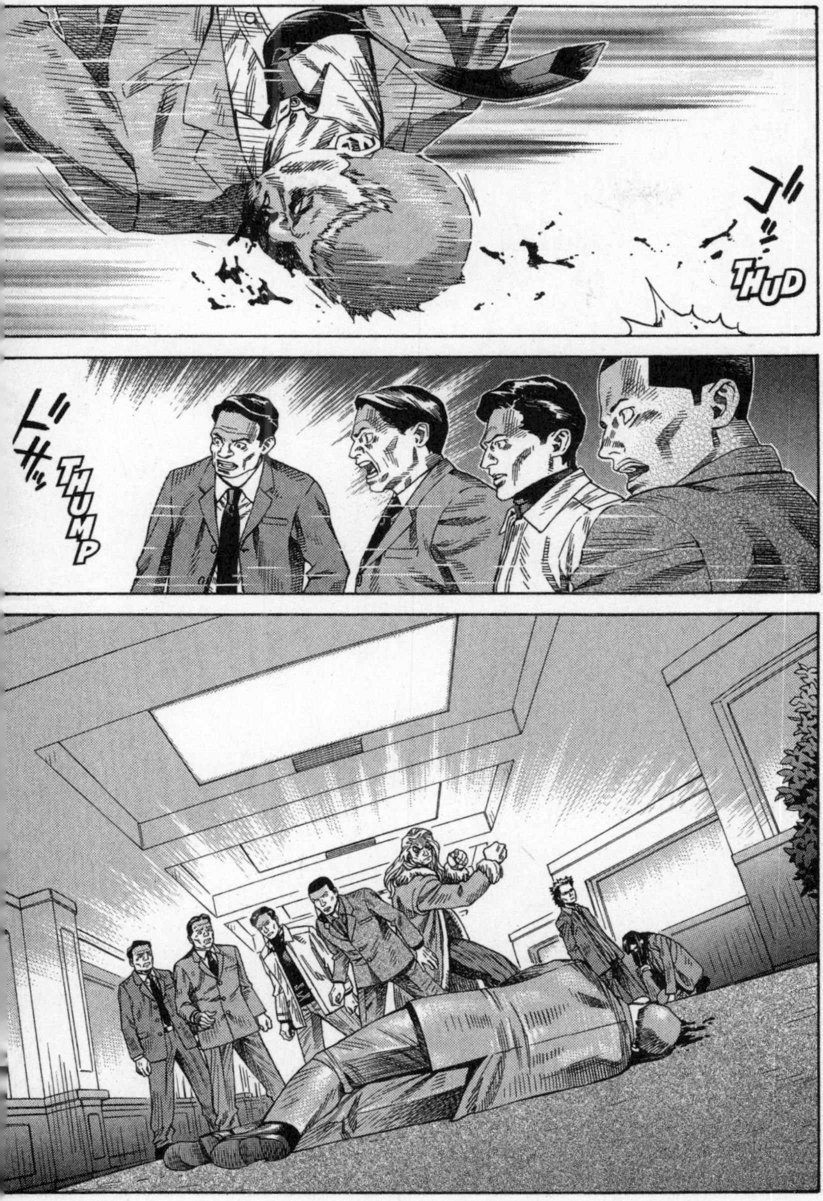
ゴッ
THUD
ドサッ
THUMP

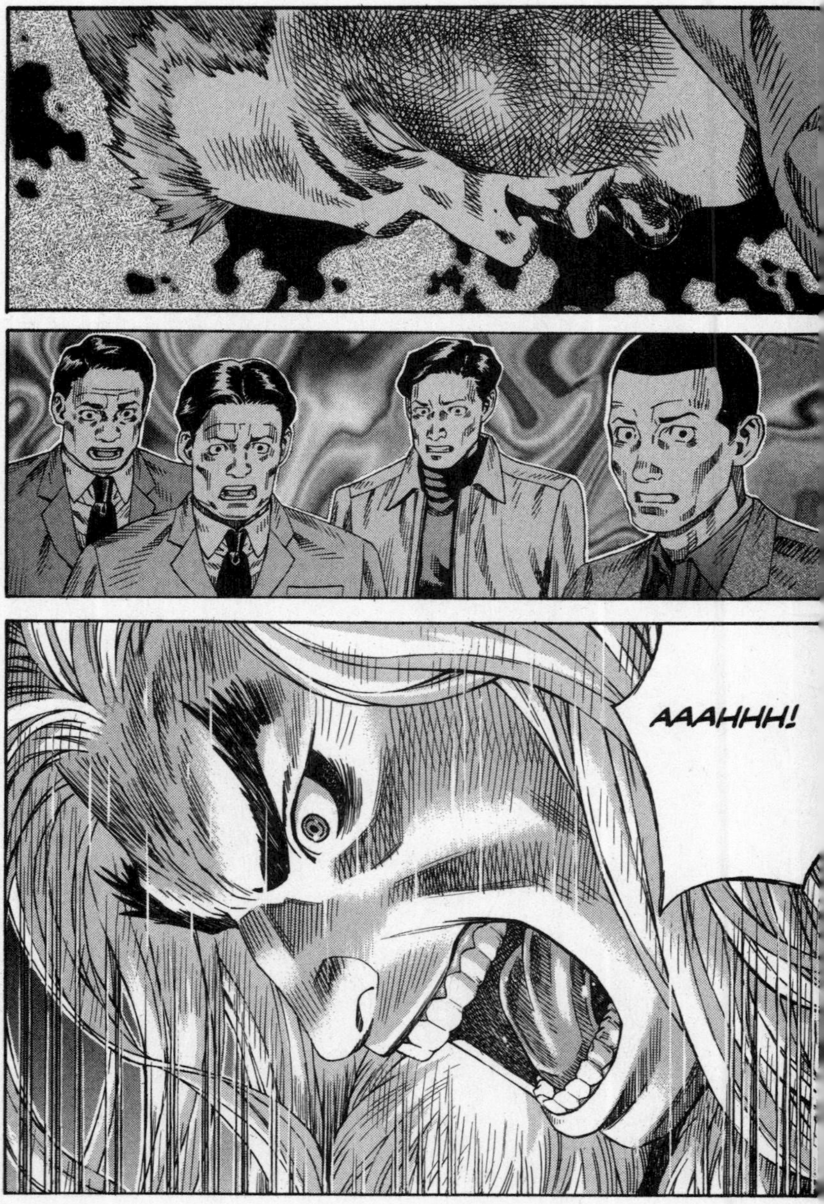
AAAHHH!

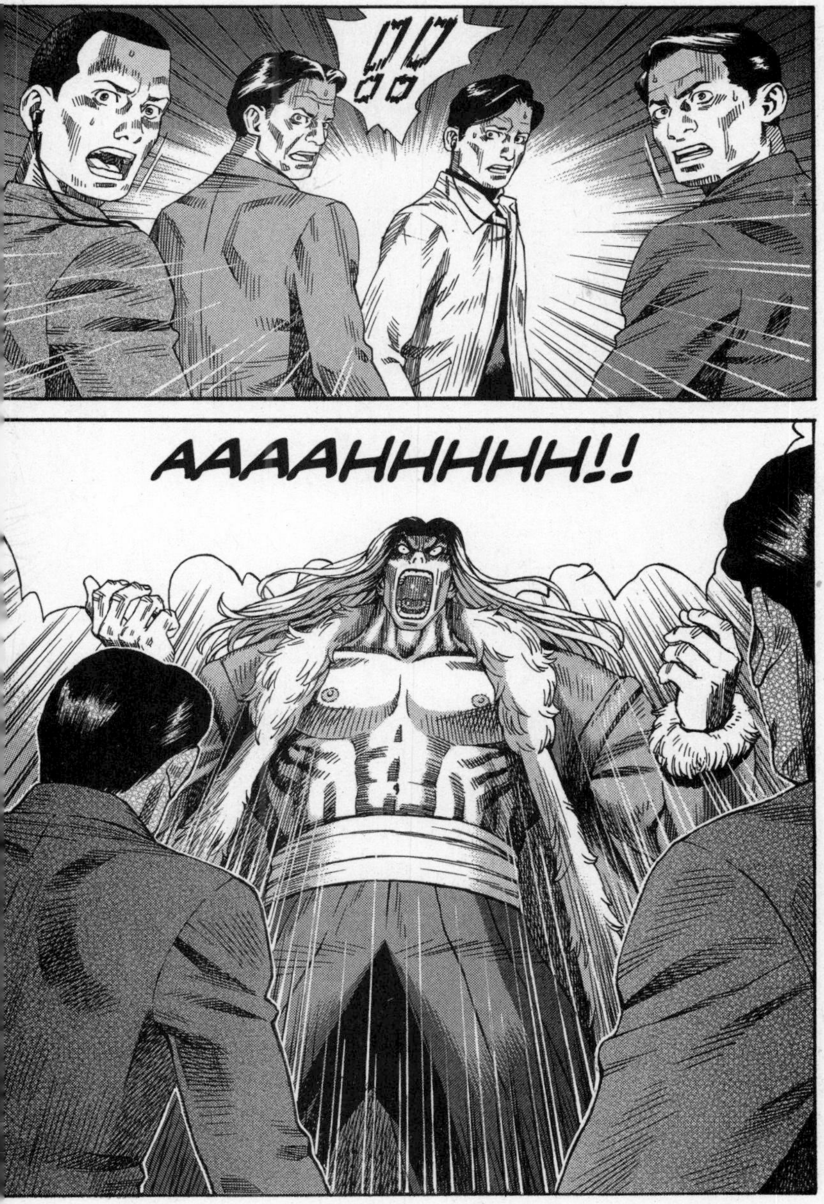
AAAAHHHHH!!

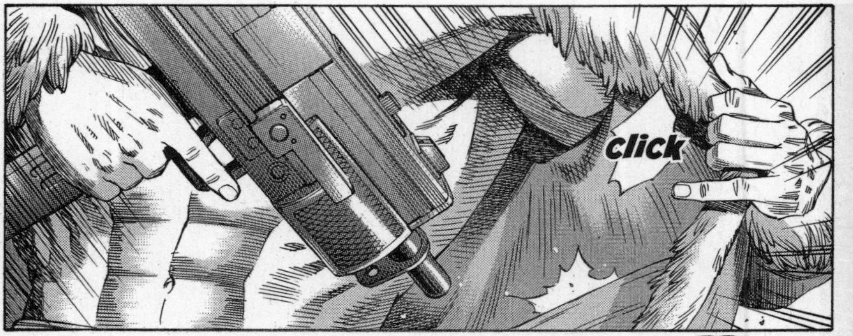
click
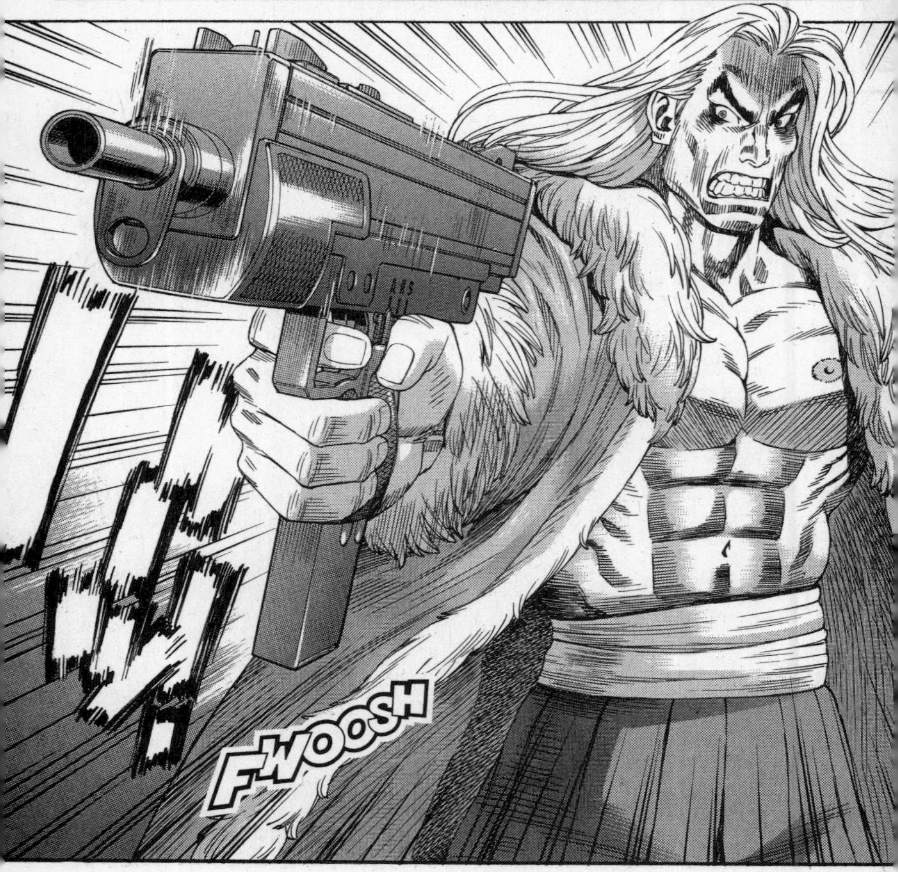
FWOOSH

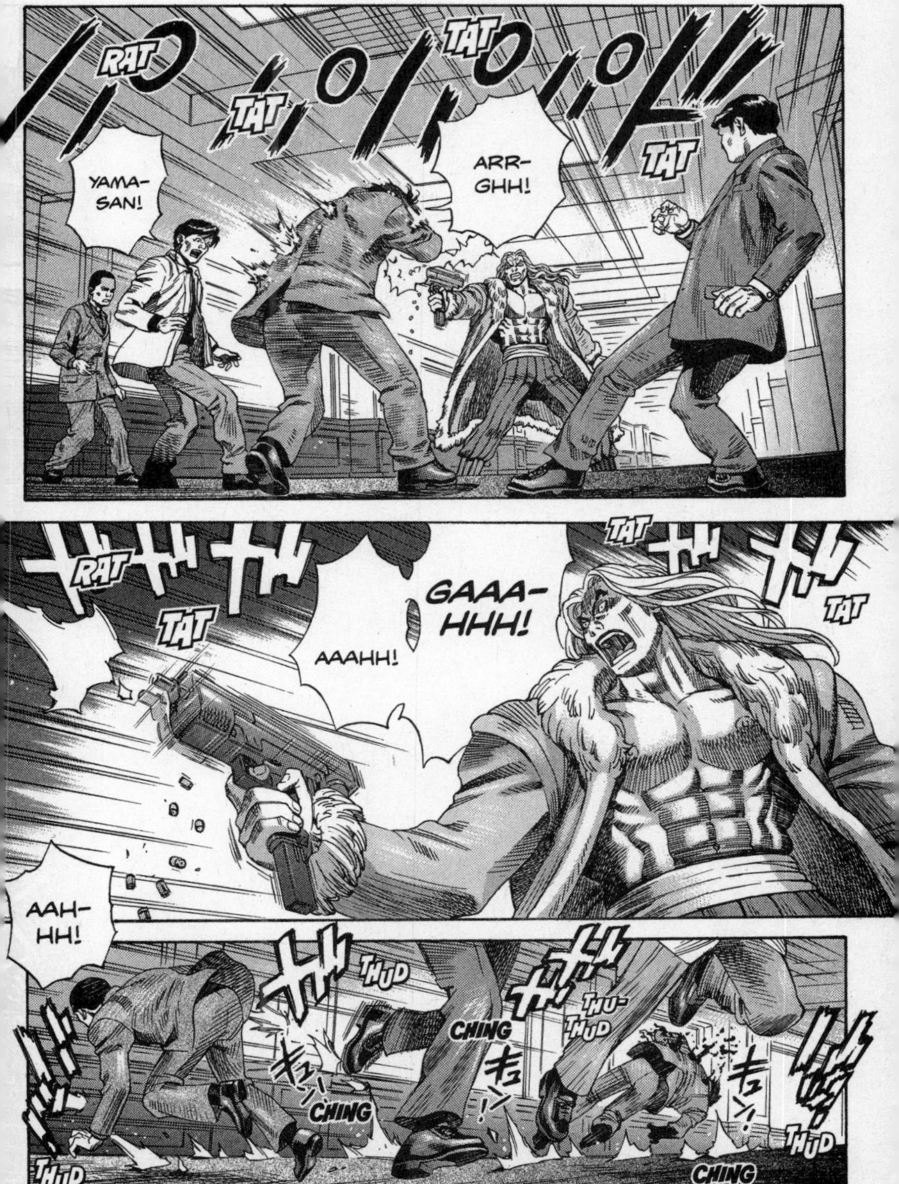
TAT
TAT
ARR-GHH!
TAT
RAT
YAMA-SAN!
TAT
TAT
GAAA-HHH!
AAAHH!
TAT
RAT
AAH-HH!
THUD
CHING
THU-THUD
CHING
THUD
CHING
THUD

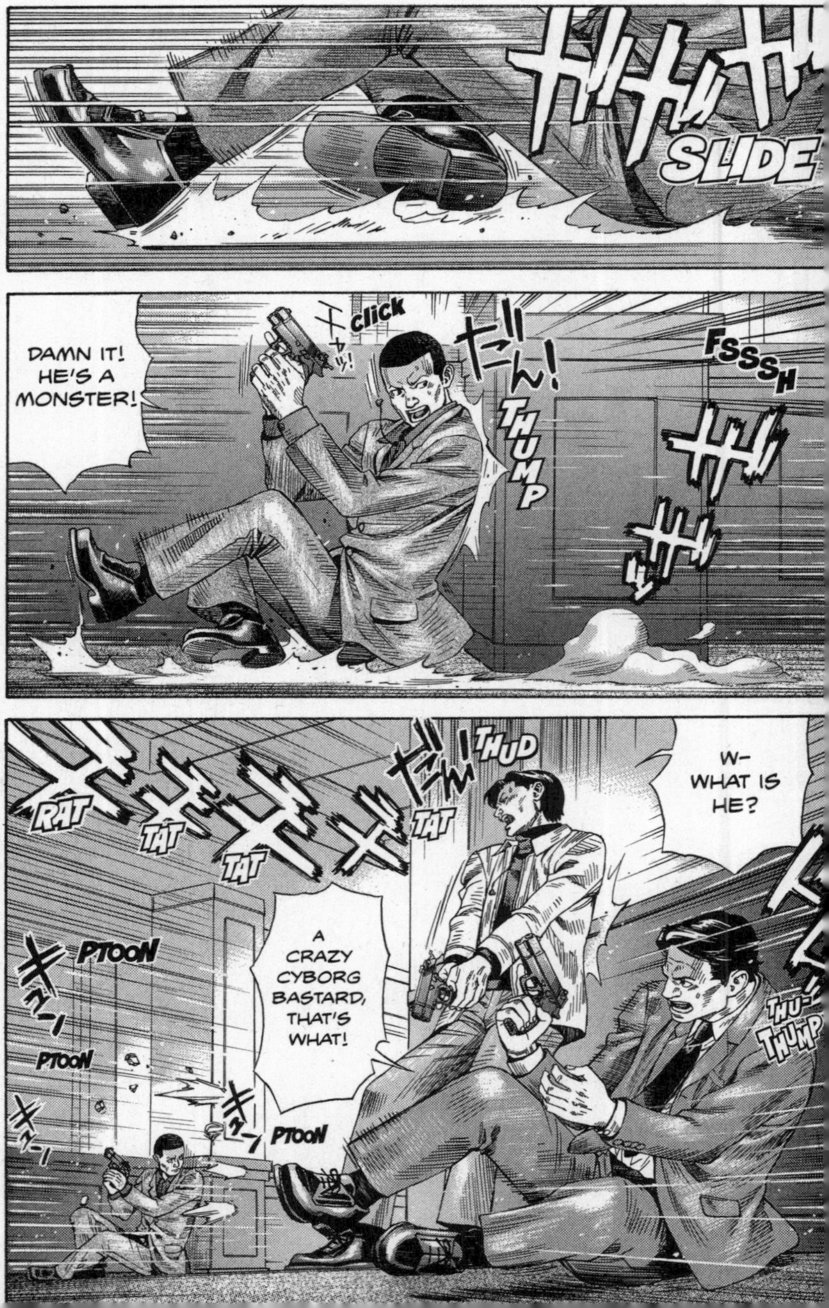
SLIDE
FSSSH
THUMP
click
DAMN IT! HE'S A MONSTER!
W- WHAT IS HE?
THU-THUMP
THUD
A CRAZY CYBORG BASTARD, THAT'S WHAT!
TAT
TAT
TAT
RAT
PTOON
PTOON
PTOON

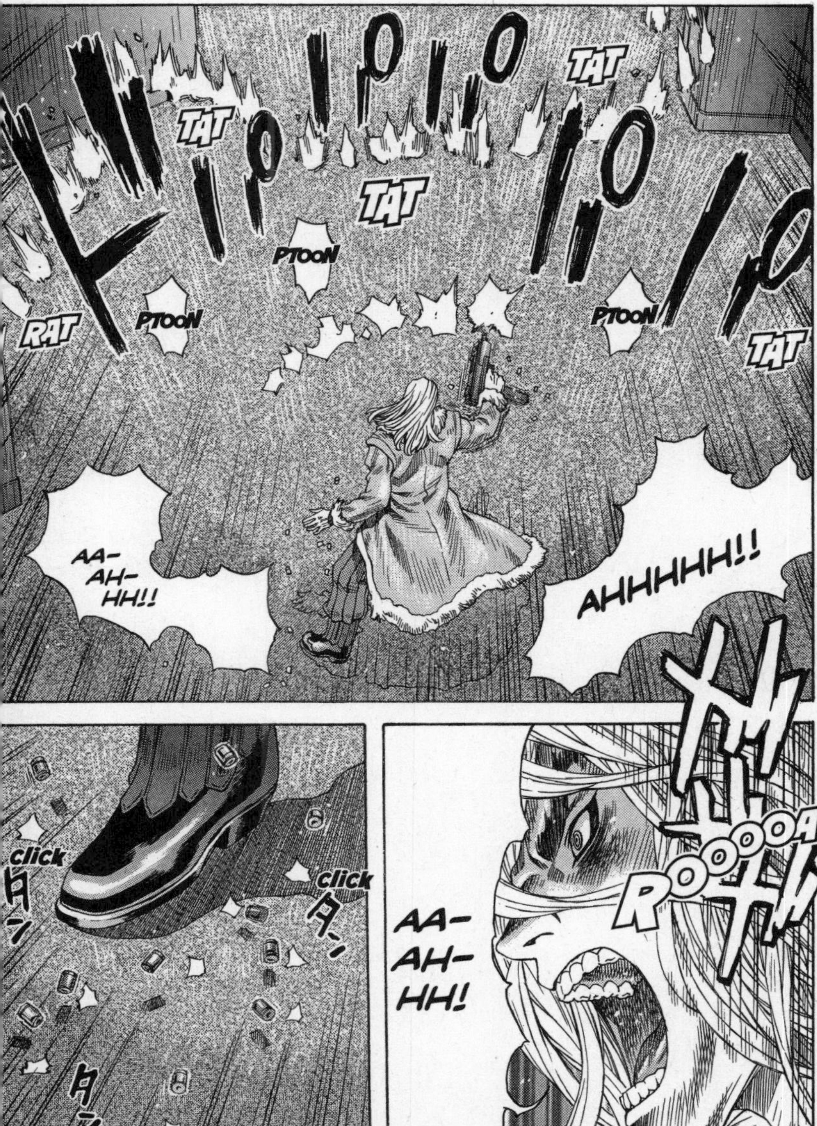
TAT
TAT
TAT
TAT
PTOON
PTOON
PTOON
RAT
AHHHHH!!
AA-
AH-
HH!!
ROOOOAR
AA-
AH-
HH!
click
click
click

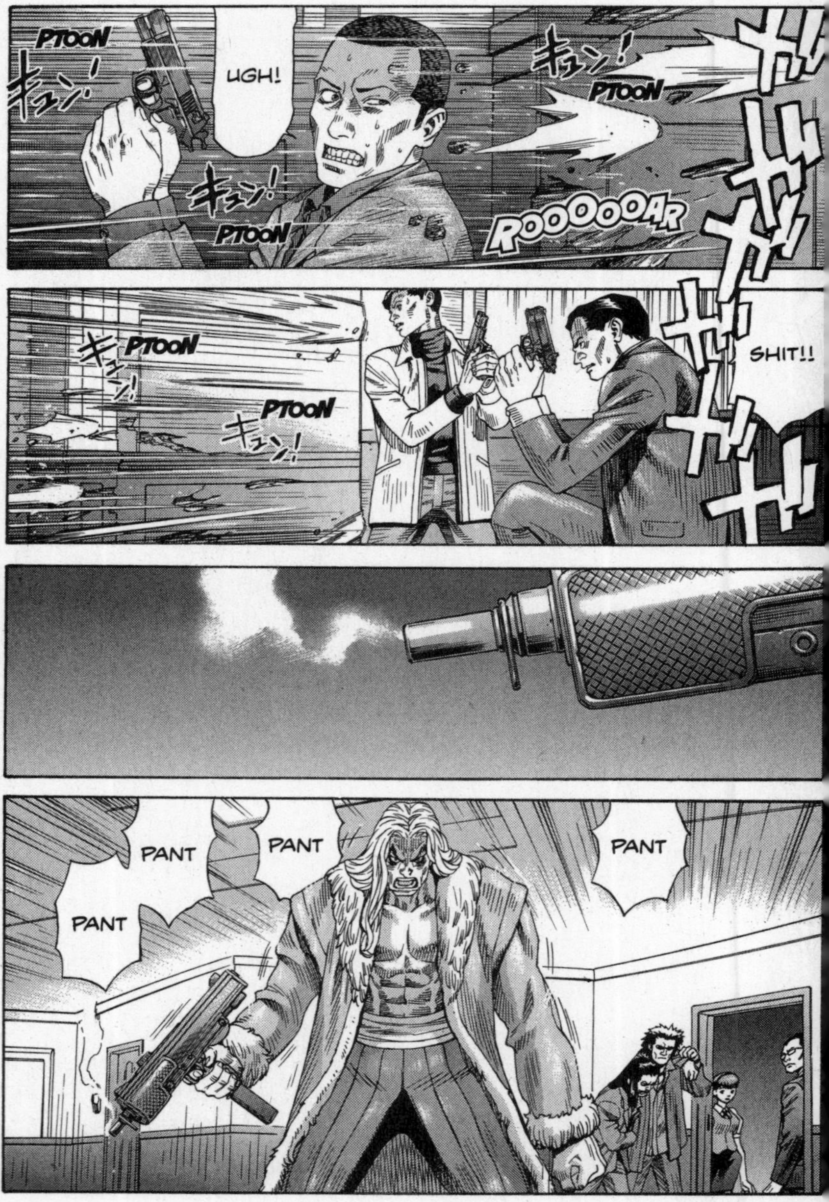
キュン!
PTOON
ROOOOOOAR
UGH!
PTOON
キュン!
キュン!
PTOON
SHIT!!
PTOON
キュン!
PTOON
キュン!
PANT
PANT
PANT
PANT

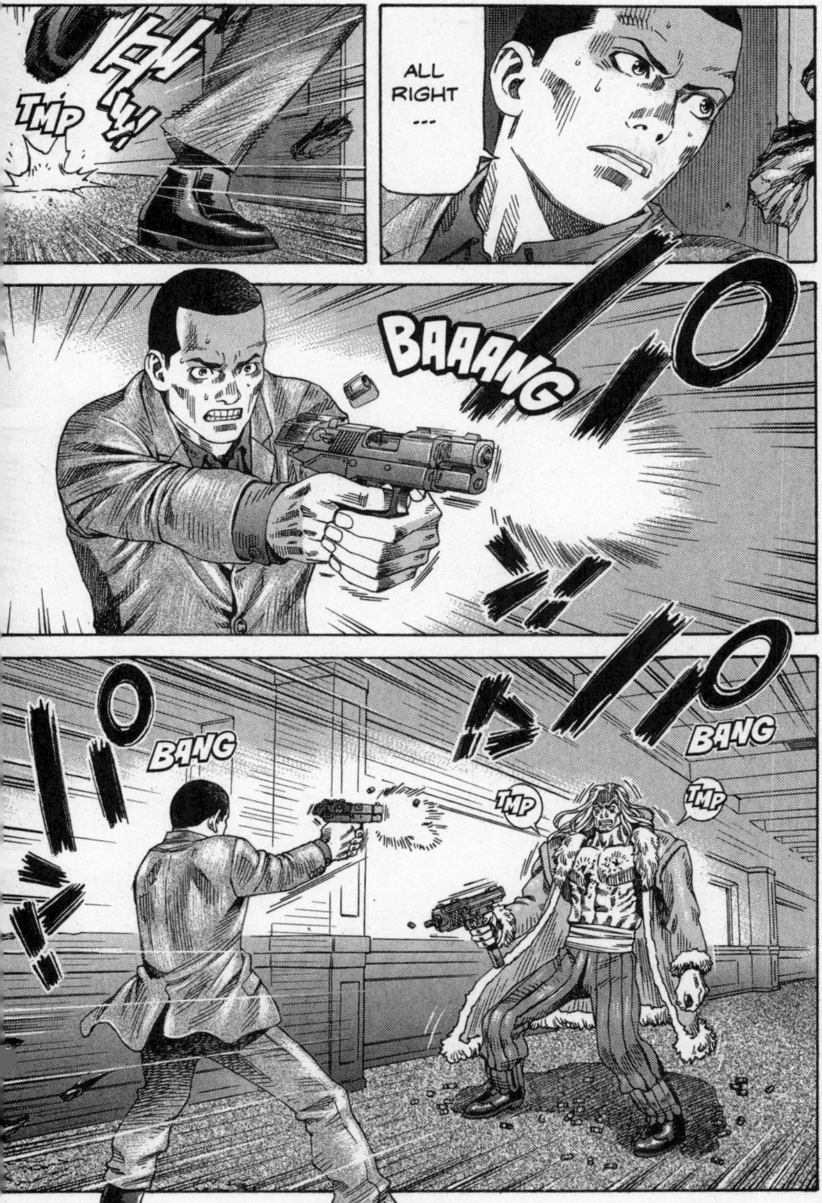
ALL RIGHT ---
TMP
BAAANG
BANG
TMP
TMP
BANG

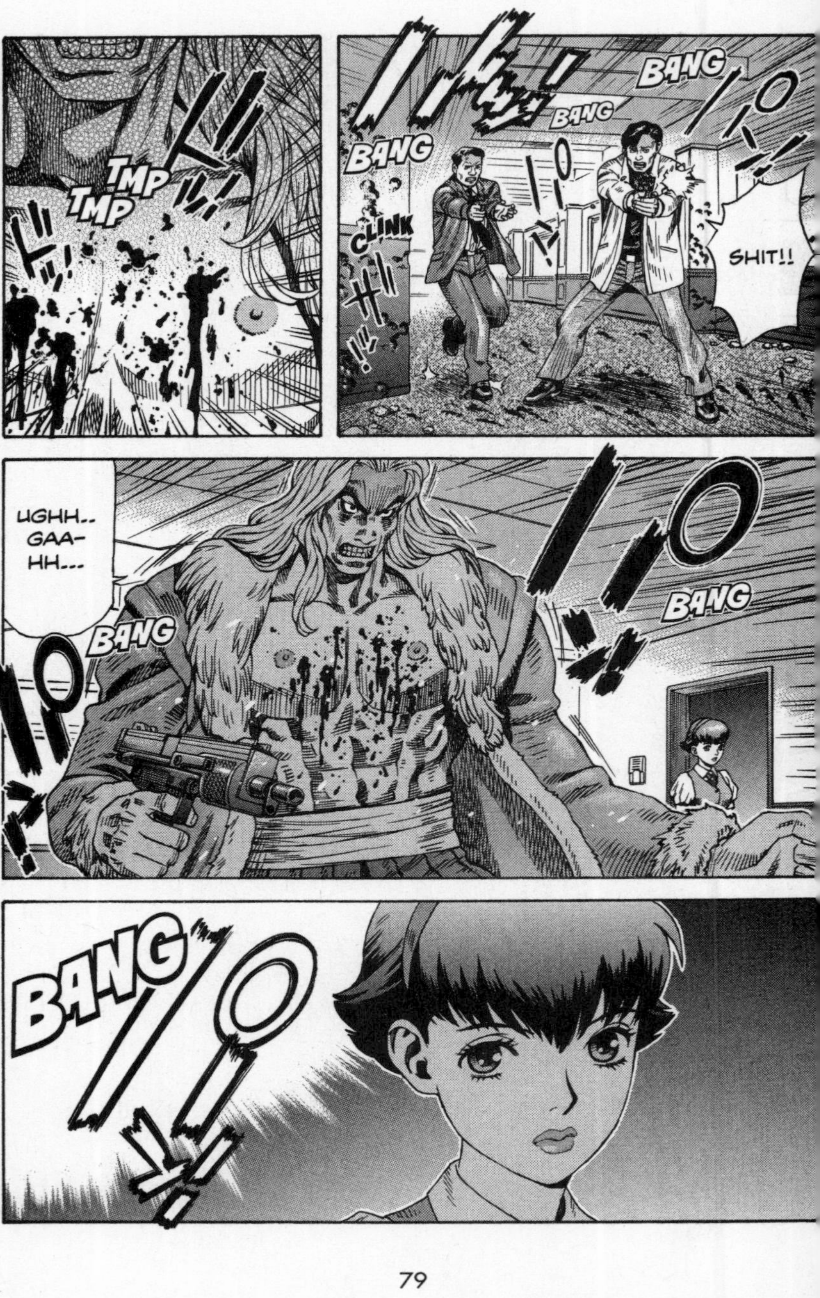
BANG
BANG
BANG
CLINK
SHIT!!
TMP
TMP
BANG
UGHH.. GAA-HH...
BANG
BANG

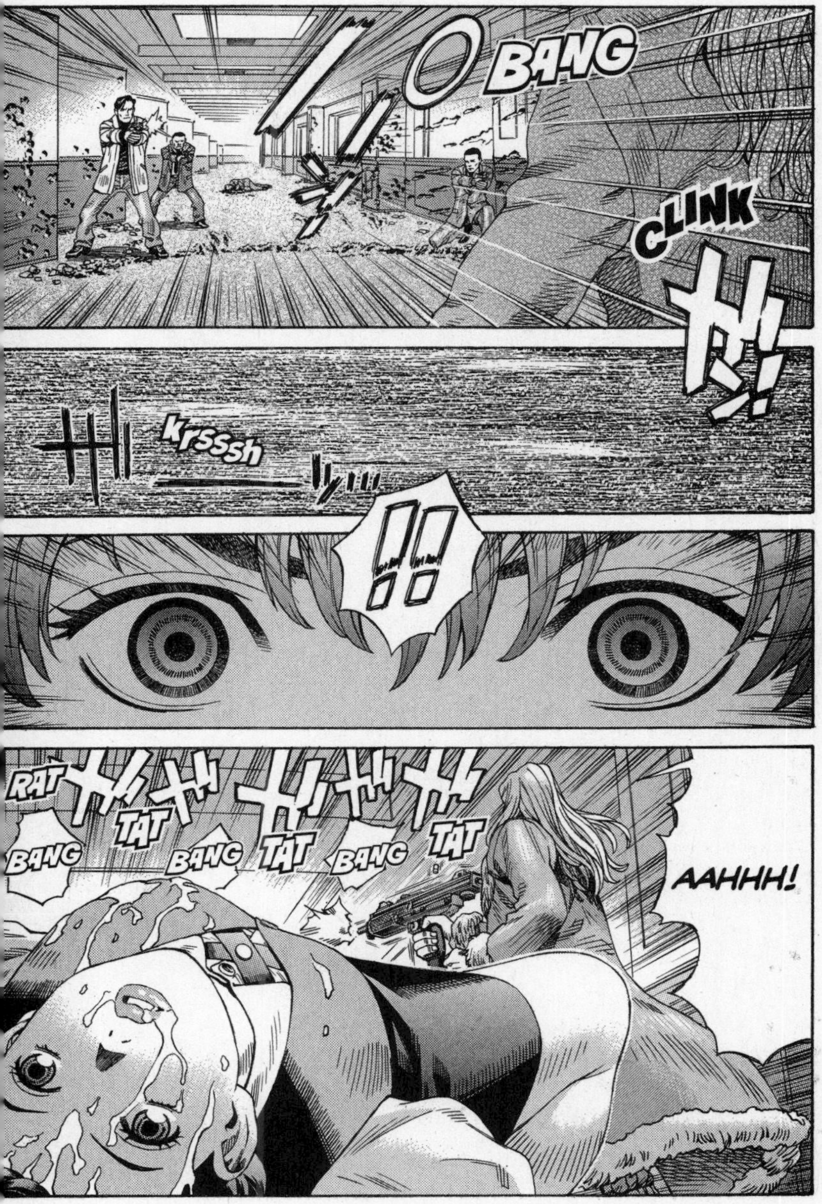
BANG
CLINK
krsssh
AAHHH!
RAT
TAT
BANG
TAT
BANG
TAT
BANG

MAJ-
OR!

GUESS SHE GOT HIT BY A STRAY BULLET...

---

THESE GUYS ARE UNDER-COVER NARCOTIC DETEC-TIVES...

..WHO'VE BEEN STAKING OUT THE HOTEL, DISGUISED AS GUESTS.

THEY'RE NOT AFTER JARTI...

THEY JUST WANT GONDŌ.

008753 P.I STOCK FILE PROTECTIO

| NAME | GON |
| NATIONALITY | JAP |
| BASEFILE | 987 |
| SEX | MA |
| HEIGHT | 5ft 9 |
| WEIGHT | 147 |
| HAIR | BLA |
| EYES | BRA |
| AGE | 57 |
| CONVICTION | 34 |
| CYBORGED | NO |
| BLOOD TYPE | B |
| FEATURES | A B |

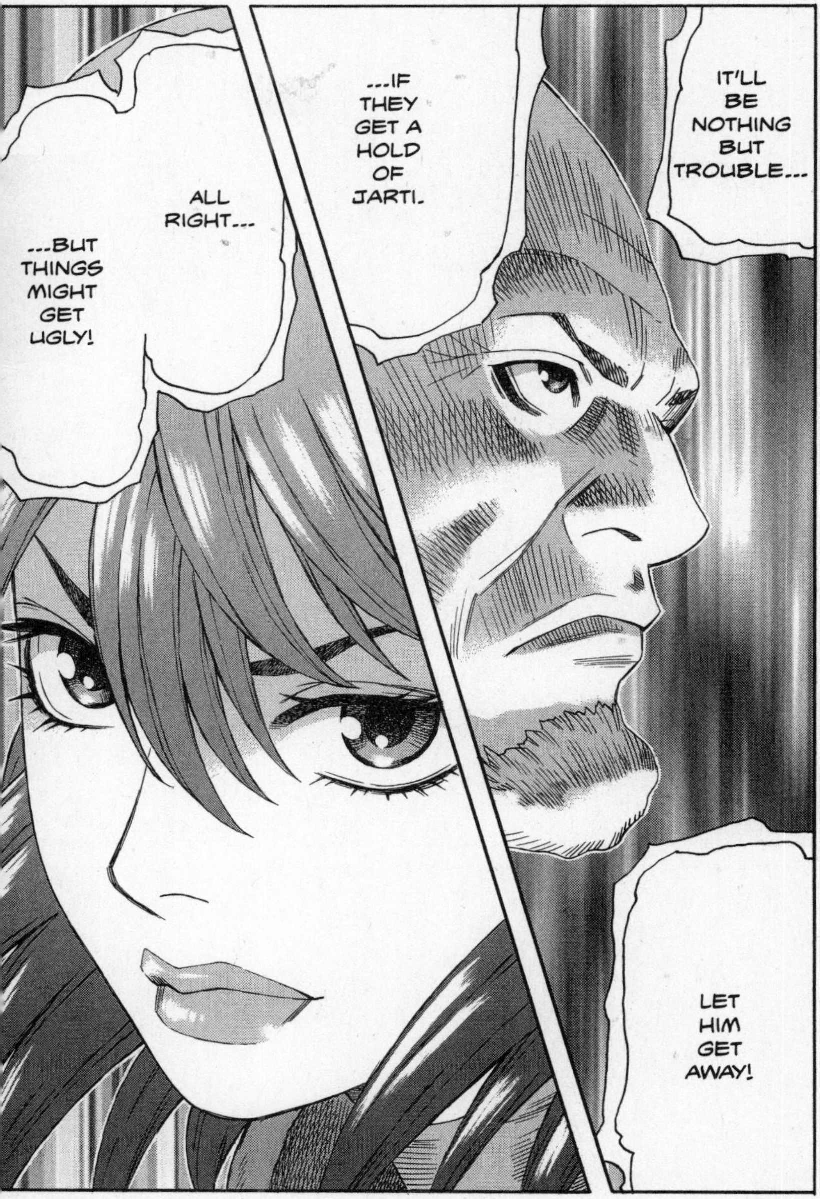
IT'LL BE NOTHING BUT TROUBLE...
...IF THEY GET A HOLD OF JARTI.
LET HIM GET AWAY!
ALL RIGHT...
...BUT THINGS MIGHT GET UGLY!

**#020: End**

# #021: Rival Showdown

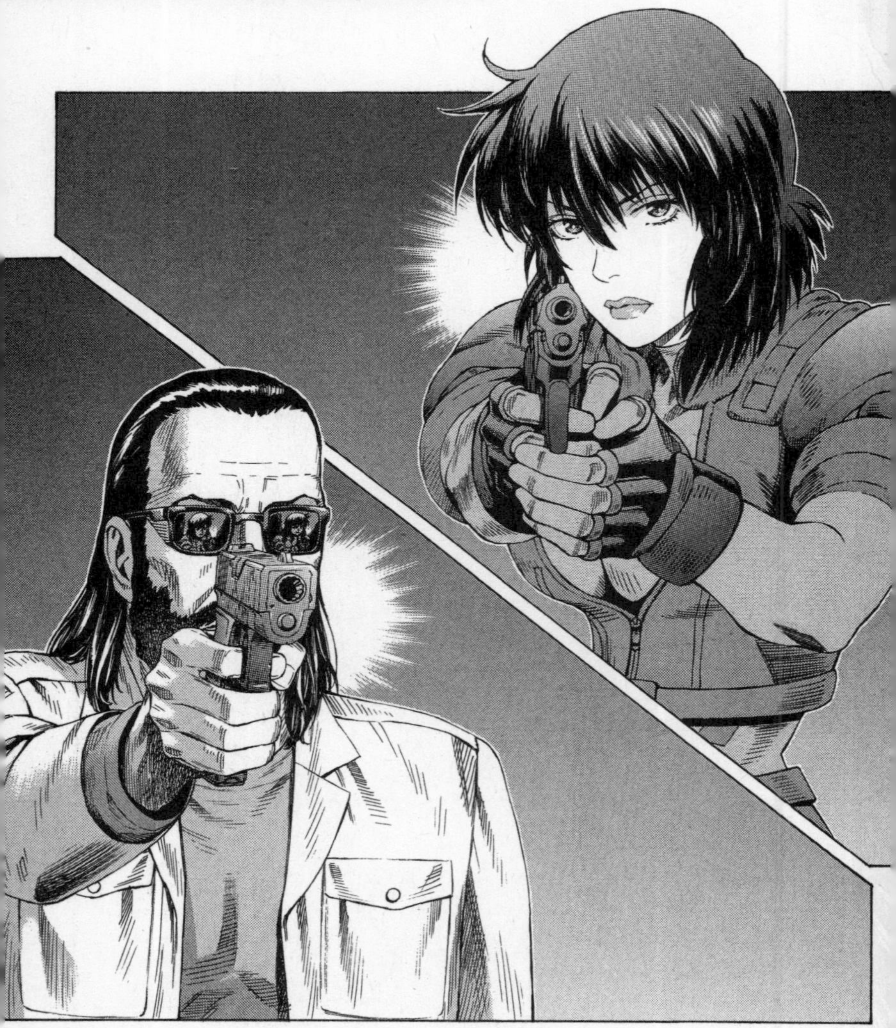

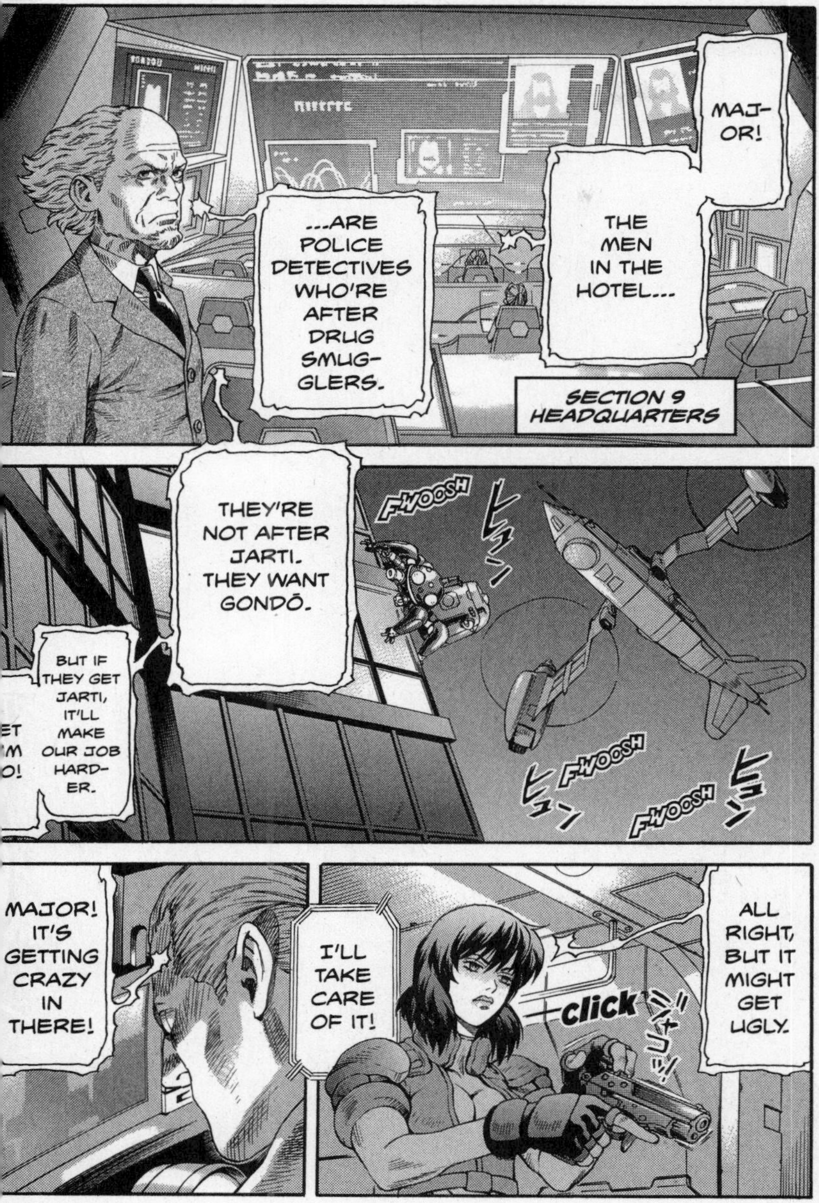
SECTION 9 HEADQUARTERS
MAJ-OR!
THE MEN IN THE HOTEL...
...ARE POLICE DETECTIVES WHO'RE AFTER DRUG SMUGGLERS.
FWOOSH
THEY'RE NOT AFTER JARTI. THEY WANT GONDŌ.
FWOOSH
FWOOSH
BUT IF THEY GET JARTI, IT'LL MAKE OUR JOB HARDER.
ALL RIGHT, BUT IT MIGHT GET UGLY.
click
I'LL TAKE CARE OF IT!
MAJOR! IT'S GETTING CRAZY IN THERE!

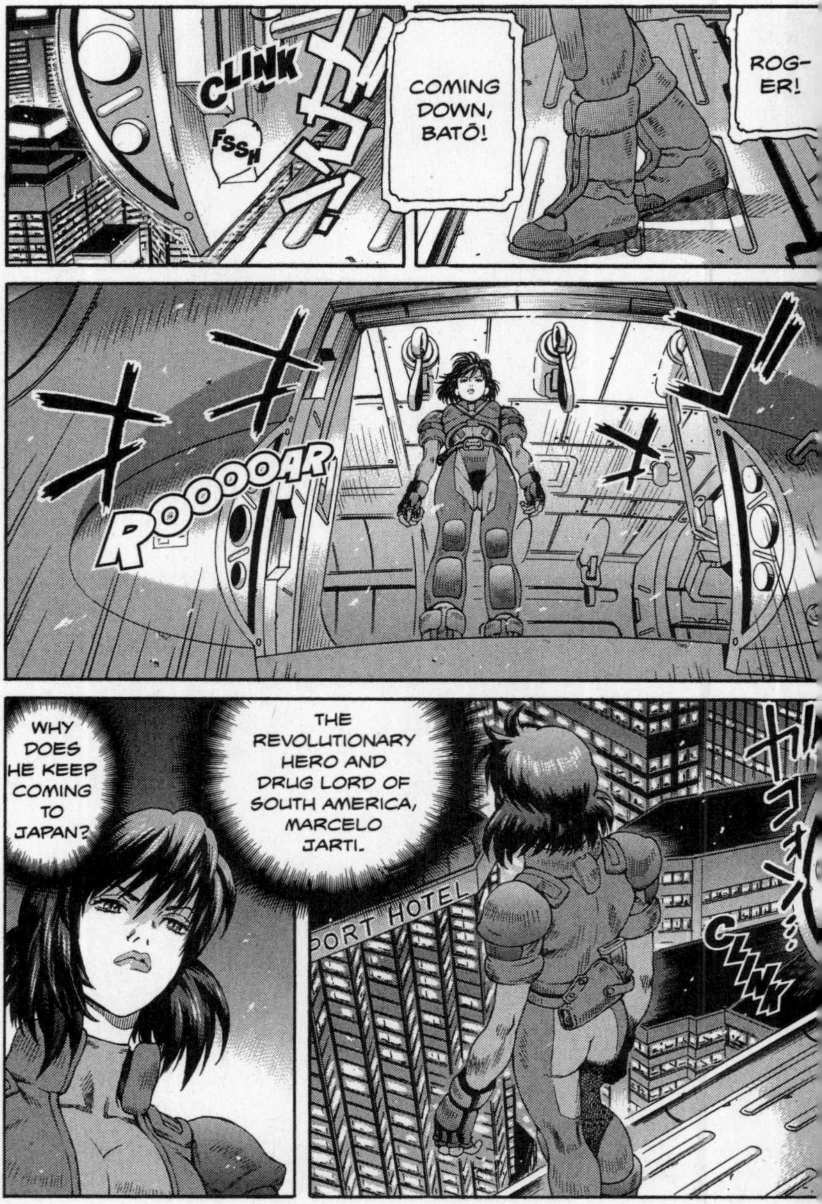
COMING DOWN, BATŌ!
ROG-ER!
CLINK
FSSH
ROOOOAR
CLINK
THE REVOLUTIONARY HERO AND DRUG LORD OF SOUTH AMERICA, MARCELO JARTI.
WHY DOES HE KEEP COMING TO JAPAN?
PORT HOTEL

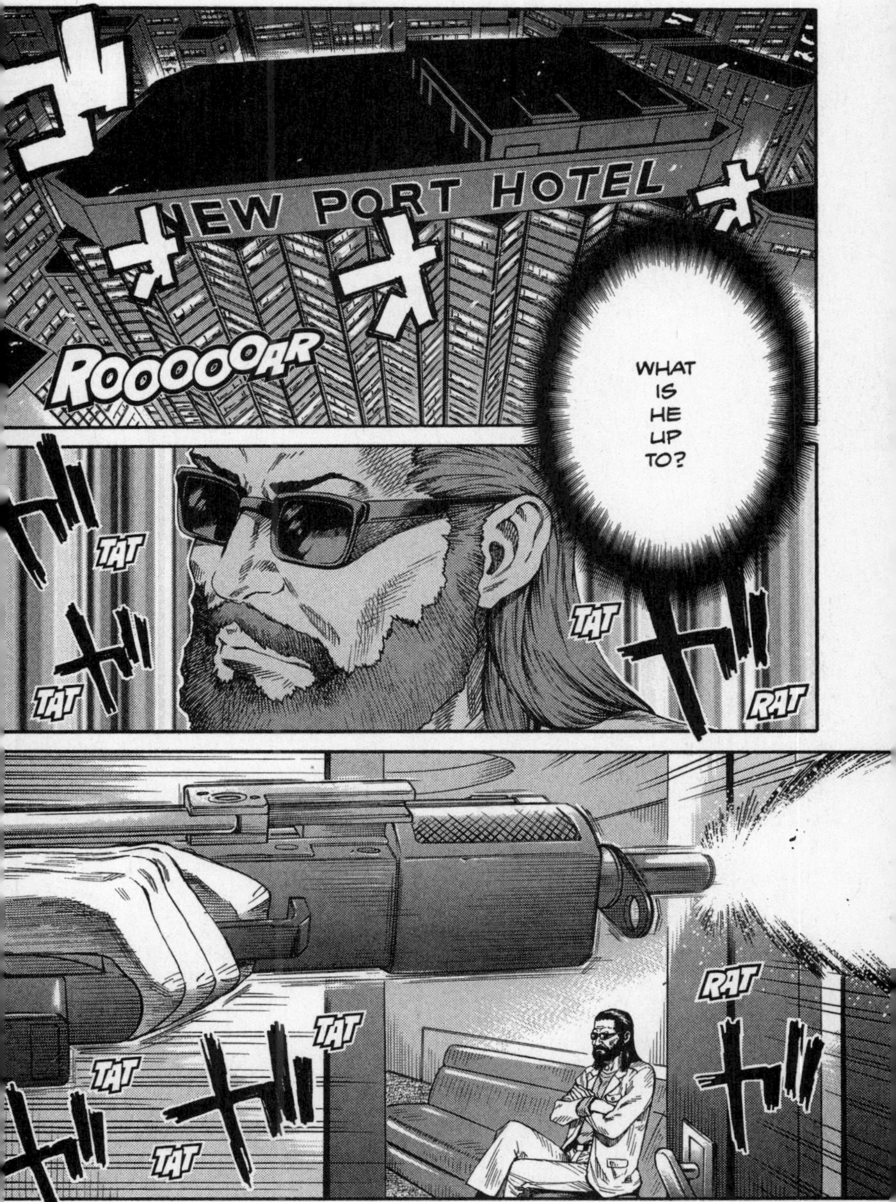
NEW PORT HOTEL
ROOOOOAR
WHAT IS HE UP TO?
RAT
TAT
TAT
TAT
RAT
TAT
TAT
TAT

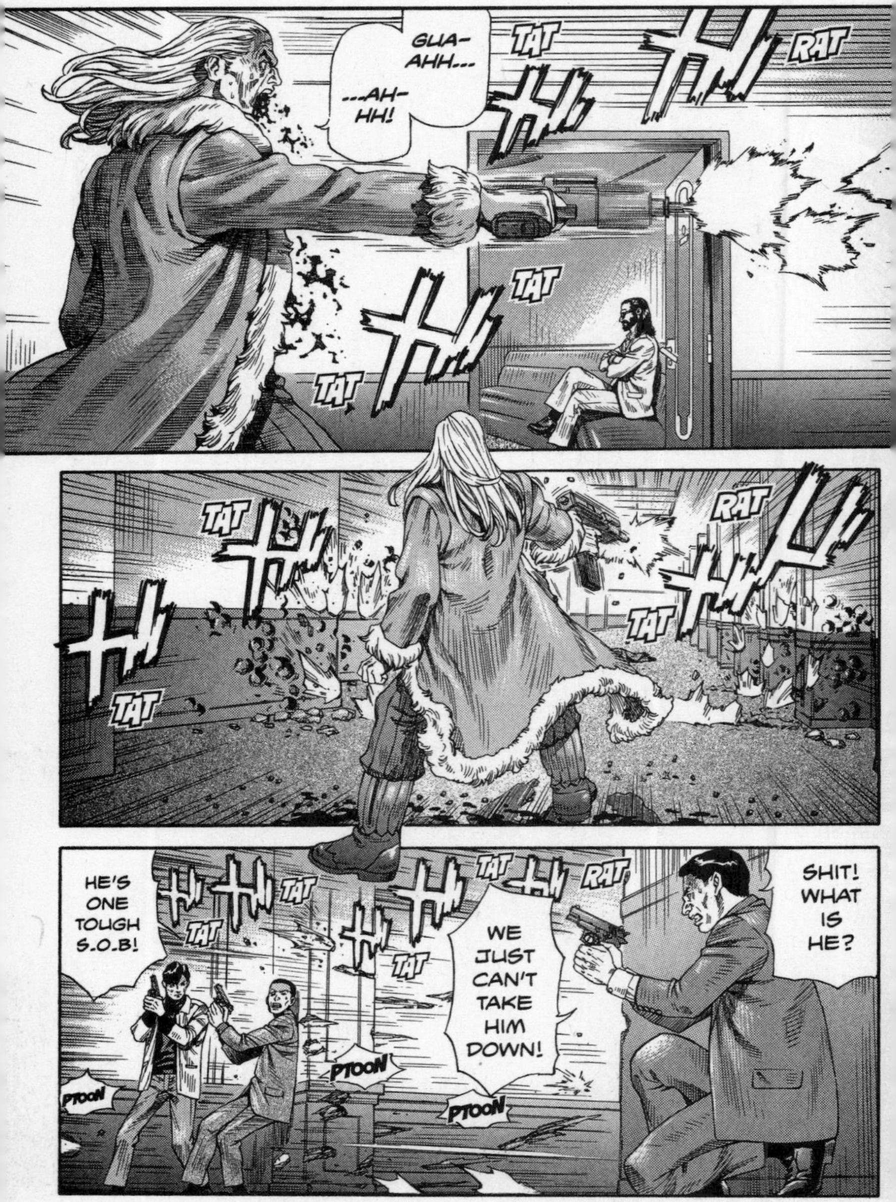
RAT
TAT
GUA-AHH...
...AH-HH!
TAT
TAT
RAT
TAT
TAT
TAT
SHIT! WHAT IS HE?
RAT
TAT
WE JUST CAN'T TAKE HIM DOWN!
TAT
TAT
TAT
HE'S ONE TOUGH S.O.B!
PTOON
PTOON
PTOON

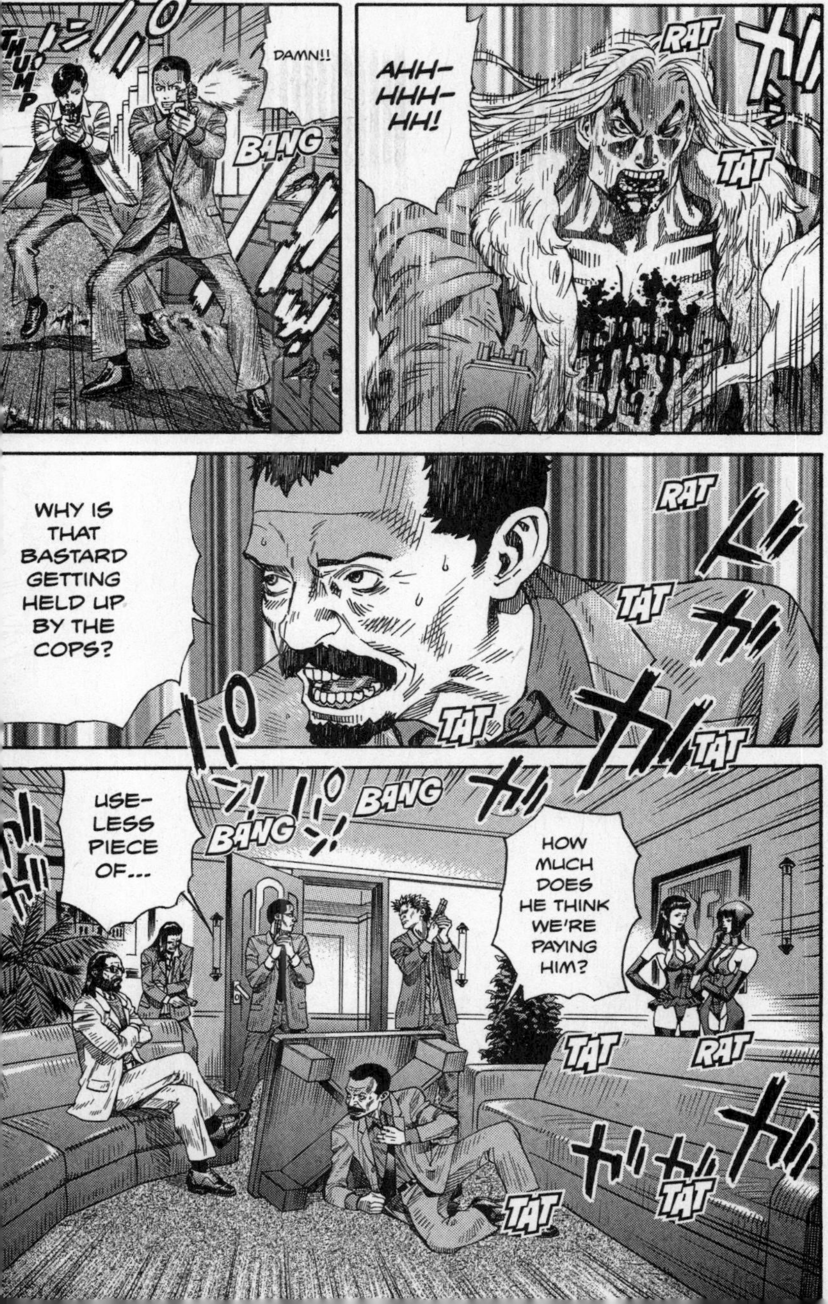
AHH-HHH-HH!
RAT
TAT
DAMN!!
THUMP
BANG
RAT
TAT
WHY IS THAT BASTARD GETTING HELD UP BY THE COPS?
TAT
TAT
BANG
BANG
HOW MUCH DOES HE THINK WE'RE PAYING HIM?
USE-LESS PIECE OF...
TAT
RAT
TAT
TAT

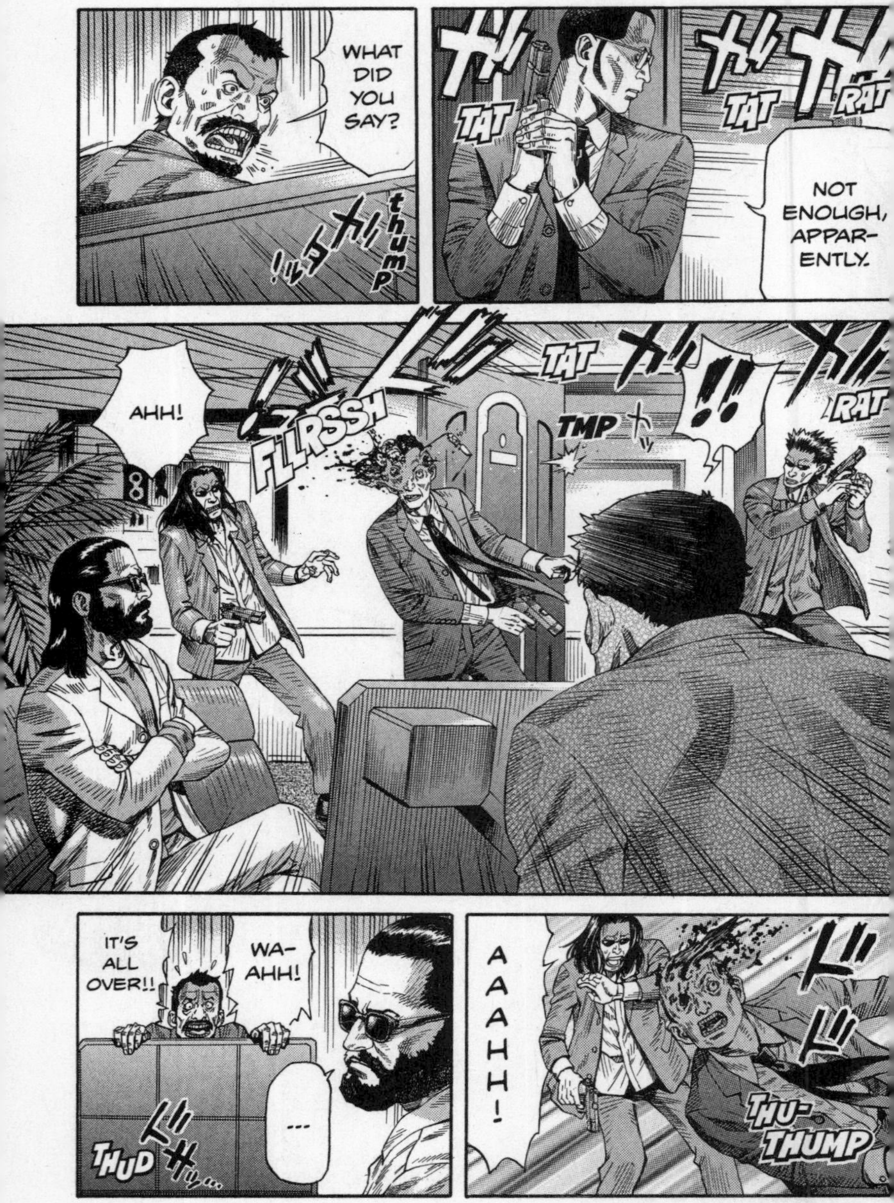
TAT
TAT
RAT
NOT ENOUGH, APPARENTLY.
WHAT DID YOU SAY?
thump
RAT
!!
TAT
TMP
FLRSSH
AHH!
AAAAHH!
THU-THUMP
WA-AHH!
IT'S ALL OVER!!
...
THUD

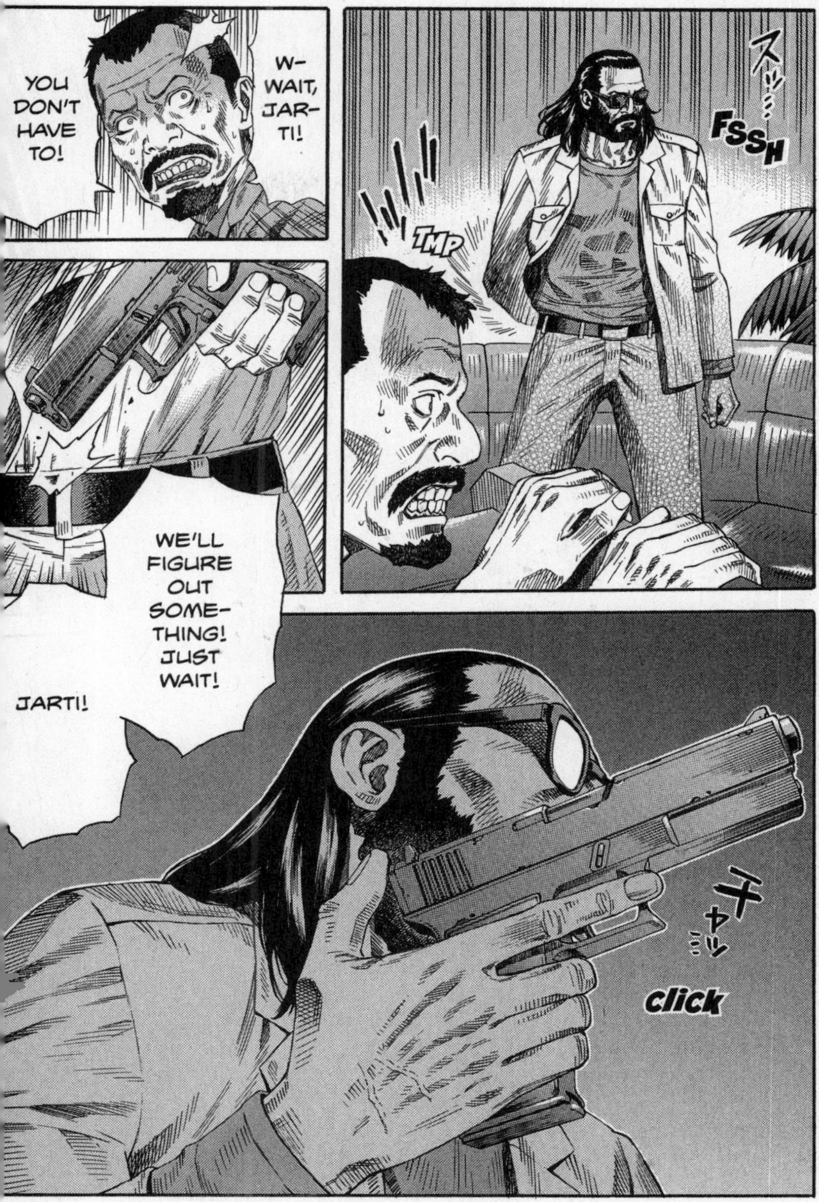
スッ
FSSH
TMP
W-WAIT, JARTI!
YOU DON'T HAVE TO!
WE'LL FIGURE OUT SOMETHING! JUST WAIT!
JARTI!
チャッ
click

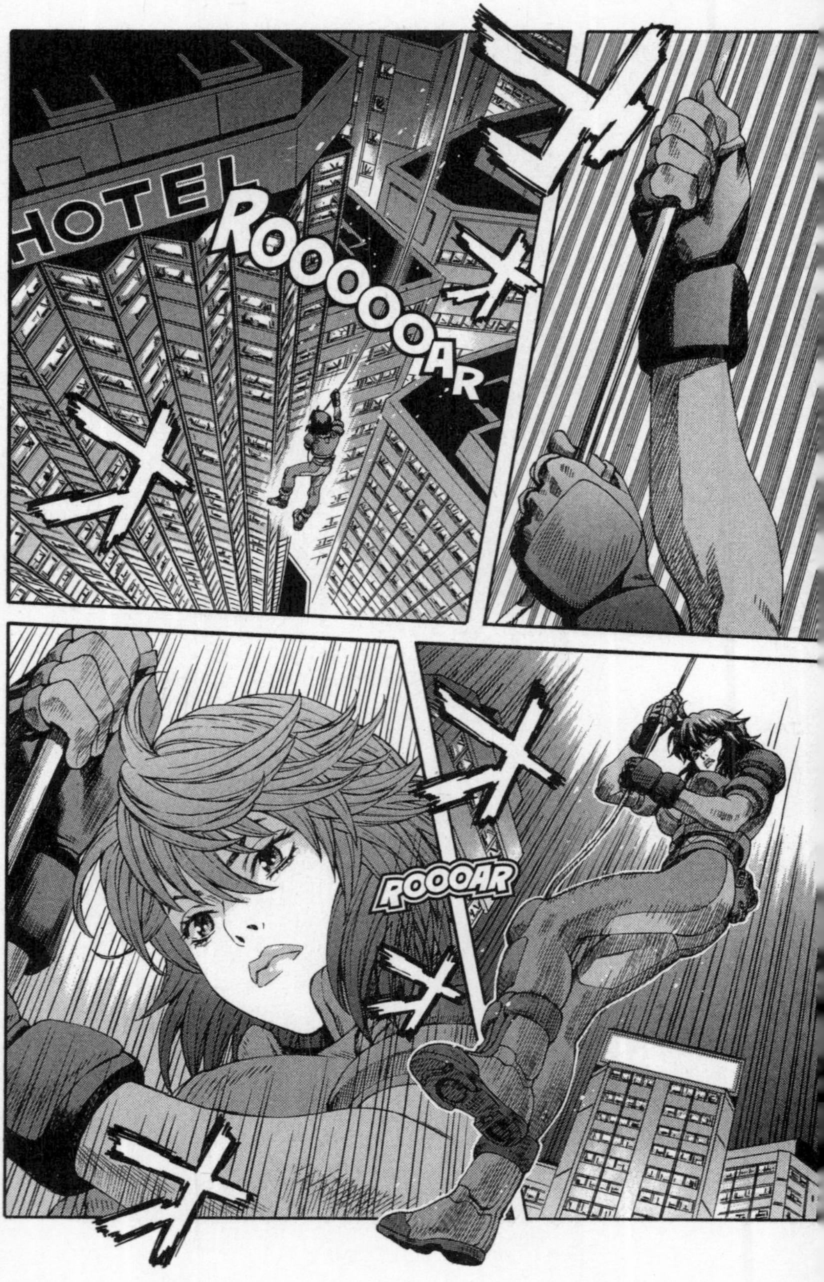
HOTEL
ROOOOOOAR
ROOOAR

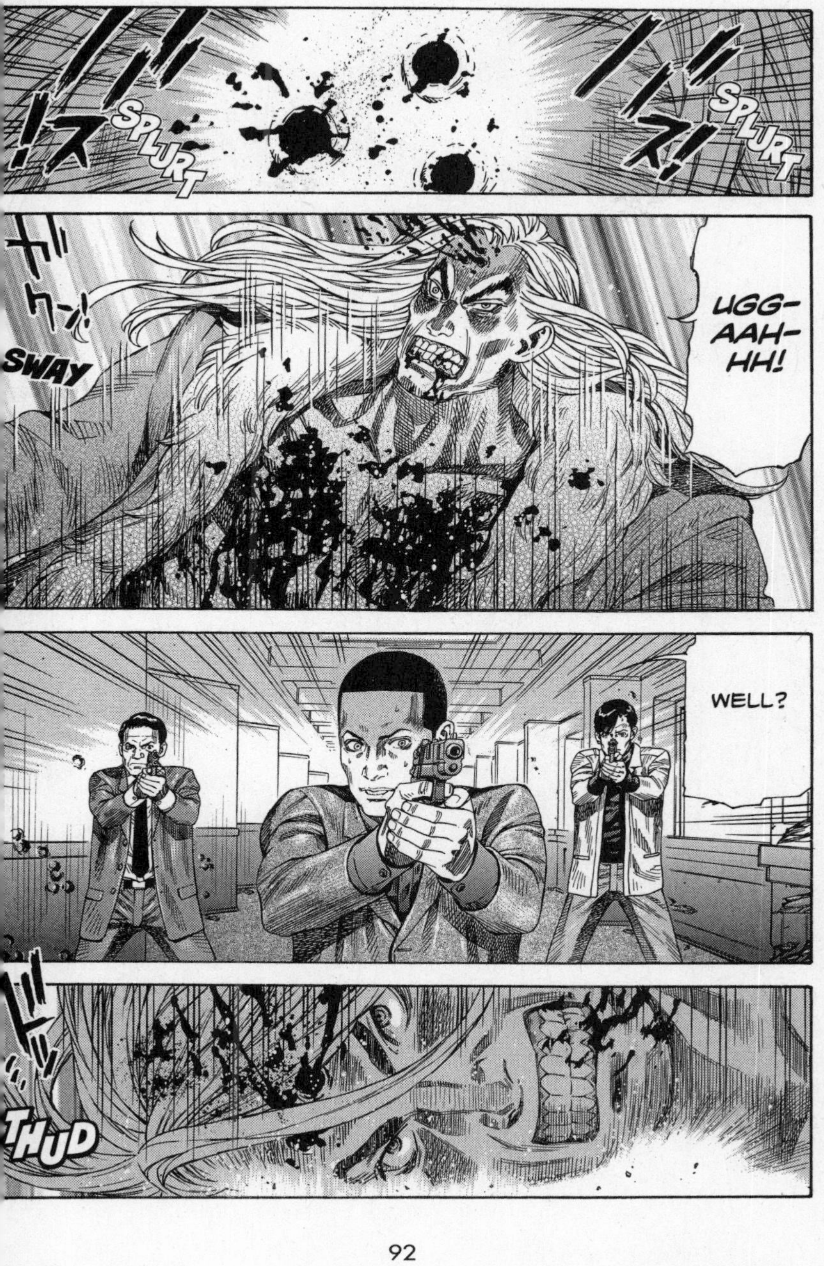
SPLURT
SPLURT
UGG-AAH-HH!
SWAY
WELL?
THUD

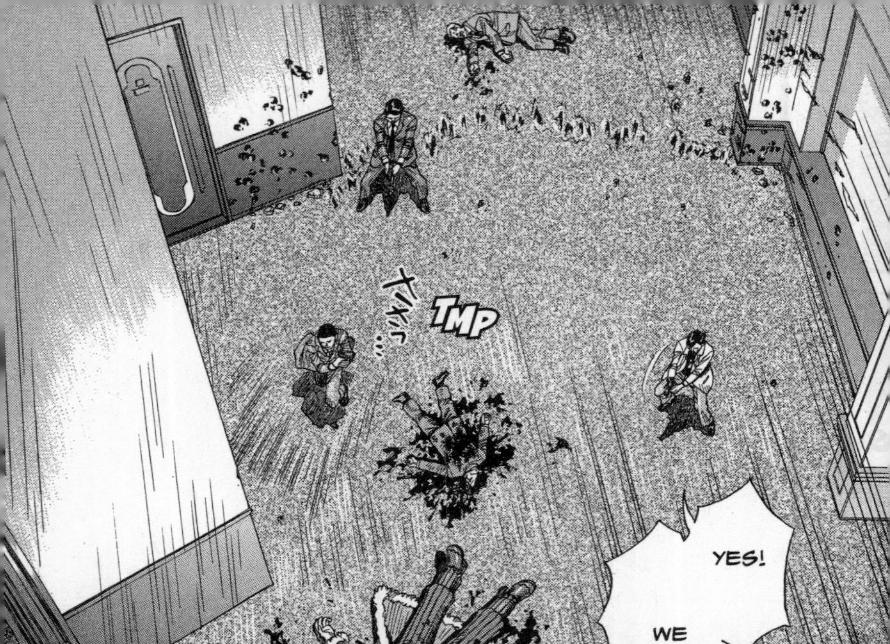
TMP
YES!
WE KILLED HIM!

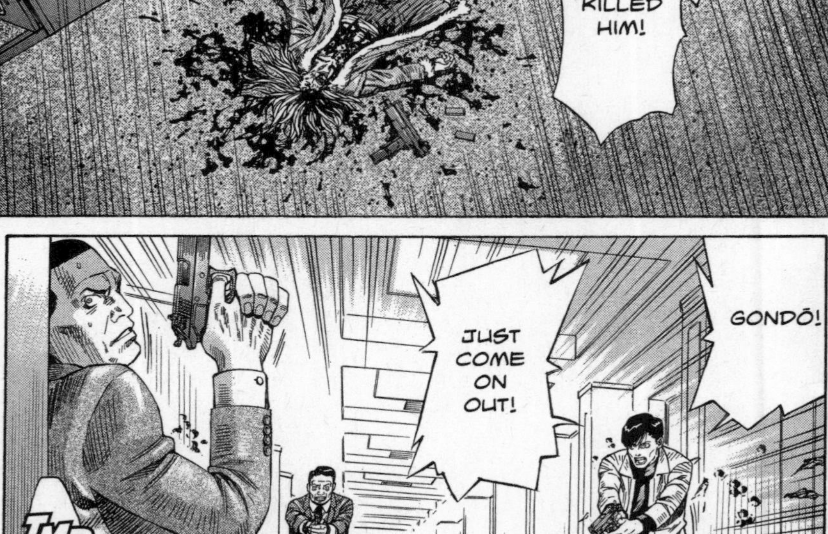
GONDŌ!
JUST COME ON OUT!
TMP

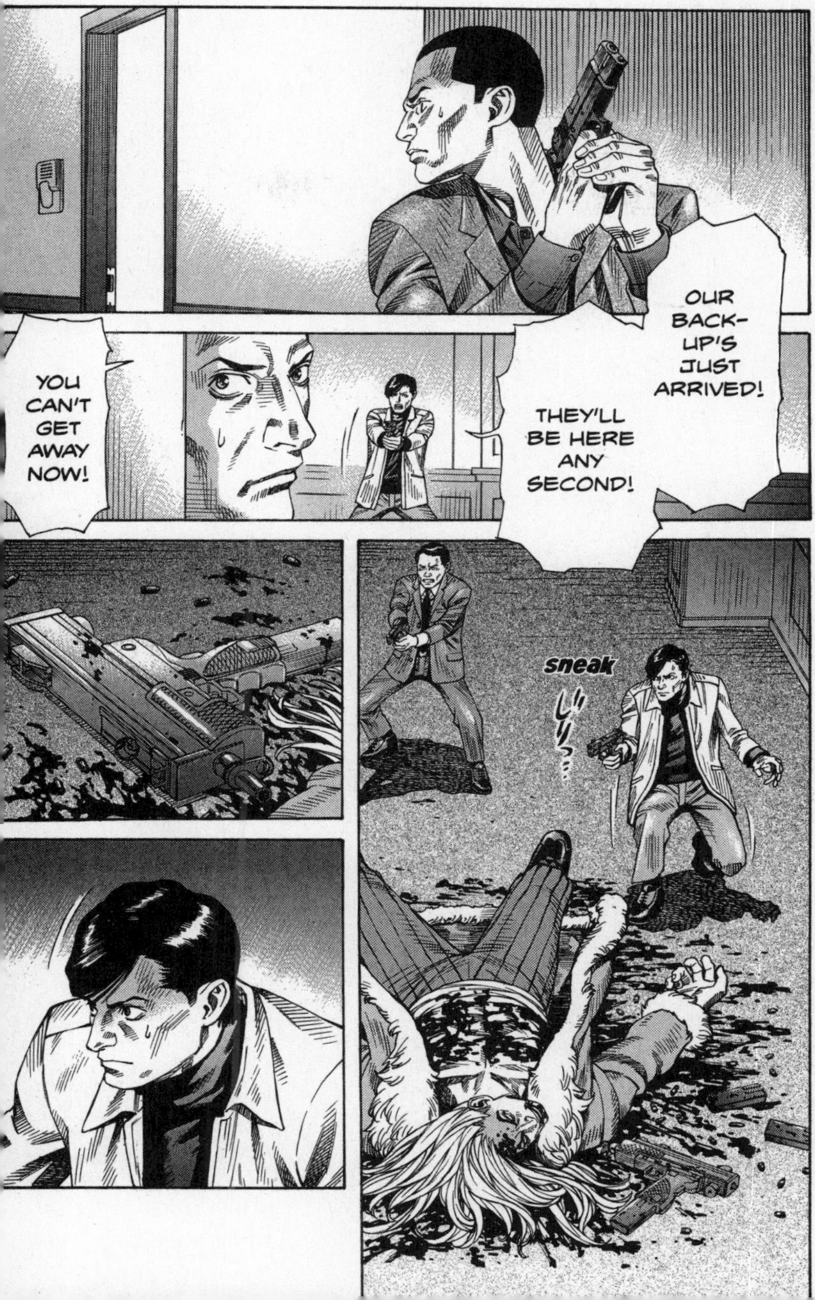
OUR BACK-UP'S JUST ARRIVED!
THEY'LL BE HERE ANY SECOND!
YOU CAN'T GET AWAY NOW!
sneak
じりっ…

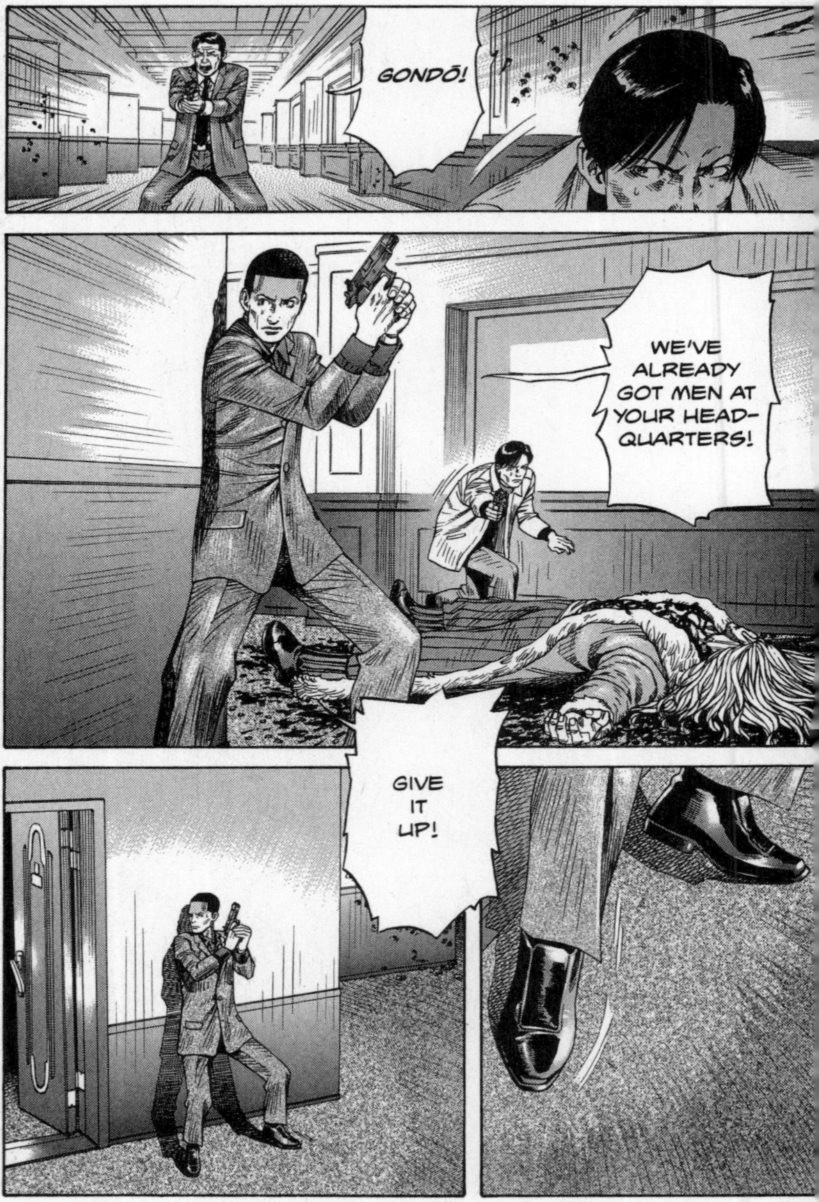
GONDŌ!
WE'VE ALREADY GOT MEN AT YOUR HEAD-QUARTERS!
GIVE IT UP!

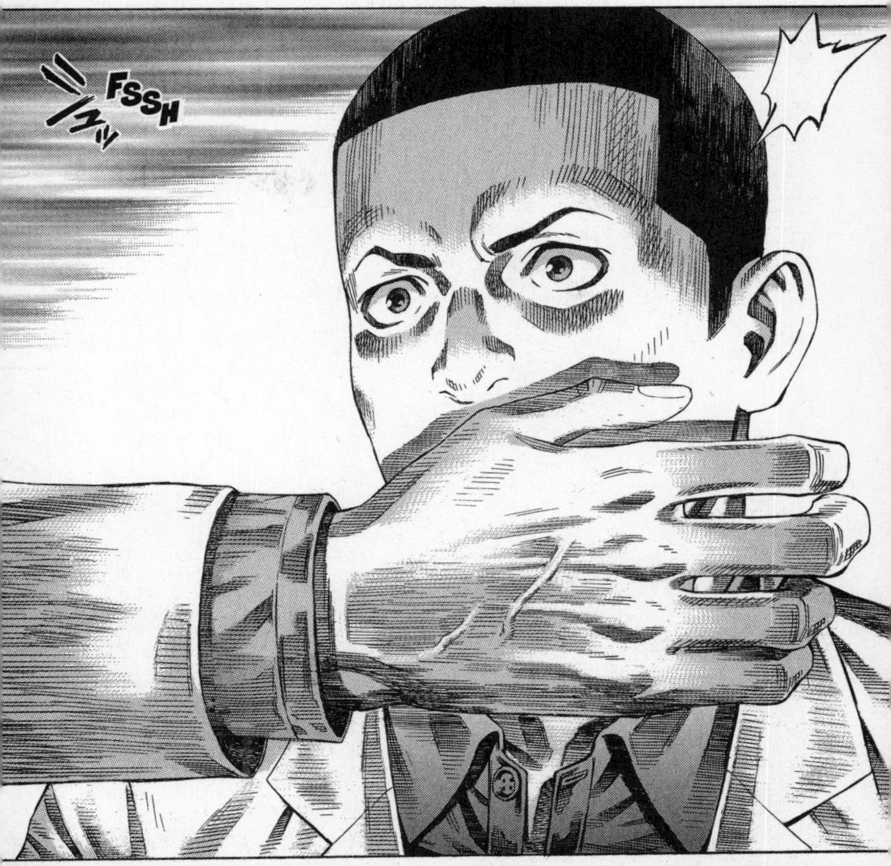
FSSH
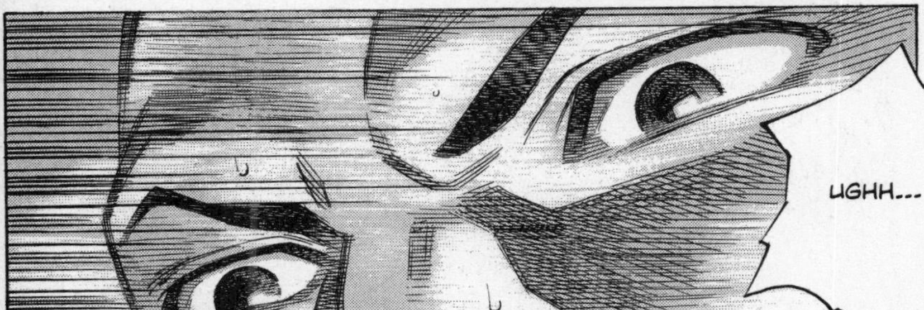
UGHH...

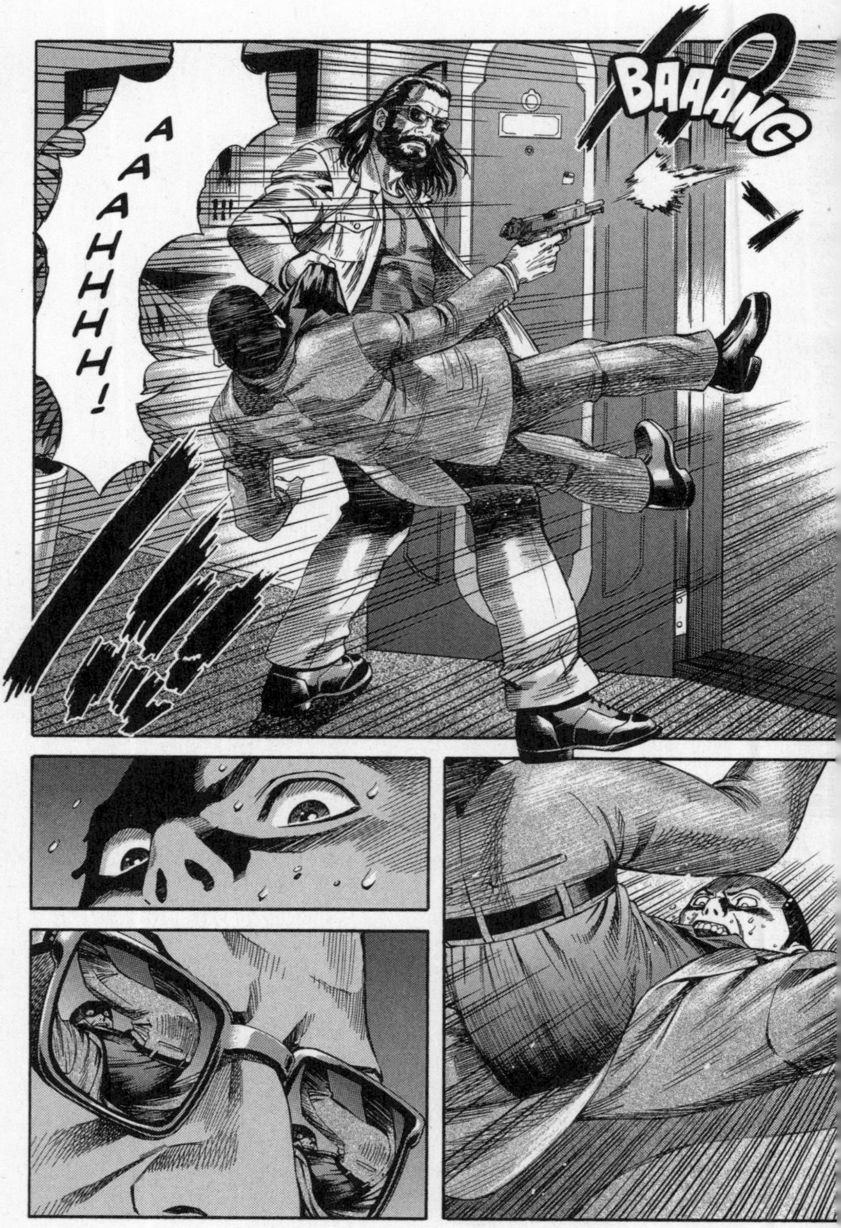
BAAANG
AAAHHHHH!

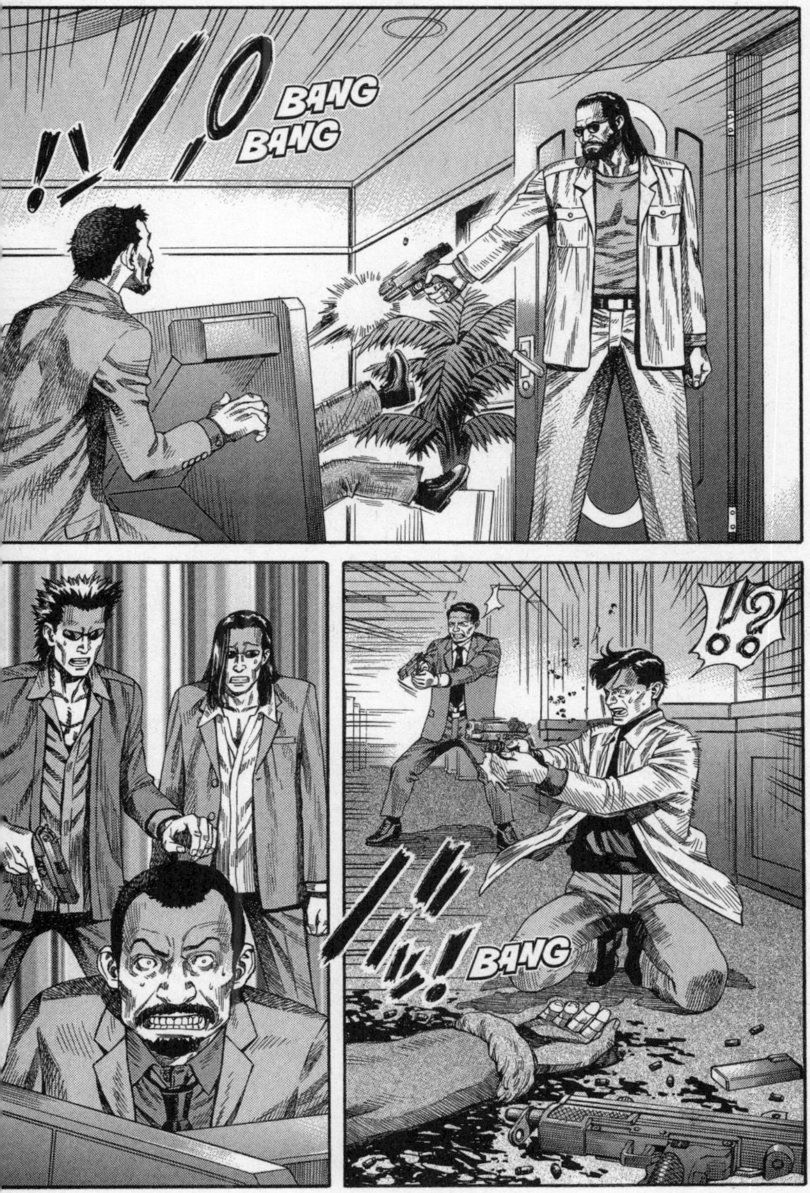
BANG
BANG
BANG

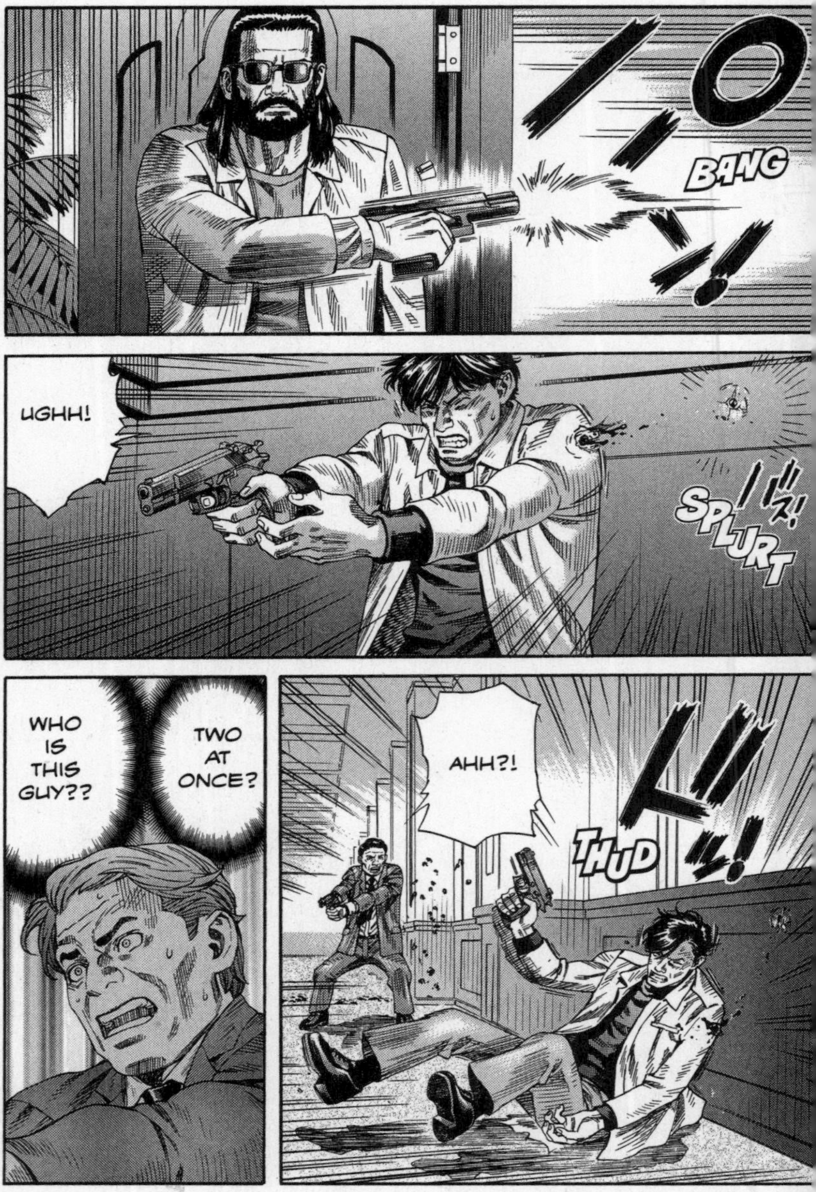

BANG
SPLURT
UGHH!
AHH?!
THUD
TWO AT ONCE?
WHO IS THIS GUY??

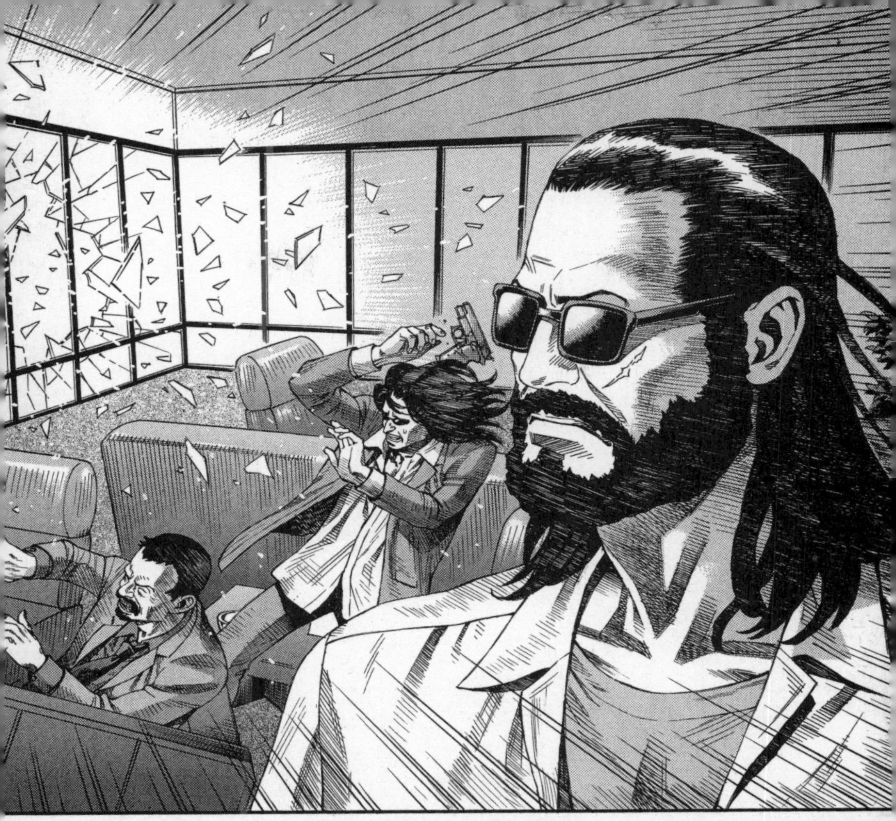

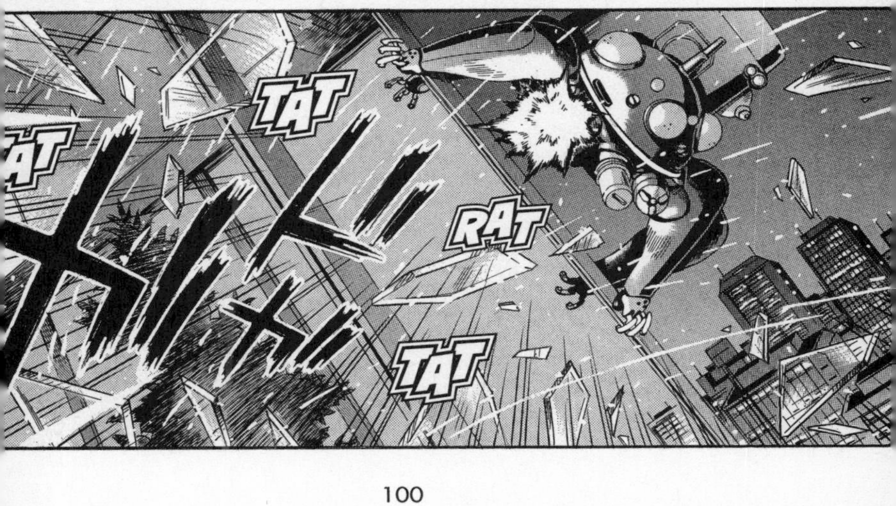
TAT
RAT
TAT

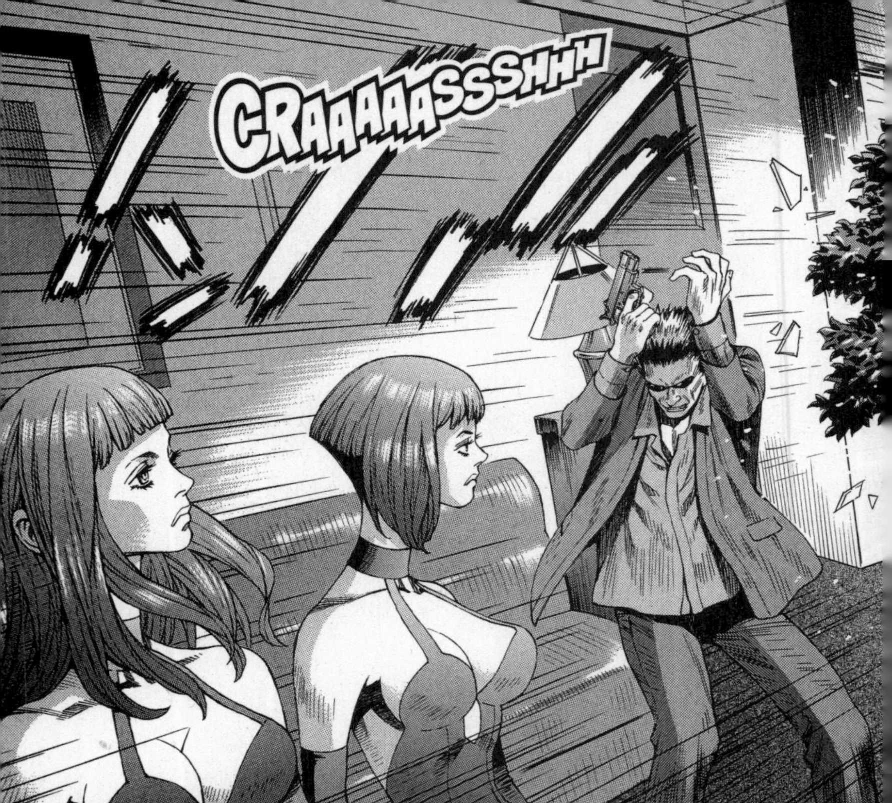
CRAAAAASSSHHH

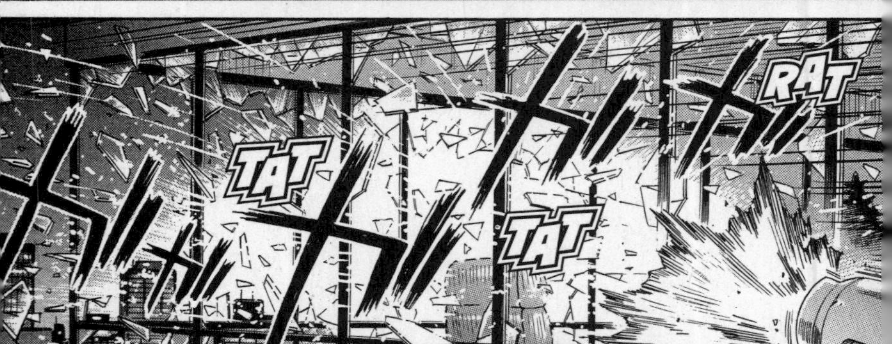
RAT
TAT
TAT
TAT

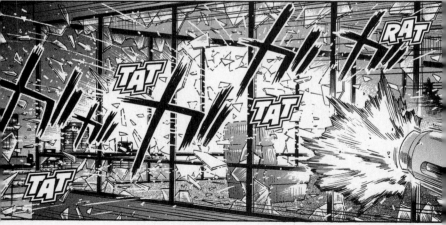

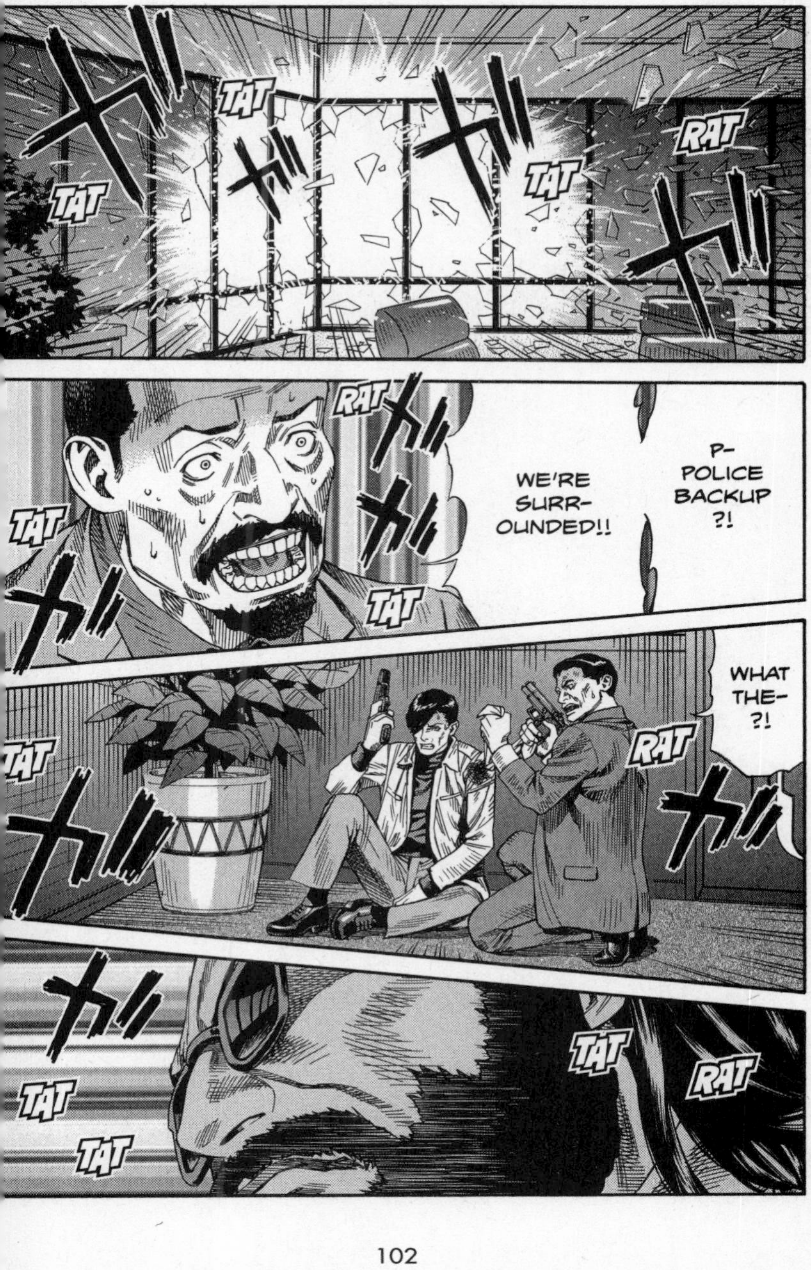
RAT
TAT
TAT
TAT
P-
POLICE
BACKUP
?!
WE'RE
SURR-
OUNDED!!
RAT
TAT
TAT
WHAT
THE-
?!
RAT
TAT
RAT
TAT
TAT
TAT

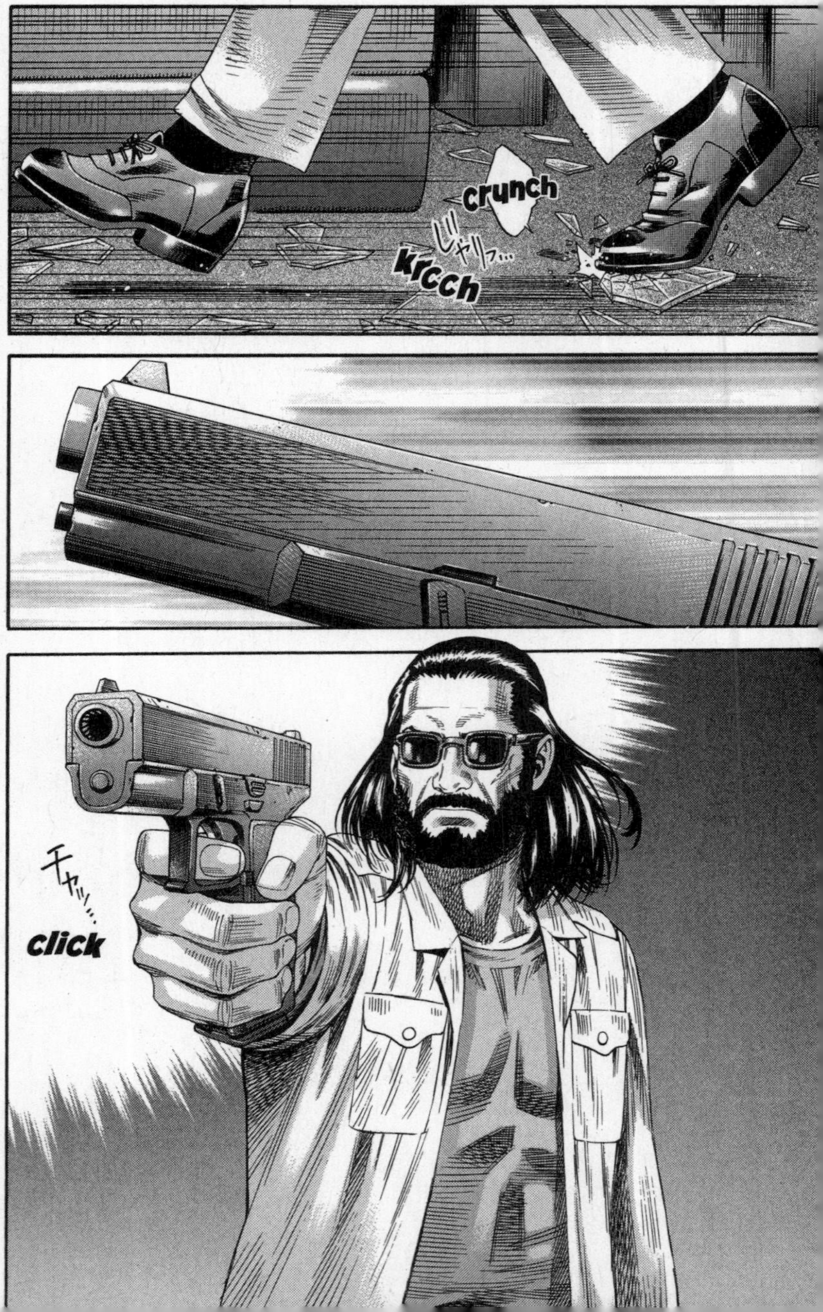
crunch
じゃりっ…
krcch
チャッ…
click

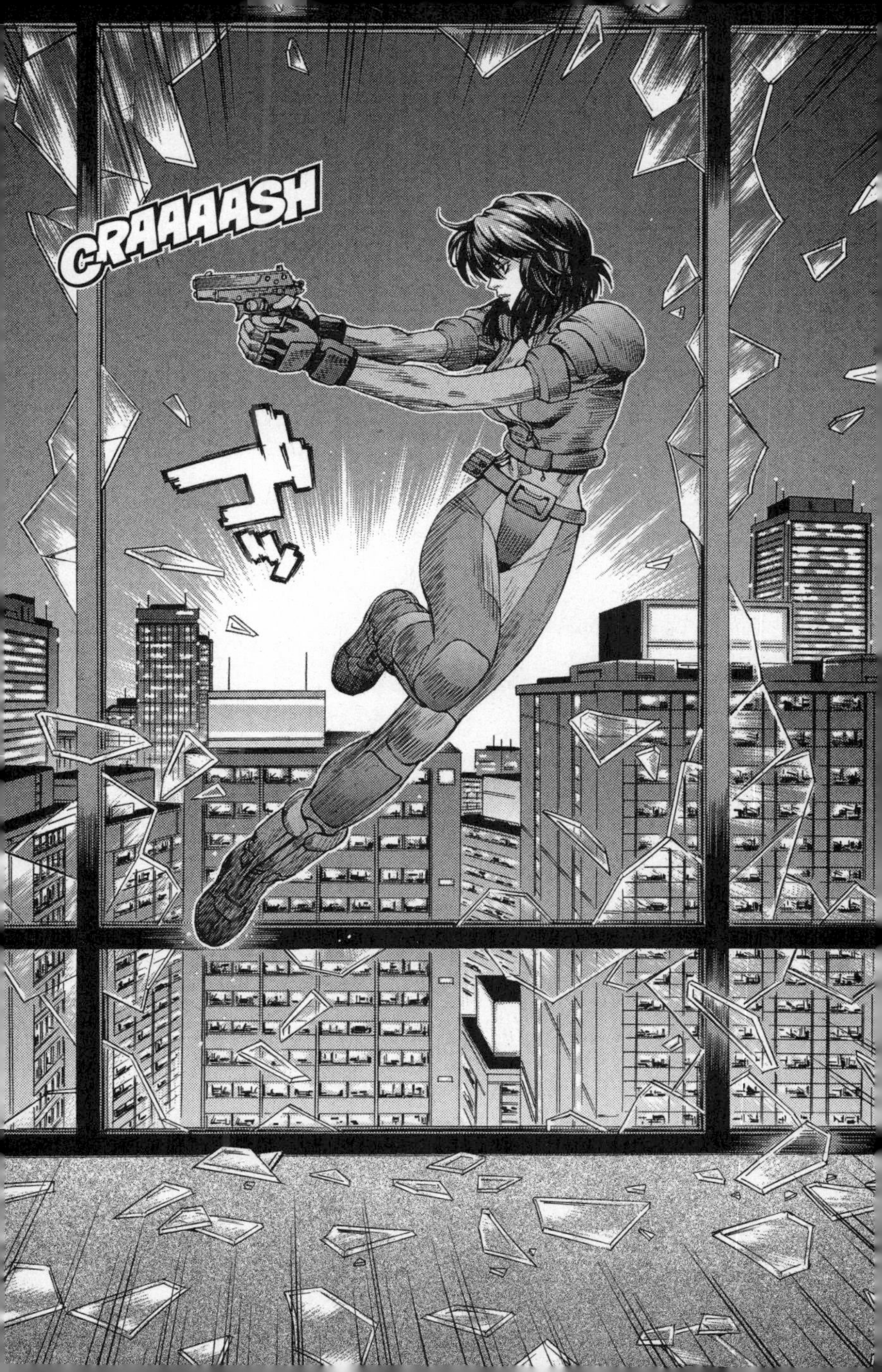
CRAAAASH

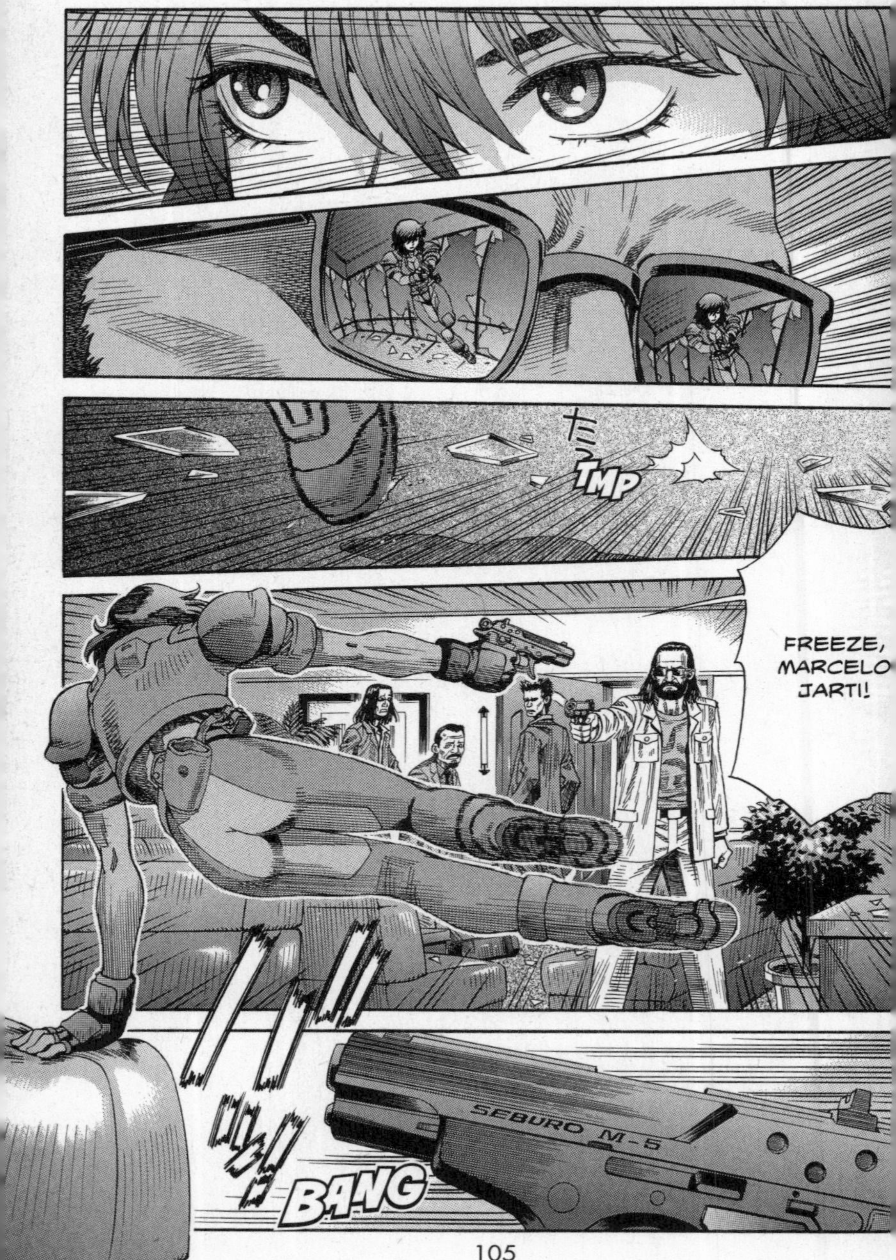
たっ
TMP
FREEZE, MARCELO JARTI!
SEBURO M-5
BANG

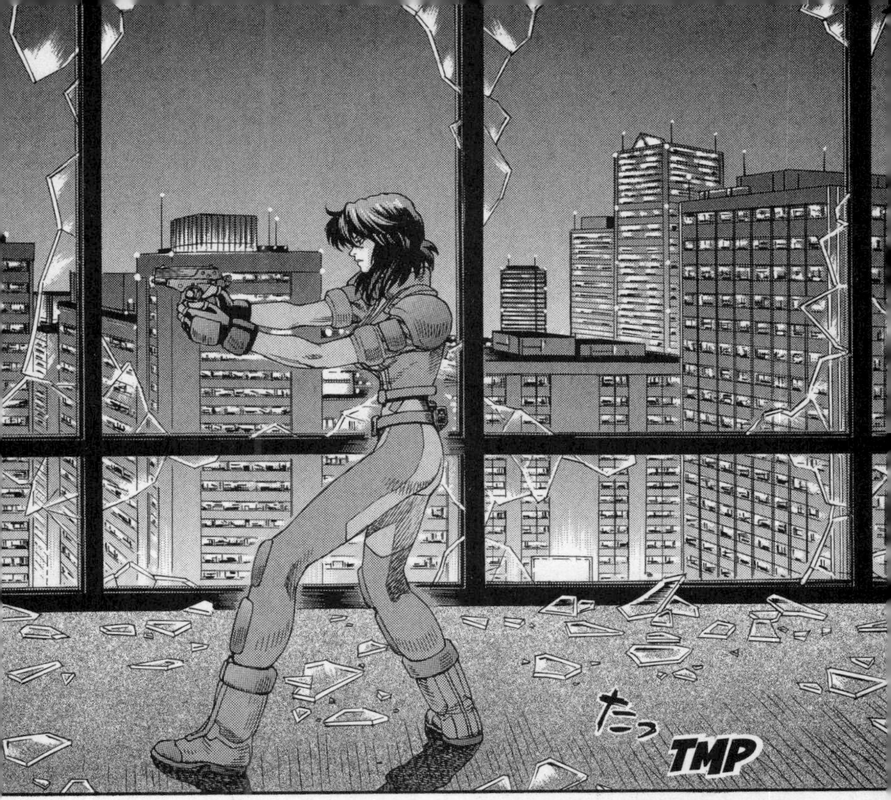
たっ
TMP
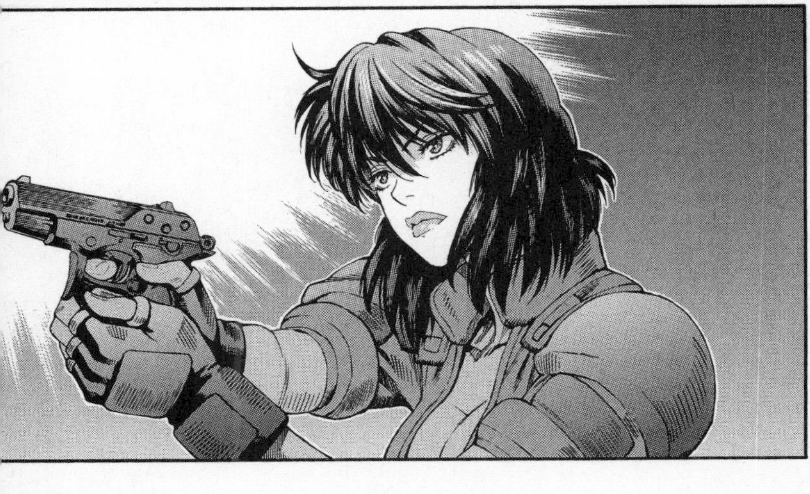

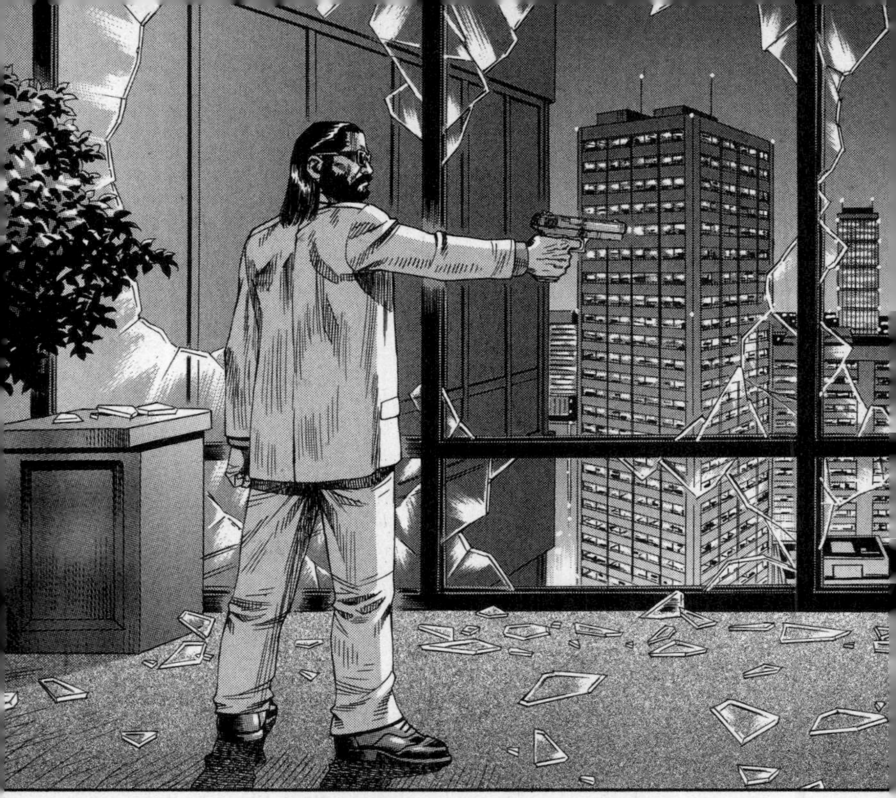
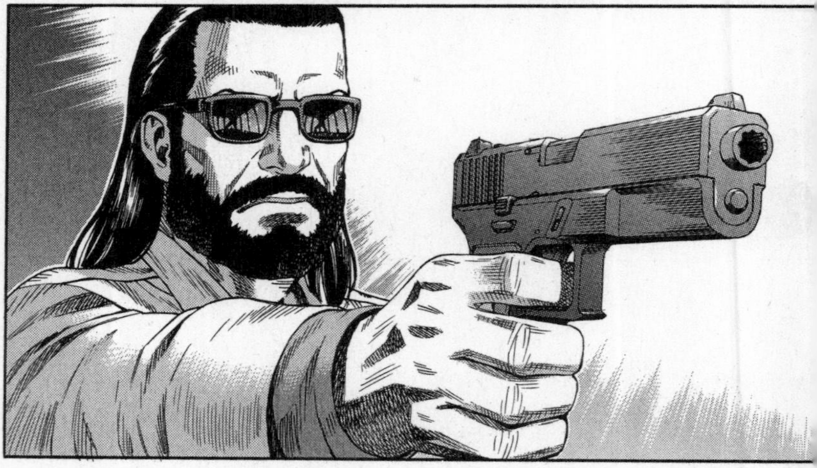

JARTI.

I'M GONNA LET YOU GO.

...THE HELL IS THAT??

W—WHO...

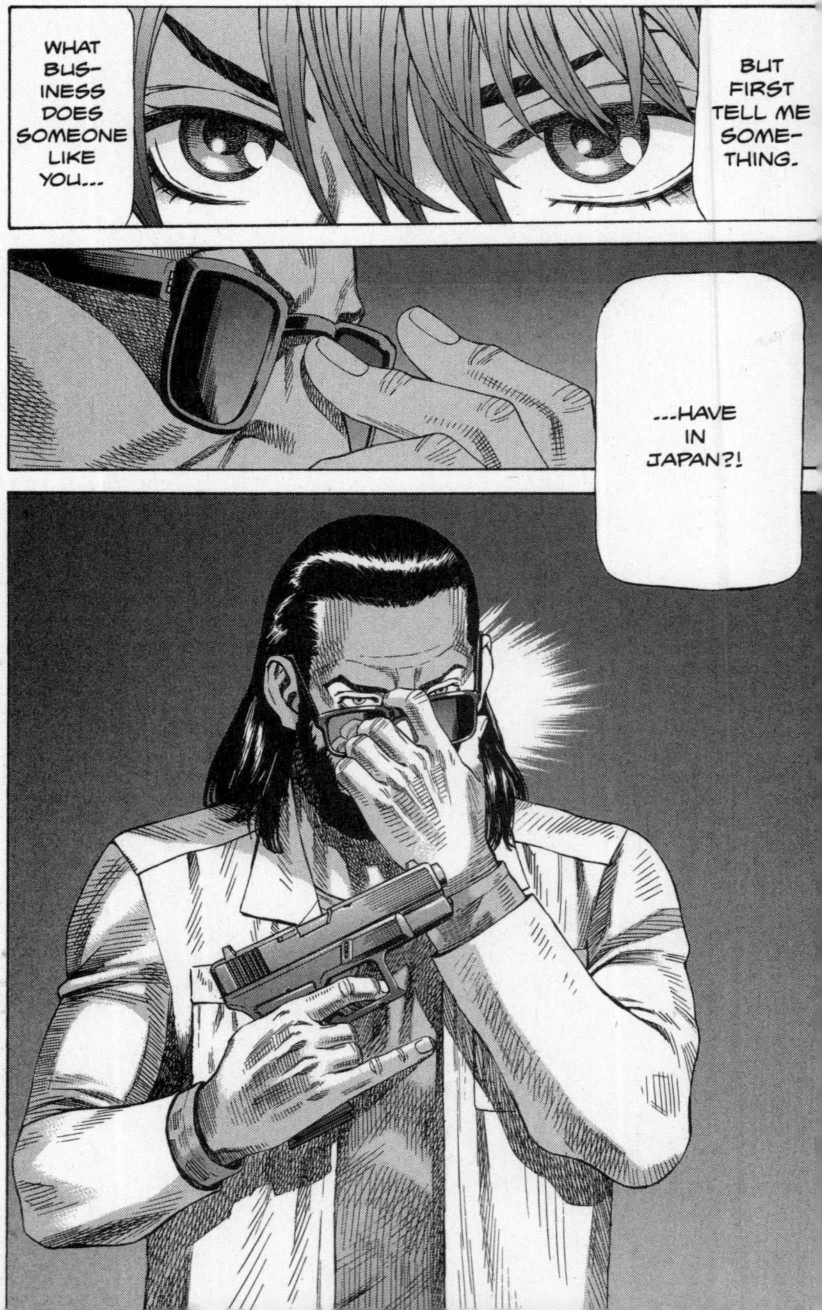
BUT FIRST TELL ME SOMETHING.
WHAT BUSINESS DOES SOMEONE LIKE YOU...
...HAVE IN JAPAN?!

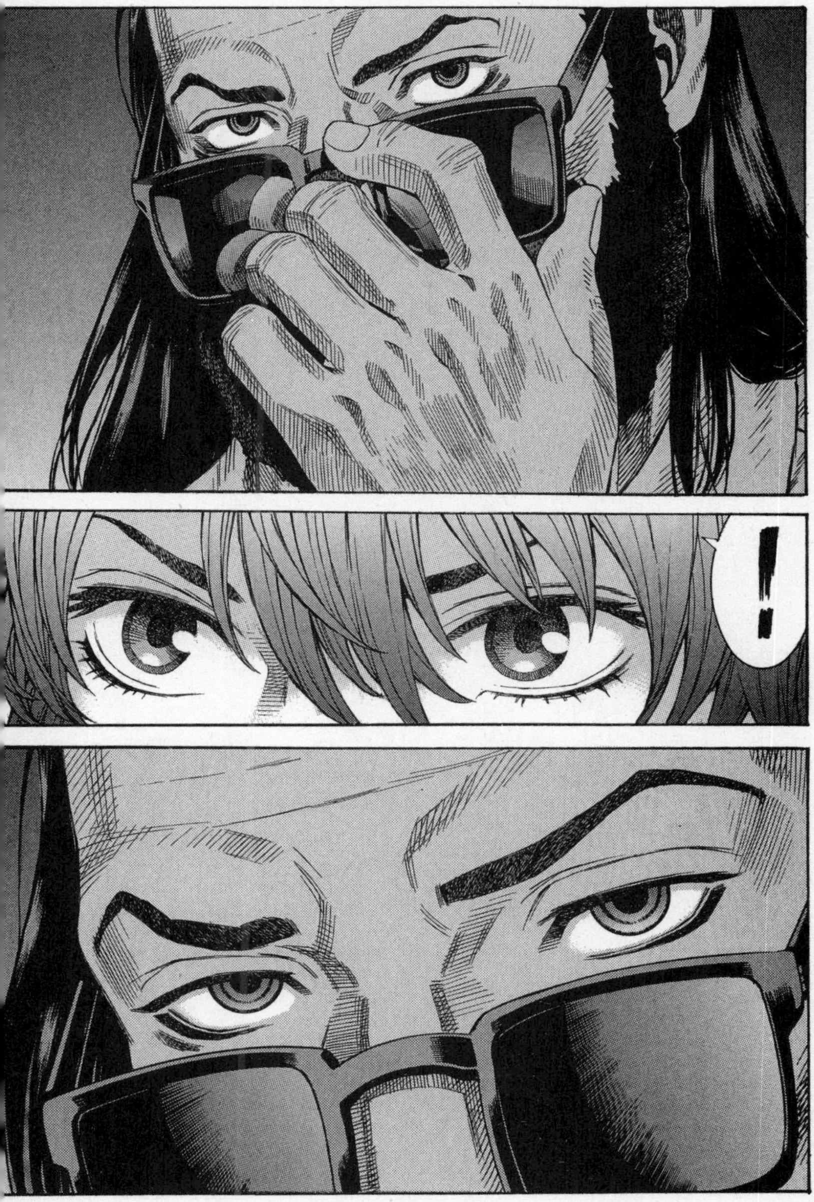
!

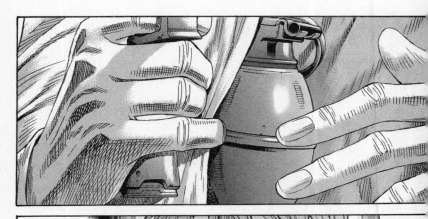

M26 GREN-ADE?!

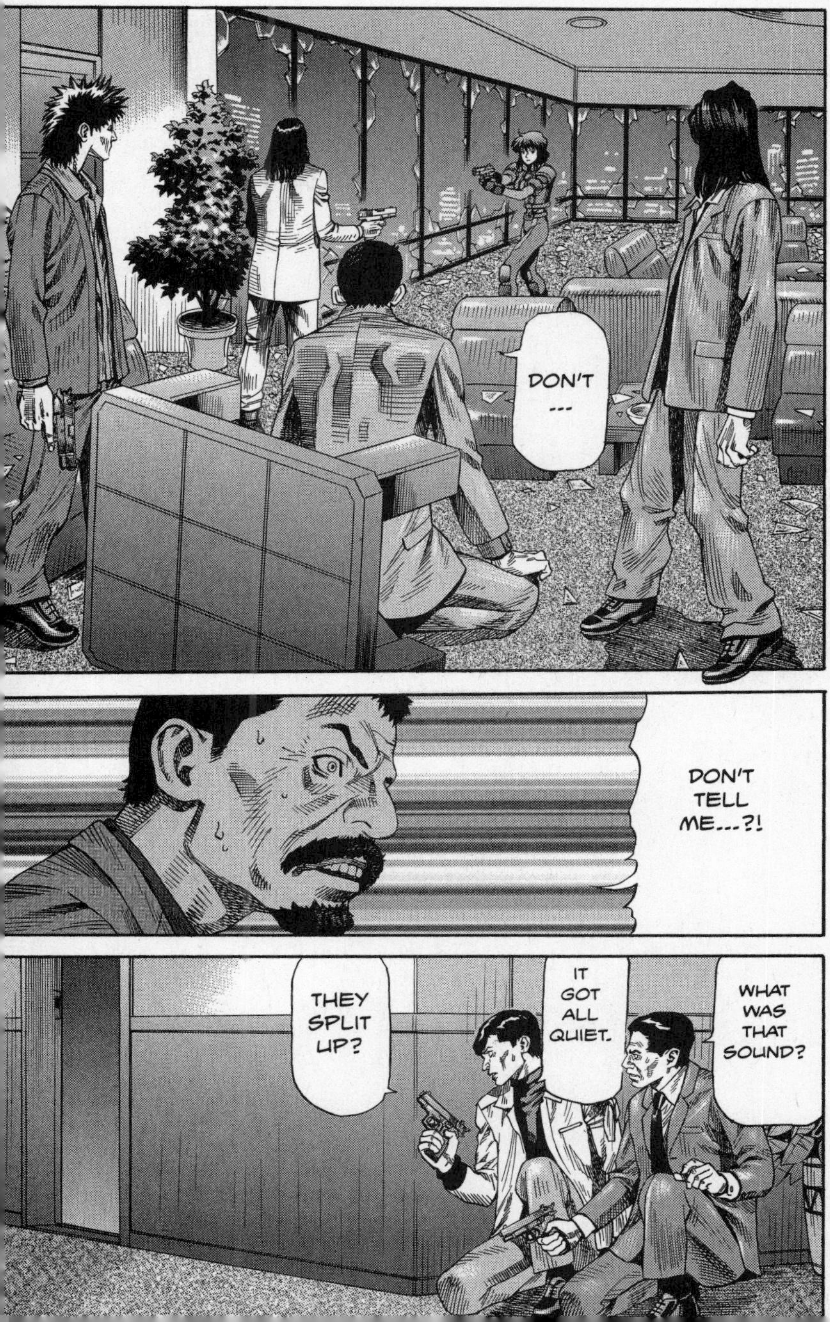
DON'T ---
DON'T TELL ME...?!
WHAT WAS THAT SOUND?
IT GOT ALL QUIET.
THEY SPLIT UP?

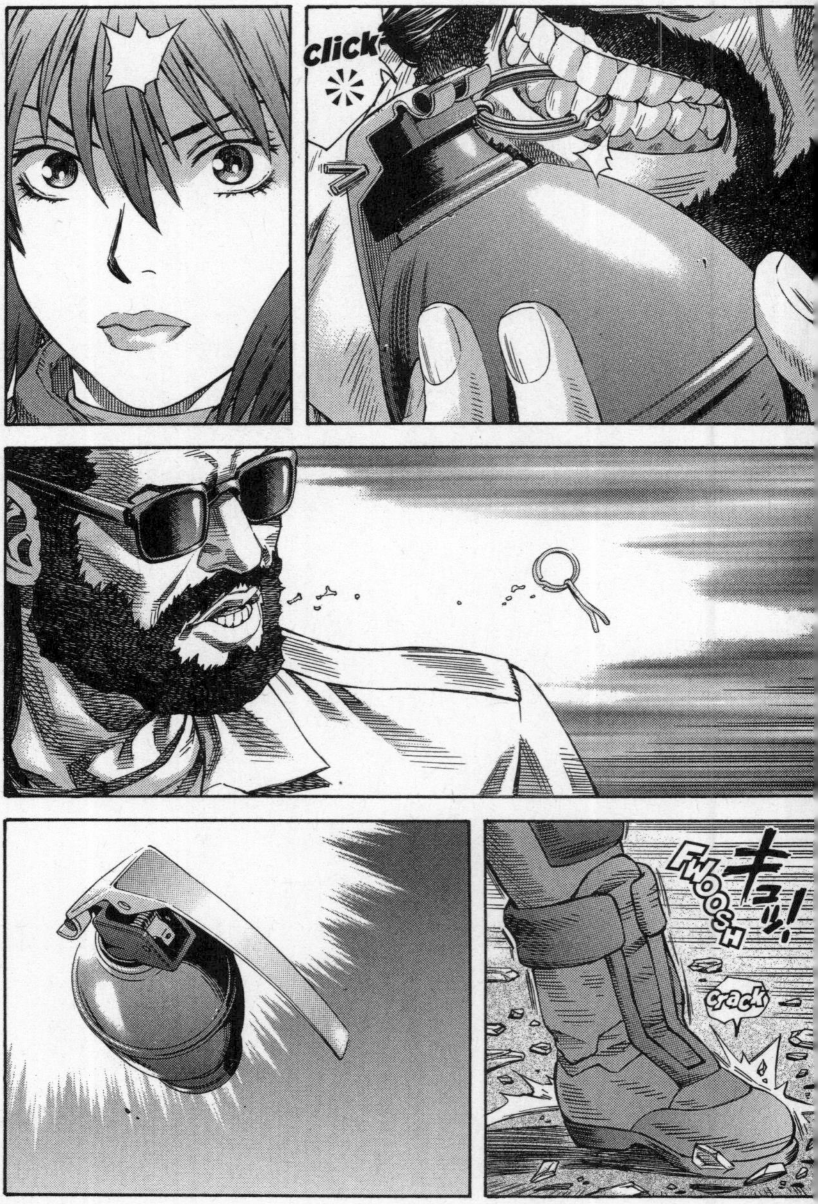
click
キュッ!
FWOOSH
crack

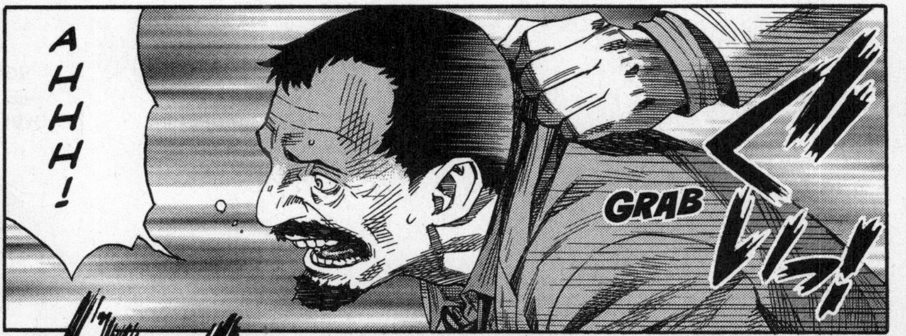
GRAB
AHHHH!

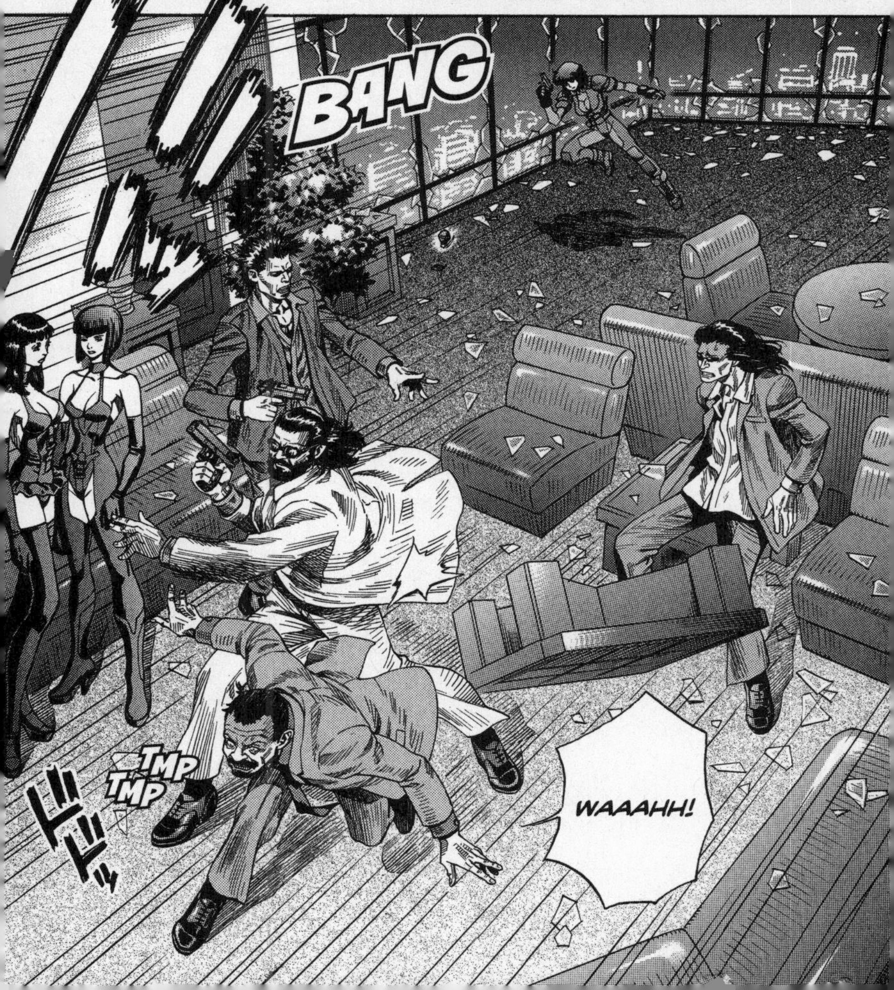
BANG
TMP
TMP
WAAAHH!

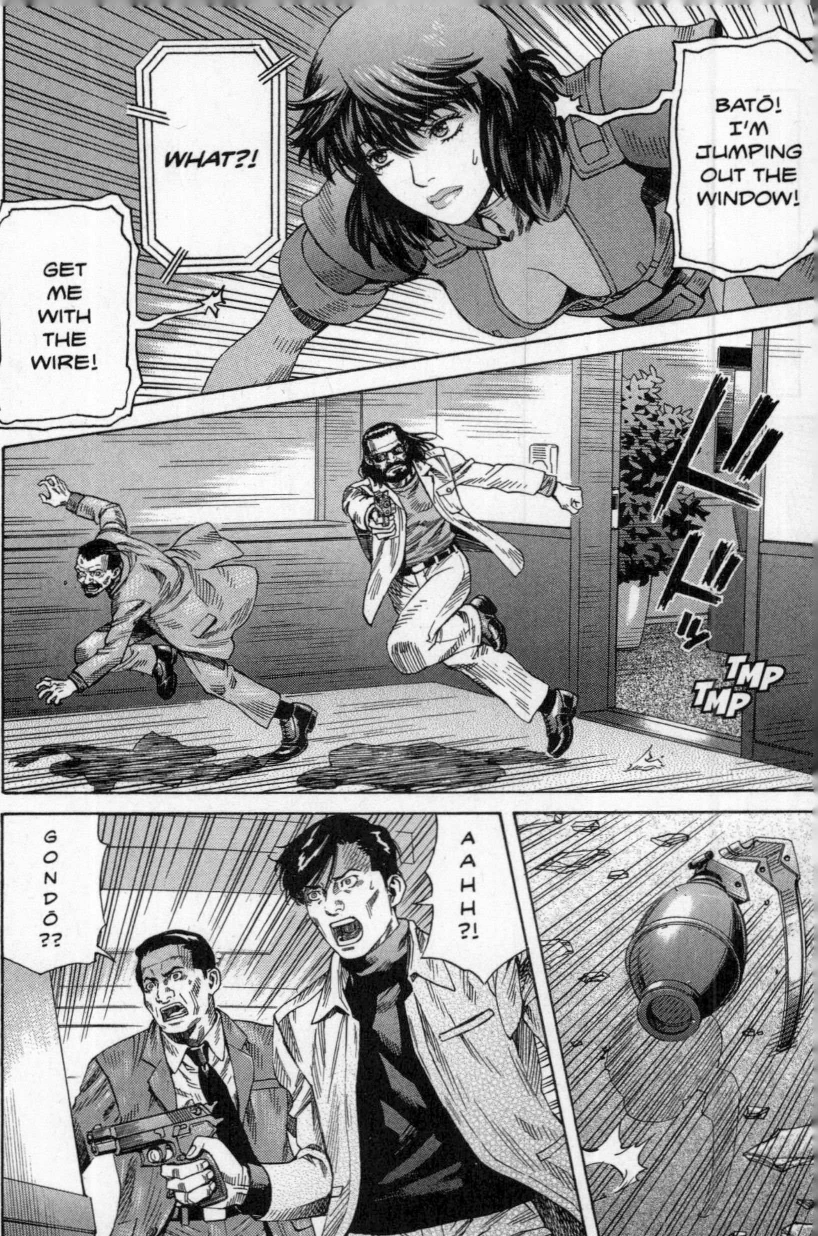
BATŌ! I'M JUMPING OUT THE WINDOW!
WHAT?!
GET ME WITH THE WIRE!
TMP TMP
AAHH?!
GONDŌ??

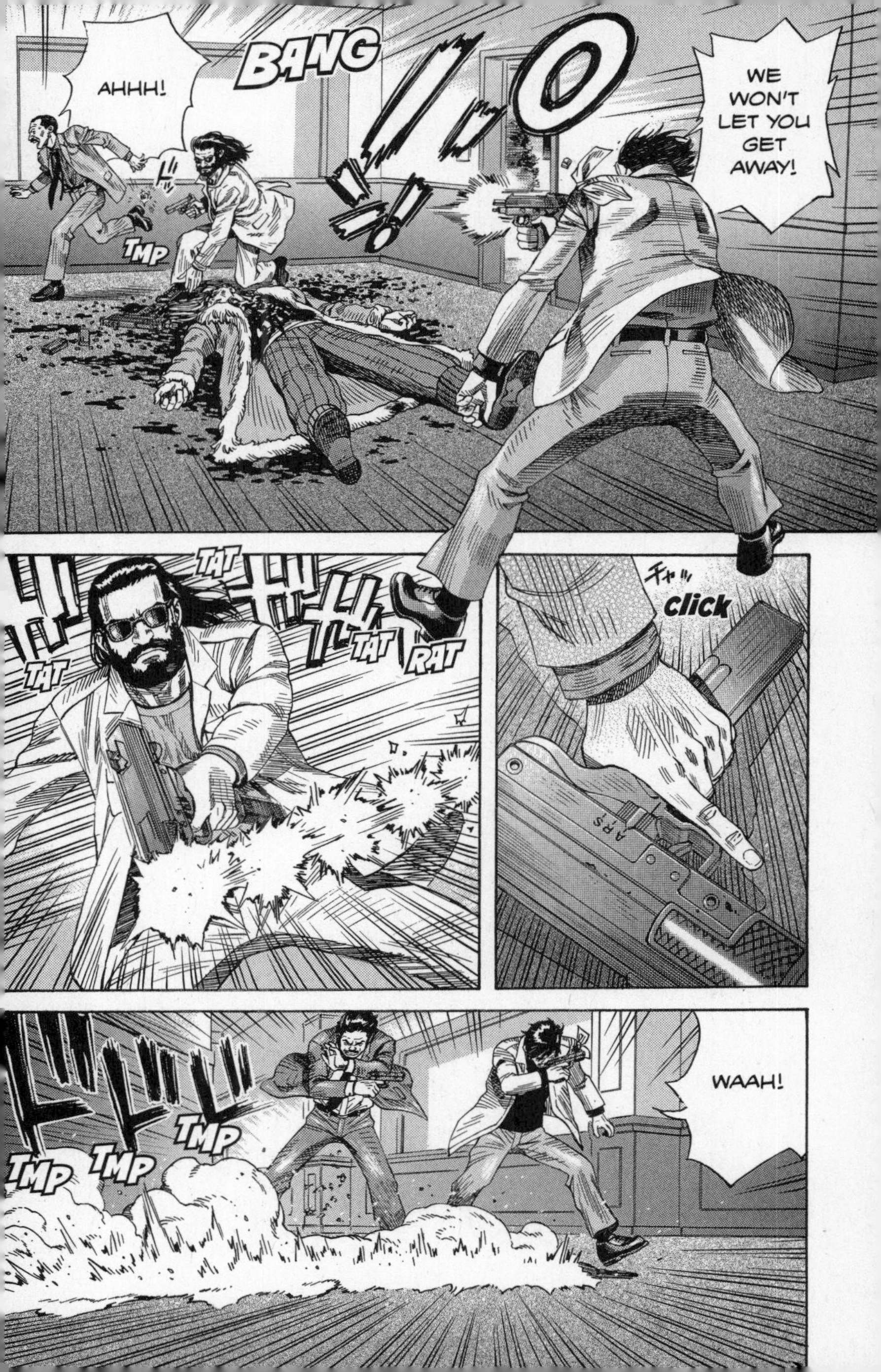
WE WON'T LET YOU GET AWAY!
BANG
AHHH!
TMP
CLICK
TAT
TAT
RAT
TAT
WAAH!
TMP
TMP
TMP

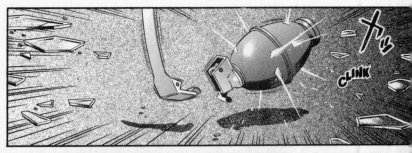

CLINK

BOOOOOOOOOOM

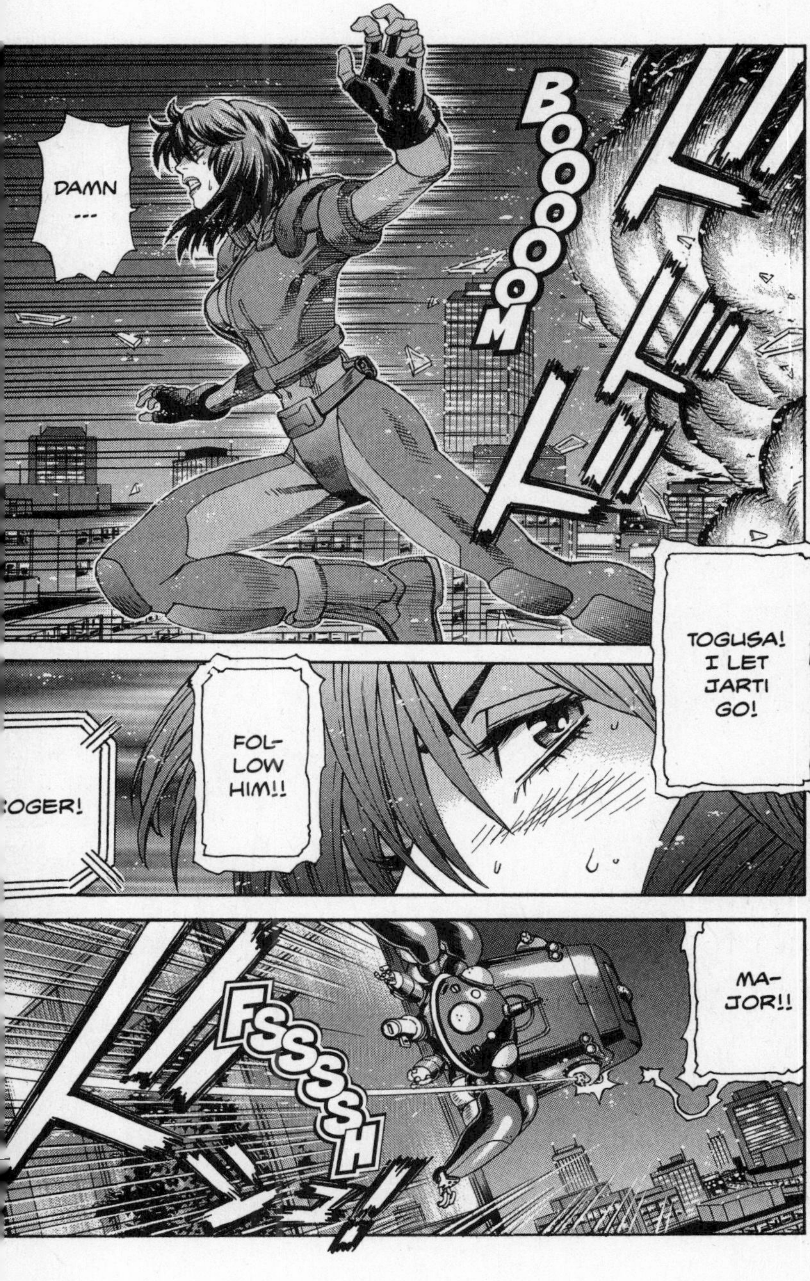
BOOOOOOM
DAMN ---
TOGUSA! I LET JARTI GO!
FOL-LOW HIM!!
ROGER!
MA-JOR!!
FSSSSH

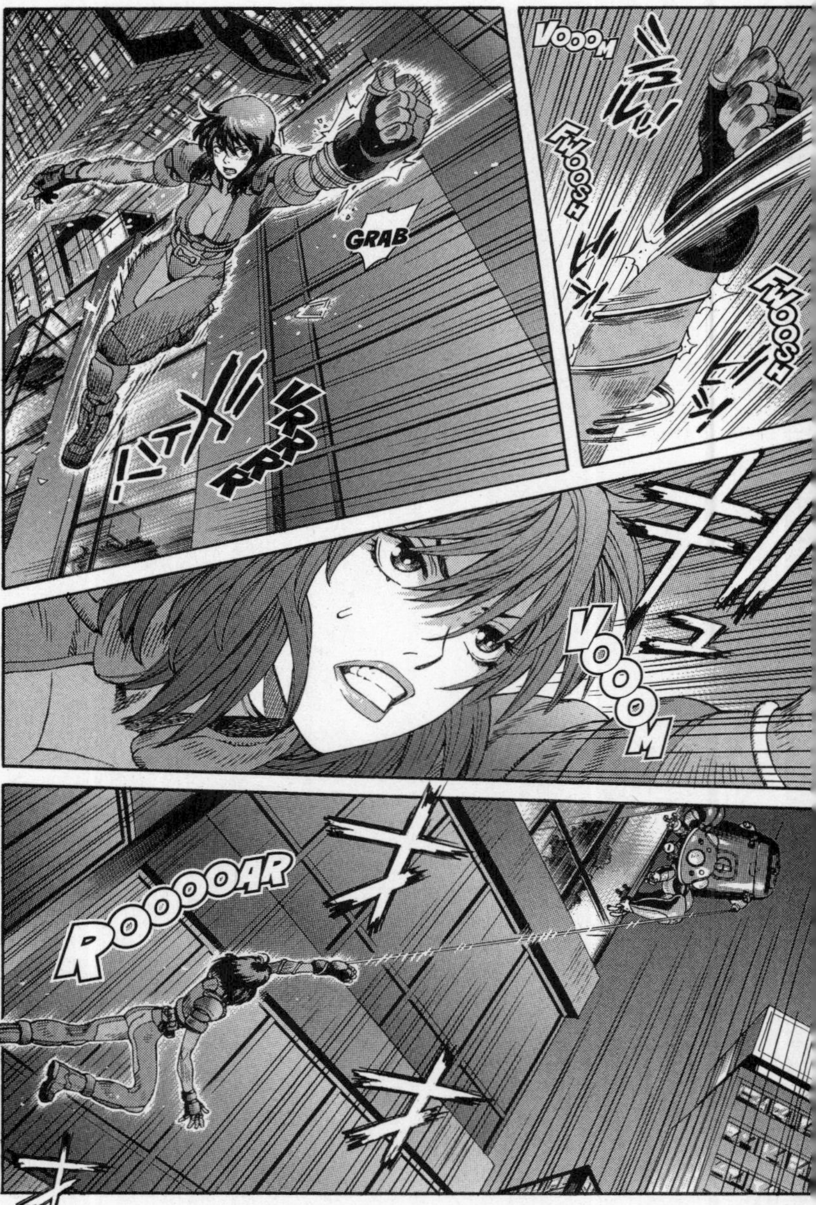

VOOOM
FWOOSH
FWOOSH
GRAB
VRRRRR
VOOOM
ROOOOOAR

TMP

THAT'S
THE REAL
MARCELO
JARTI...

BUT
---

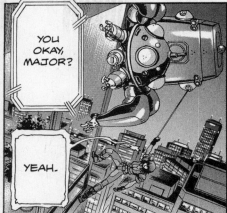

YOU
OKAY,
MAJOR?

YEAH.

WHY WERE
HIS EYES SO
VACANT??

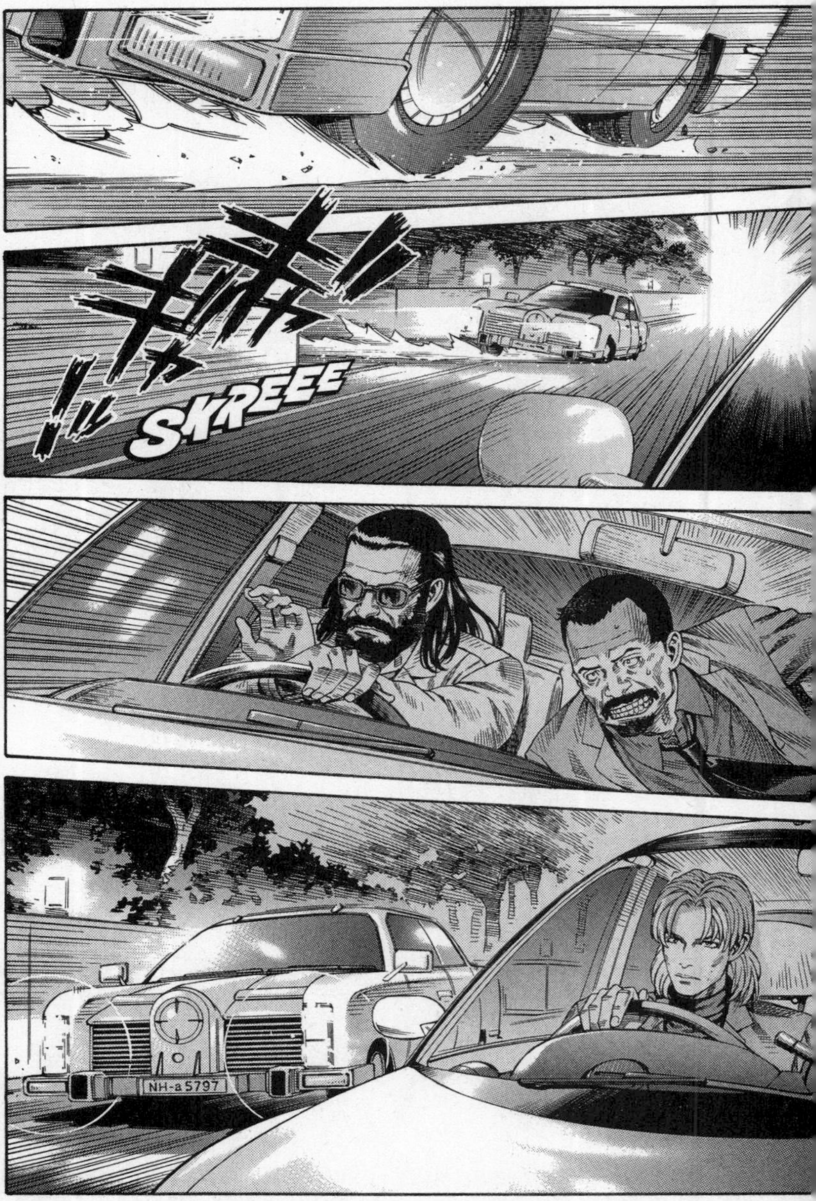
SKREEE
NH-a 5797

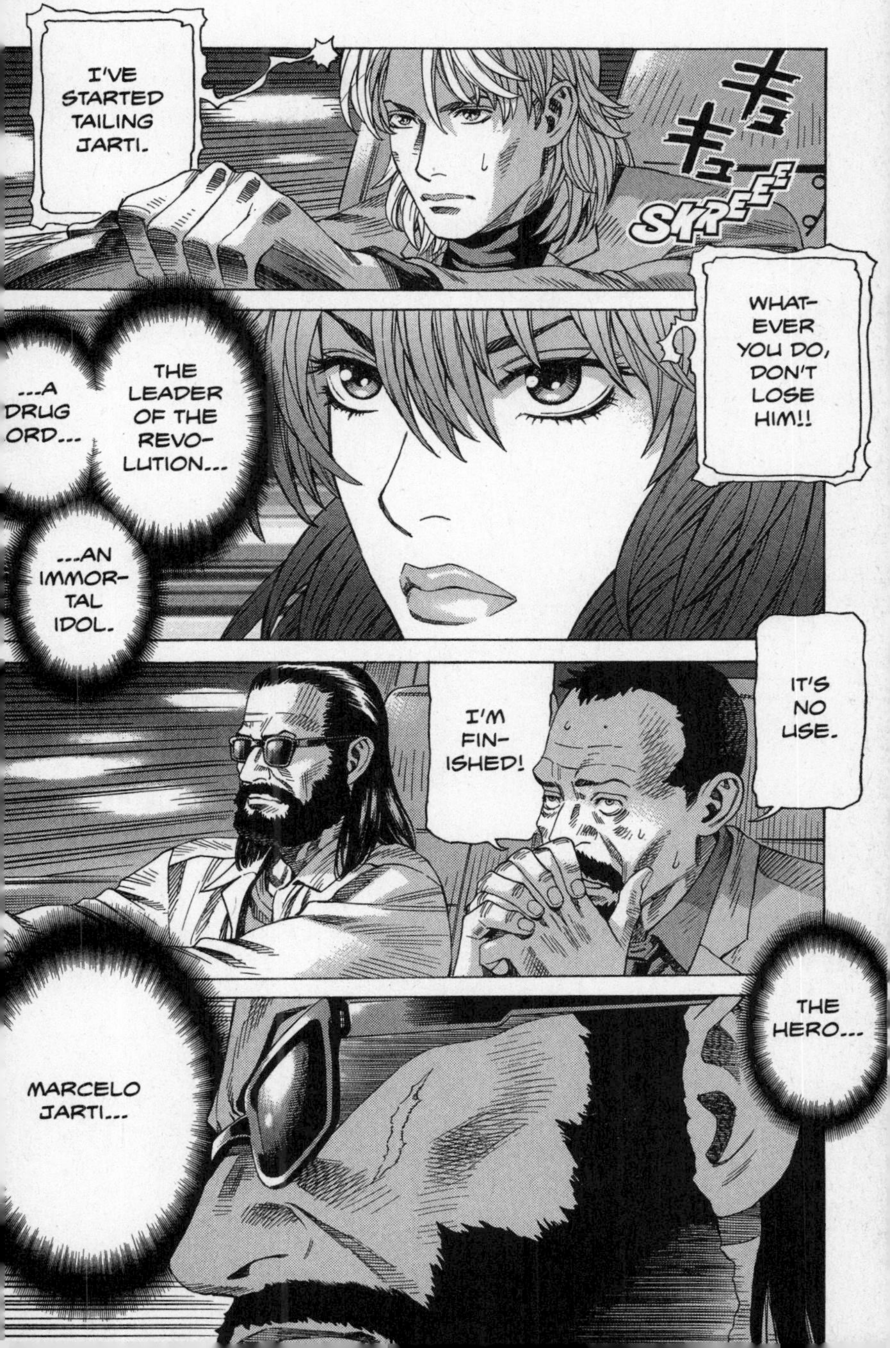
キュキュー
SKREEEE
I'VE STARTED TAILING JARTI.
WHAT-EVER YOU DO, DON'T LOSE HIM!!
THE LEADER OF THE REVO-LUTION...
...A DRUG ORD...
...AN IMMOR-TAL IDOL.
IT'S NO USE.
I'M FIN-ISHED!
THE HERO...
MARCELO JARTI...

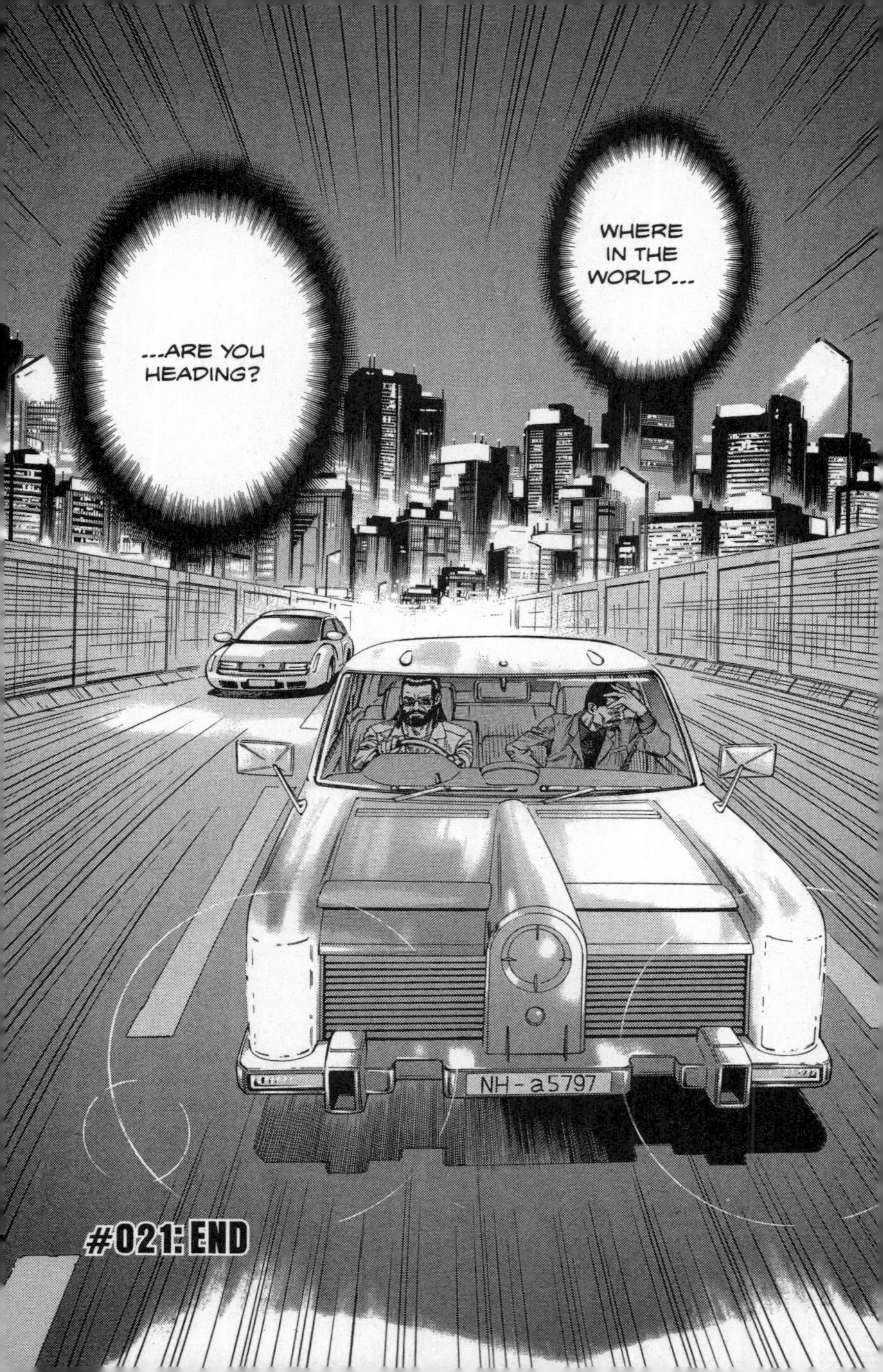
WHERE IN THE WORLD...
...ARE YOU HEADING?
NH-a5797
#021: END

# #022: Strange Circumstances

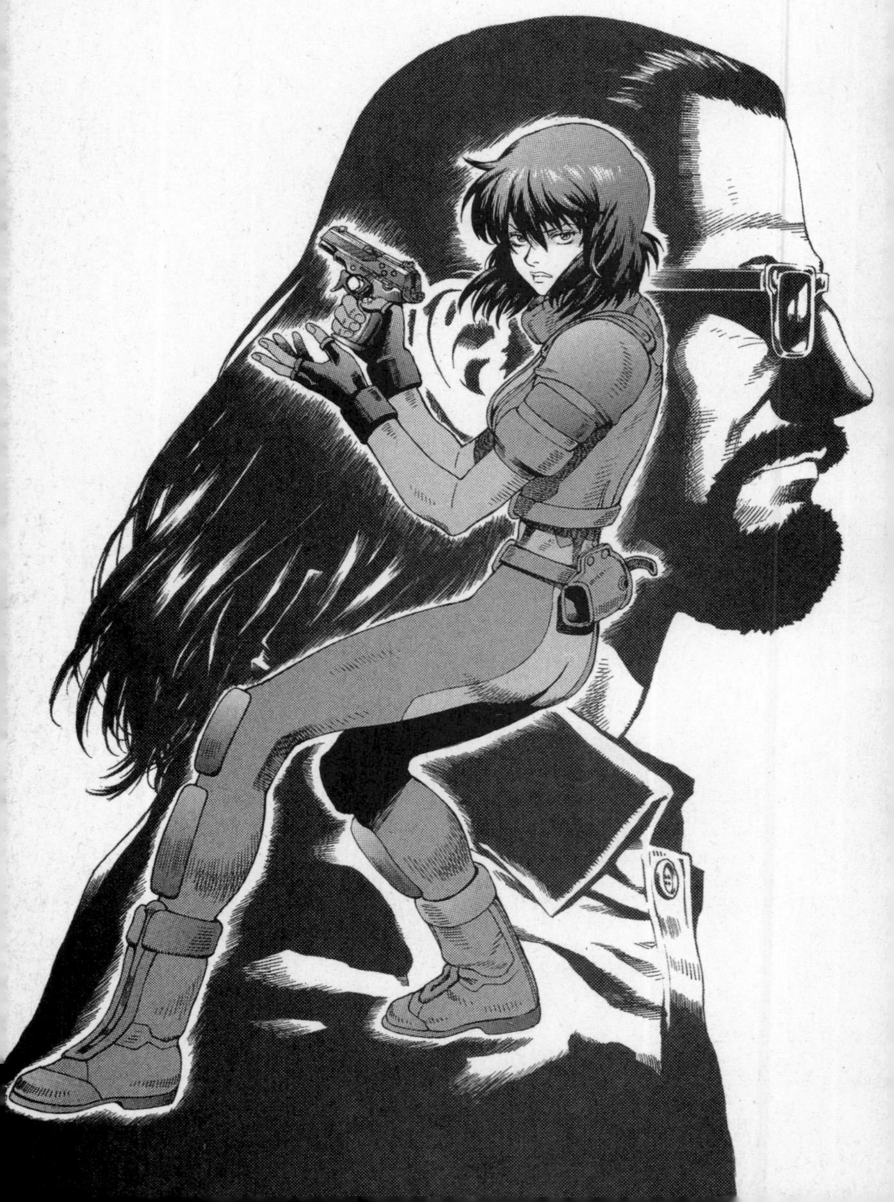

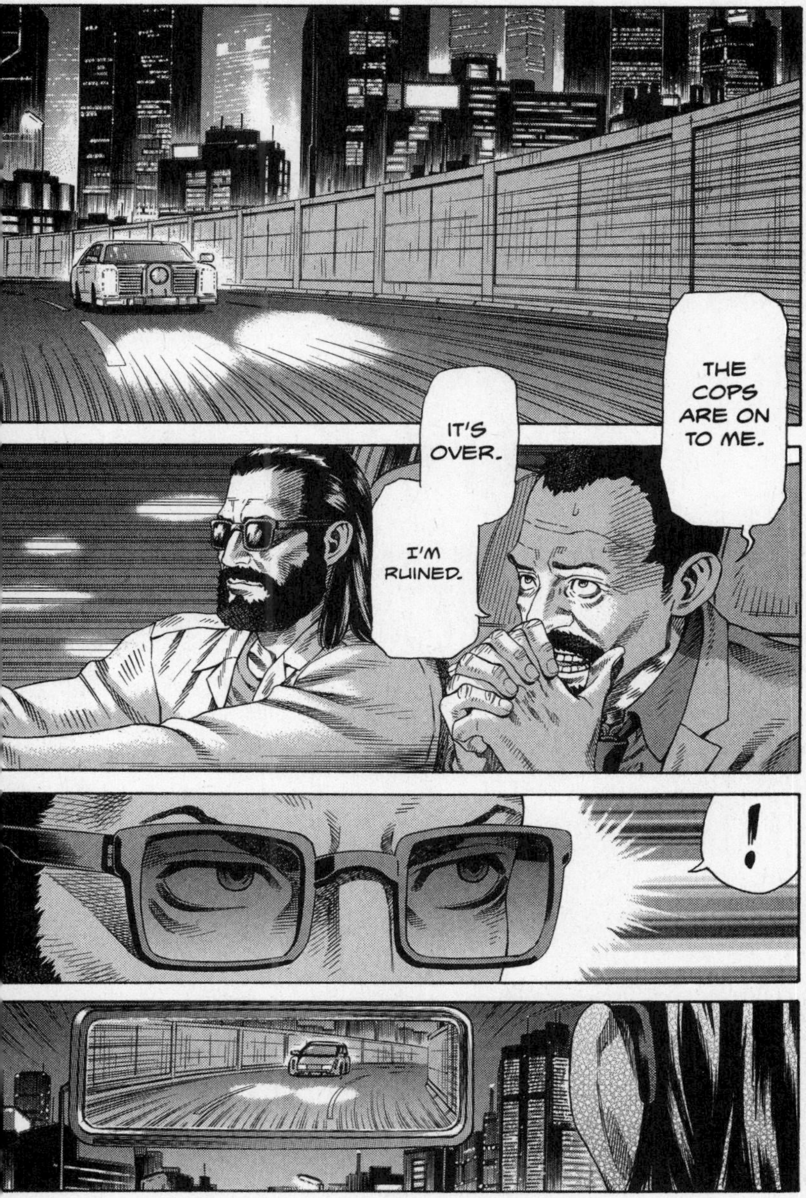
THE COPS ARE ON TO ME.
IT'S OVER.
I'M RUINED.
!

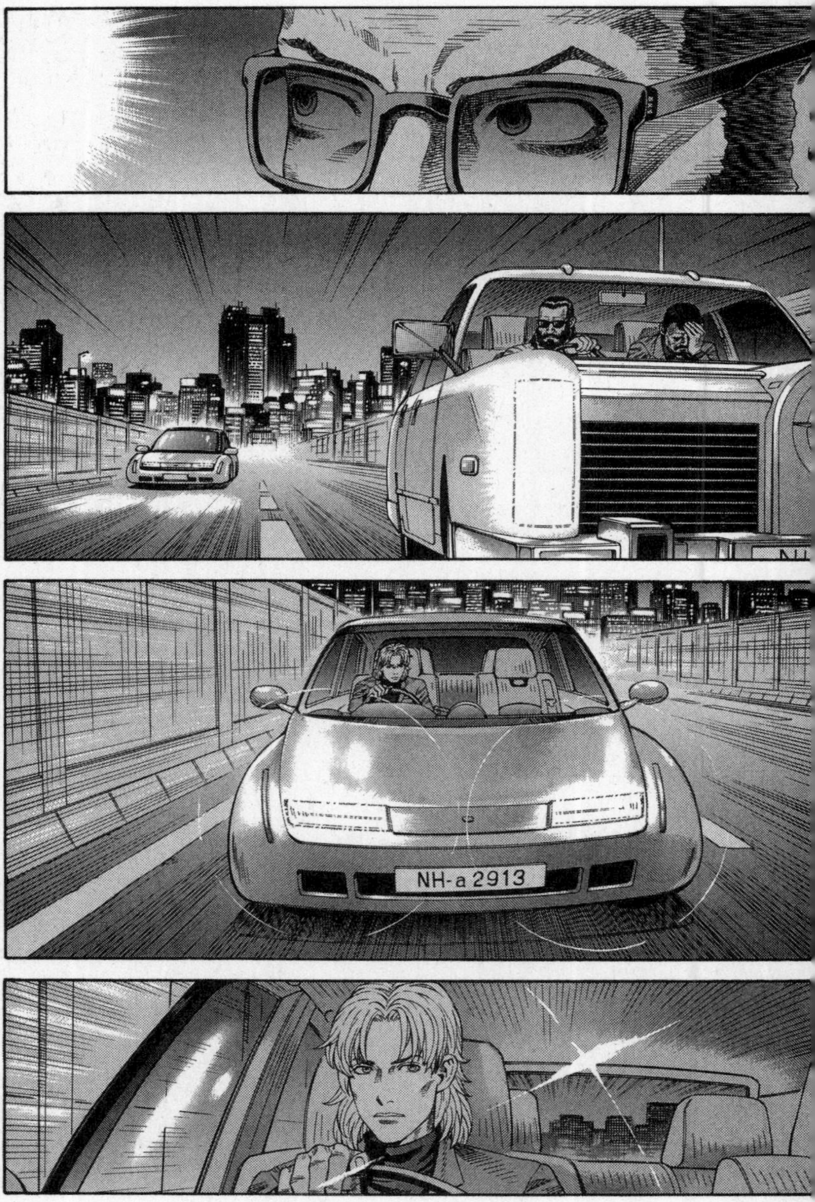
NH-a 2913

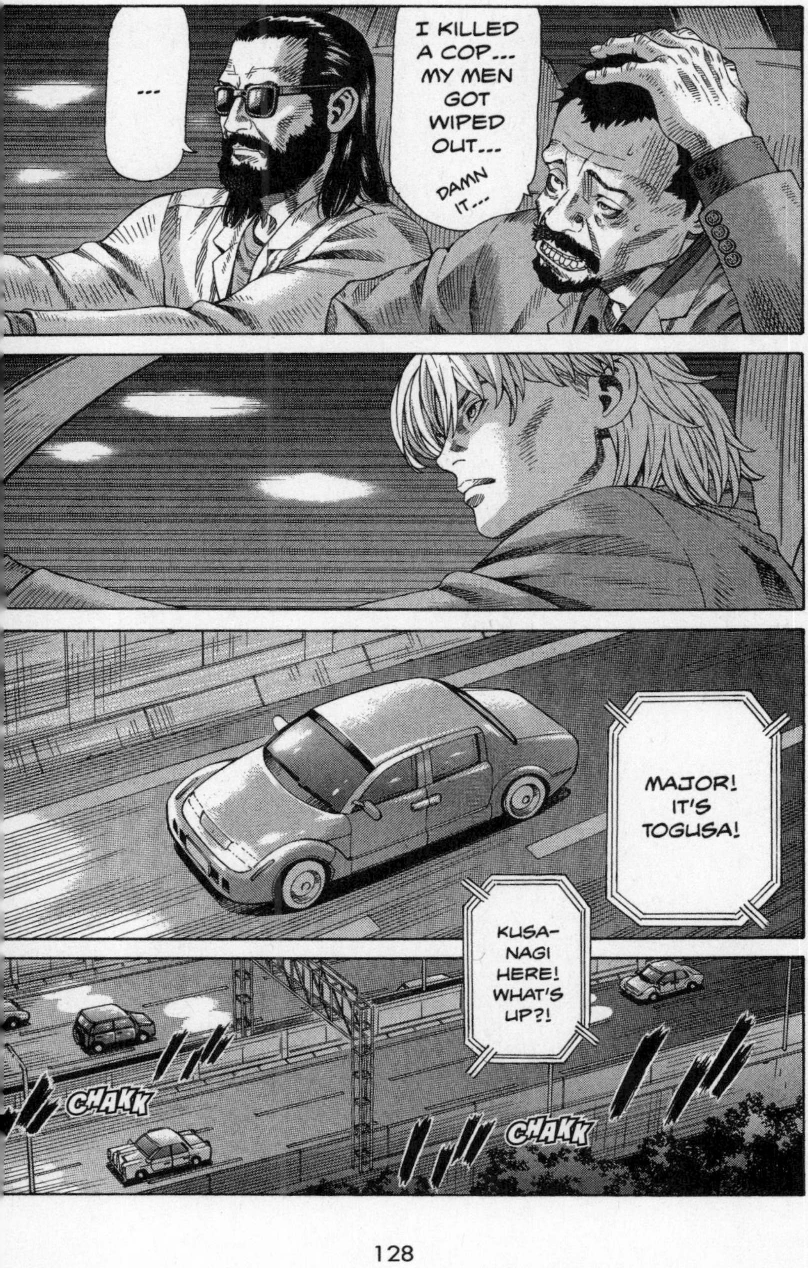
I KILLED A COP... MY MEN GOT WIPED OUT...
DAMN IT...
...
MAJOR! IT'S TOGUSA!
KUSA-NAGI HERE! WHAT'S UP?!
CHAKK
CHAKK

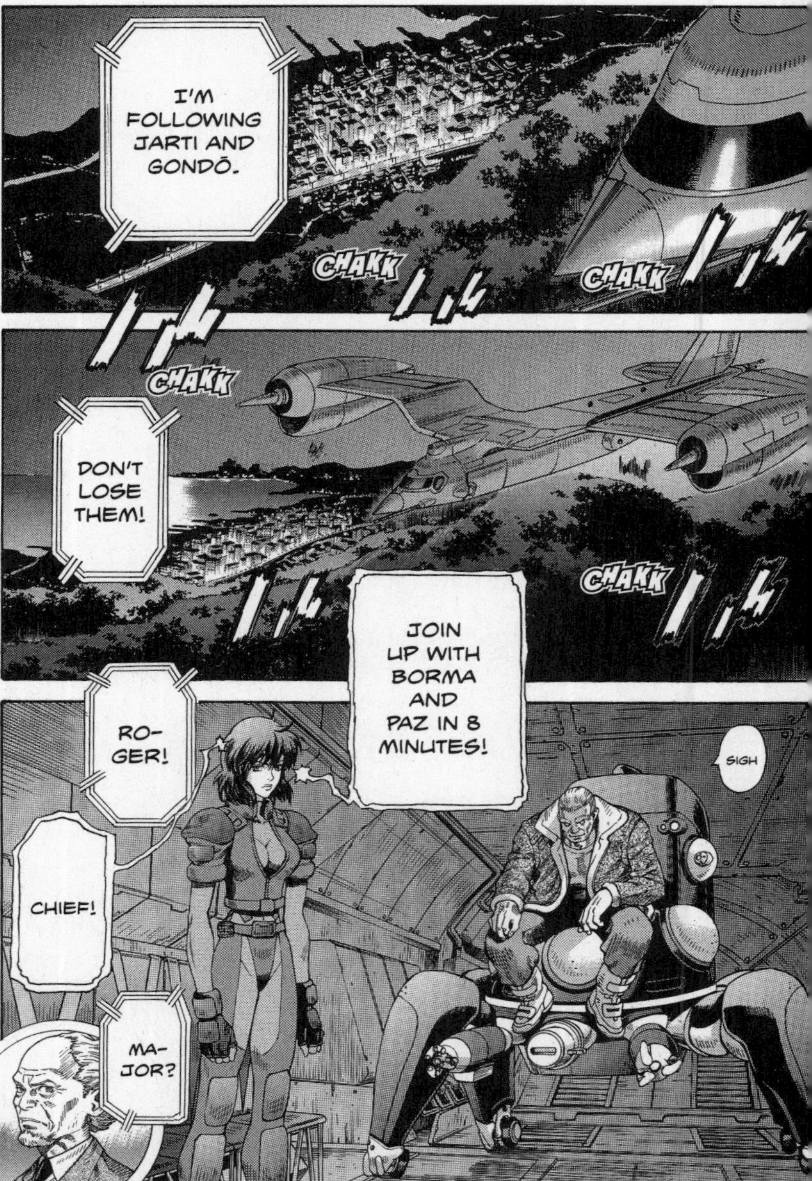
I'M FOLLOWING JARTI AND GONDŌ.
CHAKK
CHAKK
CHAKK
DON'T LOSE THEM!
CHAKK
SIGH
JOIN UP WITH BORMA AND PAZ IN 8 MINUTES!
RO-GER!
CHIEF!
MA-JOR?

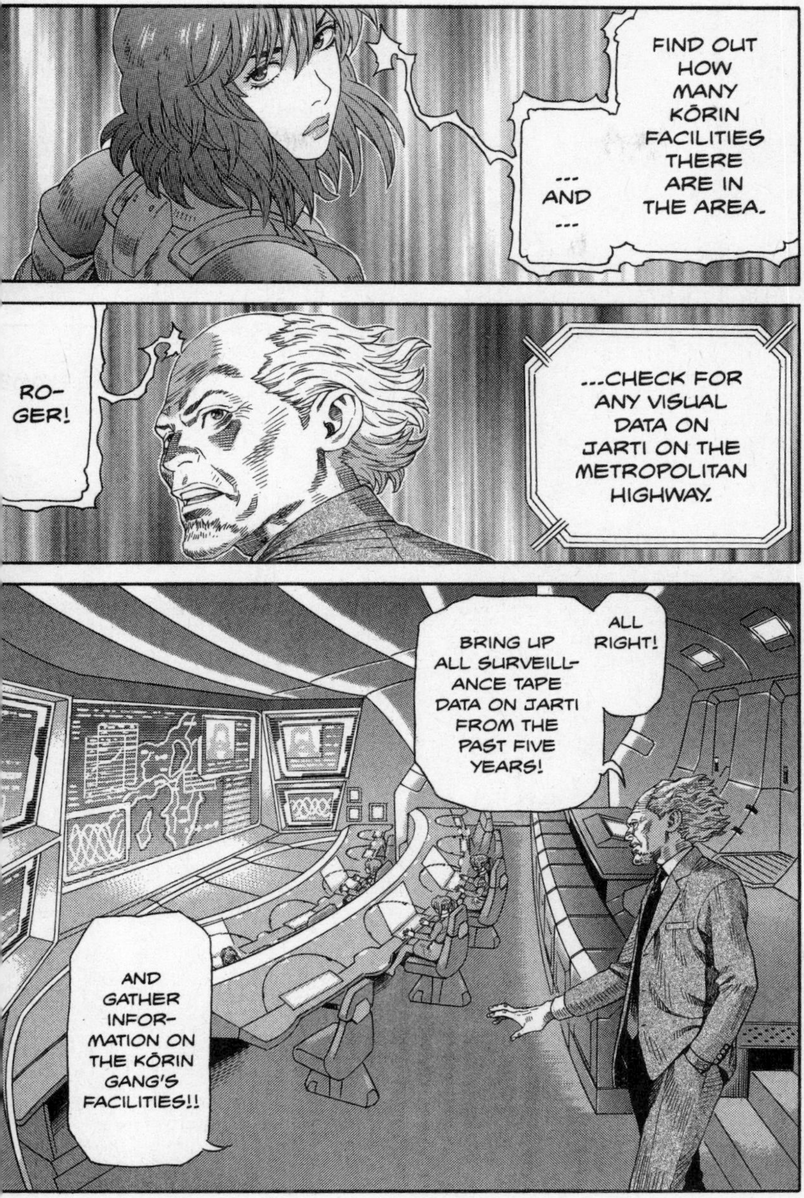
FIND OUT HOW MANY KŌRIN FACILITIES THERE ARE IN THE AREA.
...AND...
...CHECK FOR ANY VISUAL DATA ON JARTI ON THE METROPOLITAN HIGHWAY.
RO-GER!
ALL RIGHT!
BRING UP ALL SURVEILL-ANCE TAPE DATA ON JARTI FROM THE PAST FIVE YEARS!
AND GATHER INFOR-MATION ON THE KŌRIN GANG'S FACILITIES!!

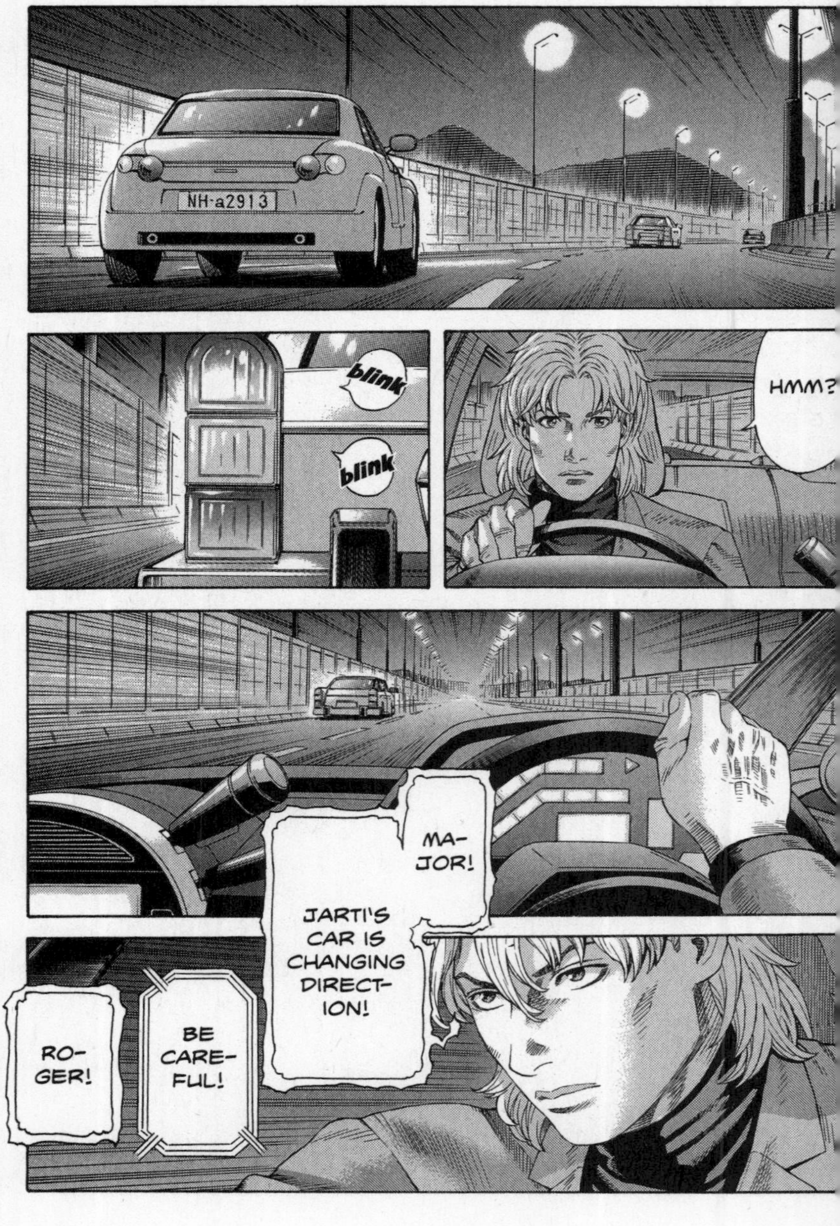
NH-a2913
HMM?
blink
blink
MA-JOR!
JARTI'S CAR IS CHANGING DIRECT-ION!
BE CARE-FUL!
RO-GER!

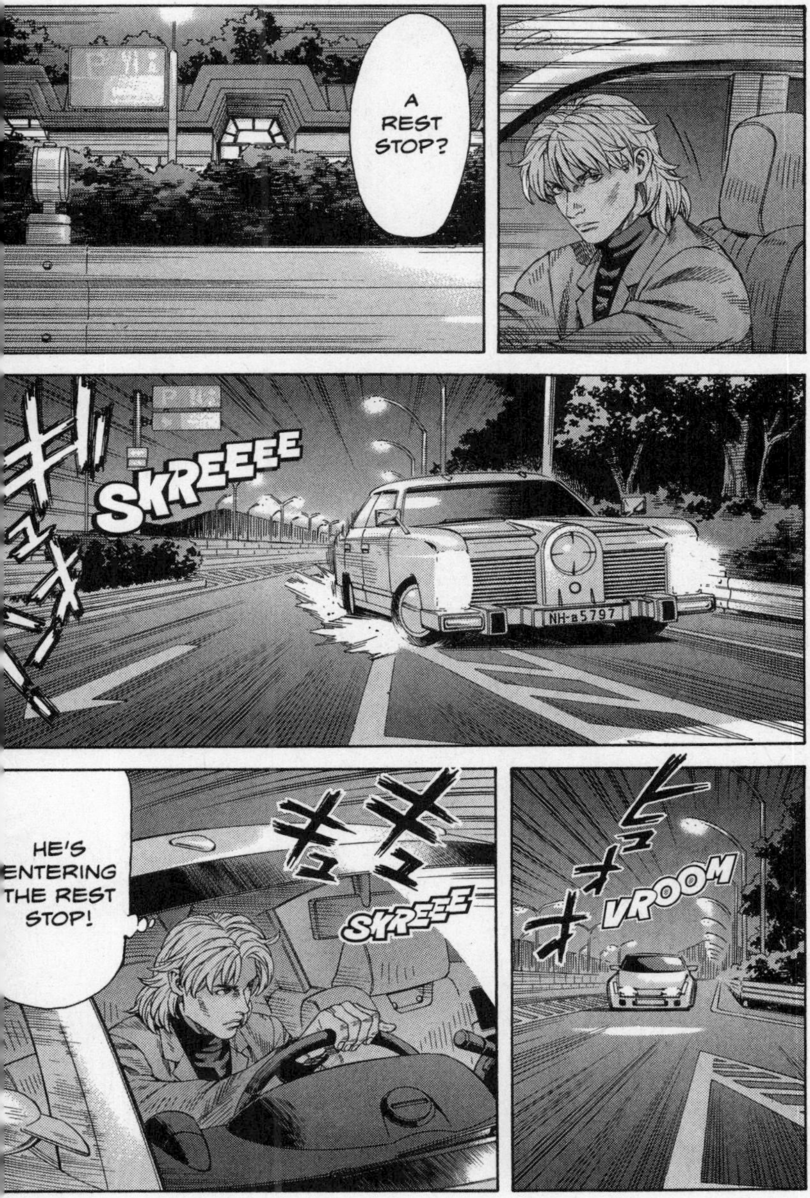
A REST STOP?
SKREEEE
NH-a5797
VROOM
SKREEE
HE'S ENTERING THE REST STOP!

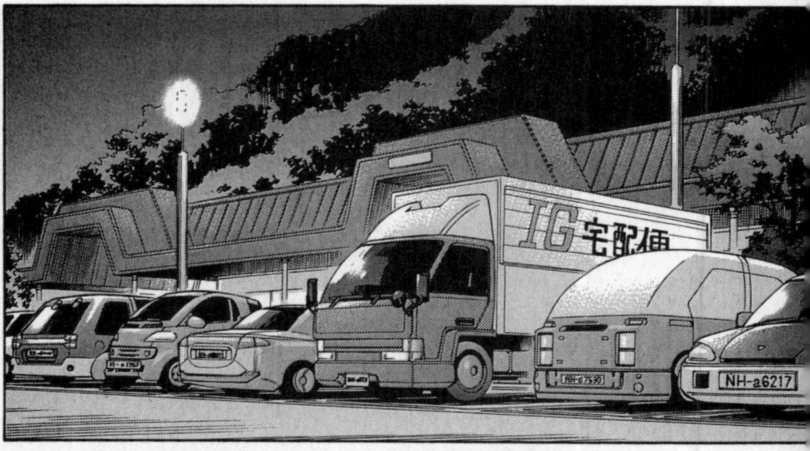
IG 宅配便
NH-a6217
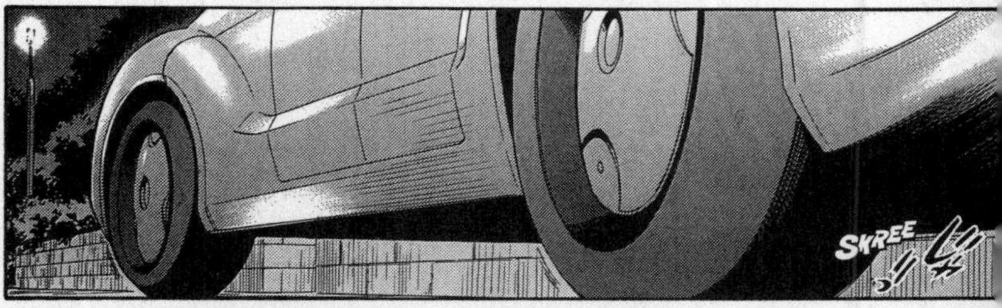
SKREE
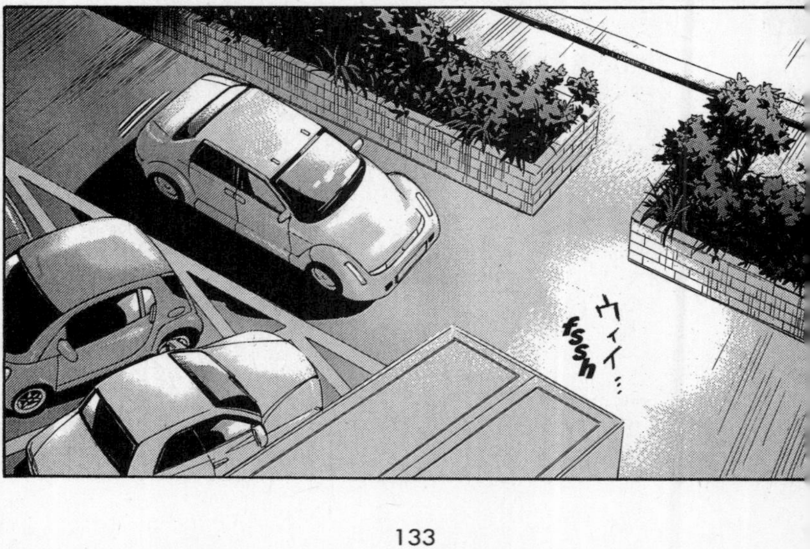
ウィイ…
fssh

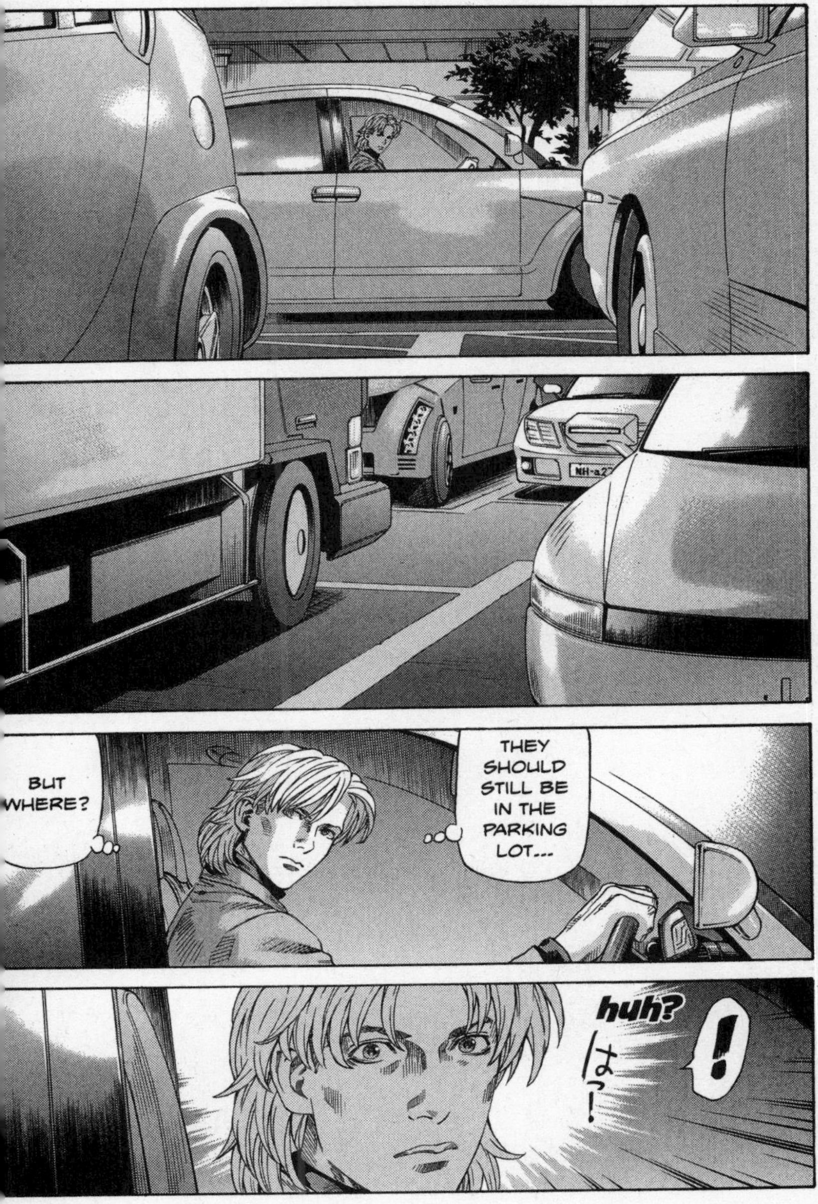
NH-a2
THEY SHOULD STILL BE IN THE PARKING LOT...
BUT WHERE?
huh?
!
はっ!

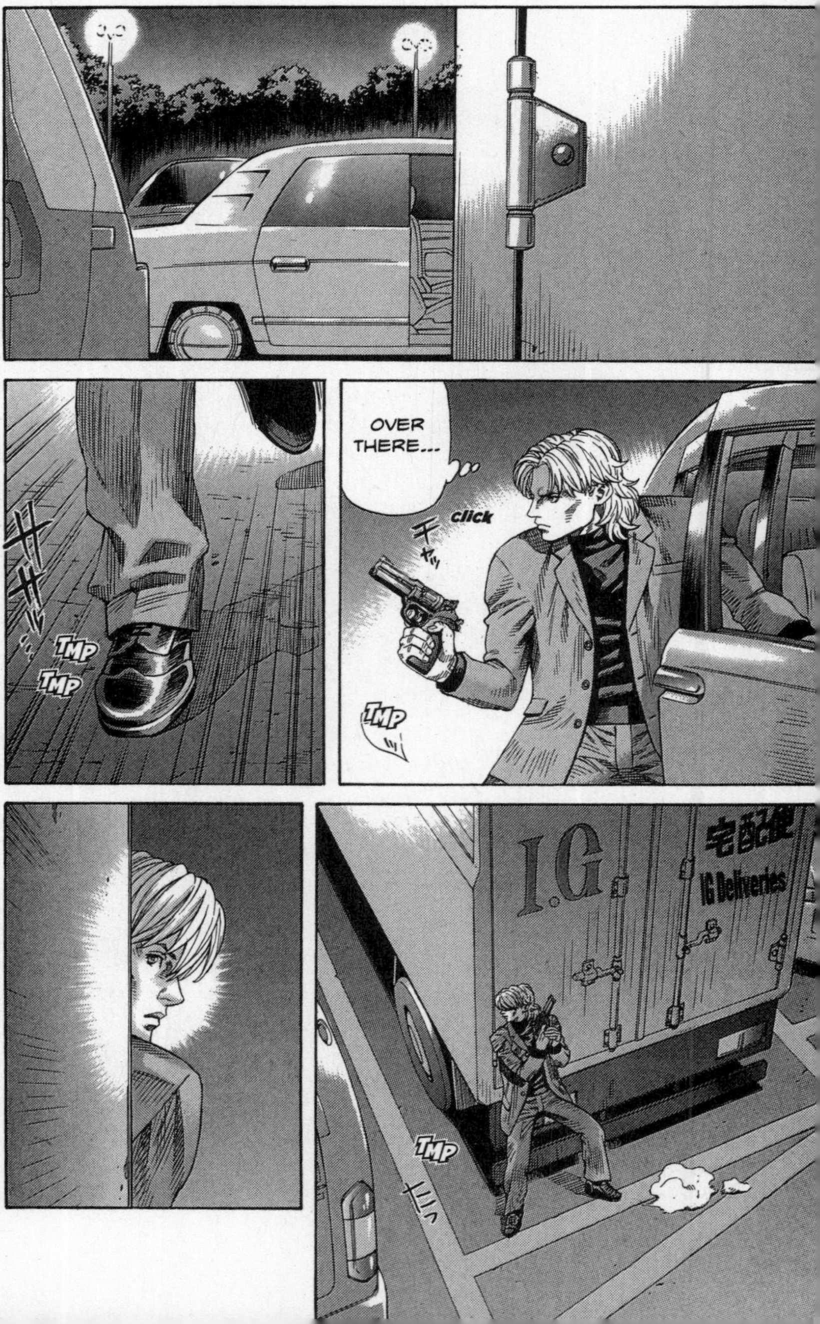
OVER THERE...
click
チャッ
TMP
TMP
TMP
宅配便
I.G
IG Deliveries
TMP

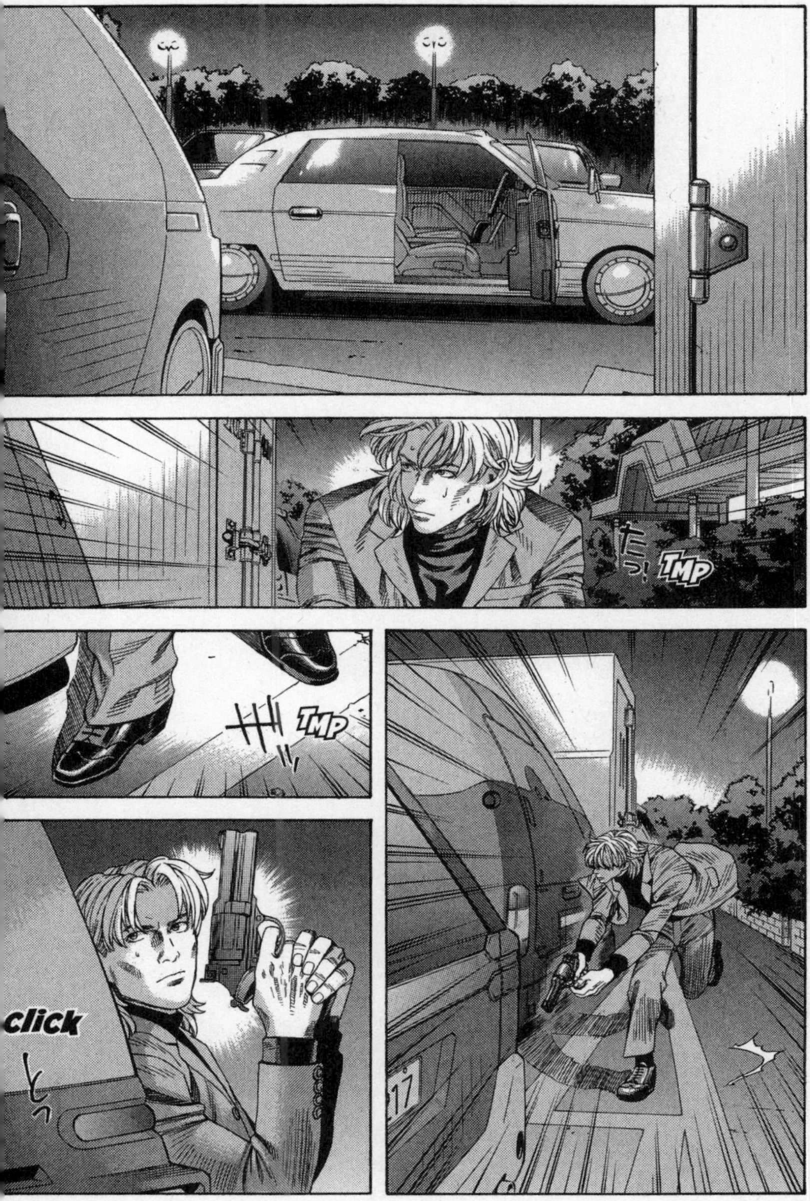
たっ!
TMP
TMP
click

NH-d7530

TMP

phew

thump

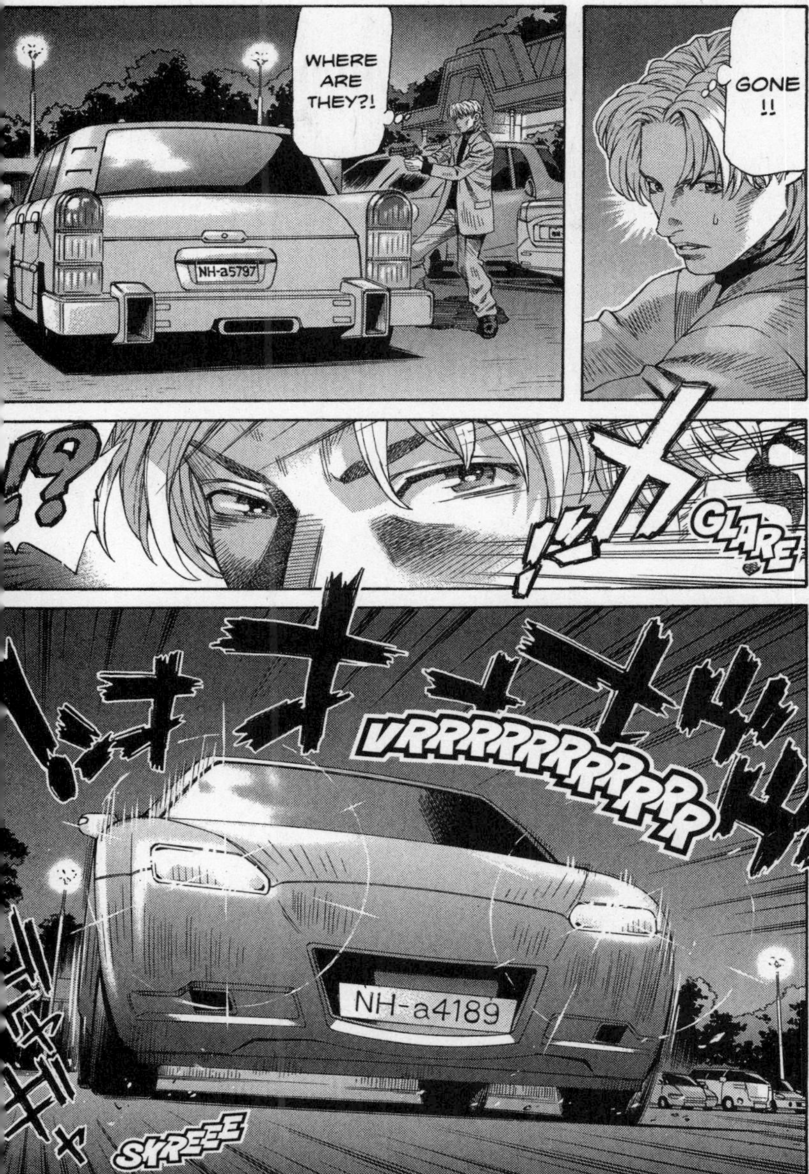
GONE !!
WHERE ARE THEY?!
NH-a5797
!?
GLARE
VRRRRRRRRRRRR
NH-a4189
SKREEE

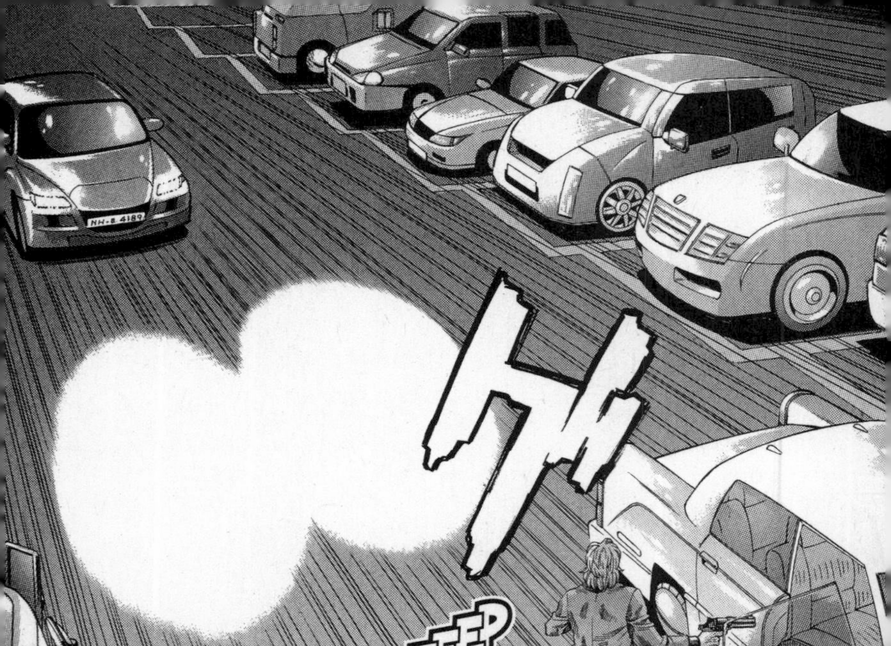
BEEEEEEEEEP

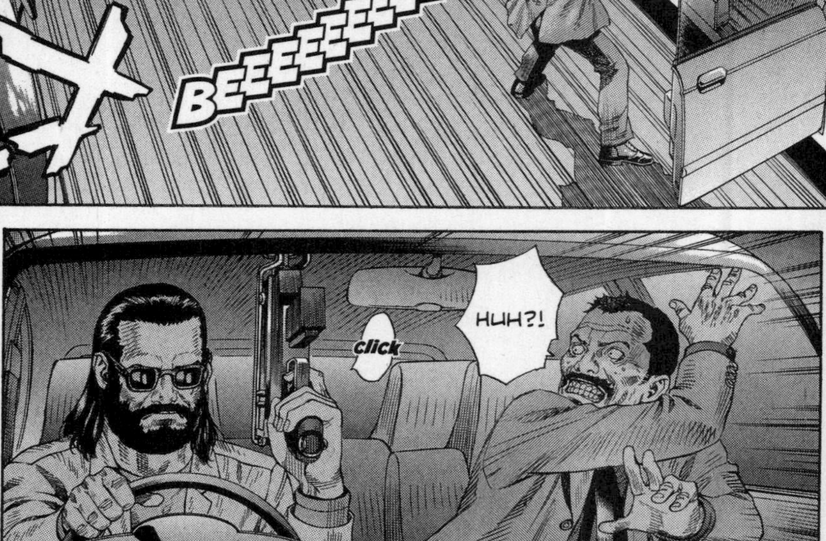
HUH?!
click

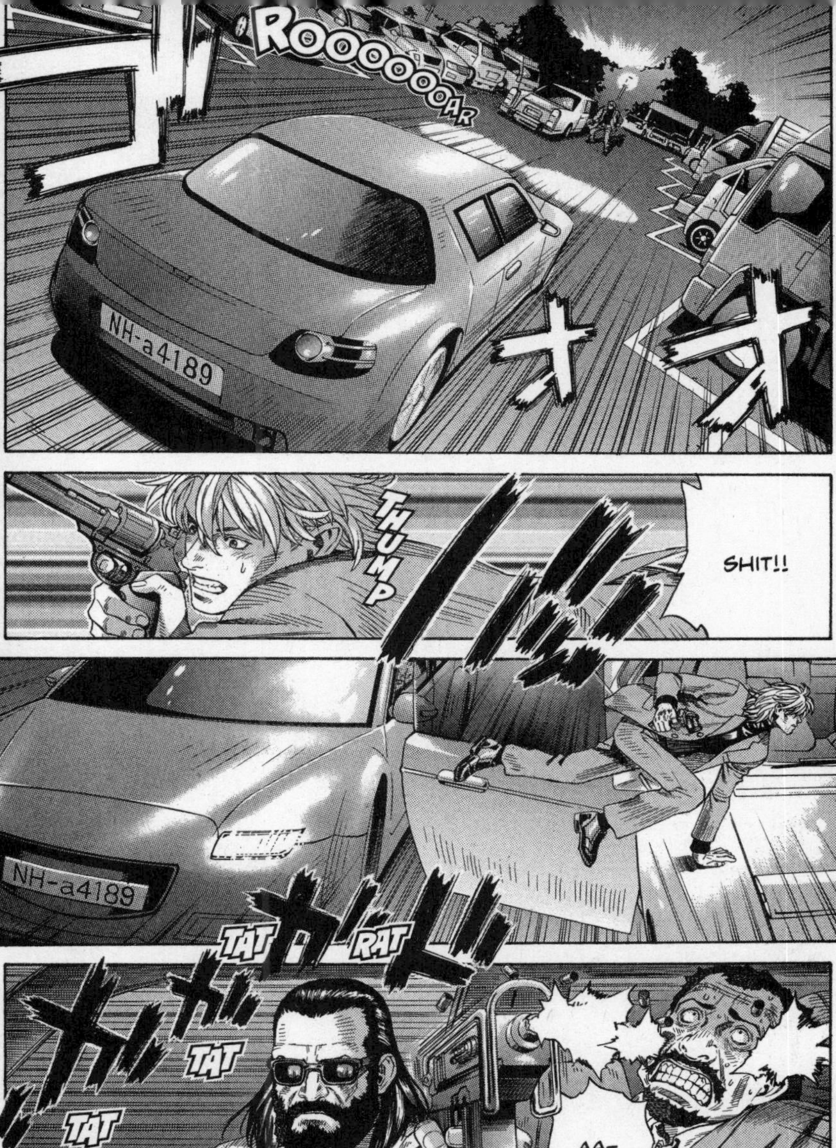
ROOOOOOOAR
NH-a4189
SHIT!!
THUMP
NH-a4189
RAT
TAT
TAT
TAT
AA-
AH-
HH-
H!

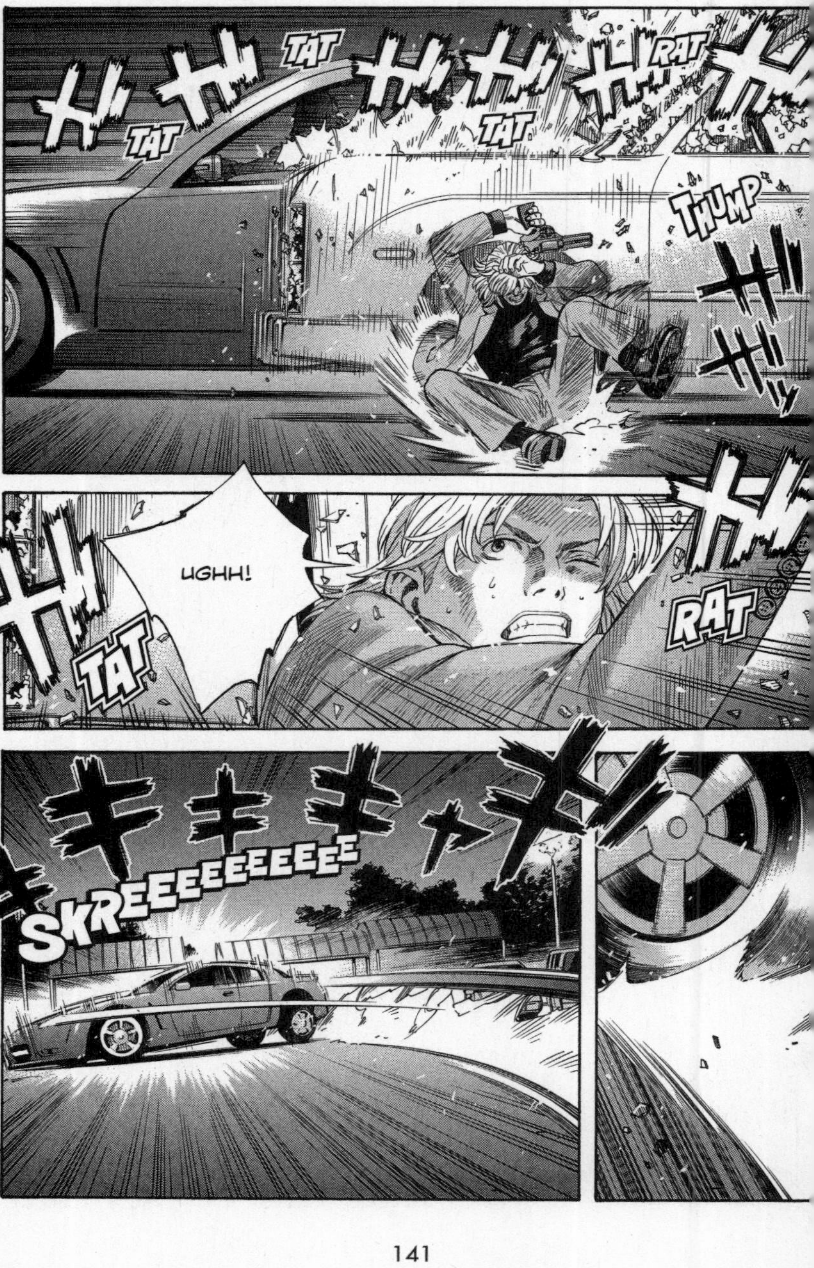
RAT
THUMP
TAT
TAT
TAT
RAT
UGHH!
TAT
SKREEEEEEEEEE

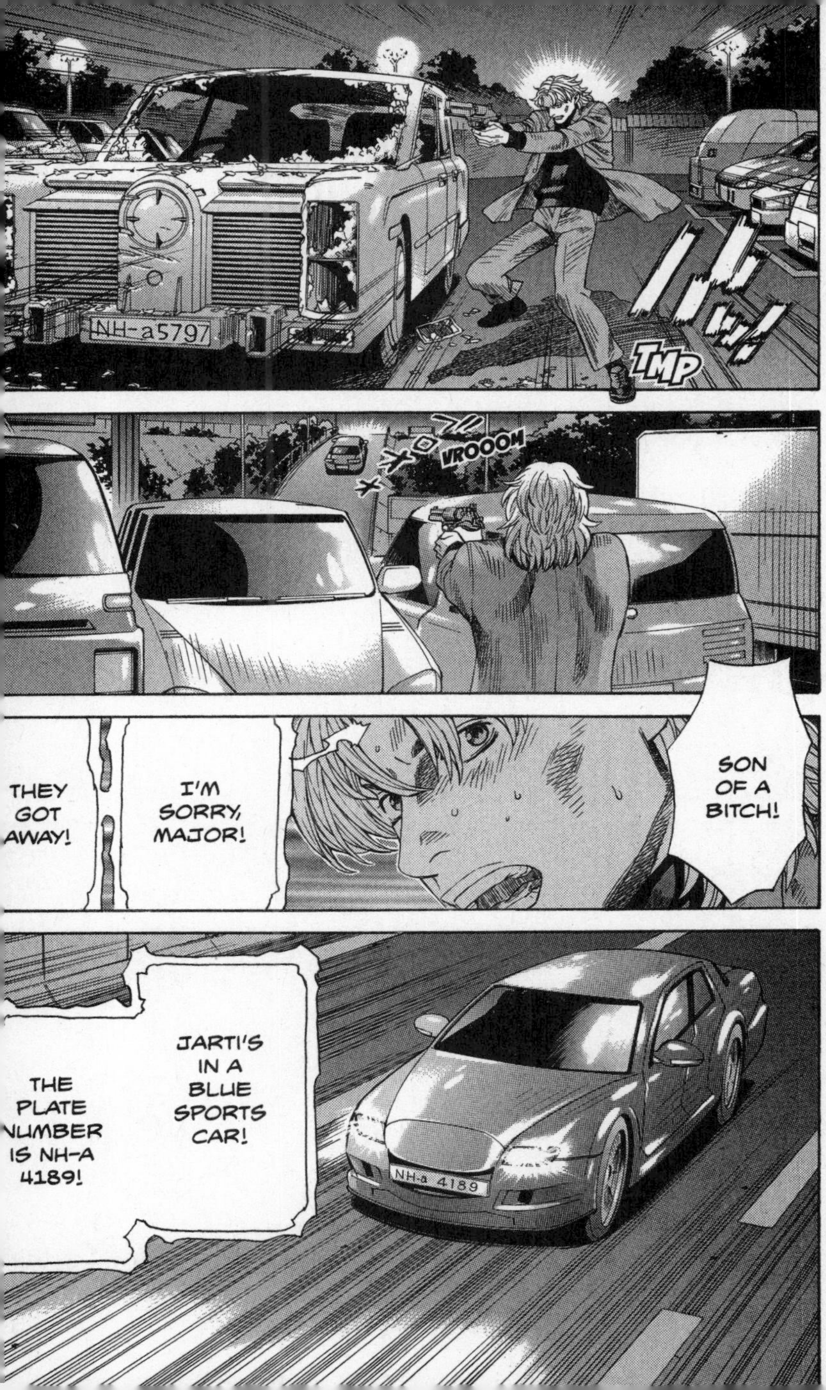
NH-a5797
TMP
VROOOM
SON OF A BITCH!
I'M SORRY, MAJOR!
THEY GOT AWAY!
JARTI'S IN A BLUE SPORTS CAR!
THE PLATE NUMBER IS NH-A 4189!
NH-a 4189

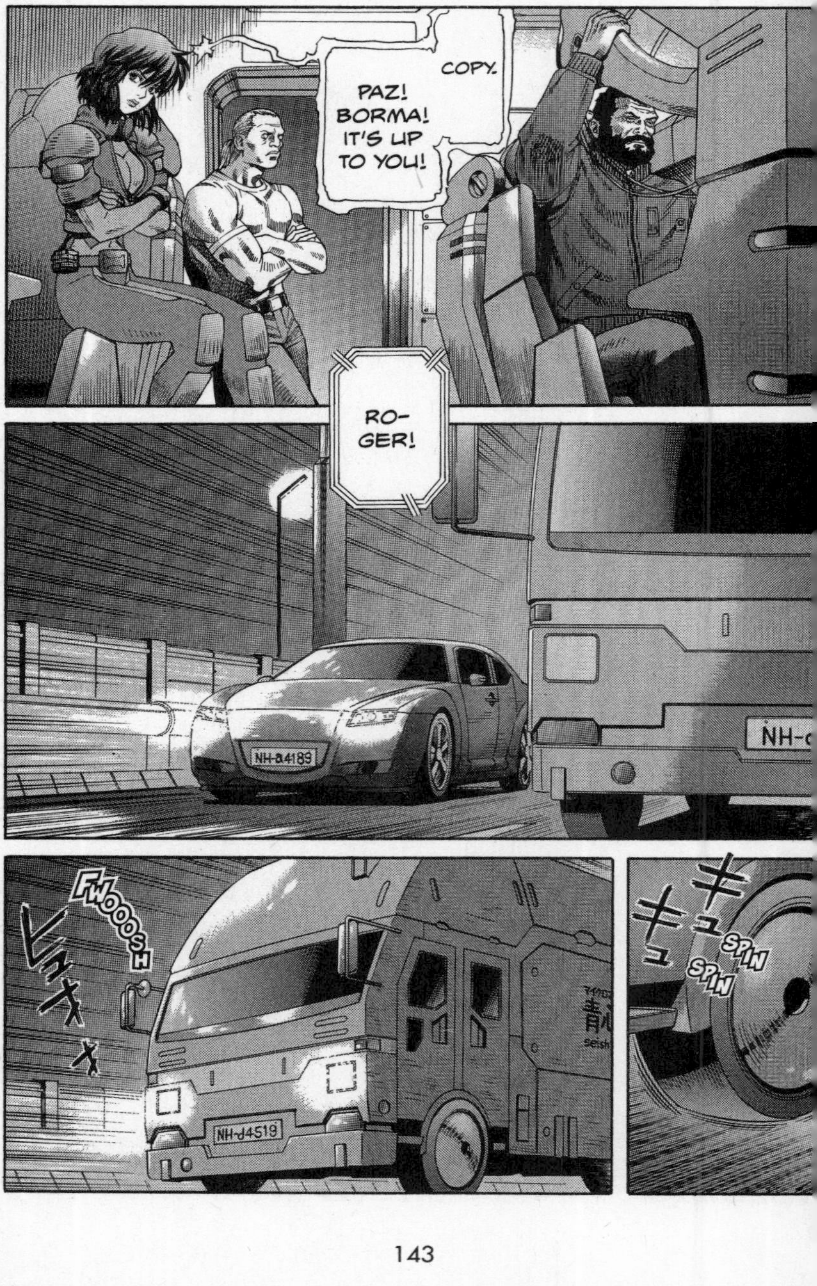
PAZ! BORMA! IT'S UP TO YOU!
COPY.
RO-
GER!
NH-a4189
SPIN
SPIN
FWOOOSH
NH-J4519

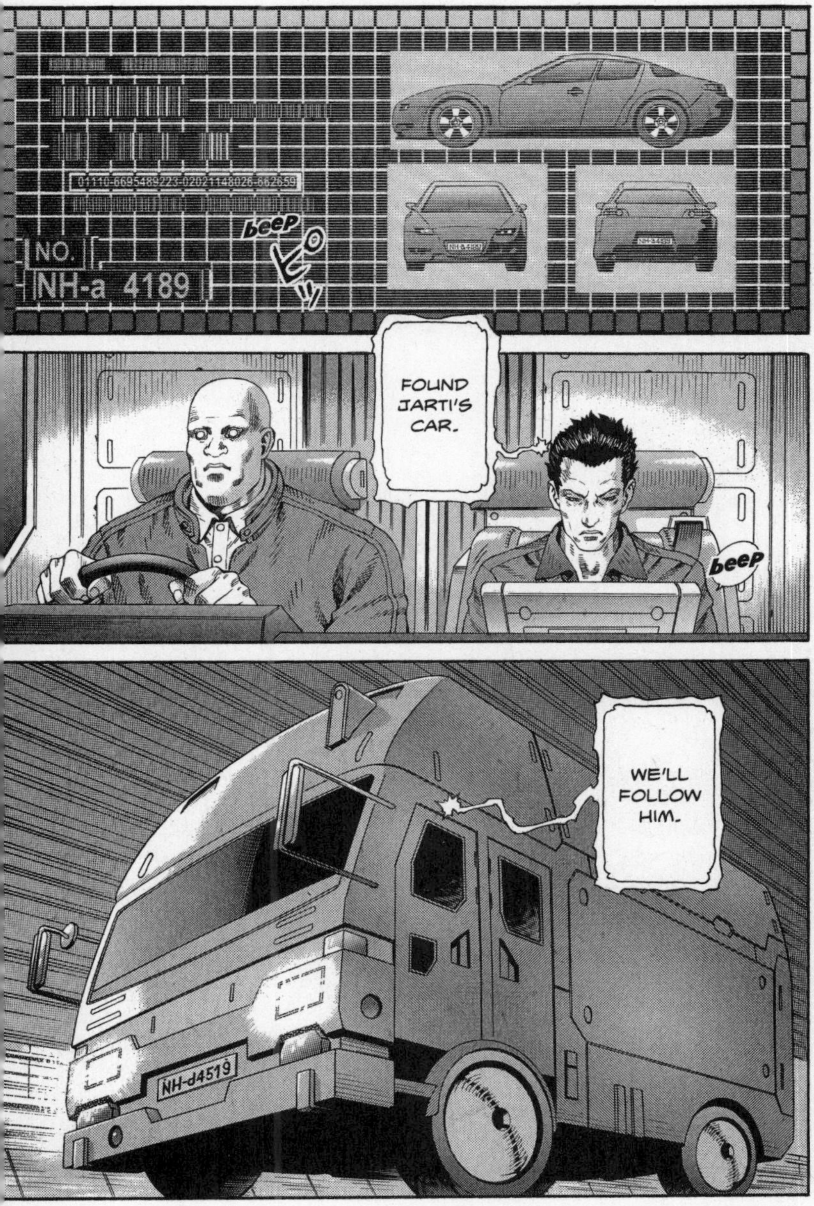
01110-669548923-02021148026-662659
NO.
NH-a 4189
beep
FOUND JARTI'S CAR.
beep
WE'LL FOLLOW HIM.
NH-d4519

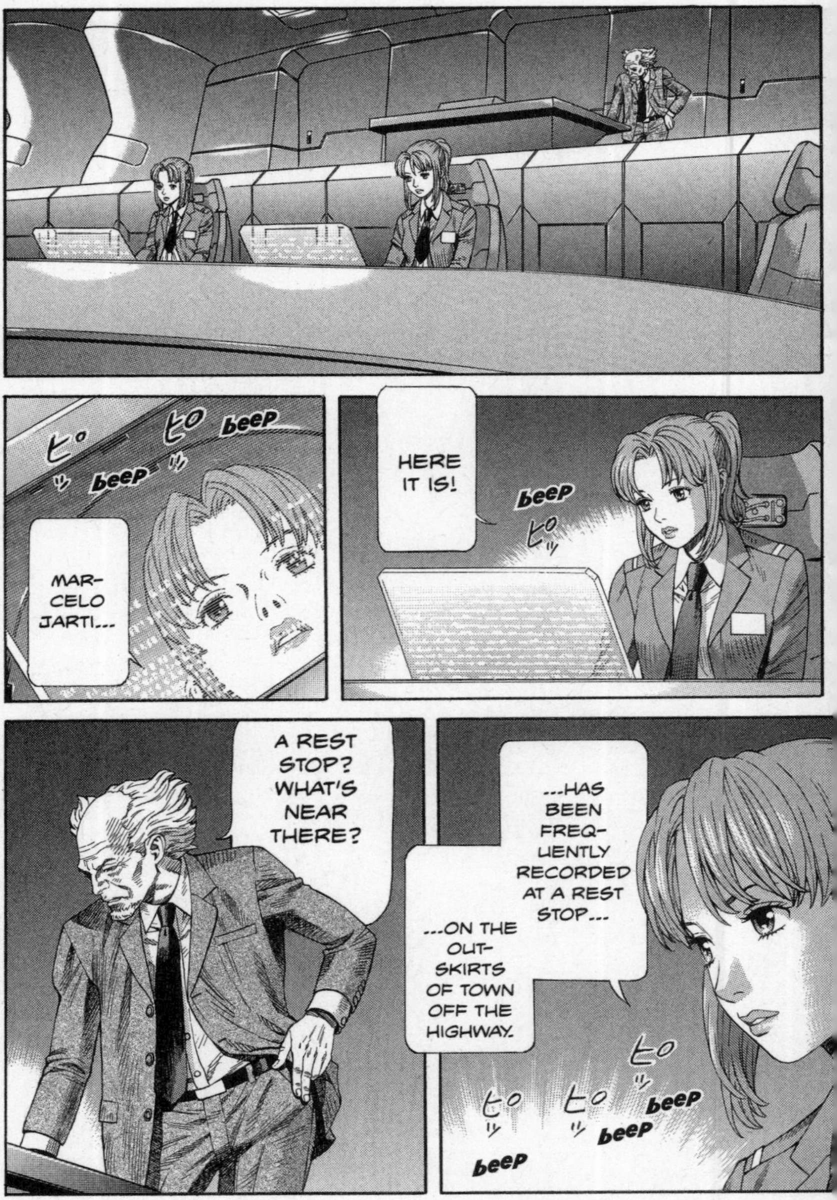
HERE IT IS!
ピッ
beep
ピッ ピッ
beep beep
MAR-CELO JARTI...
...HAS BEEN FREQ-UENTLY RECORDED AT A REST STOP...
...ON THE OUT-SKIRTS OF TOWN OFF THE HIGHWAY.
ピッ ピッ ピッ
beep beep beep
A REST STOP? WHAT'S NEAR THERE?

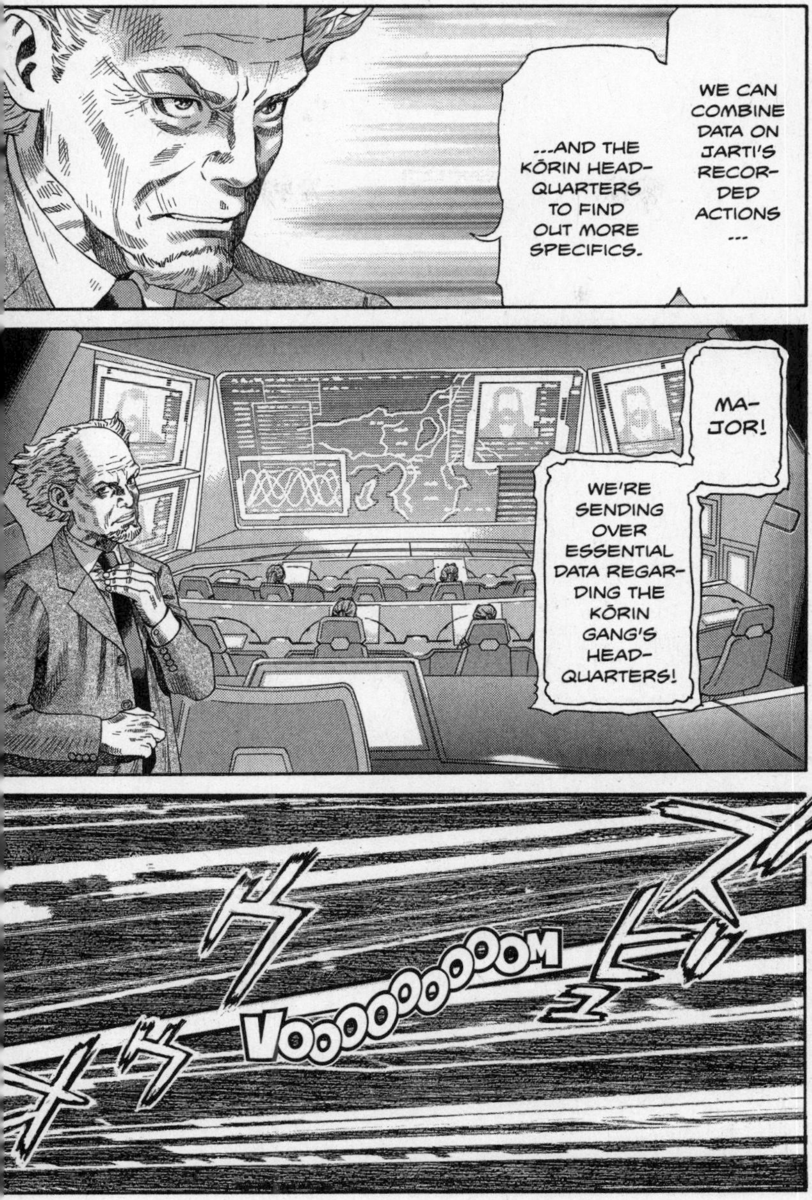
WE CAN COMBINE DATA ON JARTI'S RECORDED ACTIONS ...
...AND THE KŌRIN HEADQUARTERS TO FIND OUT MORE SPECIFICS.
MAJOR!
WE'RE SENDING OVER ESSENTIAL DATA REGARDING THE KŌRIN GANG'S HEADQUARTERS!
VOOOOOOOOOOM

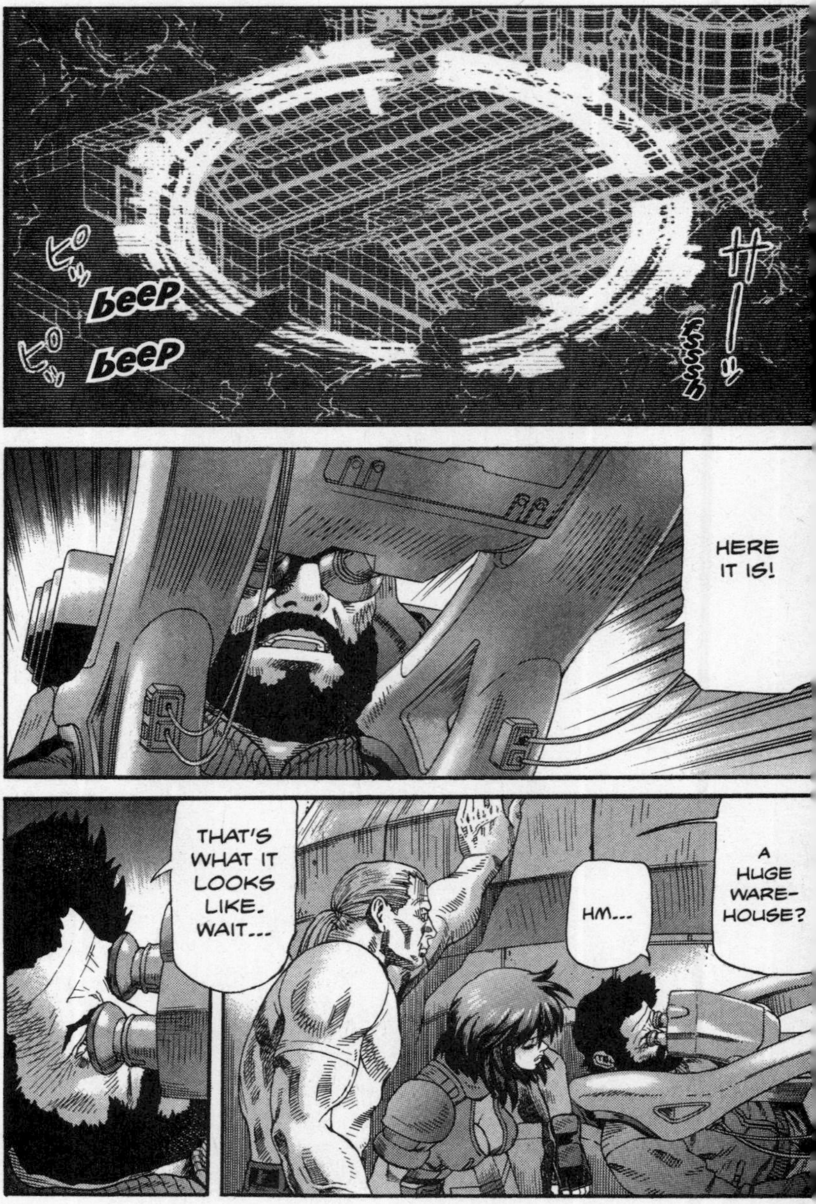
サーッ
fssssh
ピッ
beep
ピッ
beep
HERE IT IS!
A HUGE WARE-HOUSE?
HM...
THAT'S WHAT IT LOOKS LIKE. WAIT...

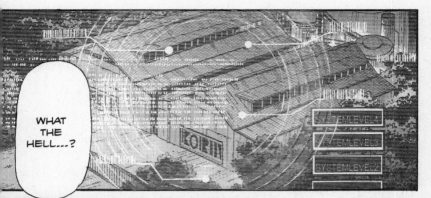

WHAT THE HELL...?

WHAT'S WRONG?

I'M GETTING SOME WEIRD DATA FROM THIS WAREHOUSE.

WHEN-EVER JARTI ENTERS THE COUNTRY...

...THERE ARE HUGE SPIKES IN POWER CONSUMPTION THERE.

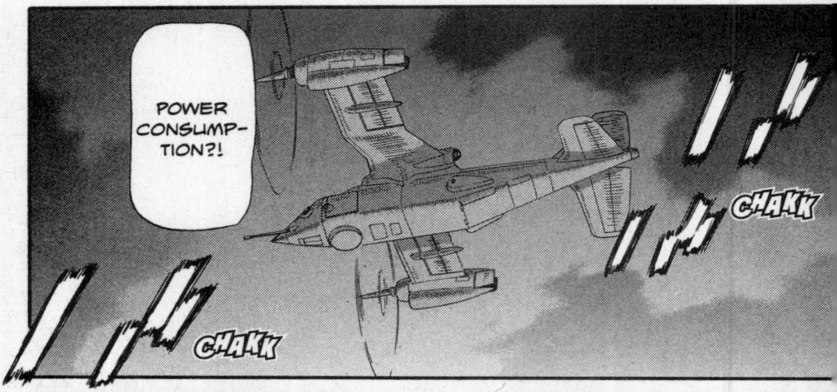
POWER CONSUMPTION?!
CHAKK
CHAKK

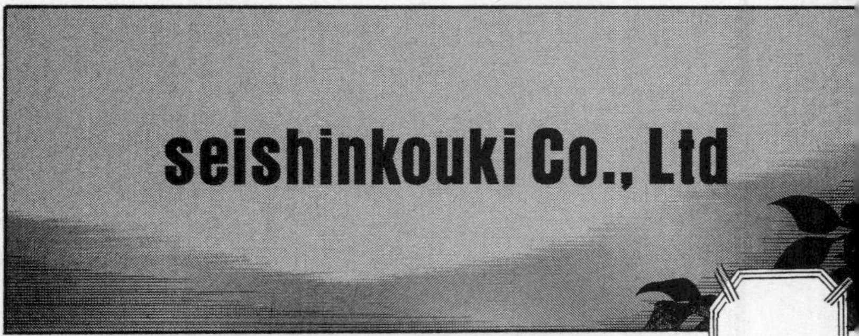
seishinkouki Co., Ltd

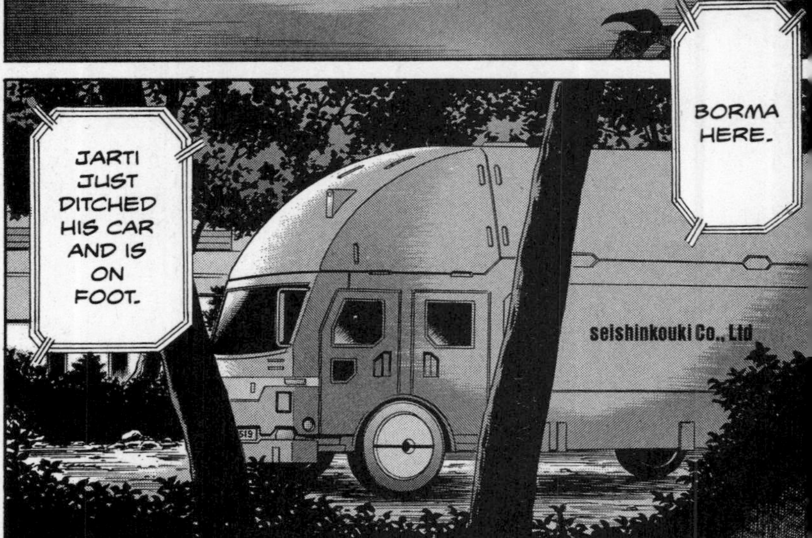
BORMA HERE.
JARTI JUST DITCHED HIS CAR AND IS ON FOOT.
seishinkouki Co., Ltd

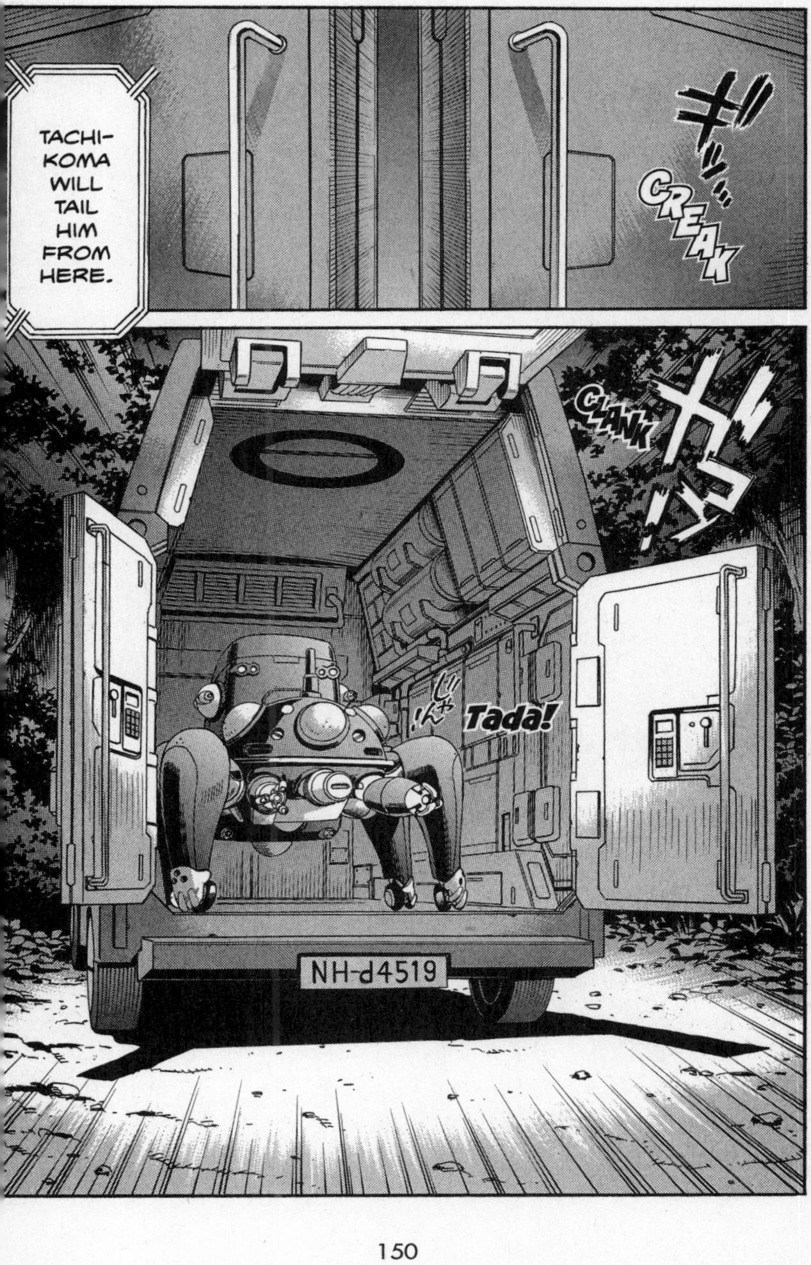

TACHI-KOMA WILL TAIL HIM FROM HERE.
CREAK
CLANK
Tada!

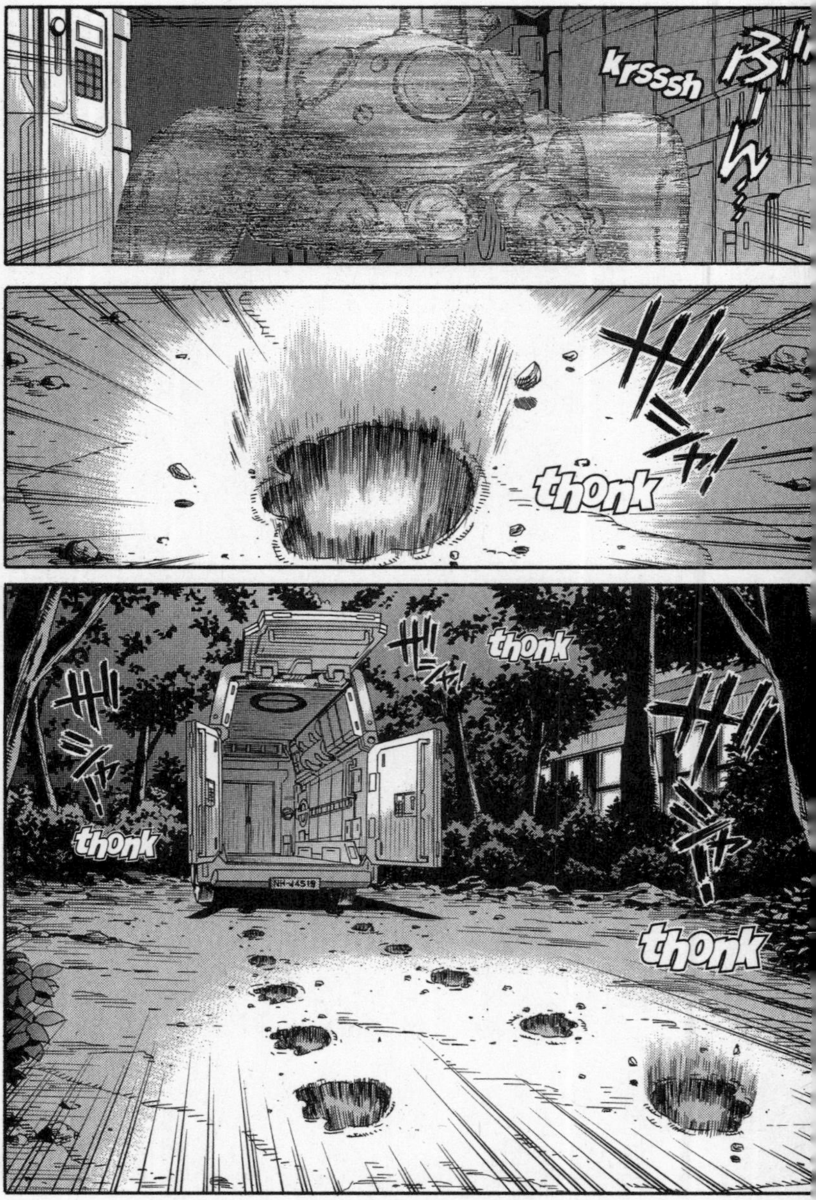
ぶーん…
krsssh
ザシャ!
thonk
ザシャ!
thonk
ザシャ!
thonk
ザシャ
thonk
NH-4519

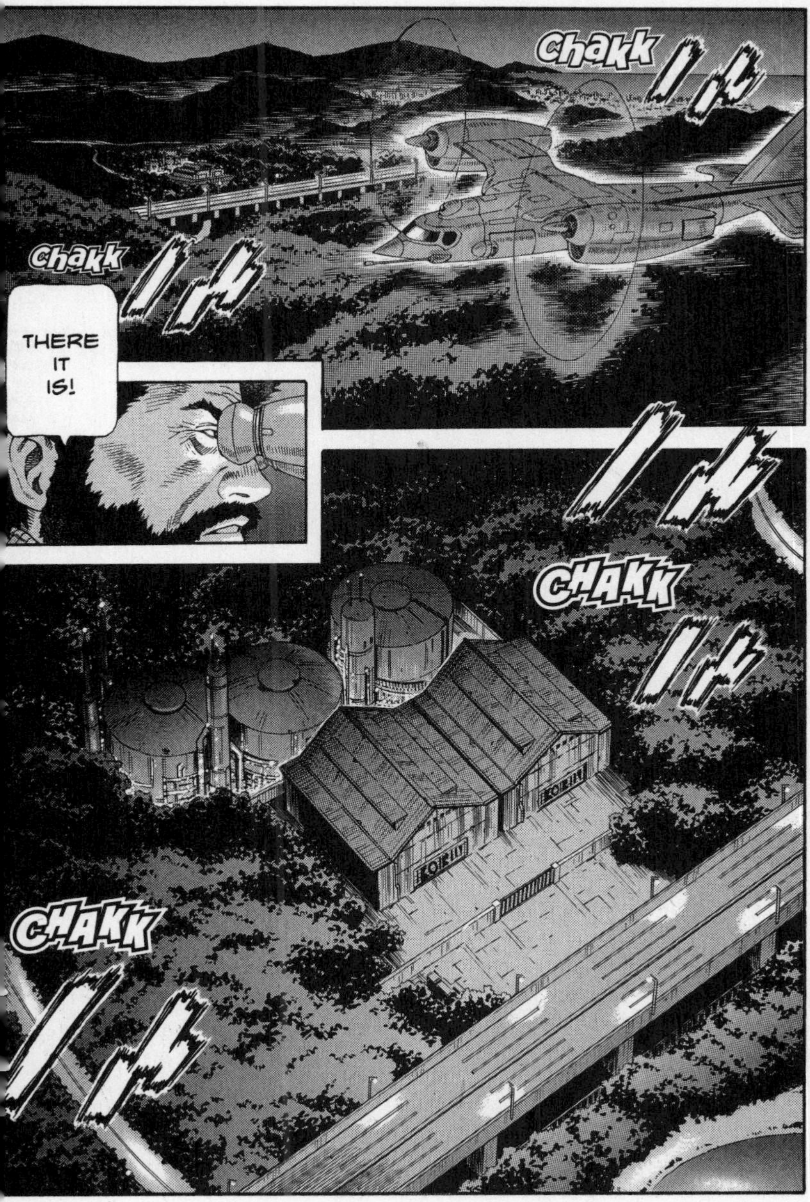
Chakk
Chakk
THERE IT IS!
CHAKK
CHAKK

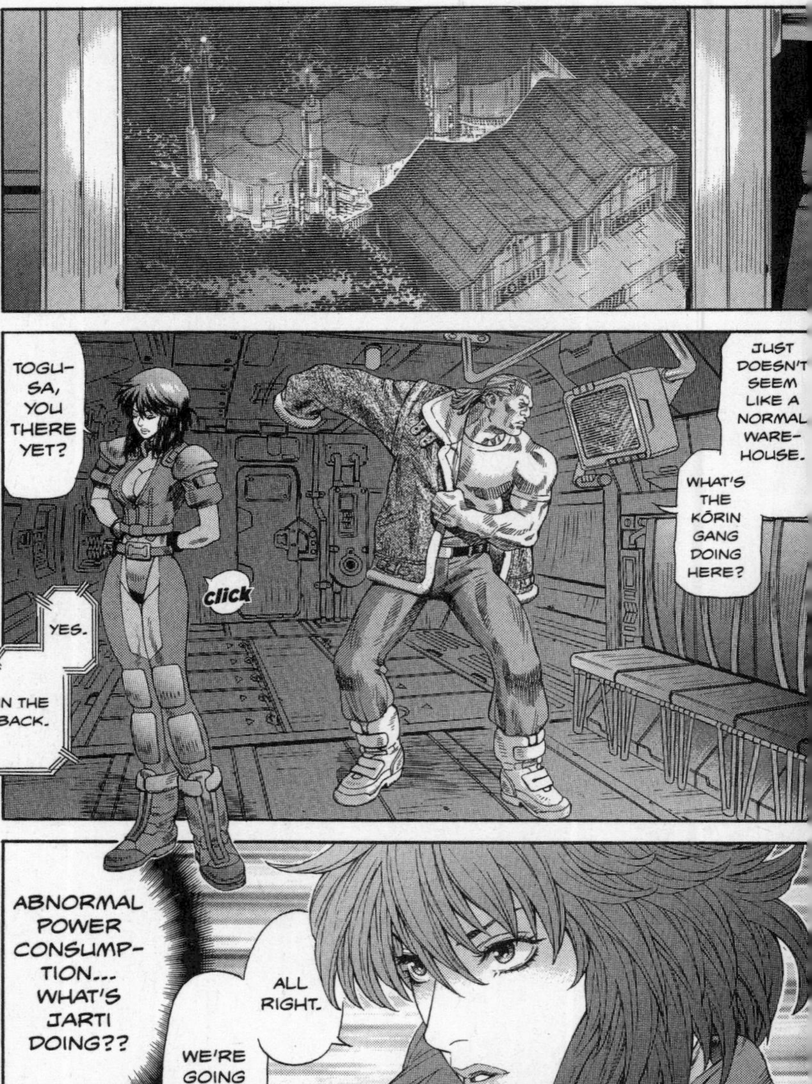
JUST DOESN'T SEEM LIKE A NORMAL WAREHOUSE.
WHAT'S THE KŌRIN GANG DOING HERE?
click
TOGUSA, YOU THERE YET?
YES.
IN THE BACK.
ALL RIGHT.
WE'RE GOING ON!
ABNORMAL POWER CONSUMPTION... WHAT'S JARTI DOING??

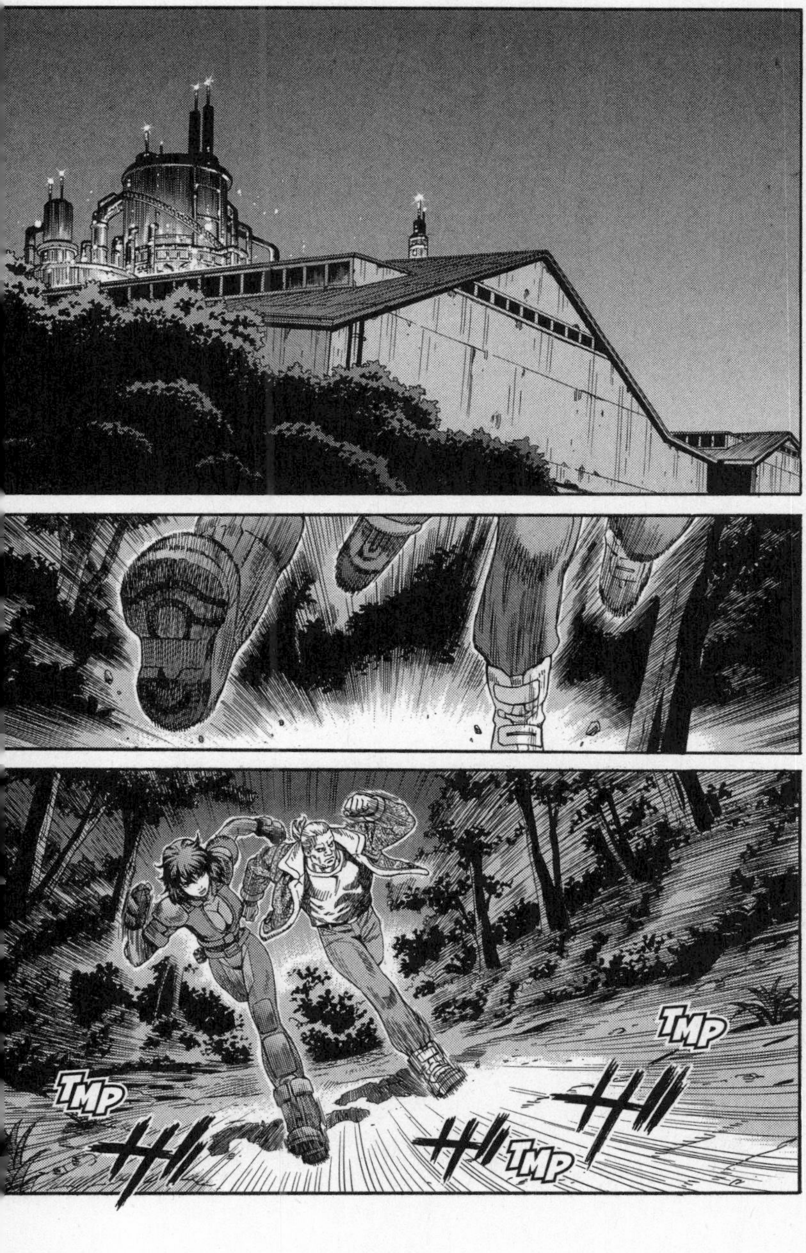
TMP
TMP
TMP

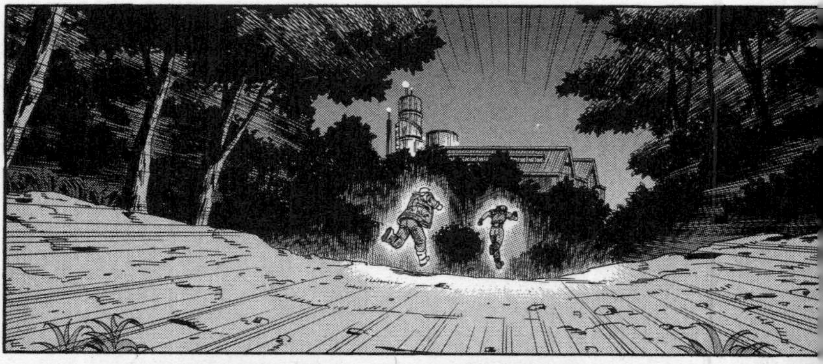

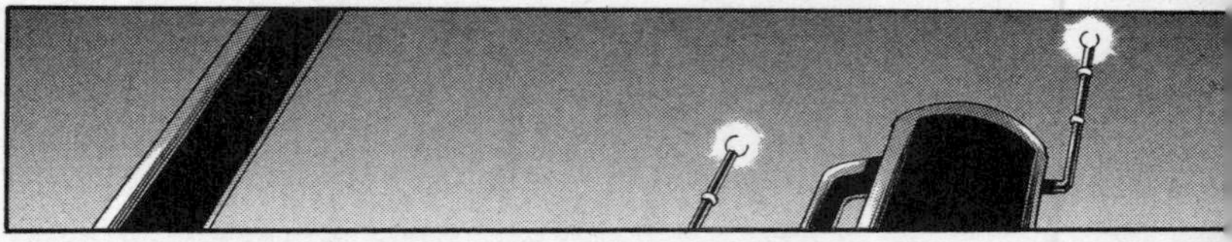

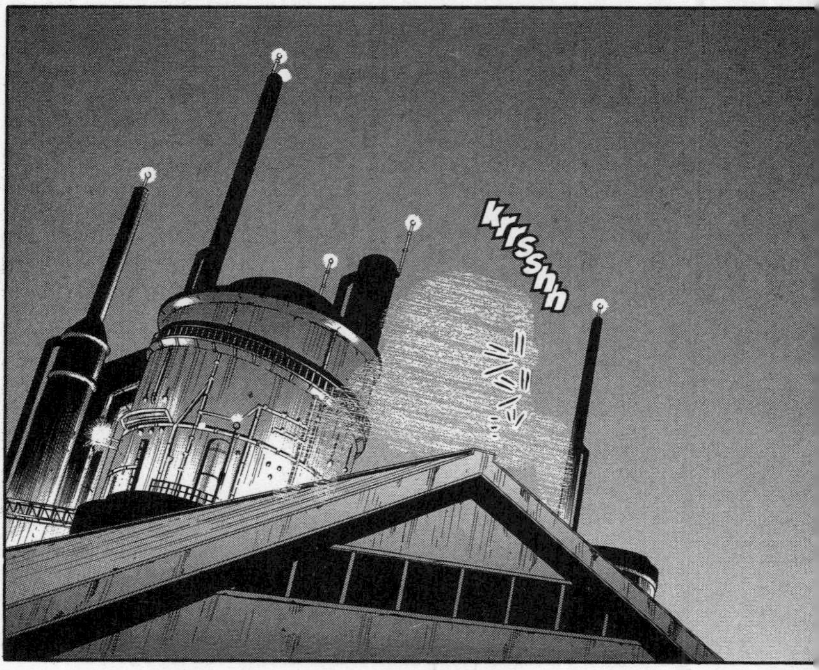
krrsshh

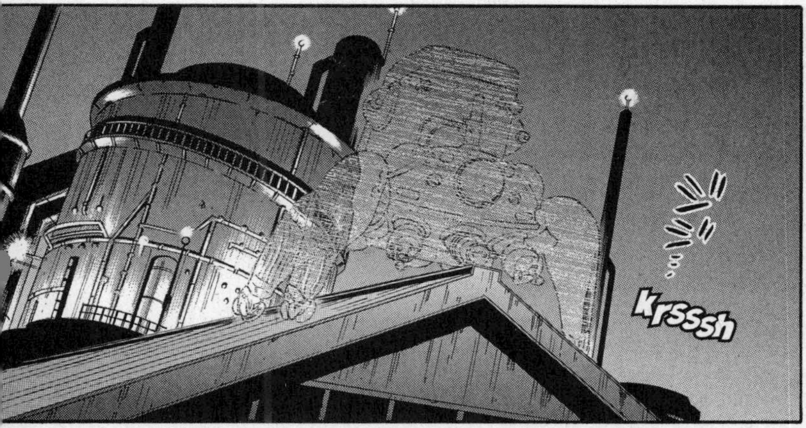
ジジジ…
krsssh

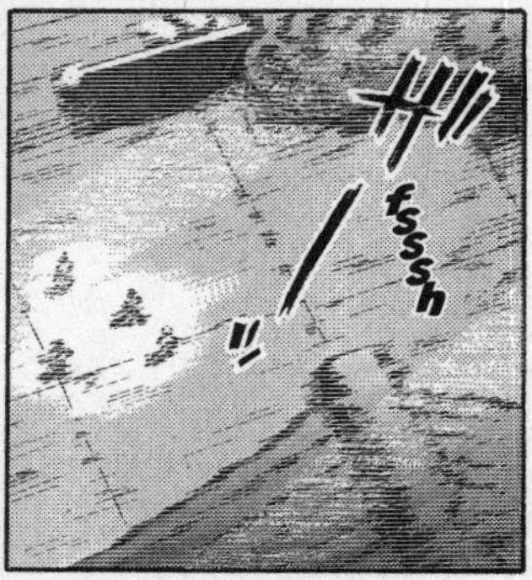
ザーッ
fsssh

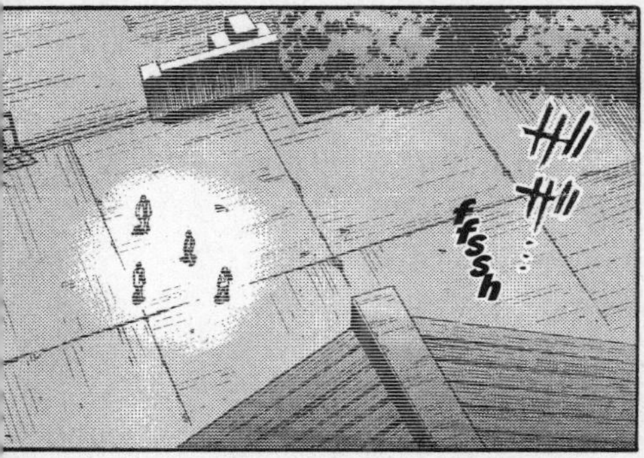
ザザ…
ffssh

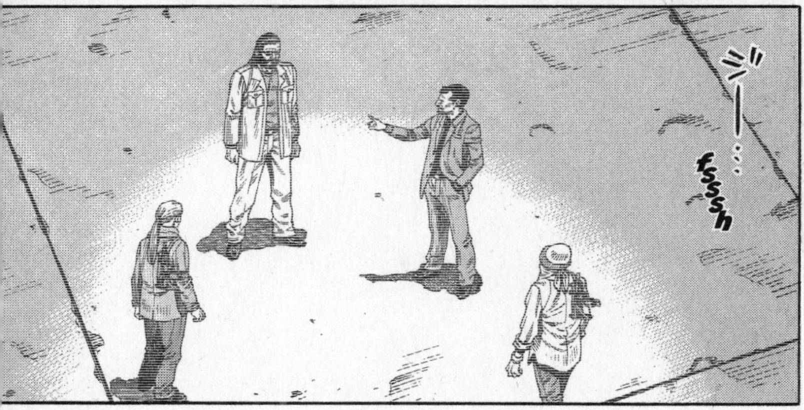
ジー…
fsssh

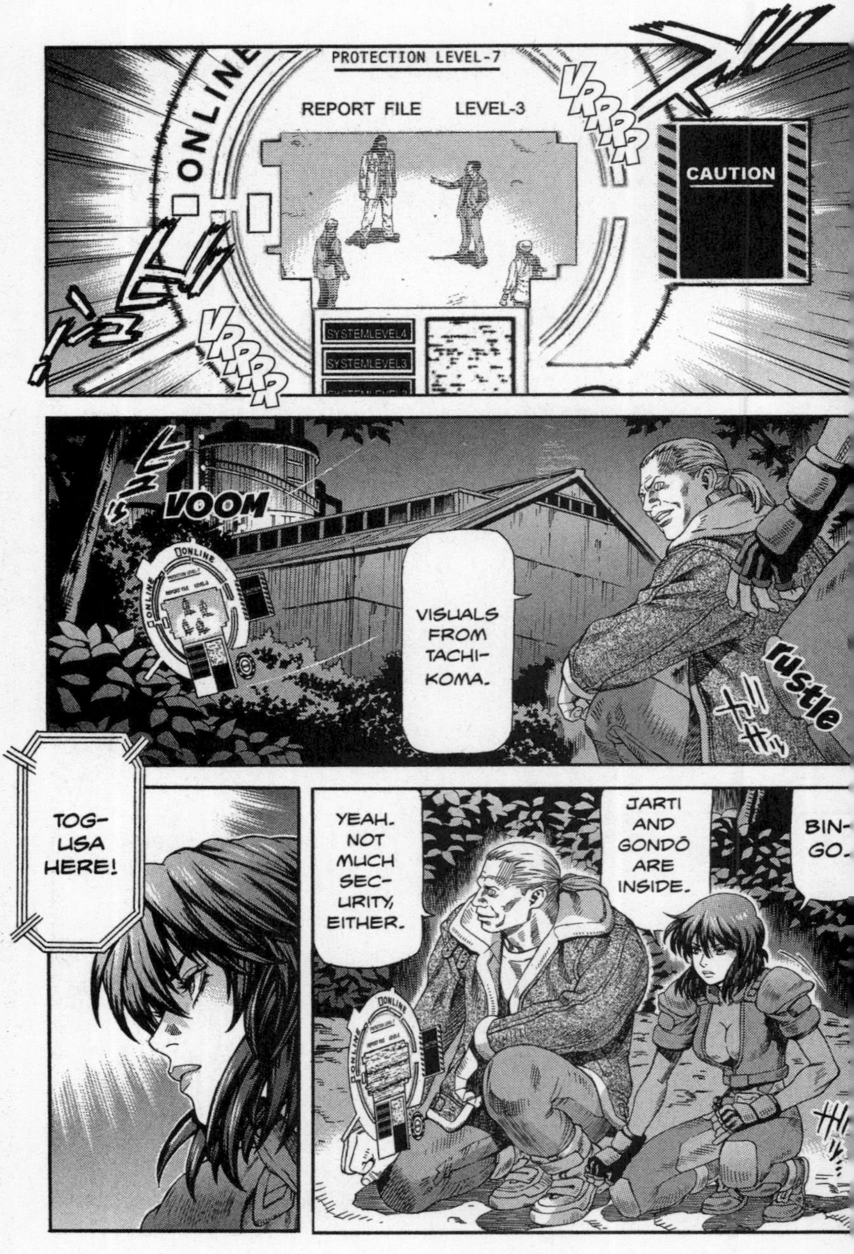
PROTECTION LEVEL-7
REPORT FILE LEVEL-3
ONLINE
VRRRR
CAUTION
SYSTEMLEVEL4
SYSTEMLEVEL3
VRRRR
VOOM
VISUALS FROM TACHI-KOMA.
rustle
BIN-GO.
JARTI AND GONDŌ ARE INSIDE.
YEAH. NOT MUCH SEC-URITY, EITHER.
TOG-USA HERE!

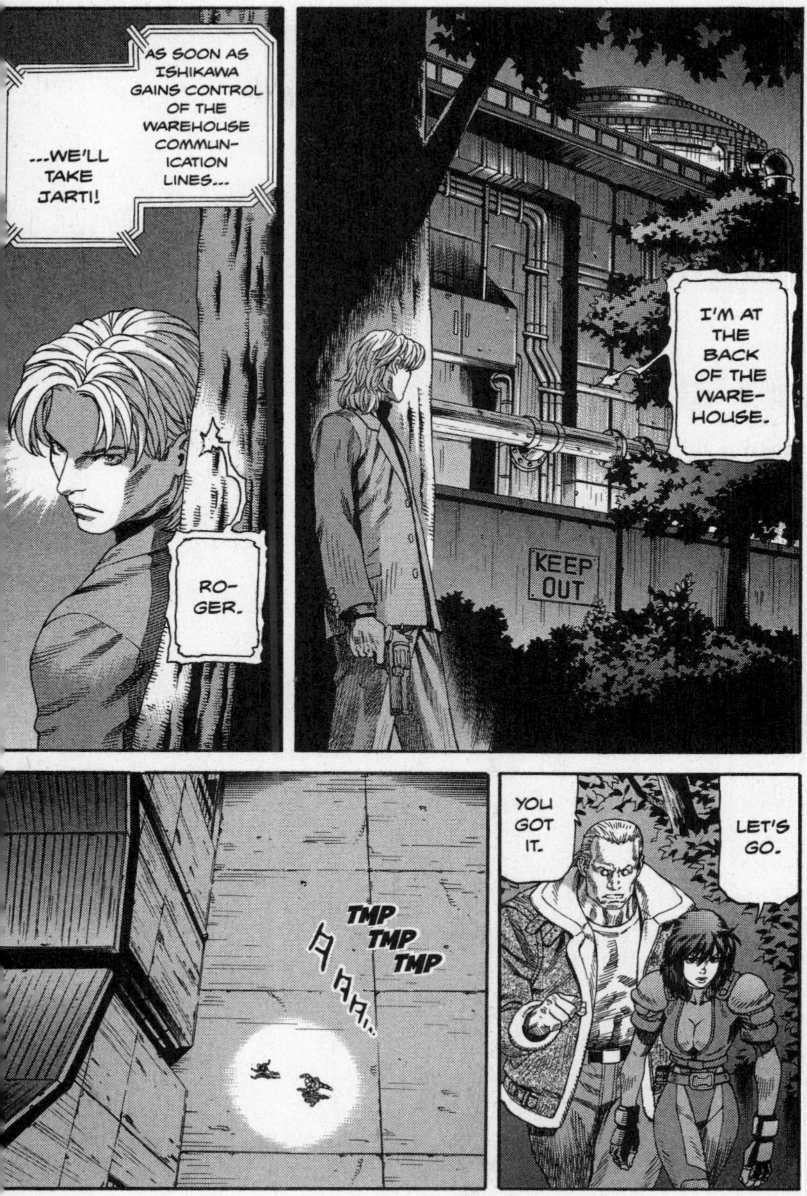
I'M AT THE BACK OF THE WAREHOUSE.
AS SOON AS ISHIKAWA GAINS CONTROL OF THE WAREHOUSE COMMUNICATION LINES...
...WE'LL TAKE JARTI!
ROGER.
KEEP OUT
LET'S GO.
YOU GOT IT.
TMP TMP TMP

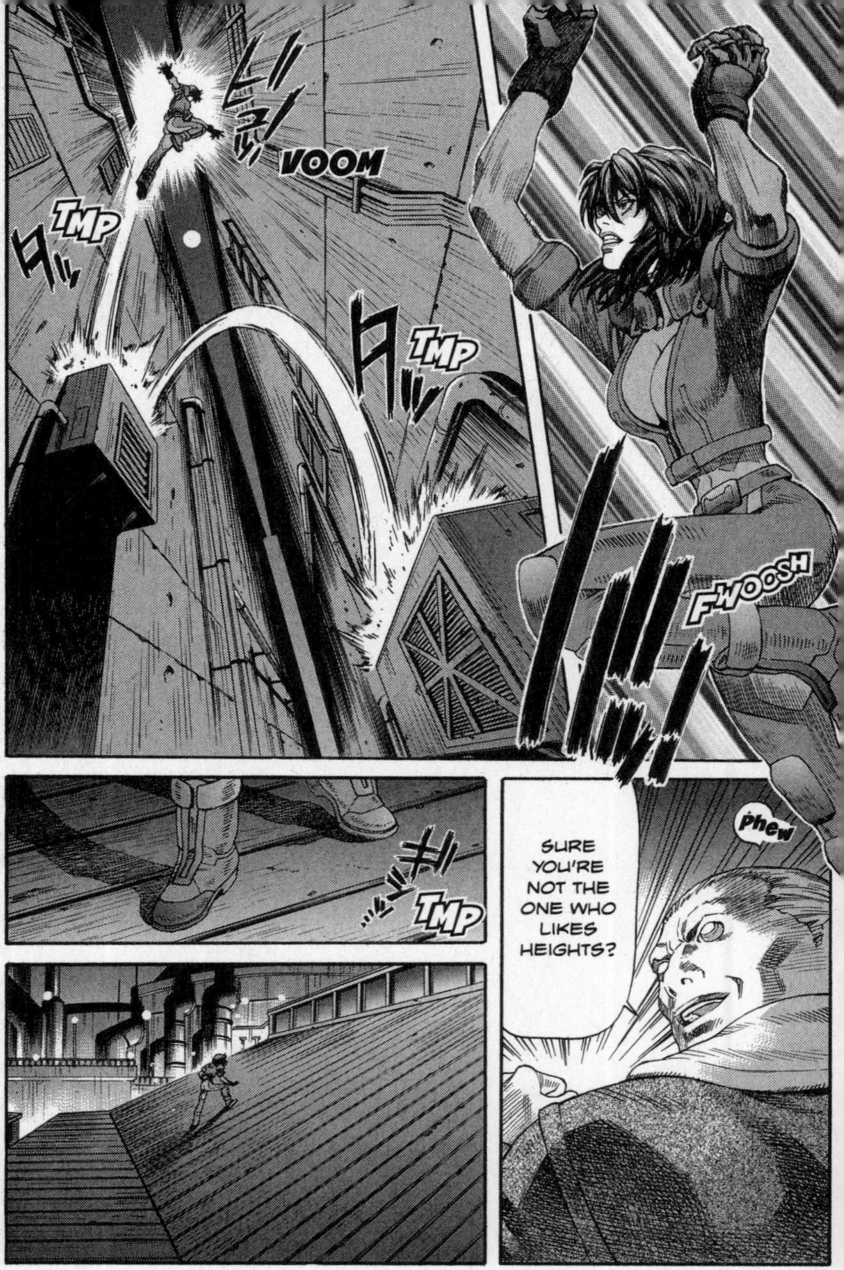
FWOOSH
VOOM
TMP
TMP
phew
SURE YOU'RE NOT THE ONE WHO LIKES HEIGHTS?
TMP

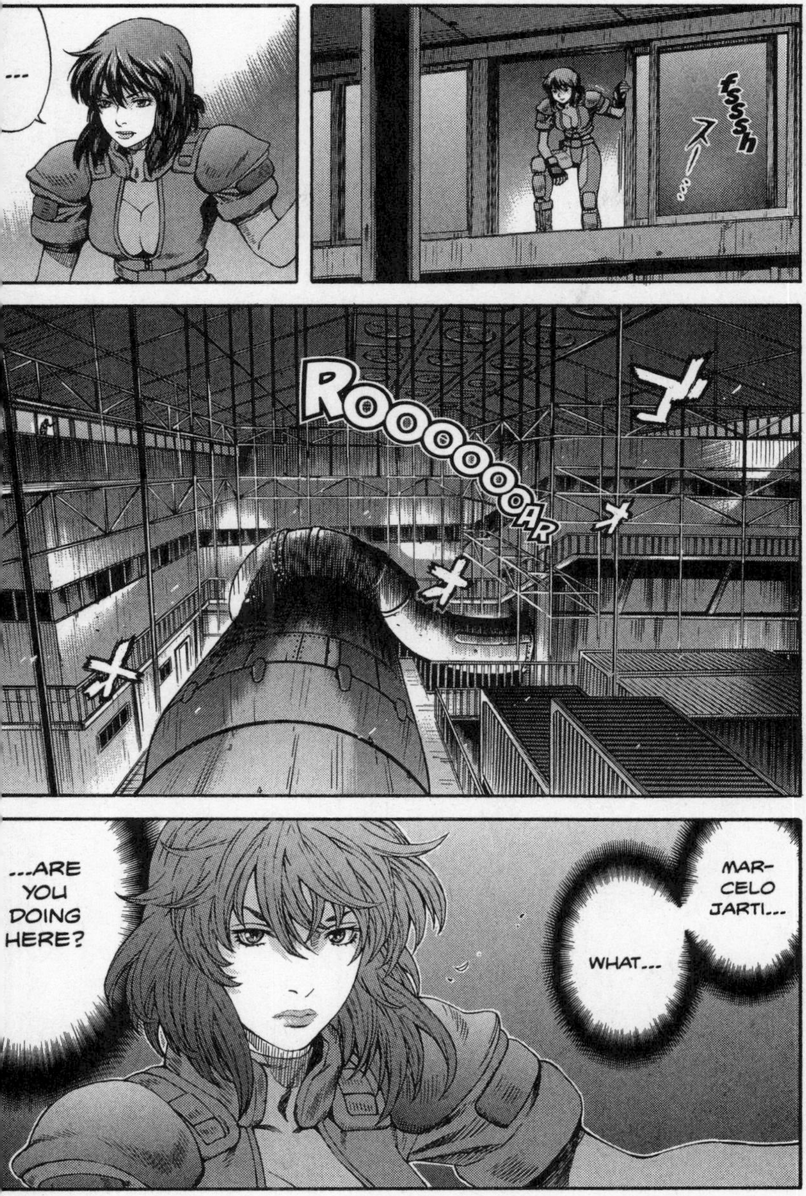
fssssh
スー…
...
ROOOOOOOAR
MAR-CELO JARTI...
WHAT...
...ARE YOU DOING HERE?

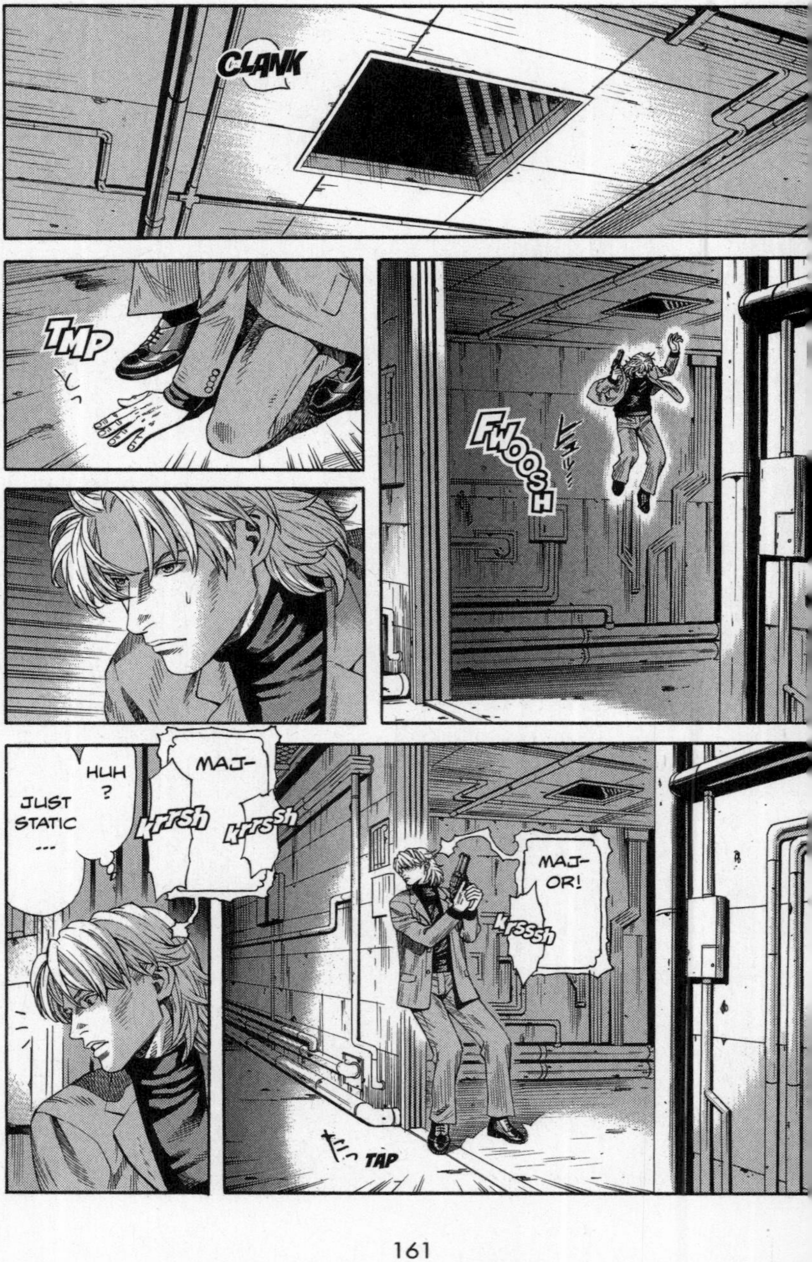
CLANK
FWOOSH
TMP
MAJ-OR!
krsssh
TAP
MAJ-
krrsh
krrssh
HUH?
JUST STATIC ...

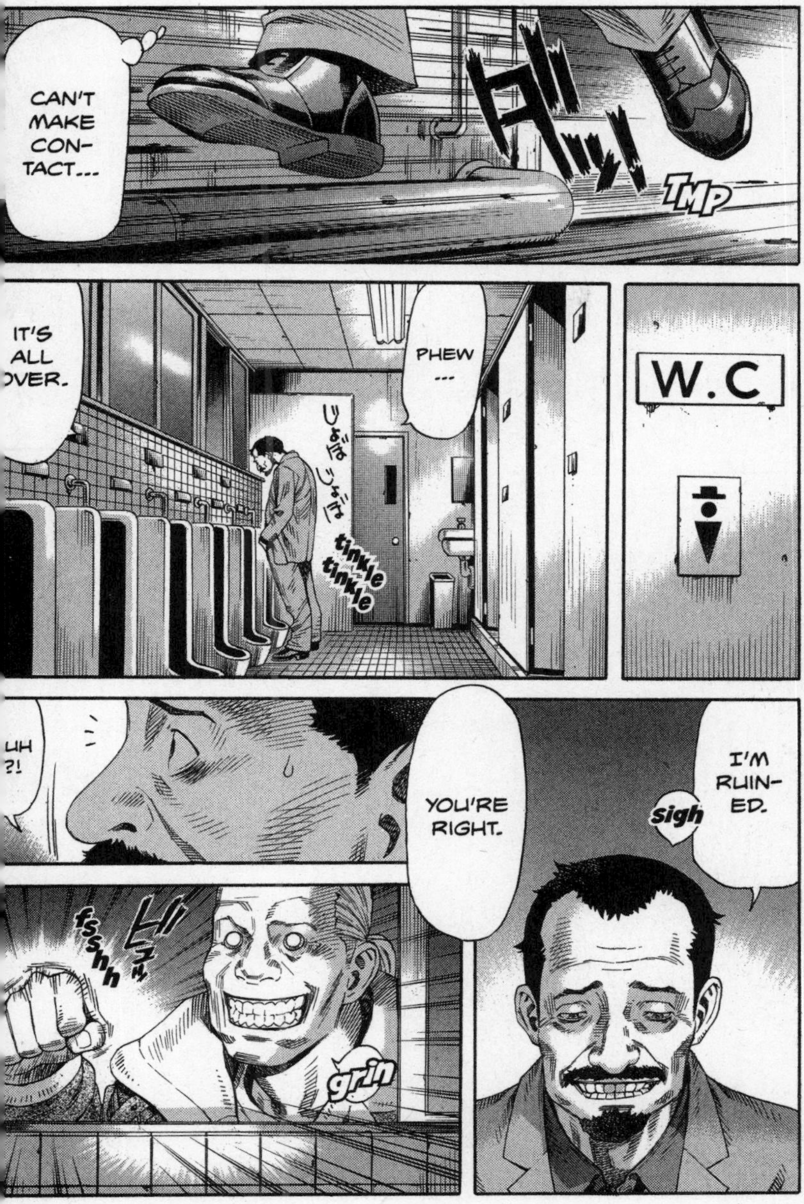
CAN'T MAKE CON-TACT...
TMP
W.C
PHEW...
じょぼじょぼ
tinkle tinkle
IT'S ALL OVER.
I'M RUIN-ED.
sigh
YOU'RE RIGHT.
UH ?!
fsshh
grin

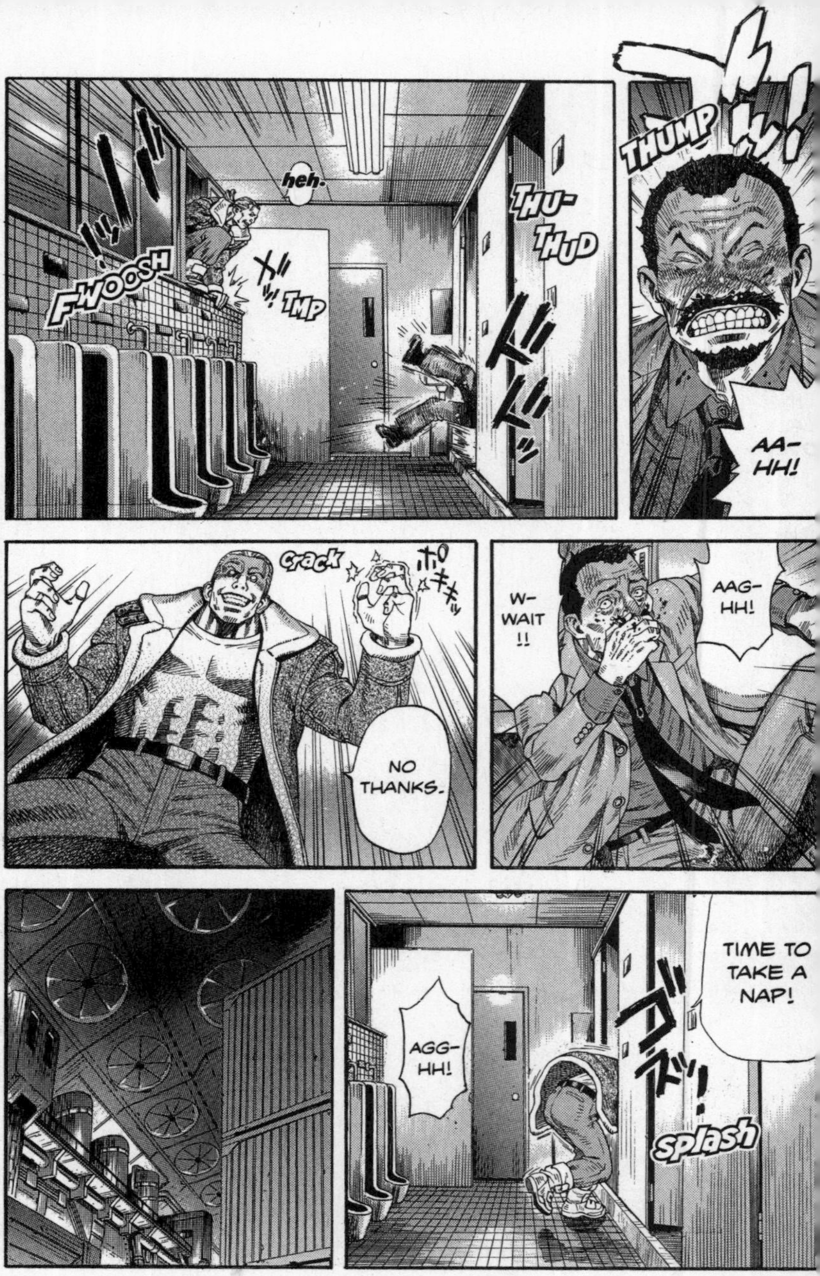
THUMP
AA-HH!
THU-THUD
heh.
TMP
FWOOSH
AAG-HH!
W-WAIT !!
crack
NO THANKS.
TIME TO TAKE A NAP!
splash
AGG-HH!

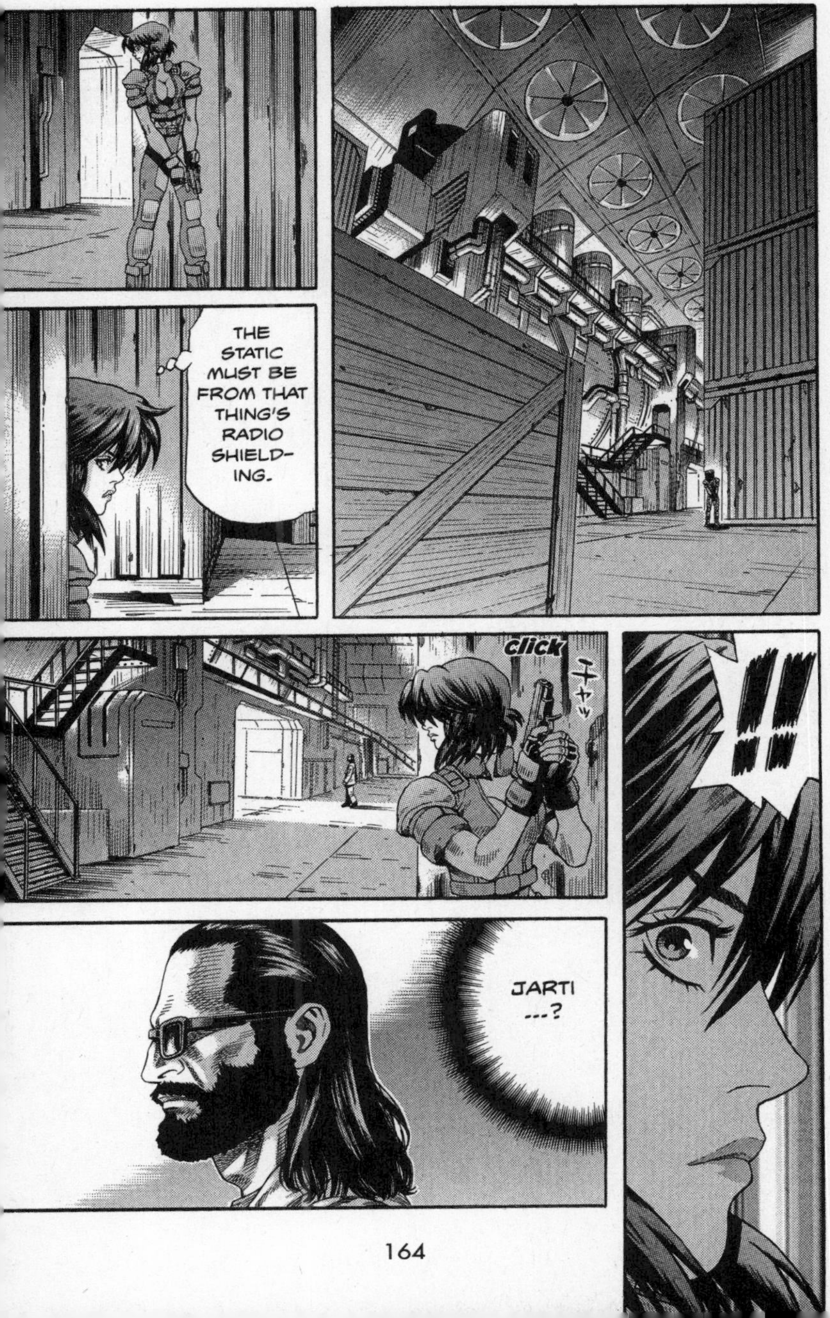
THE STATIC MUST BE FROM THAT THING'S RADIO SHIELD-ING.
!!
click
JARTI ---?

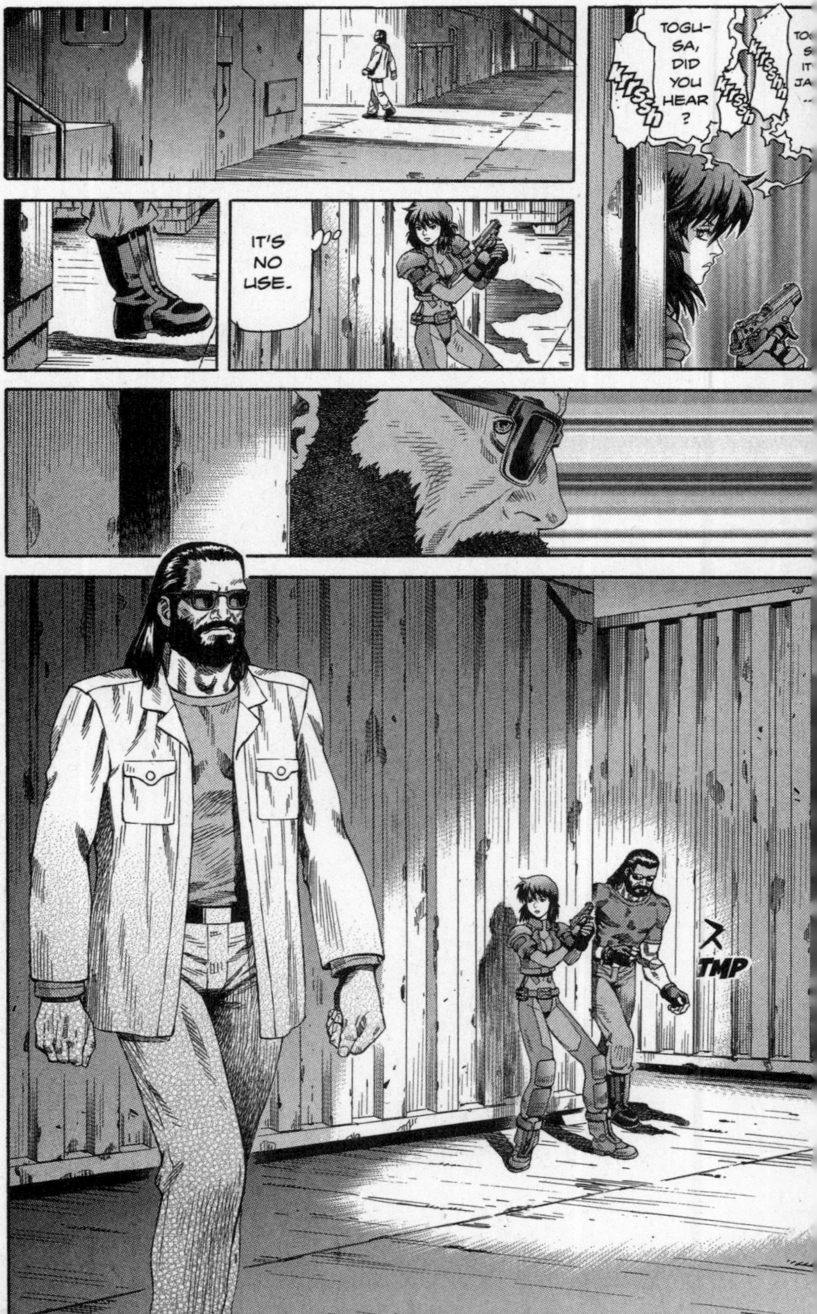
KISSH
TOGU-SA, DID YOU HEAR?
KISSH
KISSH
IT'S NO USE.
ス
TMP

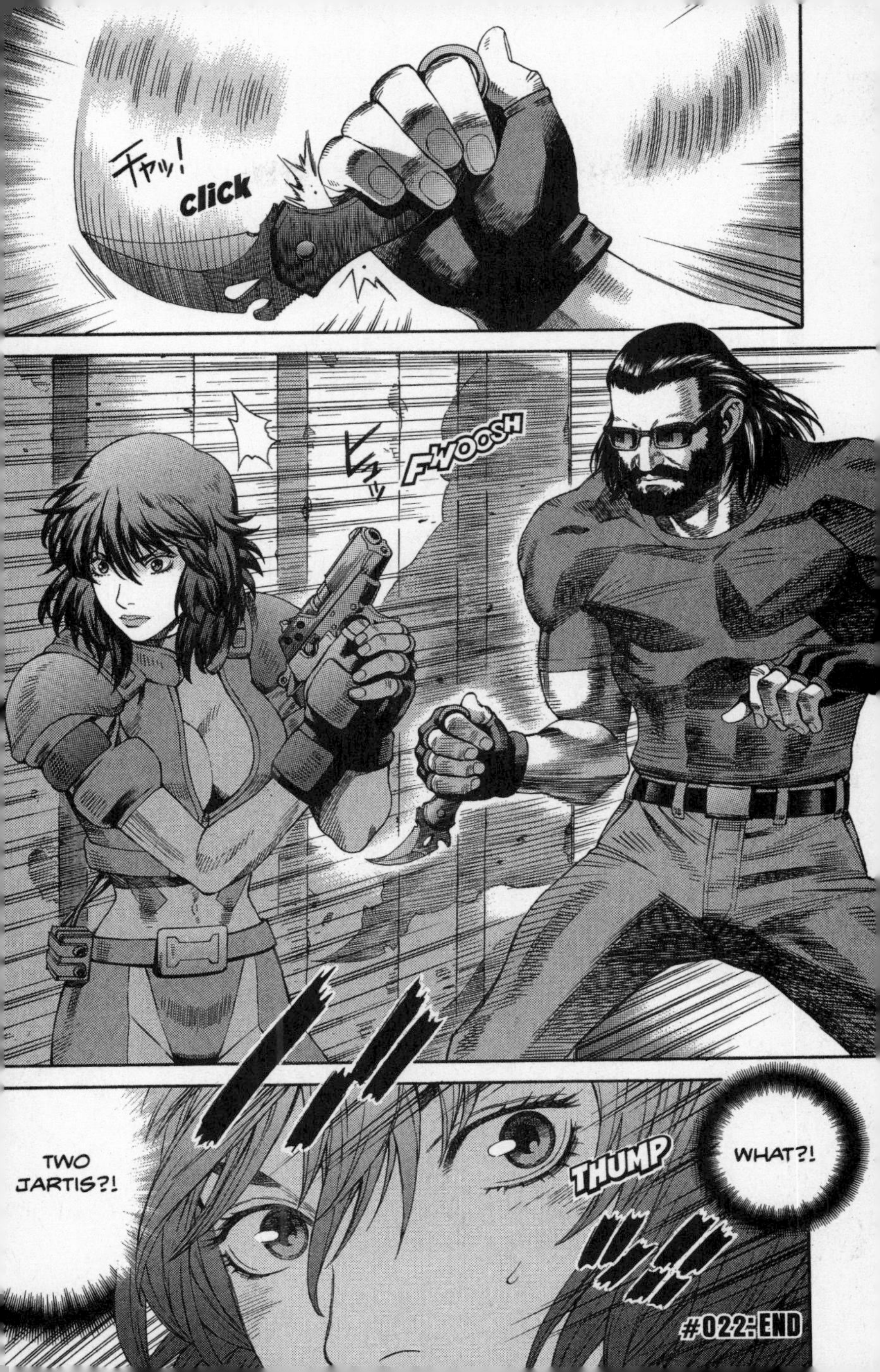
チャッ!
click
ビュッ
FWOOSH
WHAT?!
THUMP
TWO JARTIS?!
#022: END

# #023: The Hero's Secret

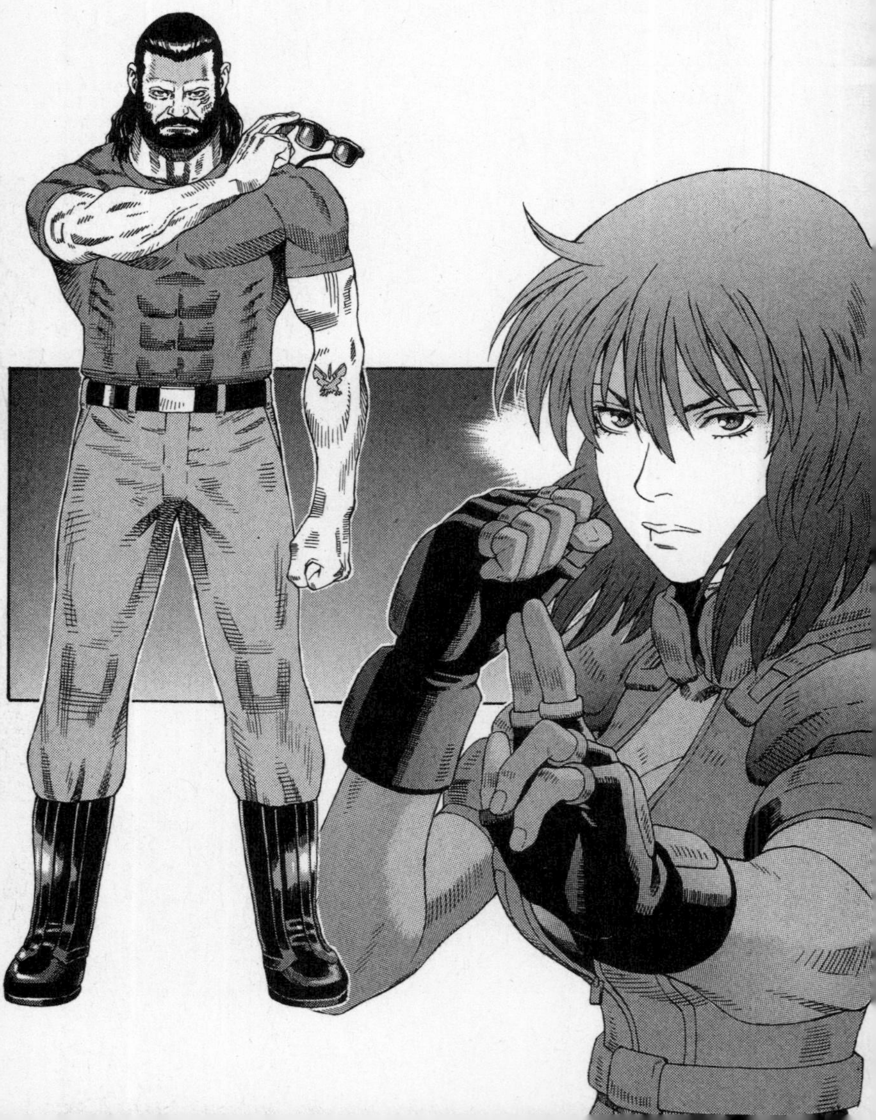

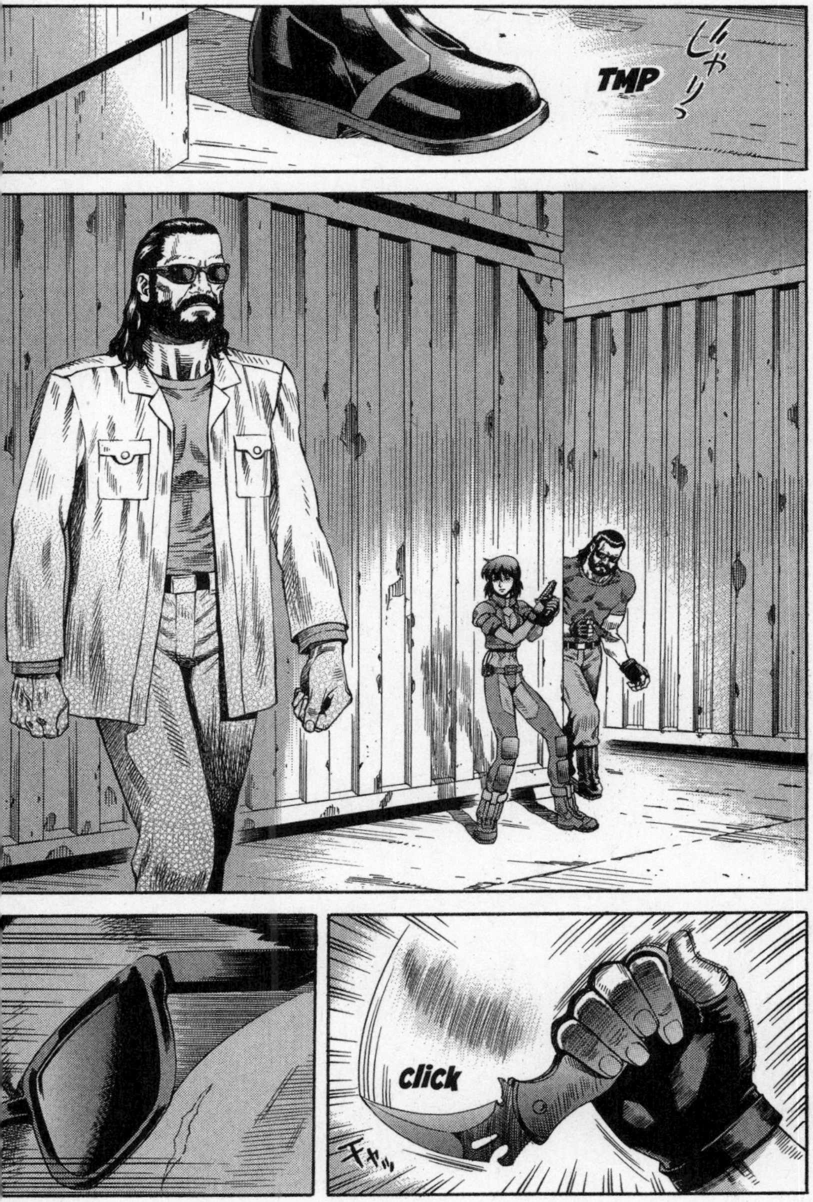
じゃりっ
TMP
click
キャッ

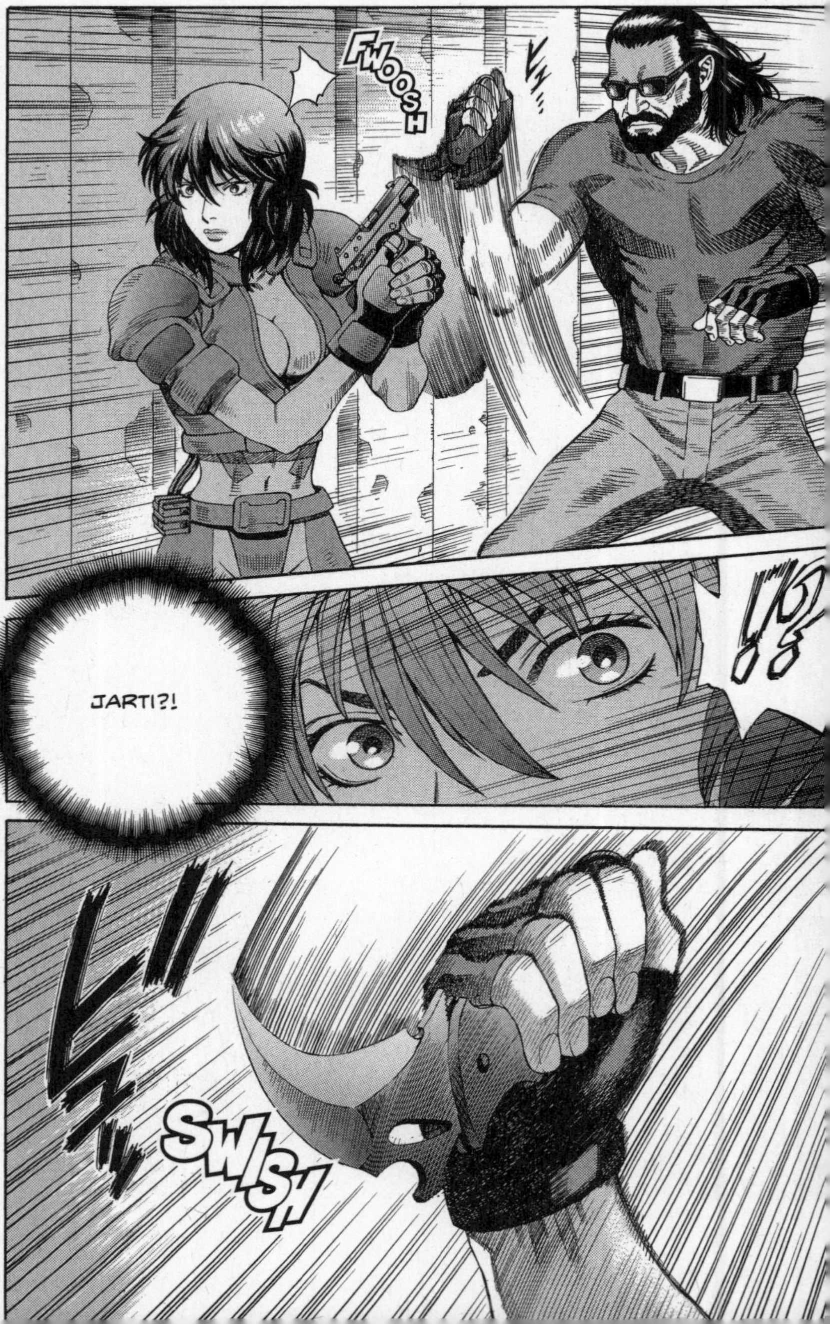
FWOOSH
JARTI?!
SWISH

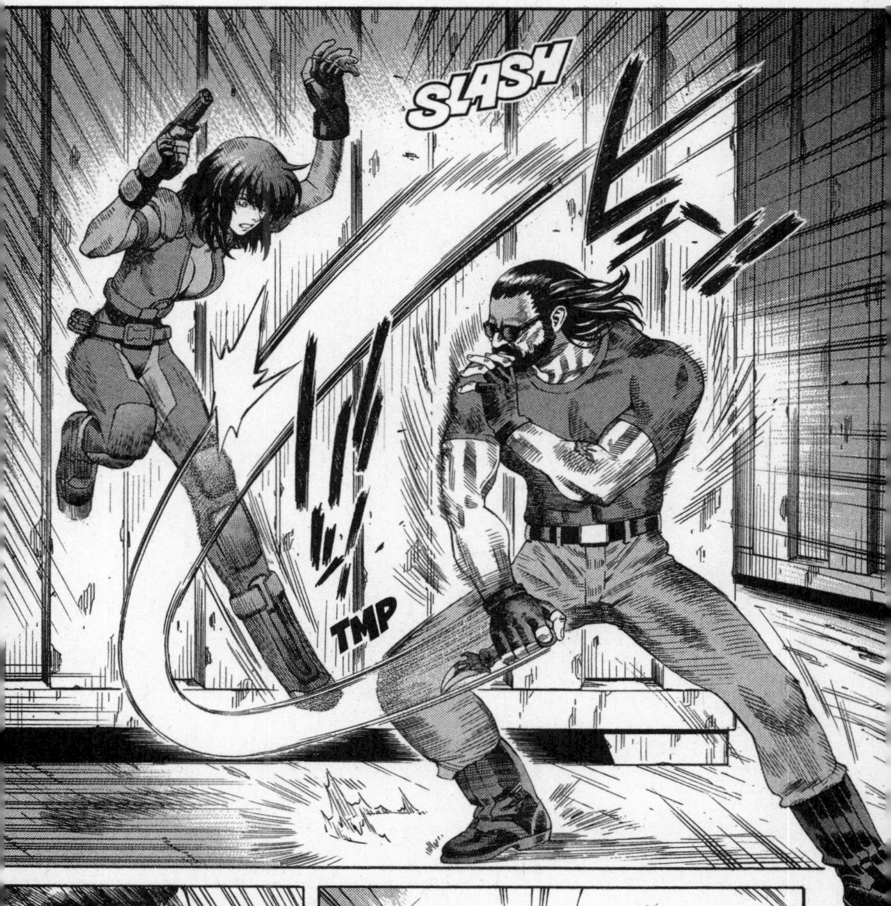
SLASH
TMP
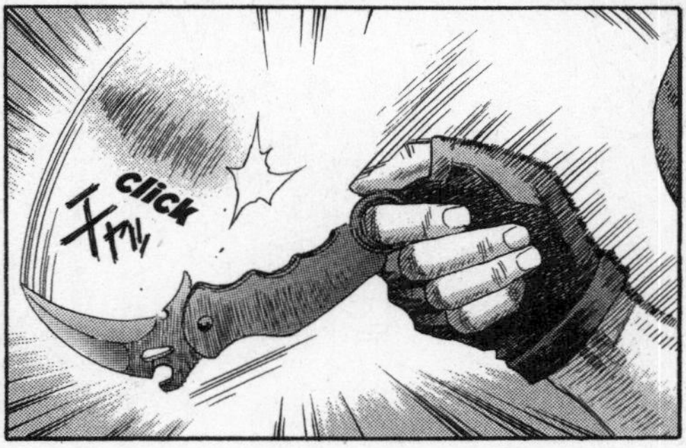
click
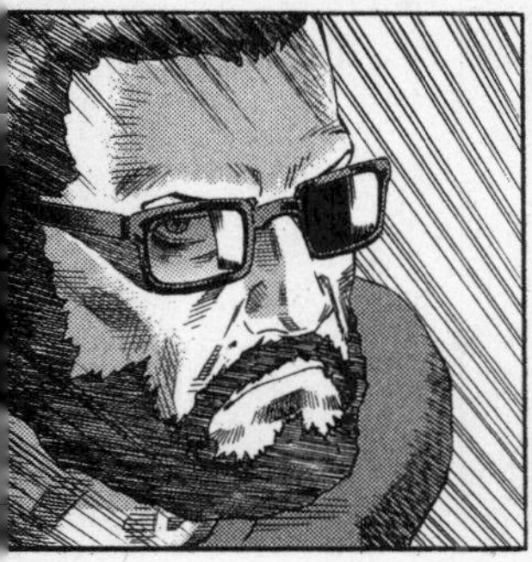

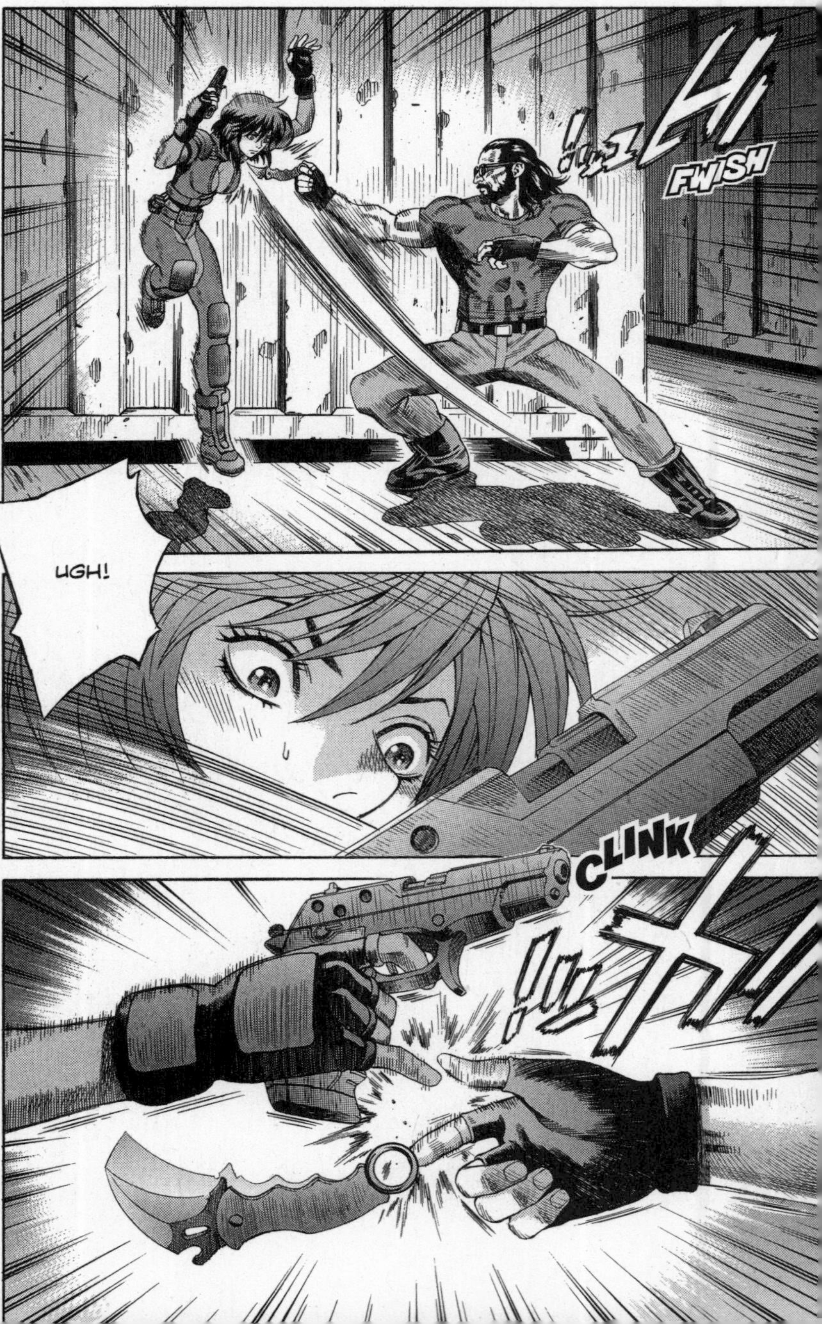
FWISH
UGH!
CLINK

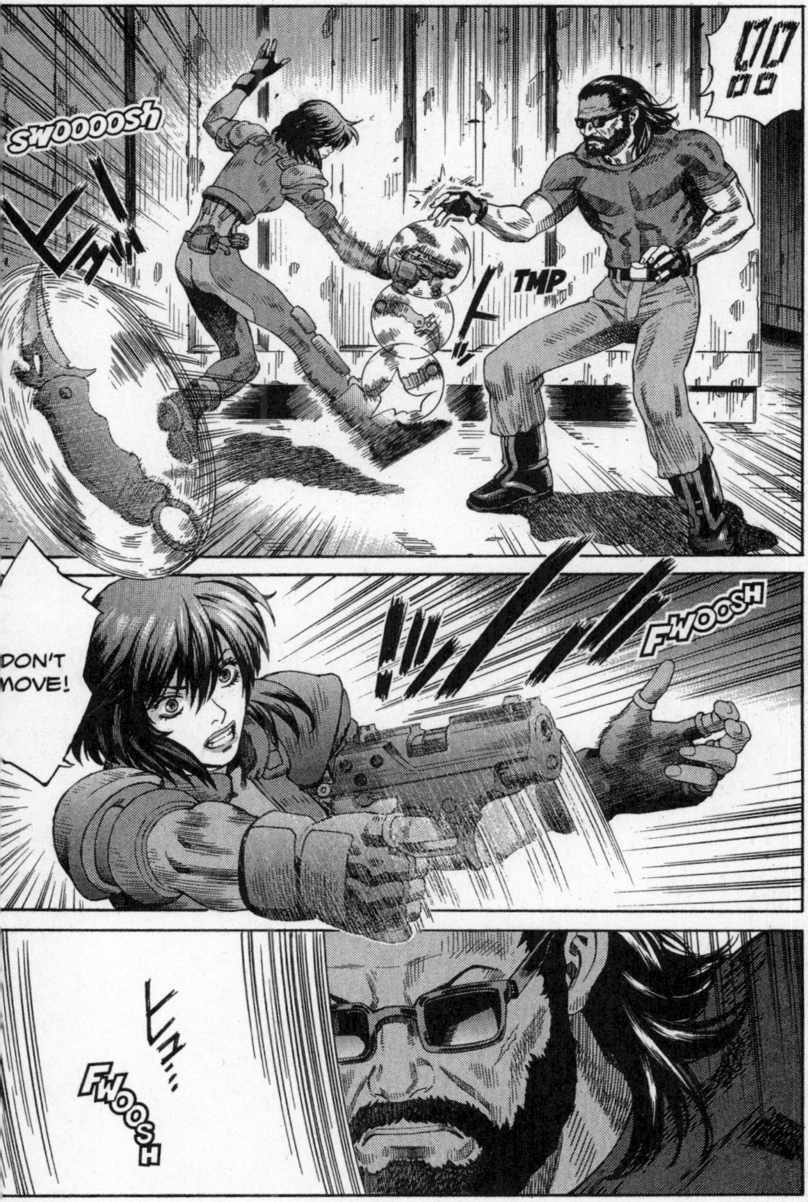
!!
SWOOOOSH
TMP
FWOOSH
DON'T MOVE!
FWOOSH

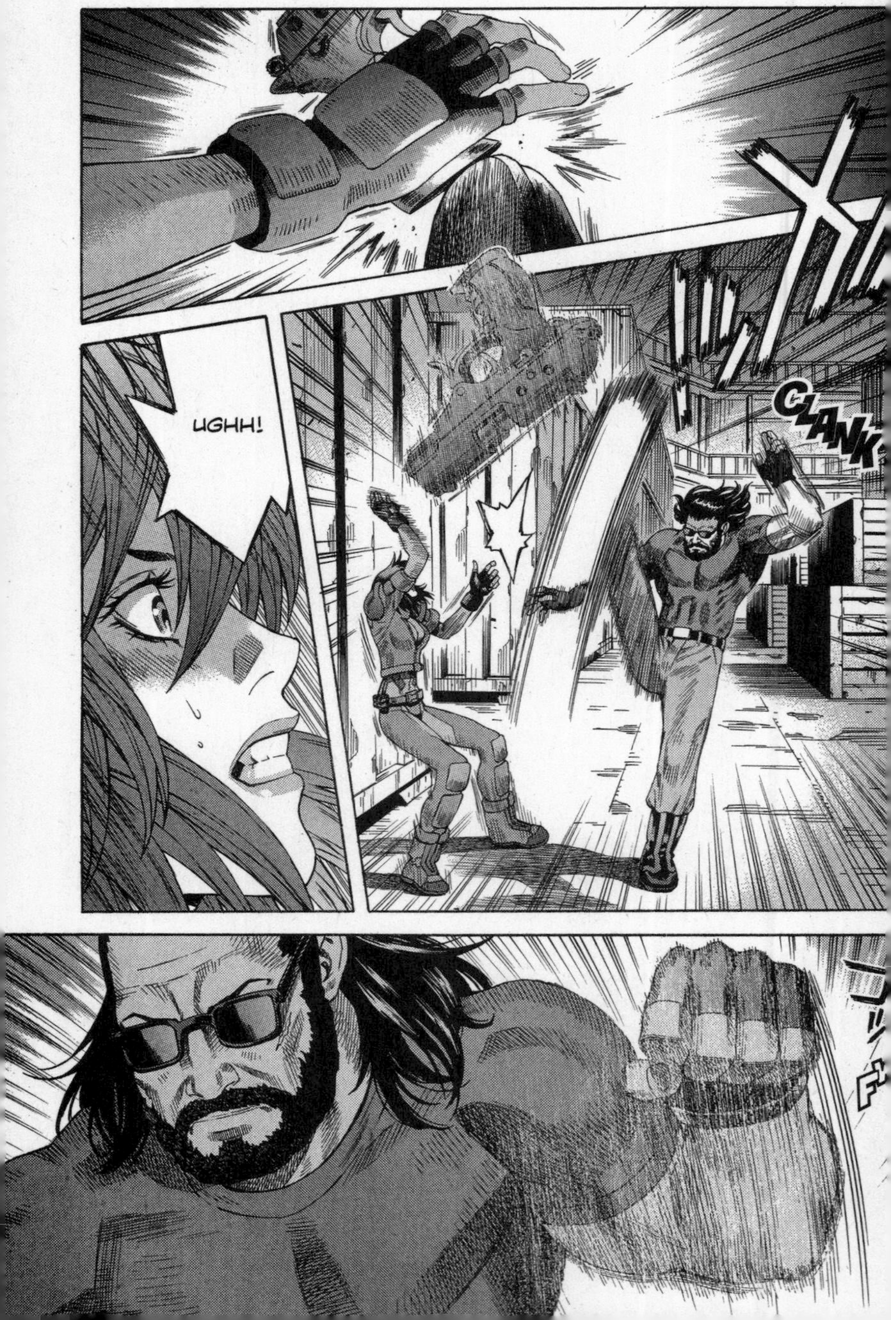
CLANK
UGHH!

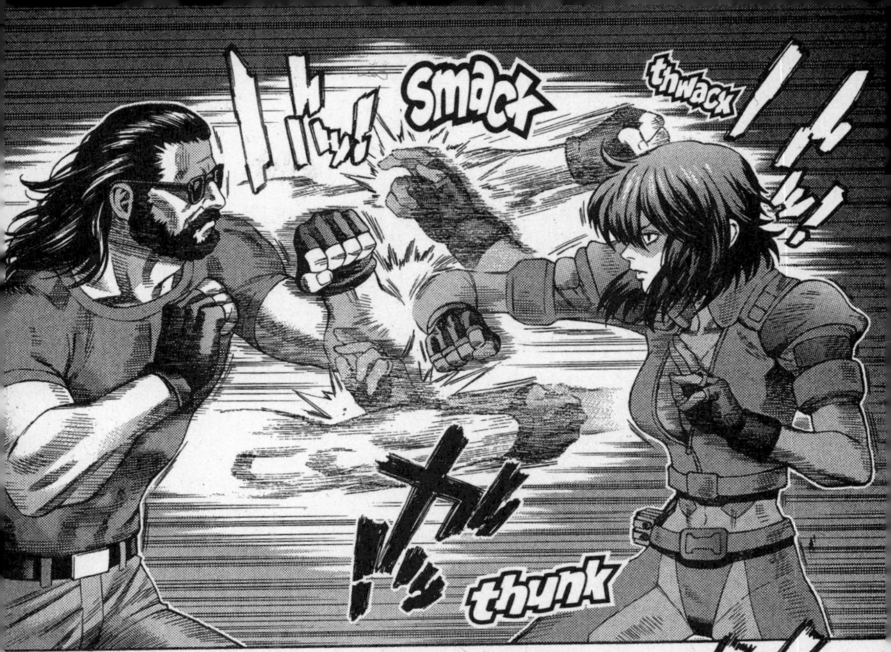
thwack
smack
thunk
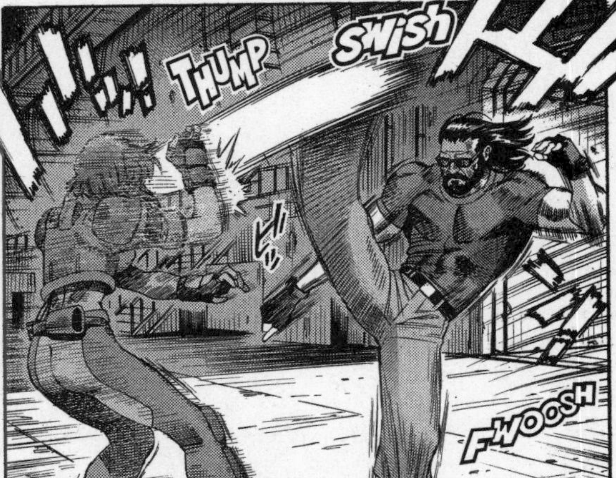
SWISH
THUMP
FWOOSH
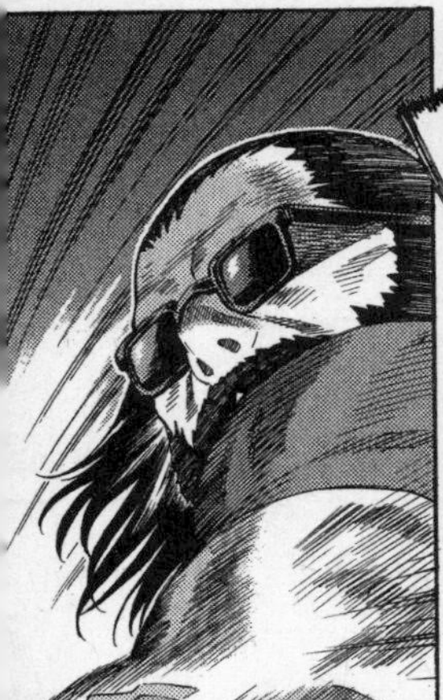

FWOOSH

TMP

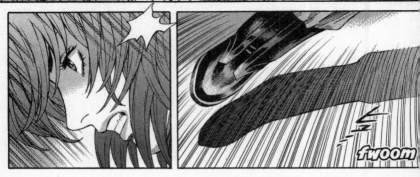

fwoom

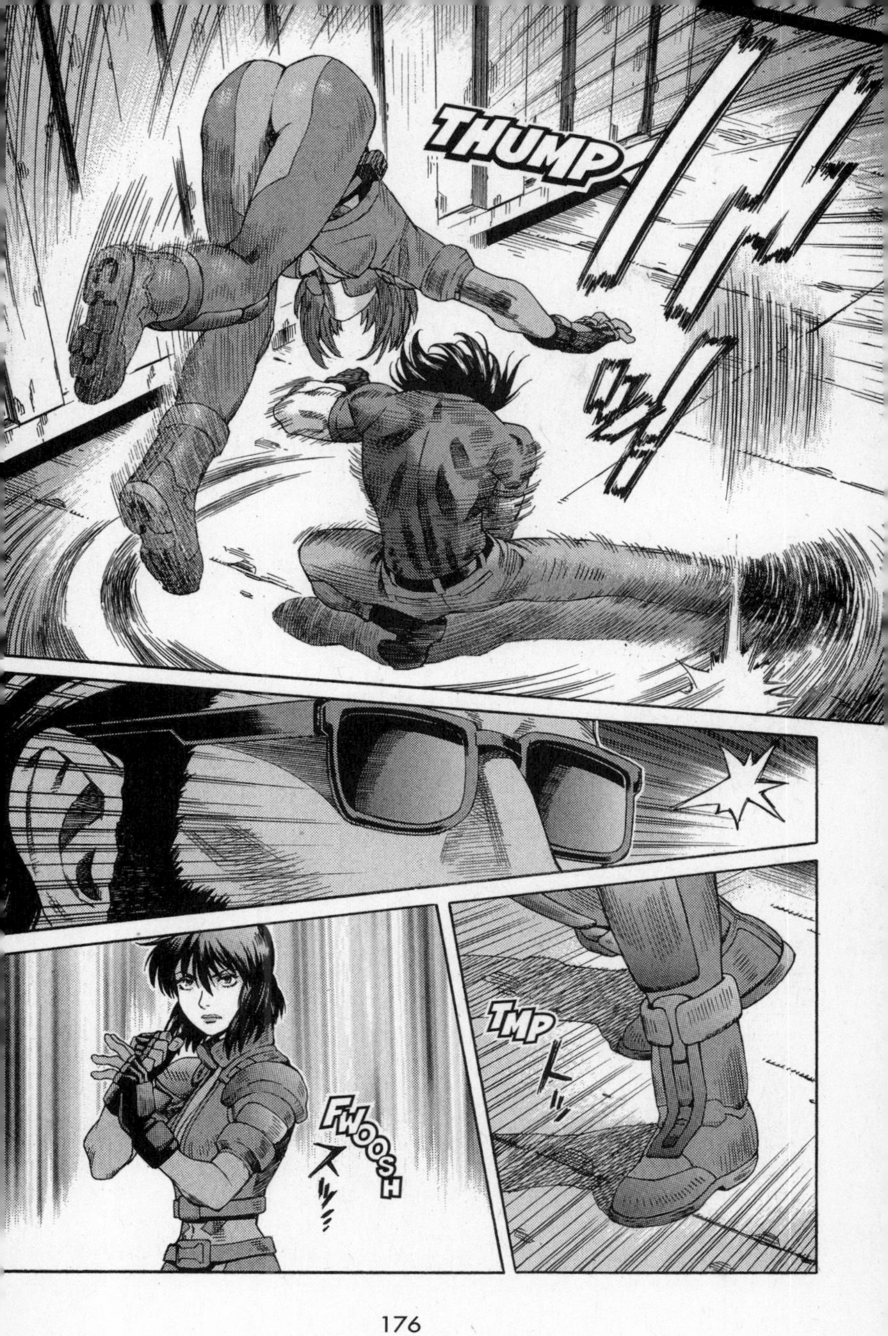
THUMP
TMP
FWOOSH

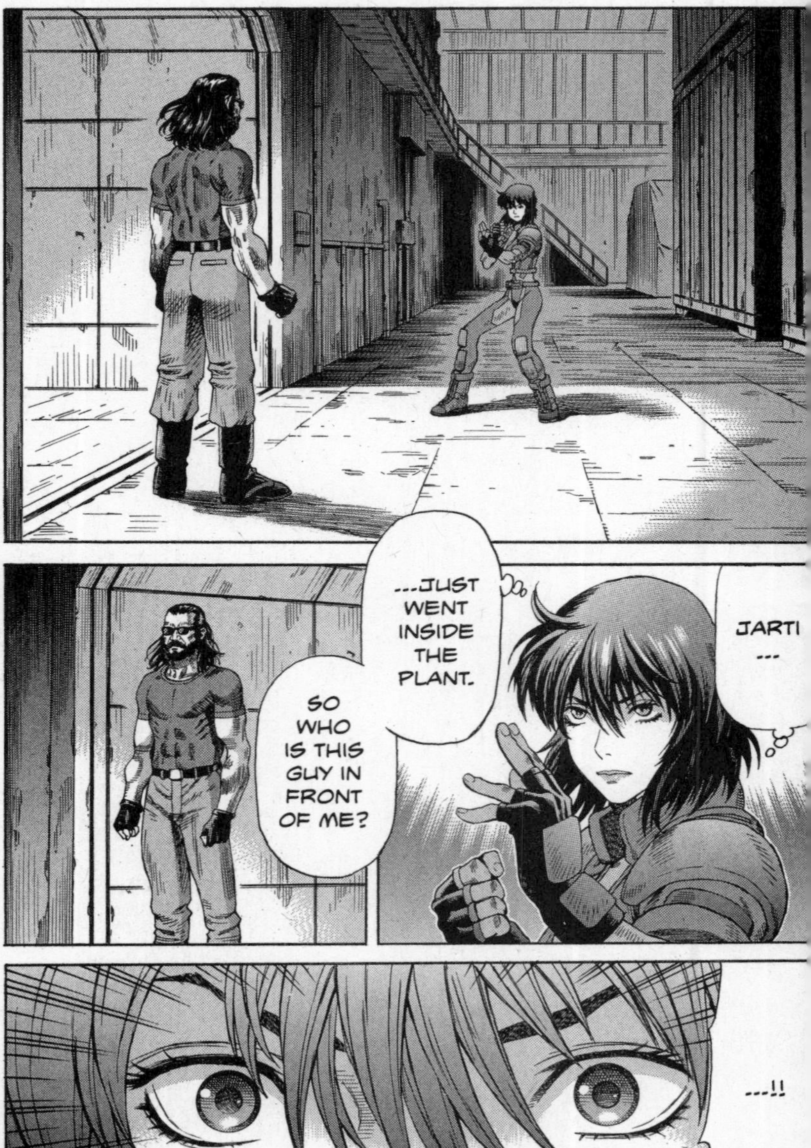
JARTI ---
---JUST WENT INSIDE THE PLANT.
SO WHO IS THIS GUY IN FRONT OF ME?
---!!

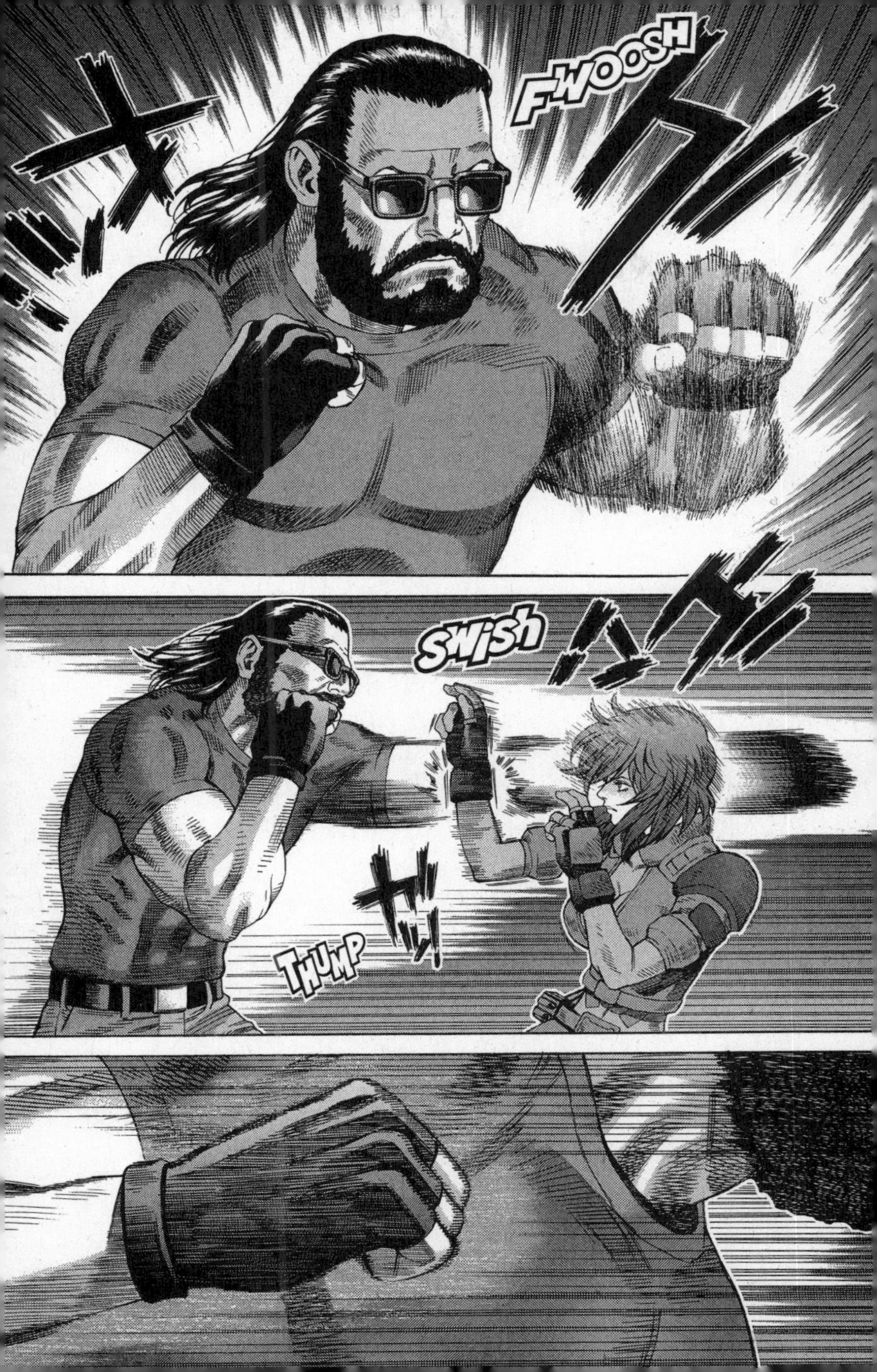
FWOOSH
SWISH
THUMP

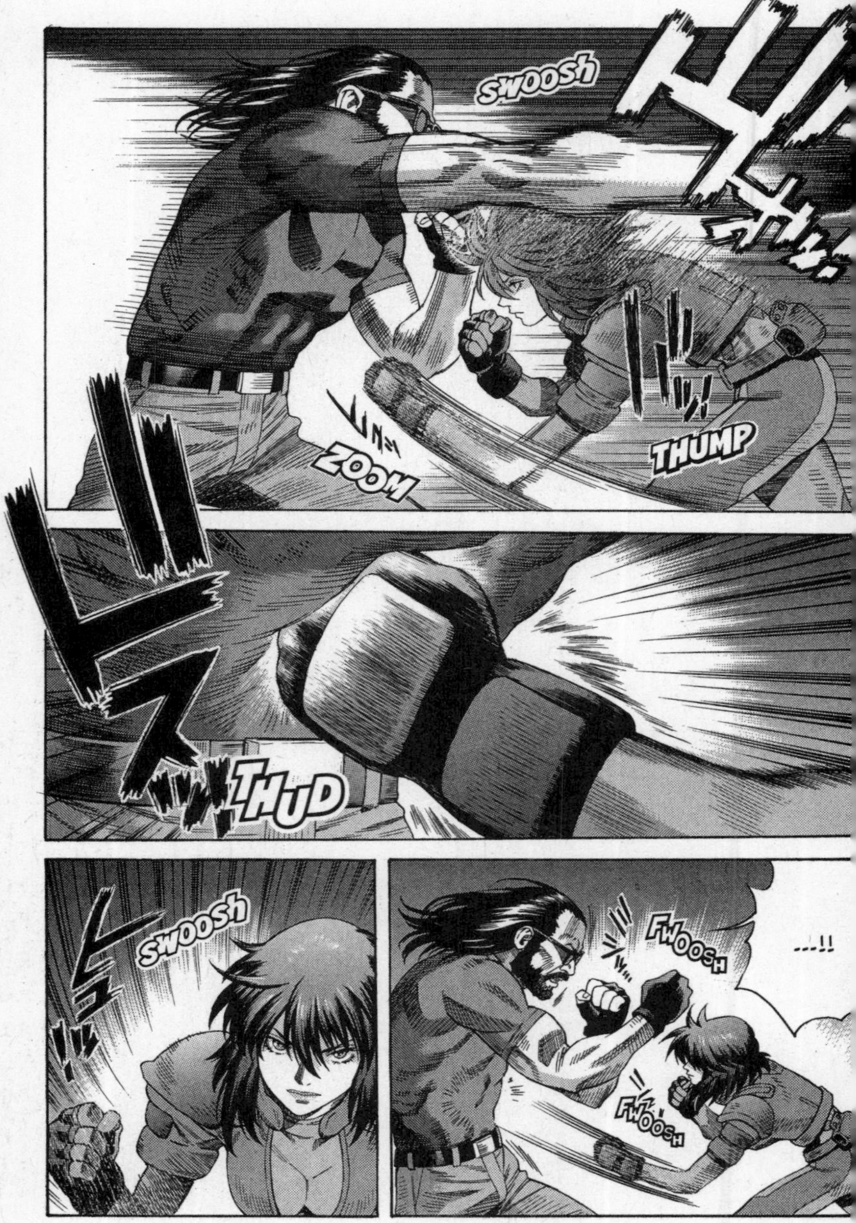
SWOOSH
THUMP
ZOOM
THUD
FWOOSH
...!!
FWOOSH
SWOOSH

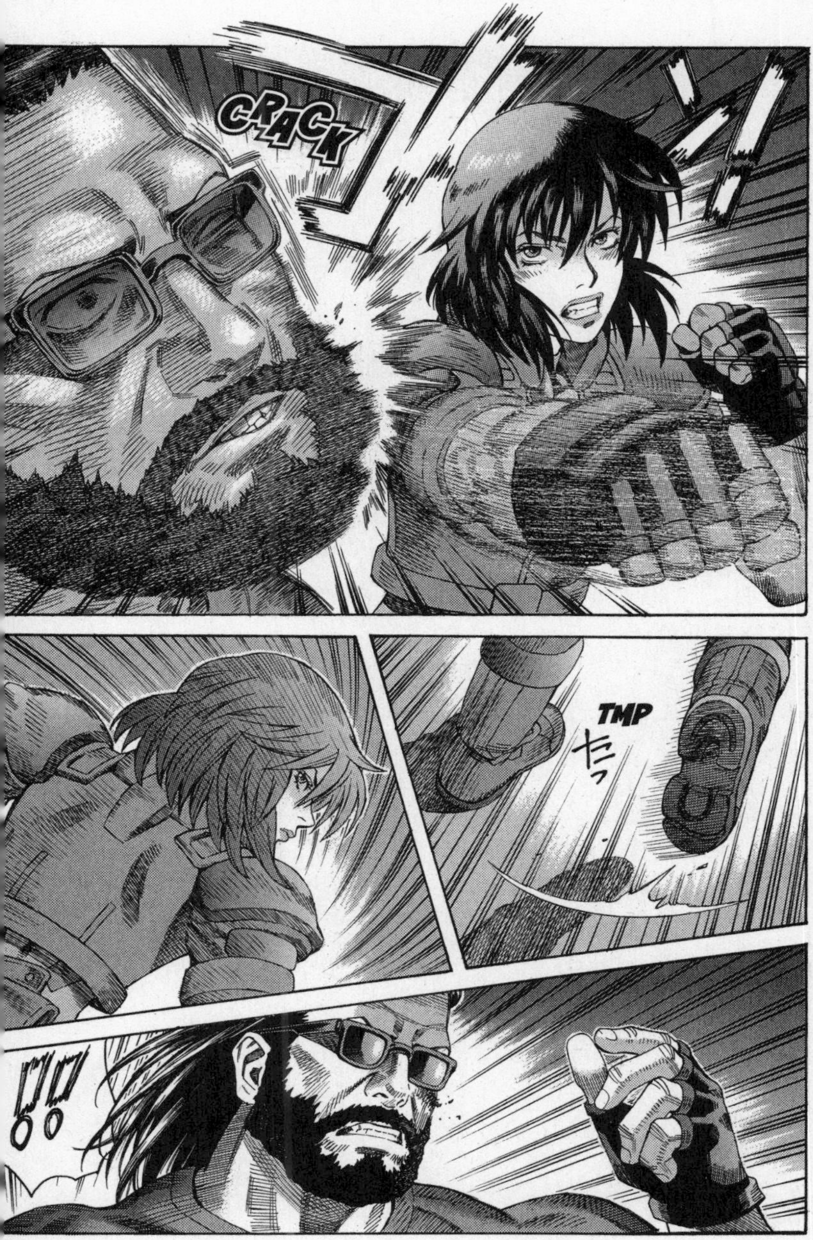
CRACK
TMP

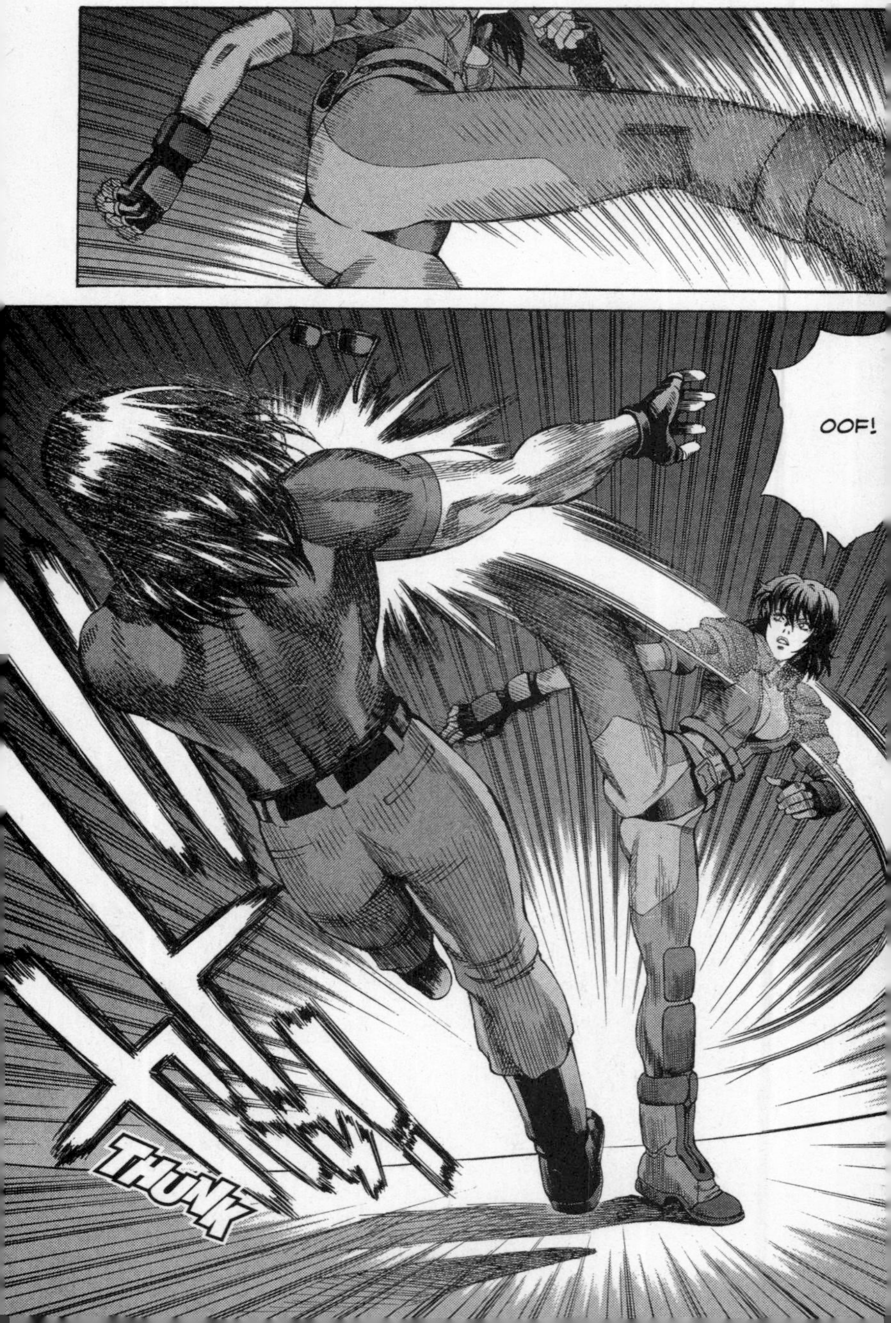
OOF!
THUNK

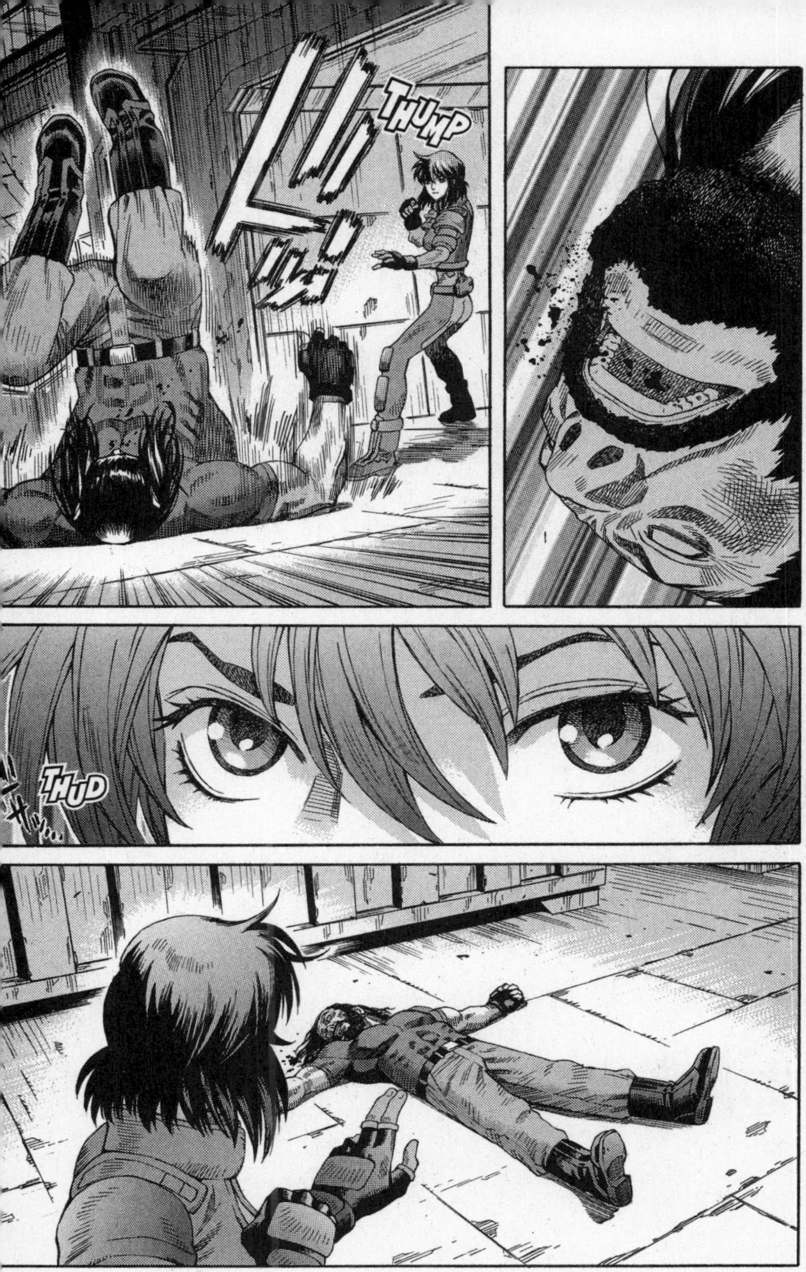
THUMP
THUD

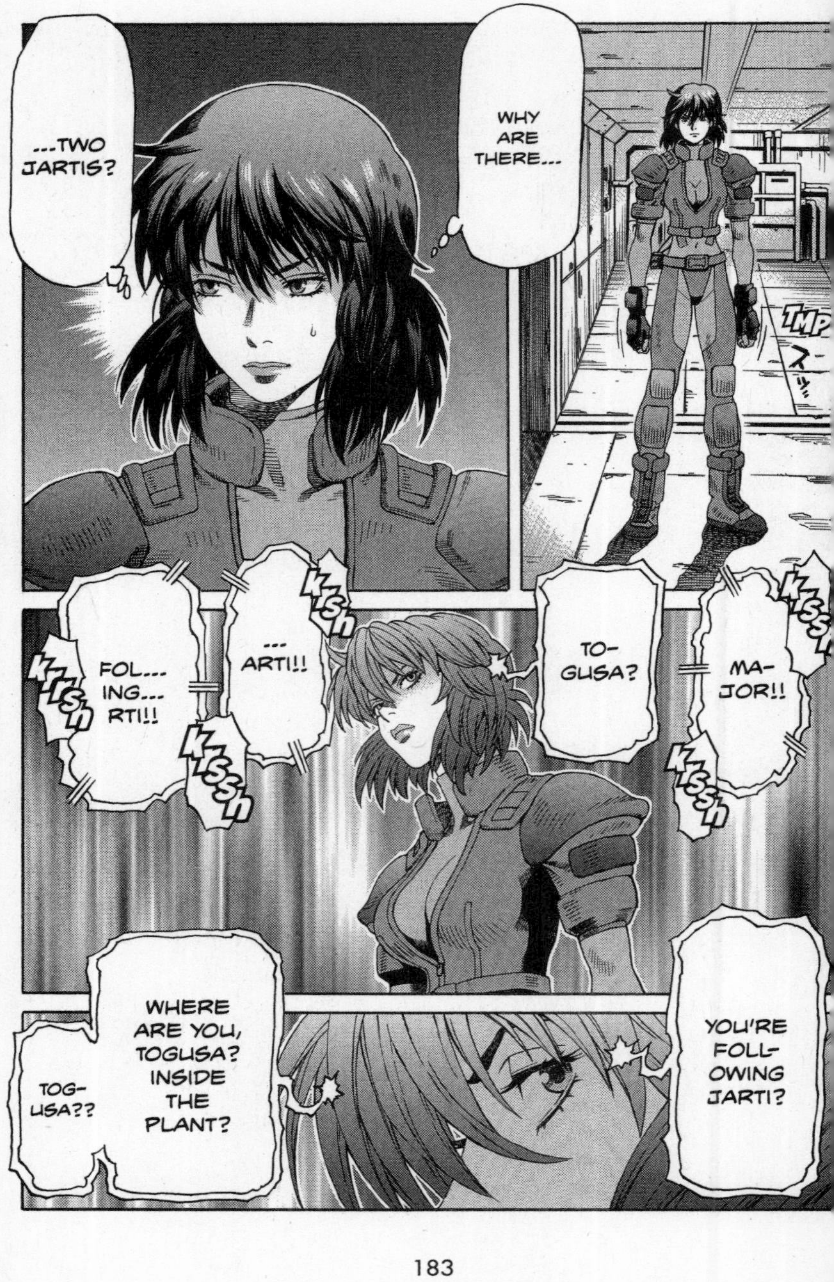
TMP
WHY ARE THERE...
...TWO JARTIS?
MA-JOR!!
TO-GUSA?
... ARTI!!
FOL... ING... RTI!!
YOU'RE FOLL-OWING JARTI?
WHERE ARE YOU, TOGUSA? INSIDE THE PLANT?
TOG-USA??

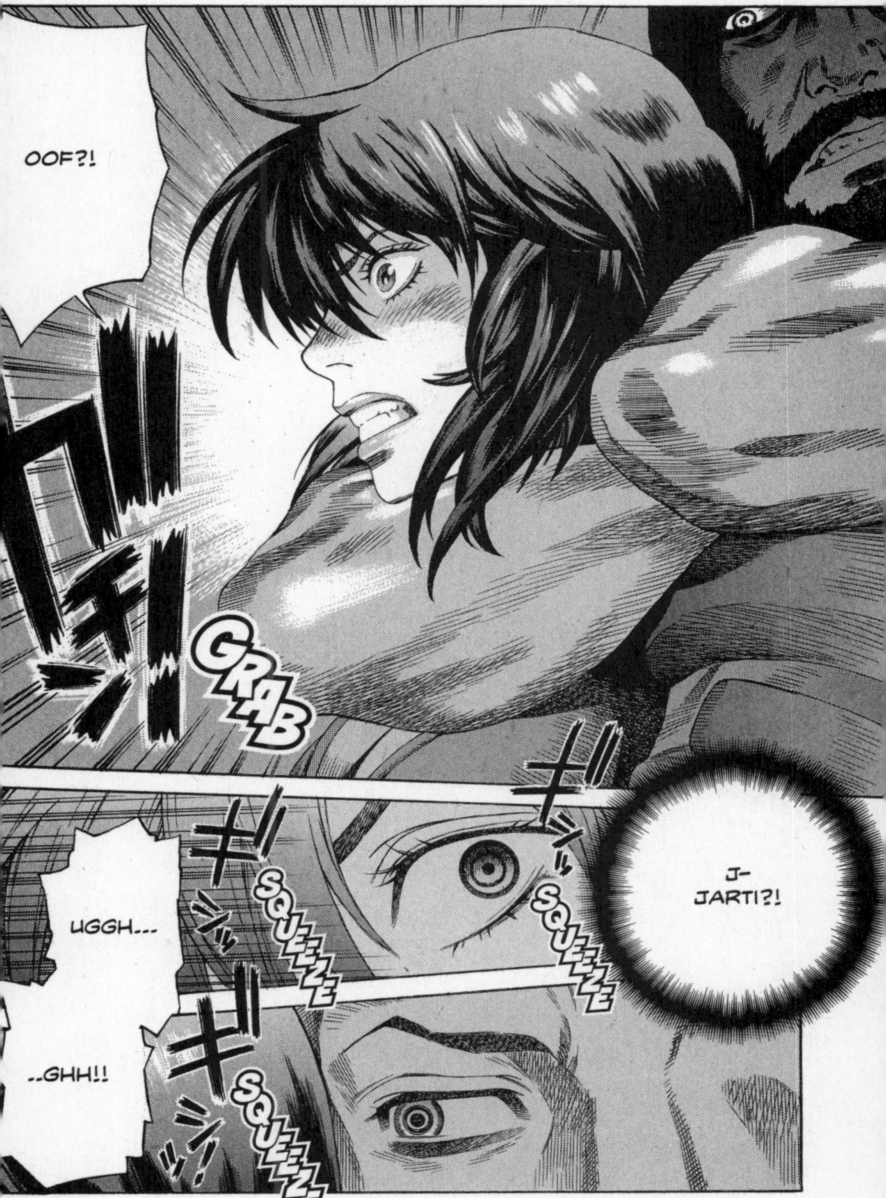
OOF?!
GRAB
J-
JARTI?!
SQUEEZE
SQUEEZE
UGGH...
..GHH!!
SQUEEZE

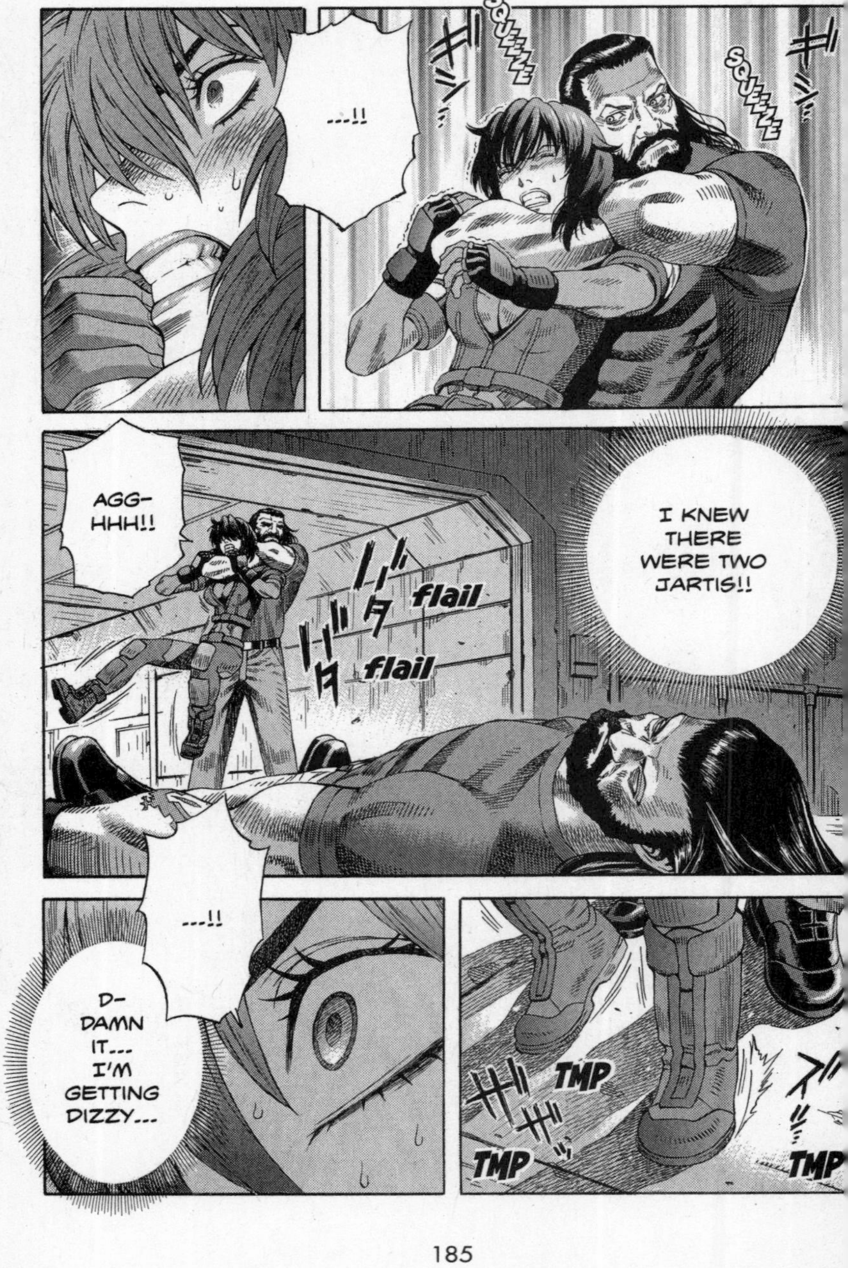
SQUEEZE
SQUEEZE
...!!
I KNEW THERE WERE TWO JARTIS!!
AGG-HHH!!
flail
flail
TMP
TMP
TMP
...!!
D-DAMN IT... I'M GETTING DIZZY...

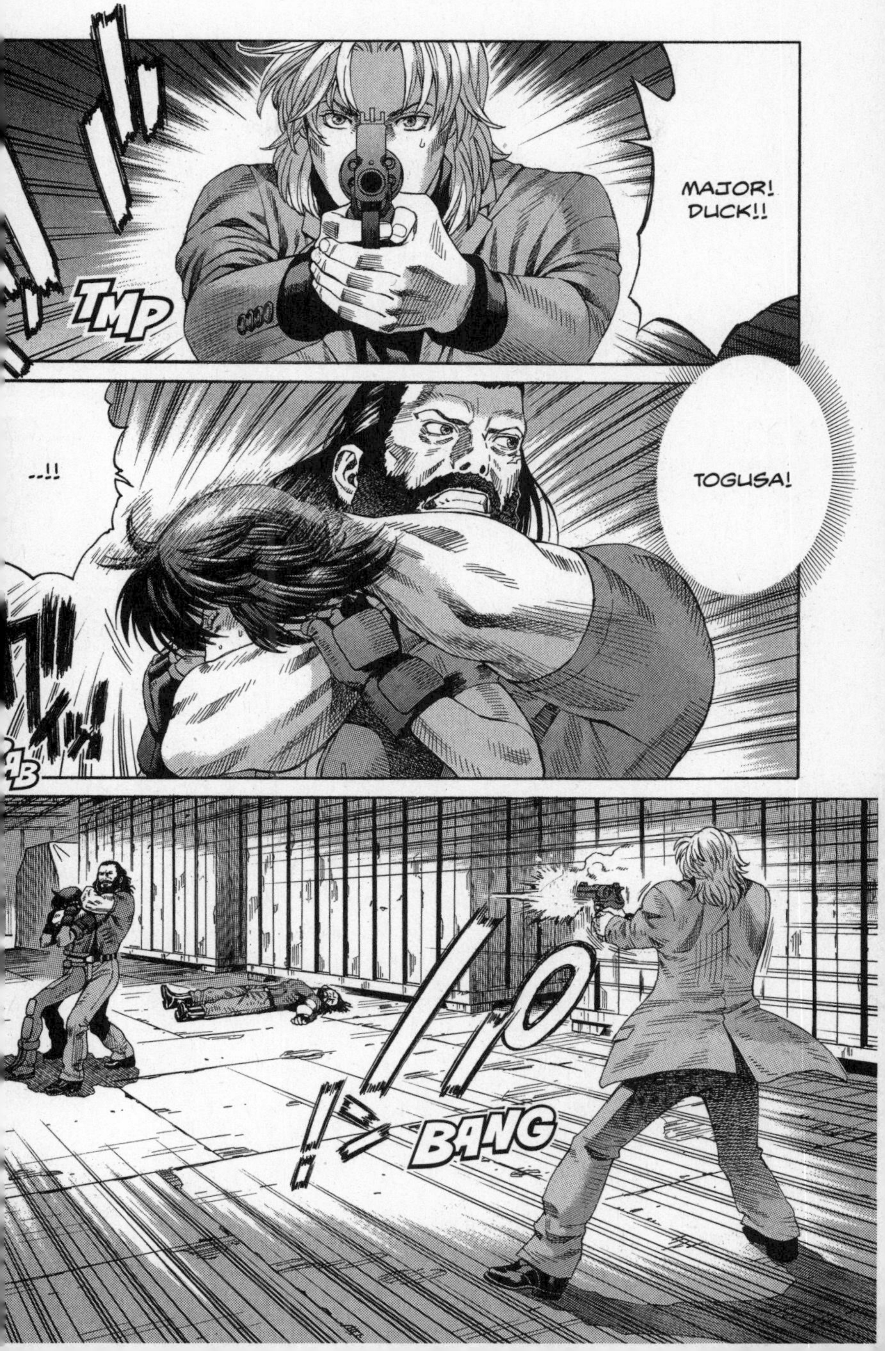
MAJOR! DUCK!!
TMP
TOGUSA!
..!!
BANG

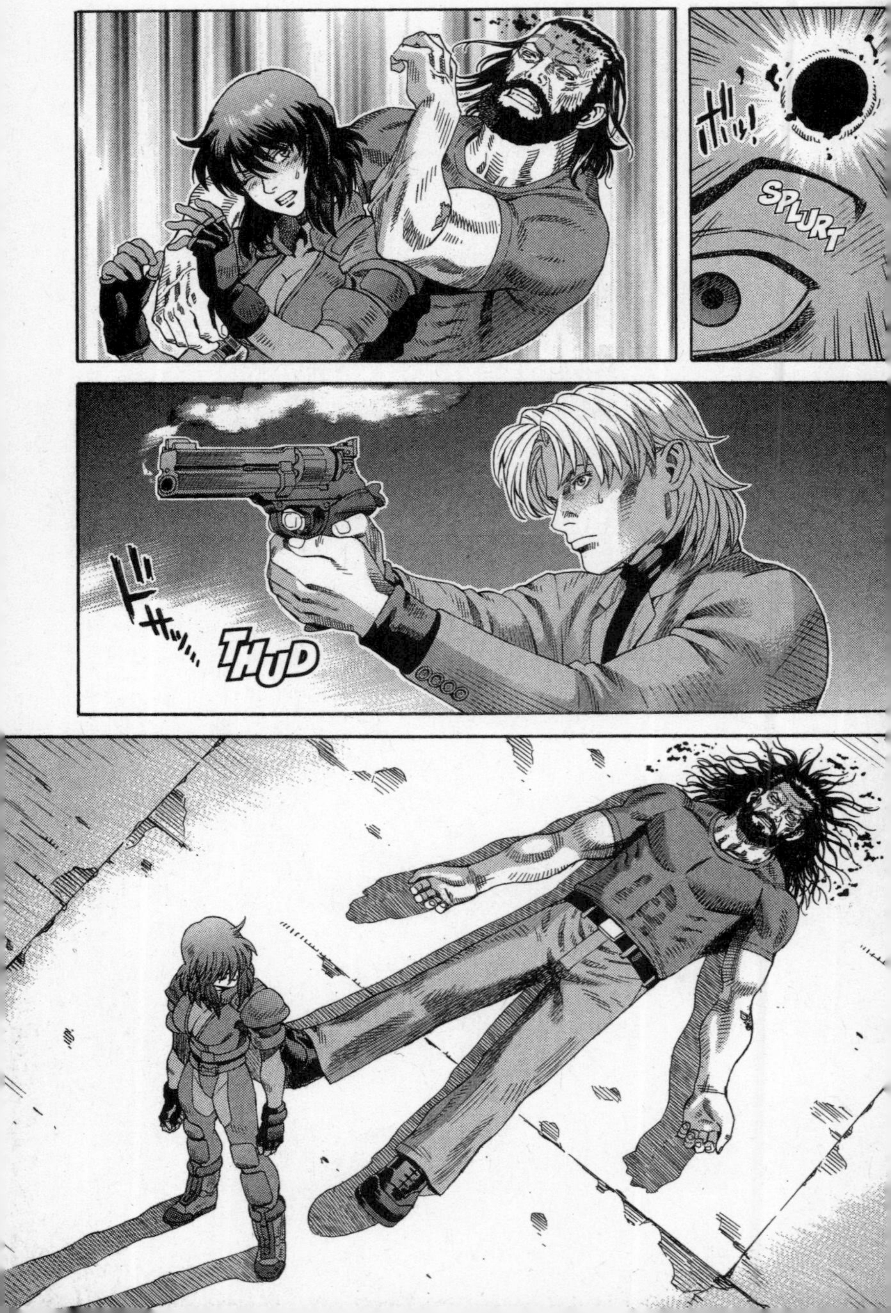
SPLURT
THUD

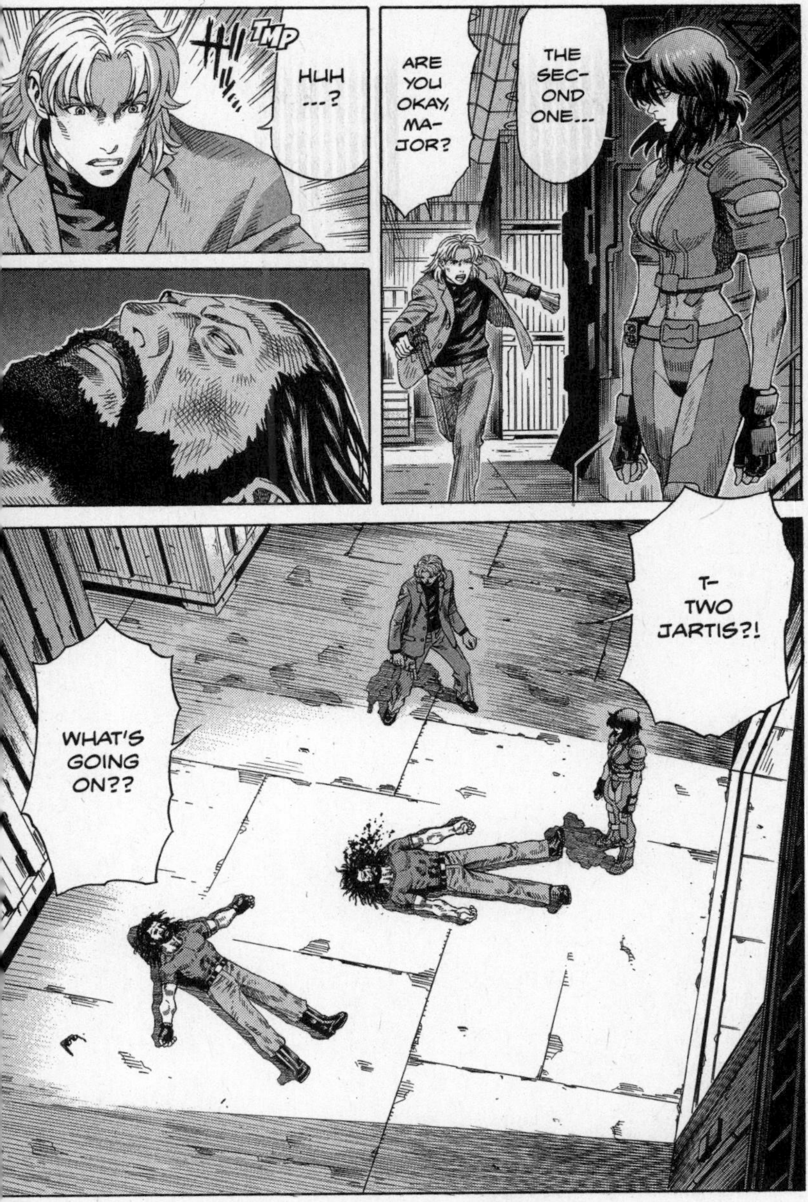
THE SECOND ONE...
ARE YOU OKAY, MAJOR?
TMP
HUH ...?
T-TWO JARTIS?!
WHAT'S GOING ON??

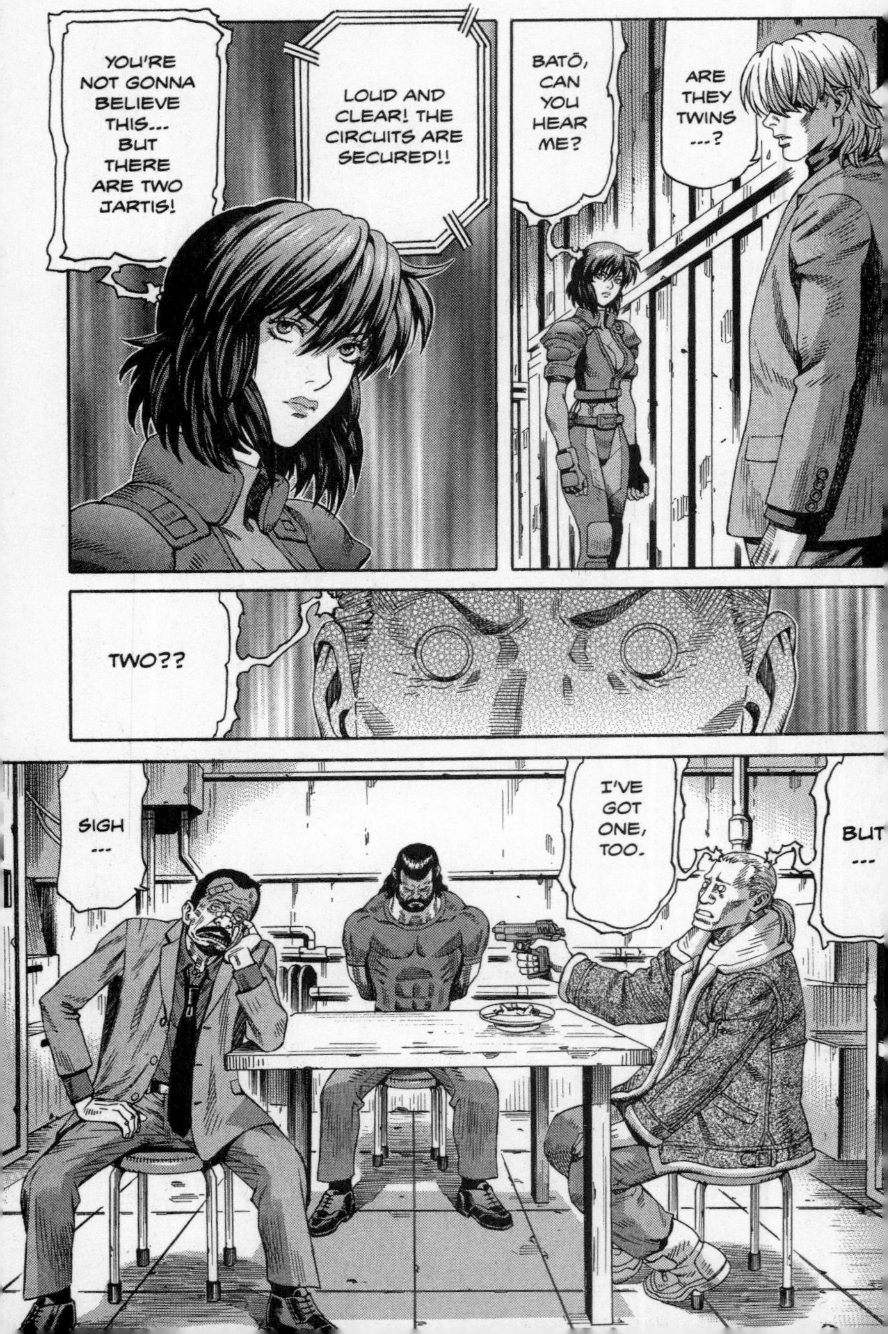
ARE THEY TWINS ---?
BATŌ, CAN YOU HEAR ME?
LOUD AND CLEAR! THE CIRCUITS ARE SECURED!!
YOU'RE NOT GONNA BELIEVE THIS... BUT THERE ARE TWO JARTIS!
TWO??
BUT ---
I'VE GOT ONE, TOO.
SIGH ---

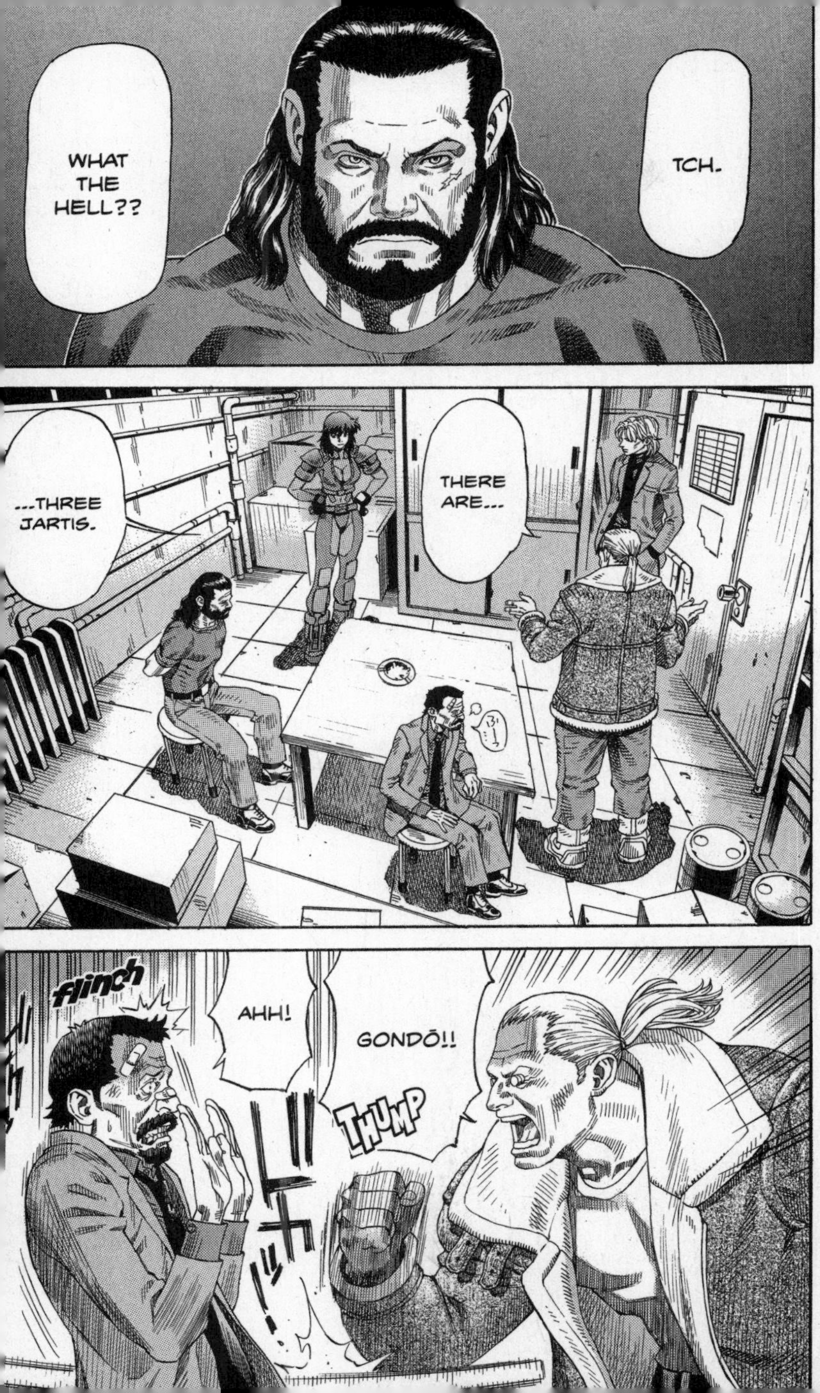
TCH.
WHAT THE HELL??
THERE ARE...
...THREE JARTIS.
GONDŌ!!
AHH!
flinch
THUMP

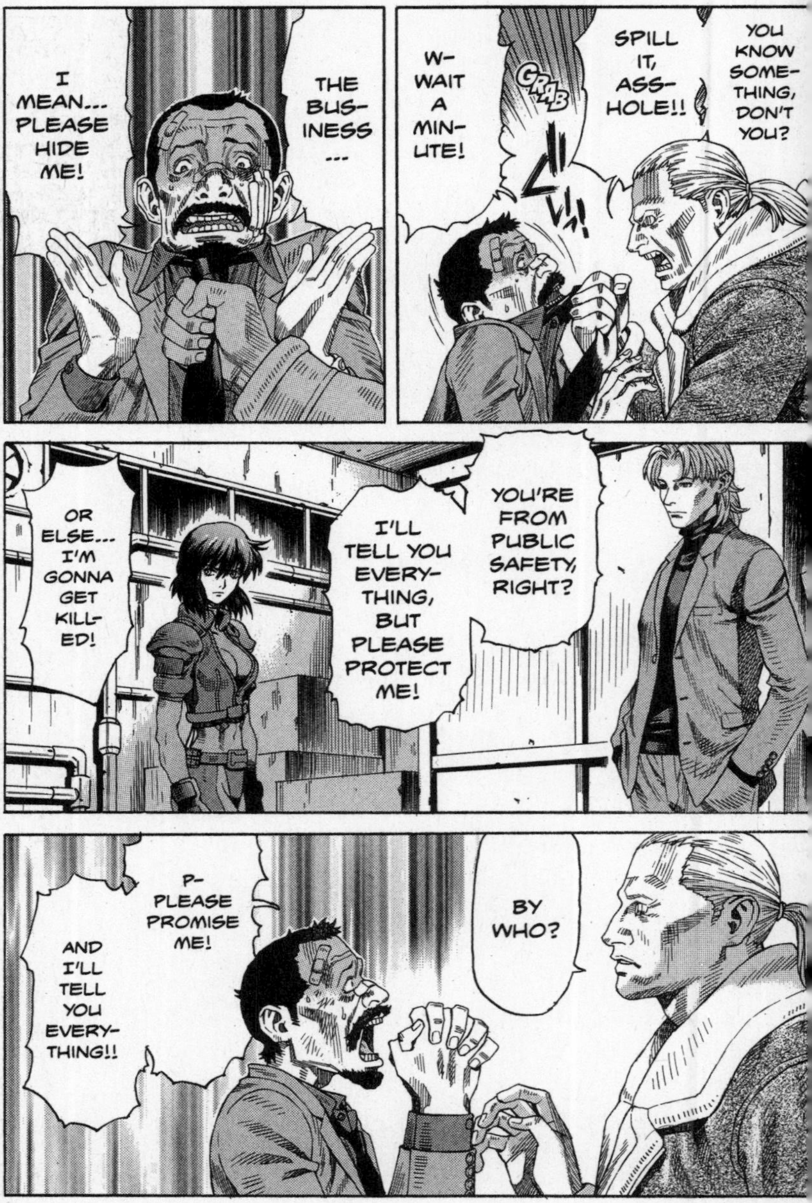
YOU KNOW SOMETHING, DON'T YOU?
SPILL IT, ASSHOLE!!
GRAB
W-WAIT A MINUTE!
THE BUSINESS...
I MEAN... PLEASE HIDE ME!
YOU'RE FROM PUBLIC SAFETY, RIGHT?
I'LL TELL YOU EVERYTHING, BUT PLEASE PROTECT ME!
OR ELSE... I'M GONNA GET KILLED!
BY WHO?
P-PLEASE PROMISE ME!
AND I'LL TELL YOU EVERYTHING!!

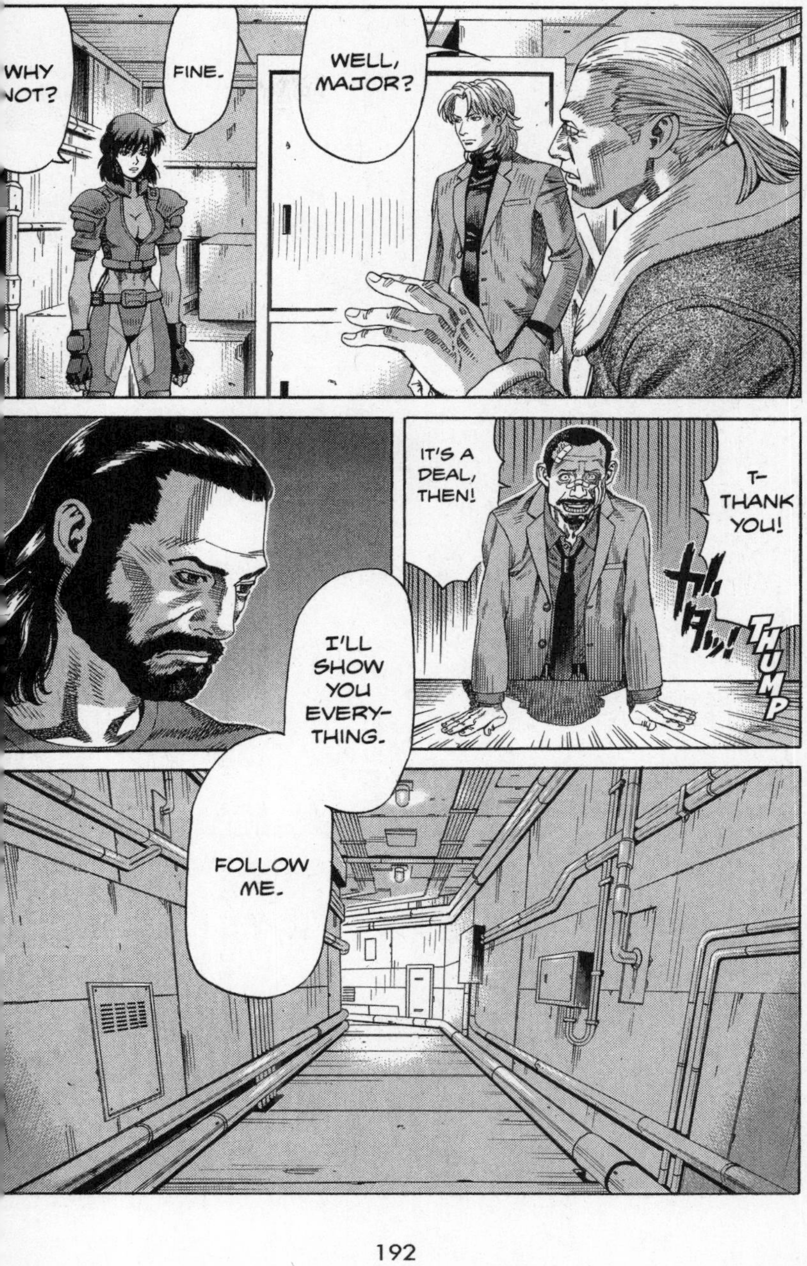
WELL, MAJOR?
FINE.
WHY NOT?
T-THANK YOU!
THUMP
IT'S A DEAL, THEN!
I'LL SHOW YOU EVERYTHING.
FOLLOW ME.

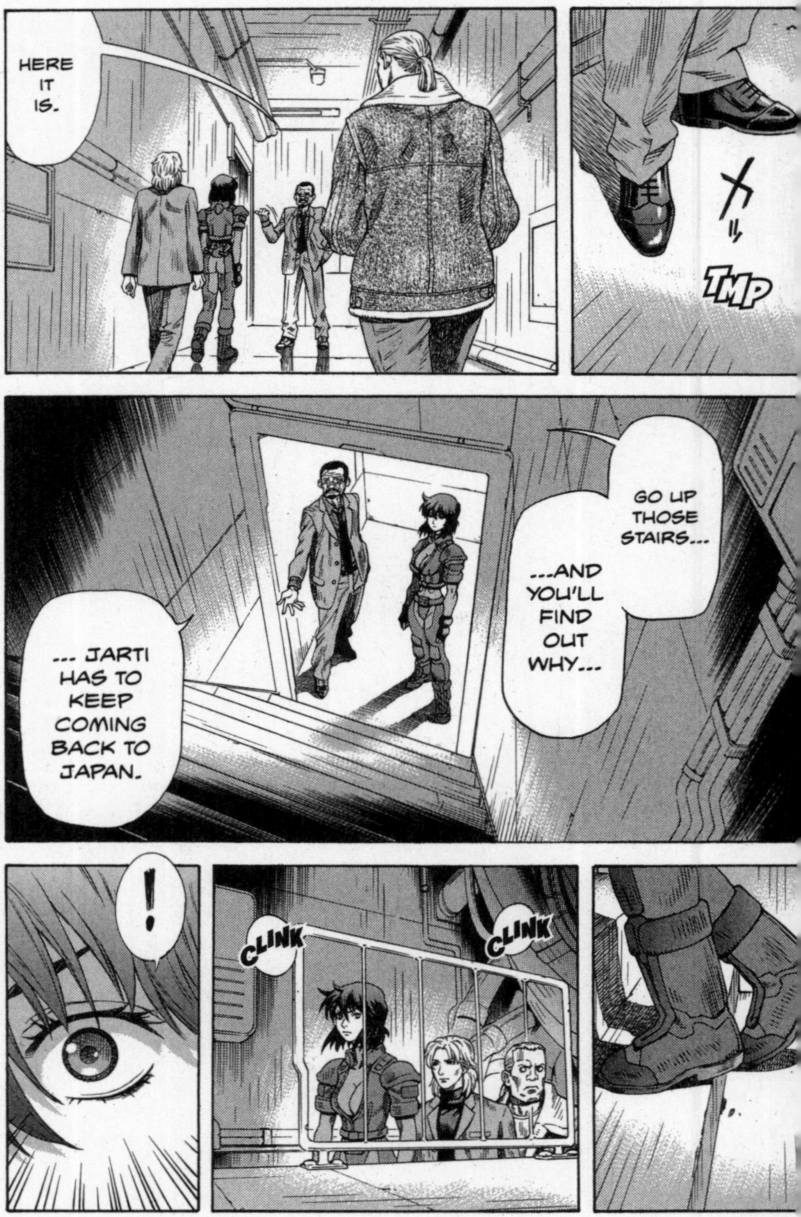
TMP
HERE IT IS.
GO UP THOSE STAIRS...
...AND YOU'LL FIND OUT WHY...
... JARTI HAS TO KEEP COMING BACK TO JAPAN.
CLINK
CLINK
!

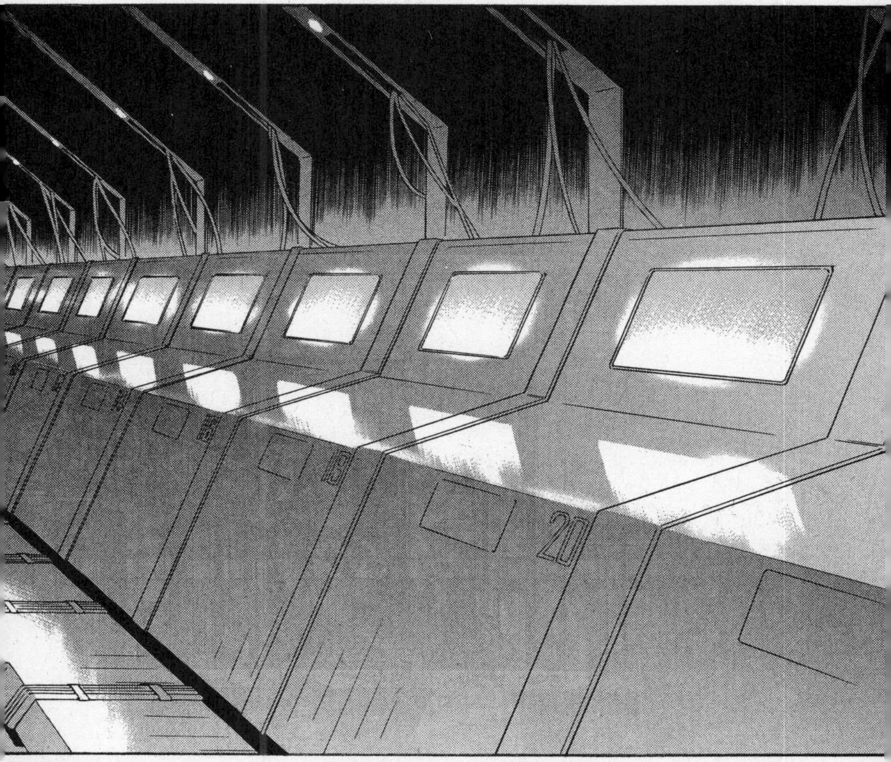
20
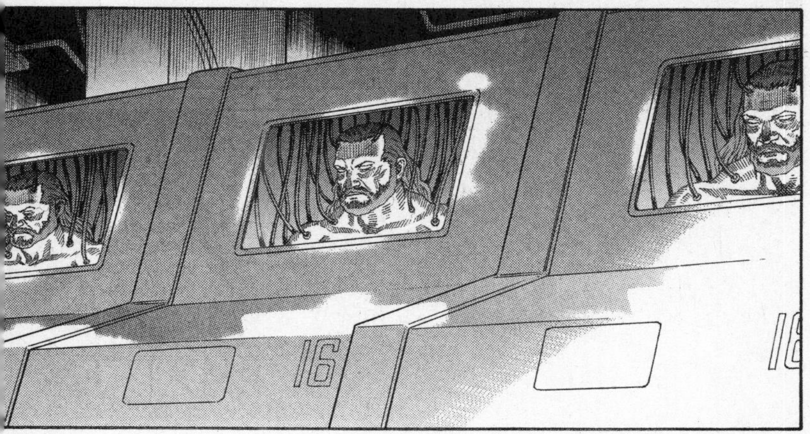
16

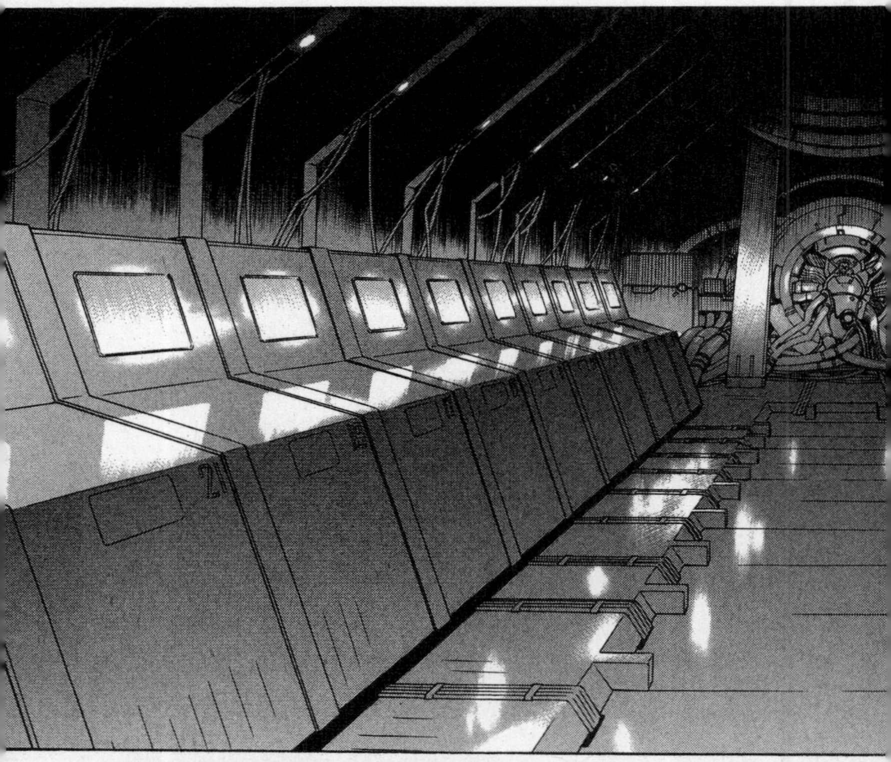

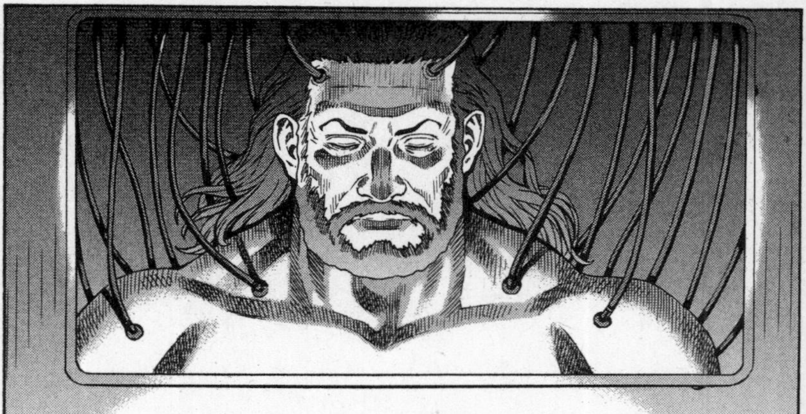

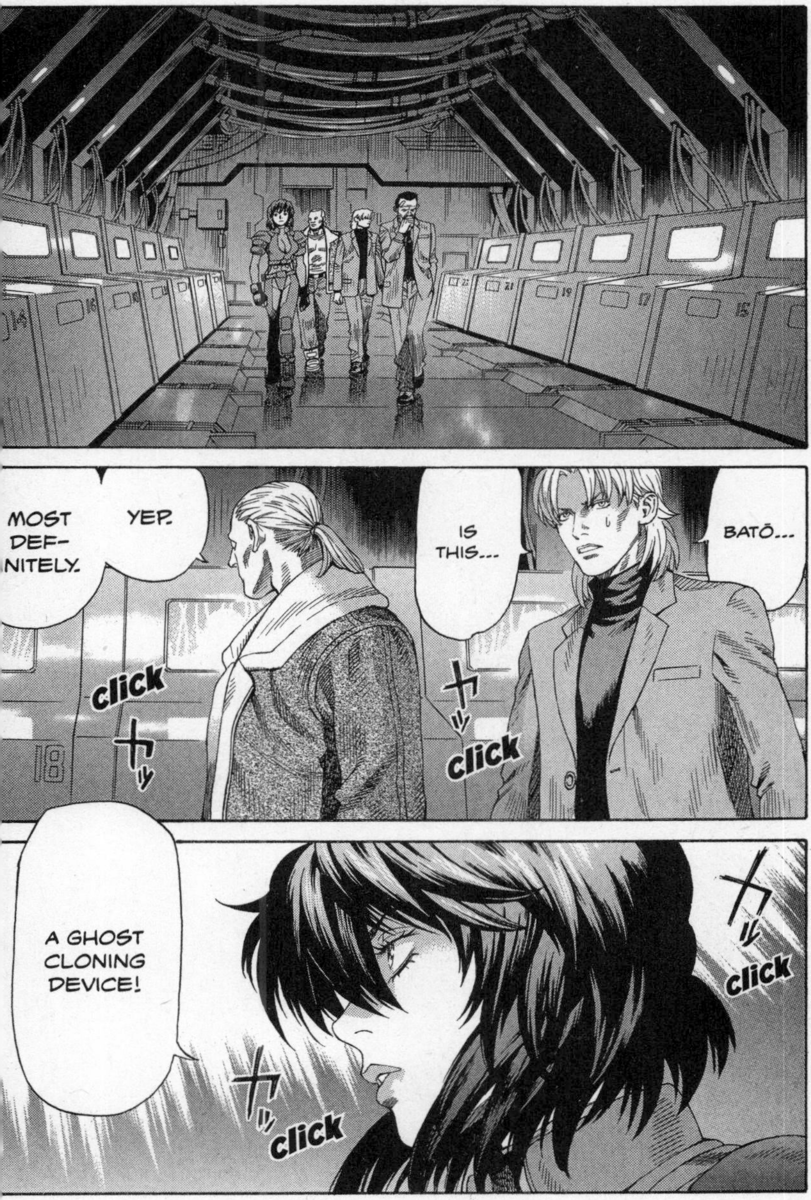
BATŌ...
IS THIS...
click
YEP.
MOST DEF-NITELY.
click
click
A GHOST CLONING DEVICE!
click

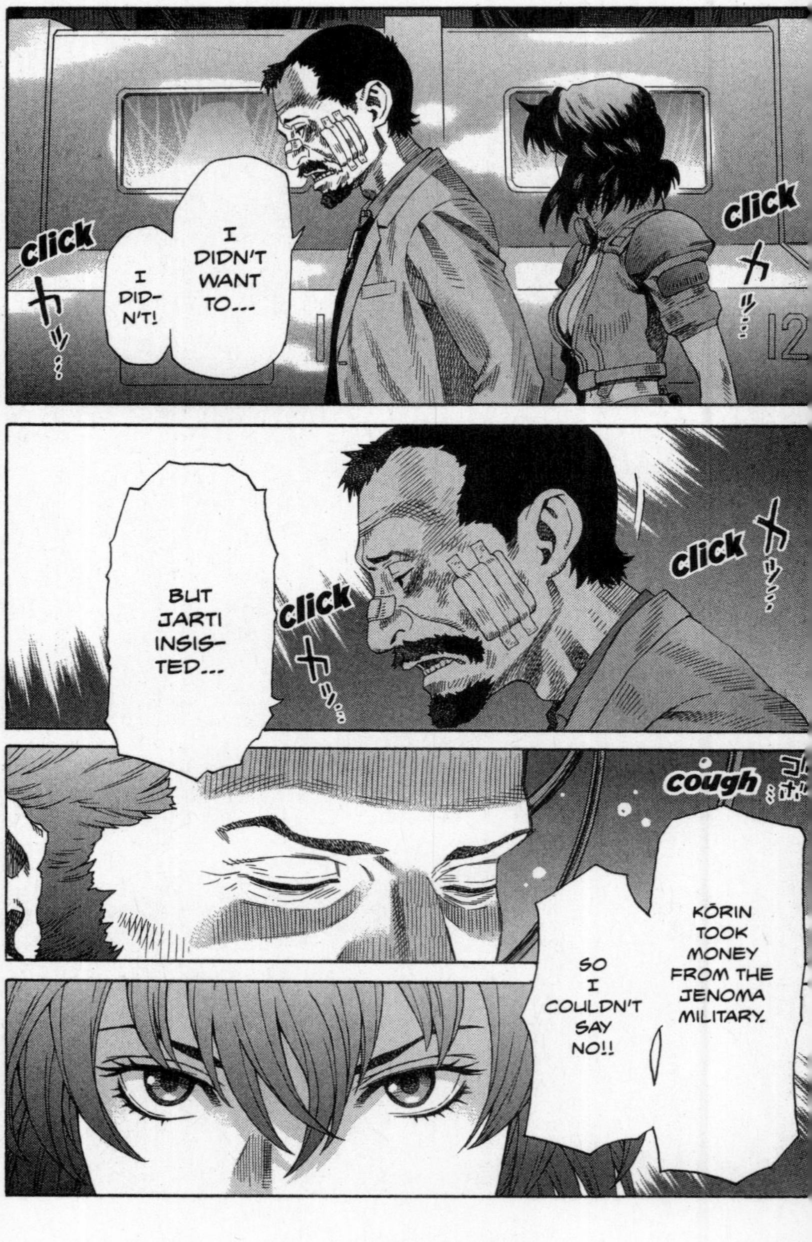
click
カッ…
I DIDN'T WANT TO...
I DID-N'T!
click
カッ…
click
カッ…
BUT JARTI INSIS-TED...
click
カッ…
cough
ゴボ…
KŌRIN TOOK MONEY FROM THE JENOMA MILITARY.
SO I COULDN'T SAY NO!!

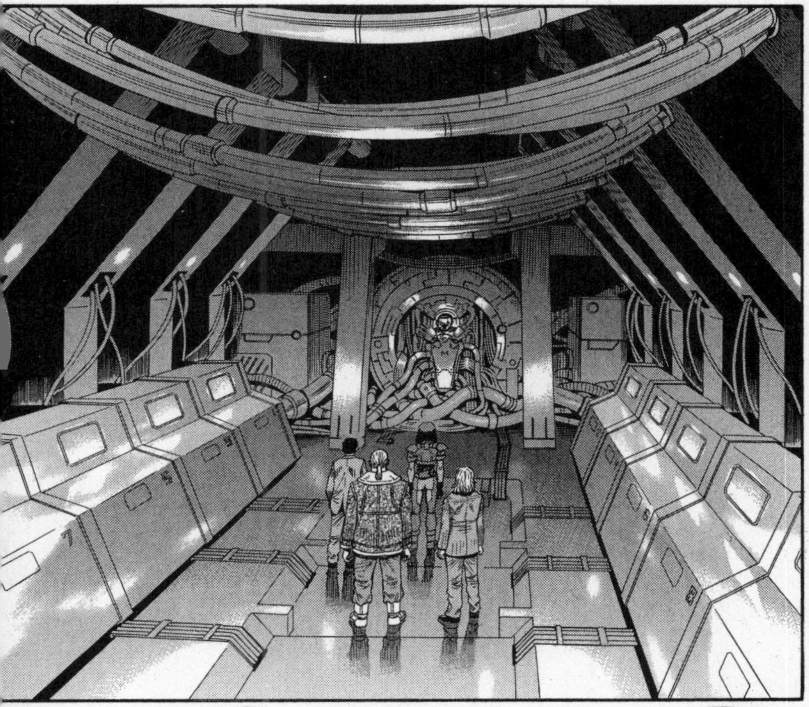

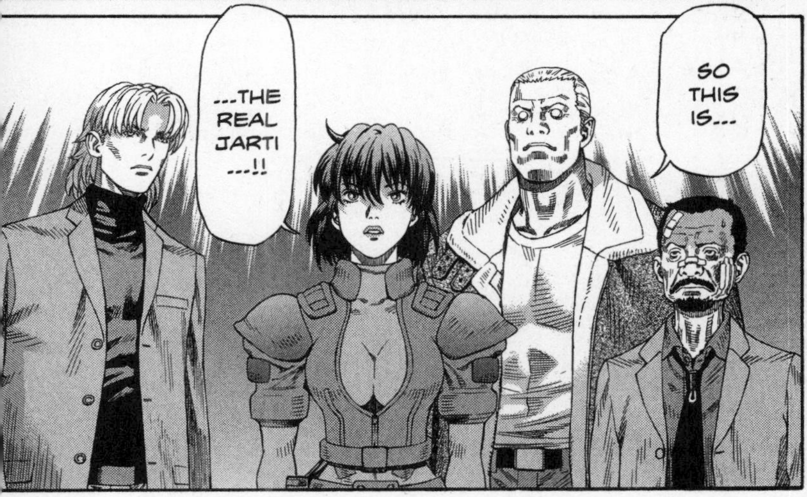
SO THIS IS...
...THE REAL JARTI ...!!

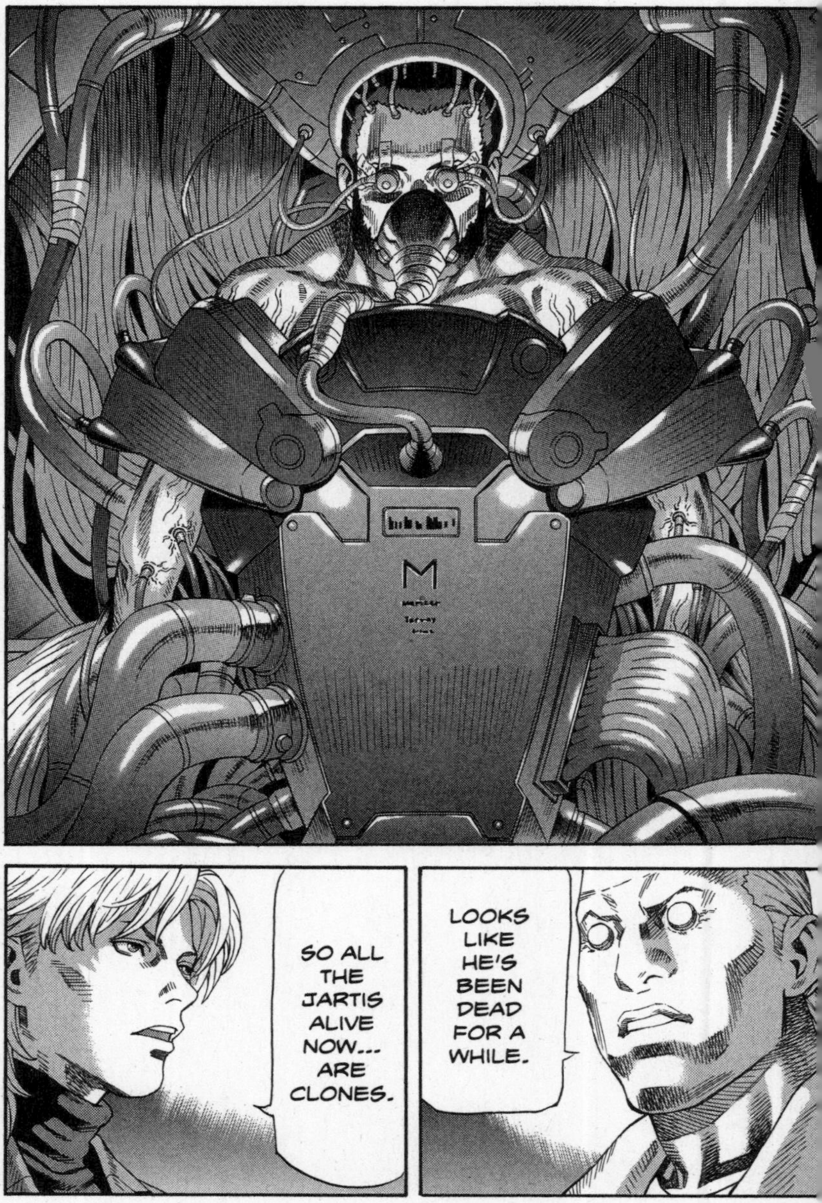
M
LOOKS LIKE HE'S BEEN DEAD FOR A WHILE.
SO ALL THE JARTIS ALIVE NOW... ARE CLONES.

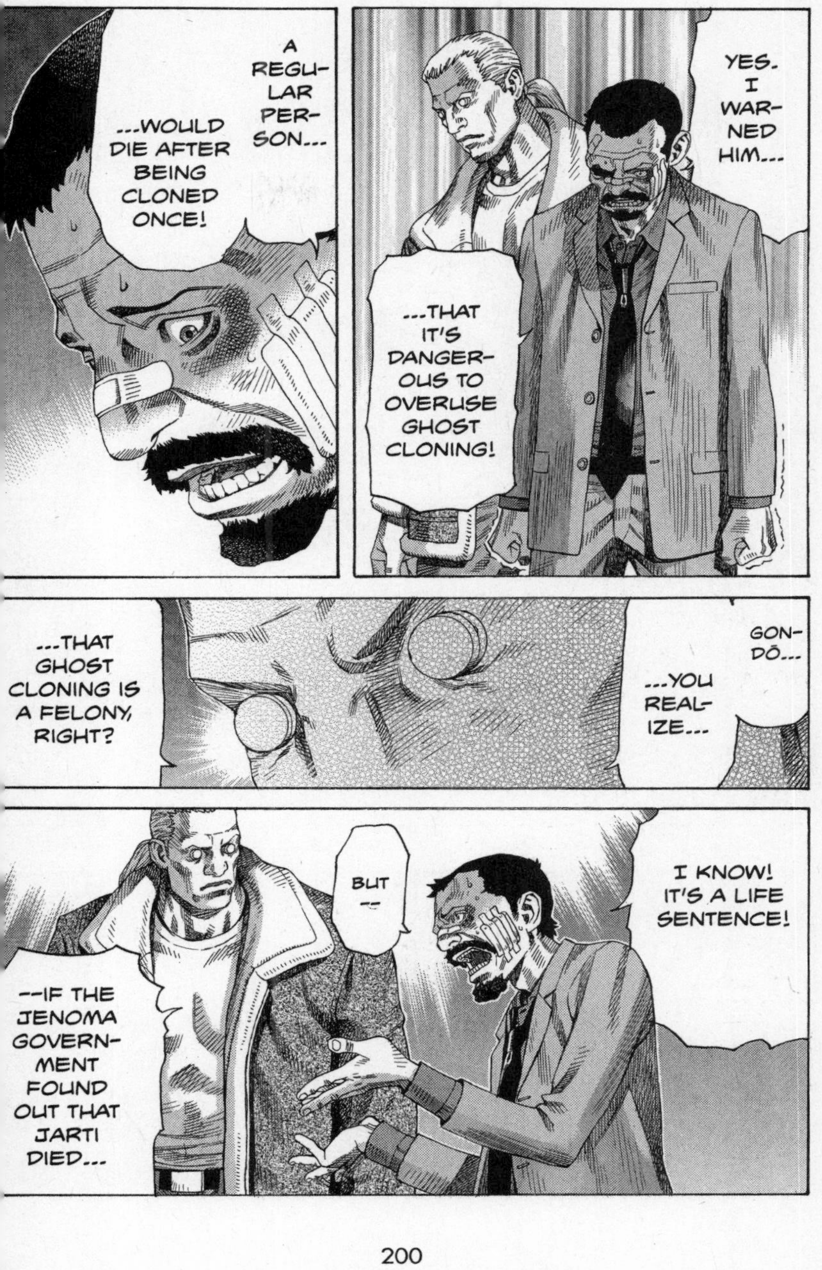
YES. I WARNED HIM...
...THAT IT'S DANGEROUS TO OVERUSE GHOST CLONING!
A REGULAR PERSON...
...WOULD DIE AFTER BEING CLONED ONCE!
GONDŌ...
...YOU REALIZE...
...THAT GHOST CLONING IS A FELONY, RIGHT?
I KNOW! IT'S A LIFE SENTENCE!
BUT --
--IF THE JENOMA GOVERNMENT FOUND OUT THAT JARTI DIED...

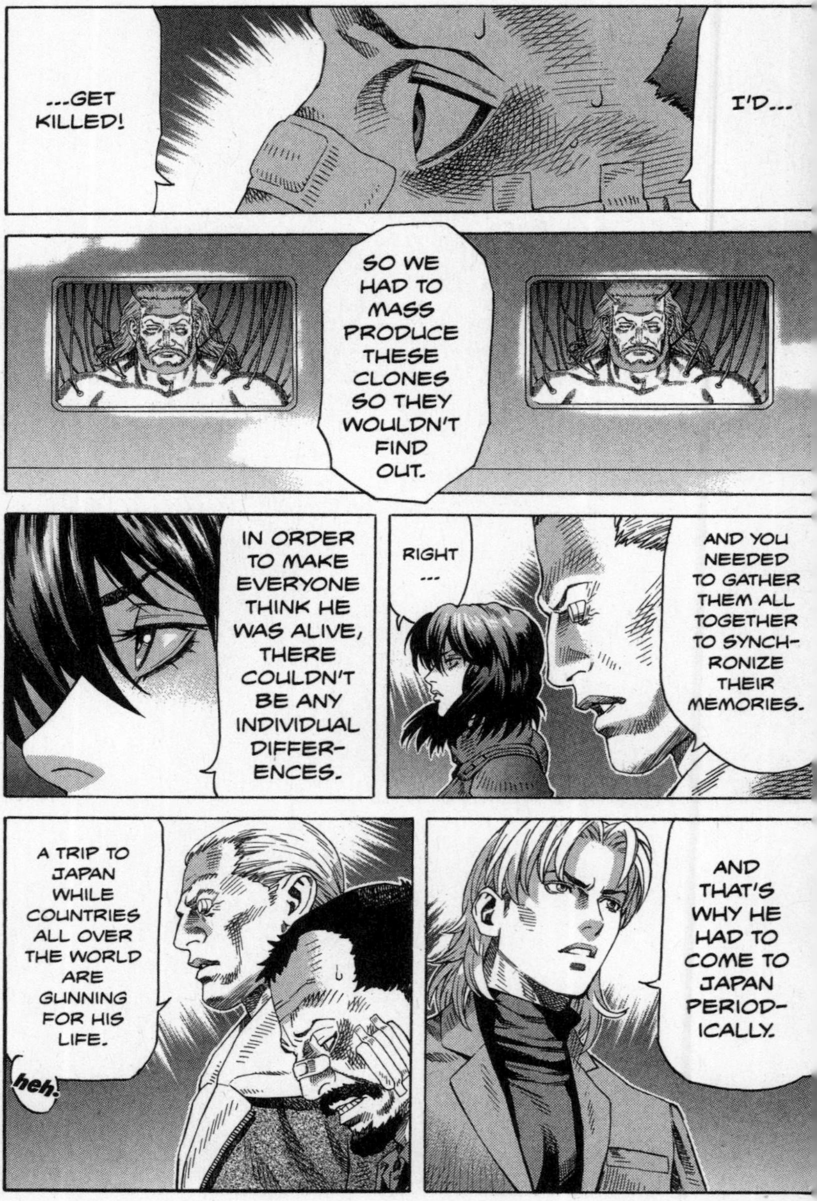
I'D...
...GET KILLED!
SO WE HAD TO MASS PRODUCE THESE CLONES SO THEY WOULDN'T FIND OUT.
AND YOU NEEDED TO GATHER THEM ALL TOGETHER TO SYNCHRONIZE THEIR MEMORIES.
RIGHT ---
IN ORDER TO MAKE EVERYONE THINK HE WAS ALIVE, THERE COULDN'T BE ANY INDIVIDUAL DIFFERENCES.
AND THAT'S WHY HE HAD TO COME TO JAPAN PERIODICALLY.
A TRIP TO JAPAN WHILE COUNTRIES ALL OVER THE WORLD ARE GUNNING FOR HIS LIFE.
heh.

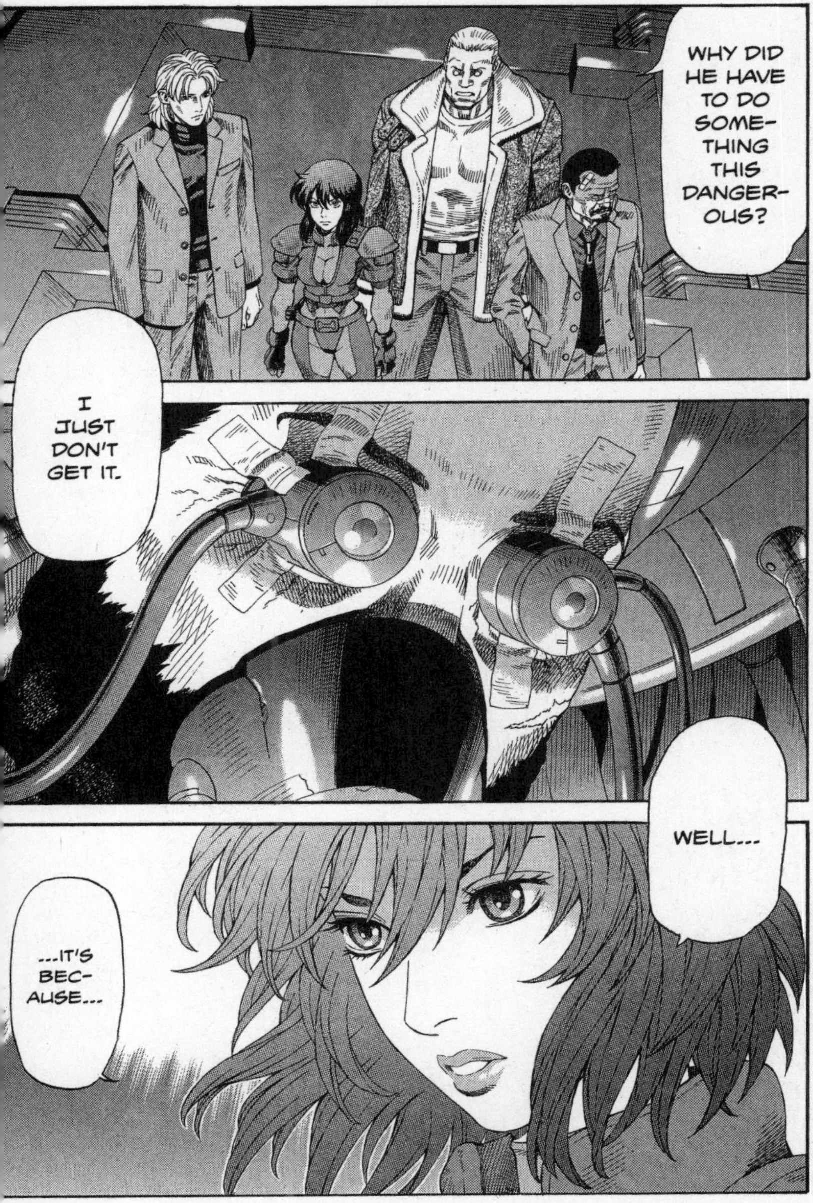
WHY DID HE HAVE TO DO SOME-THING THIS DANGER-OUS?
I JUST DON'T GET IT.
WELL...
...IT'S BEC-AUSE...

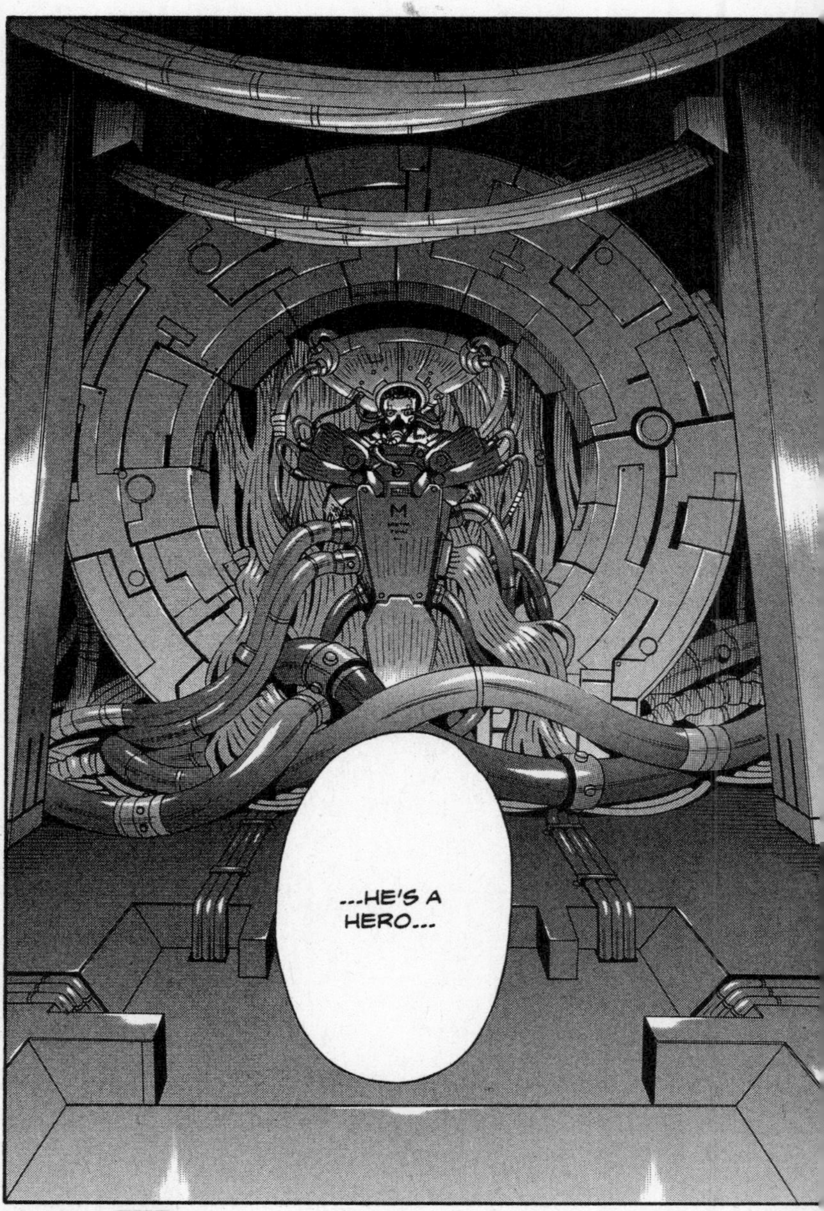
...HE'S A HERO...

#023: END

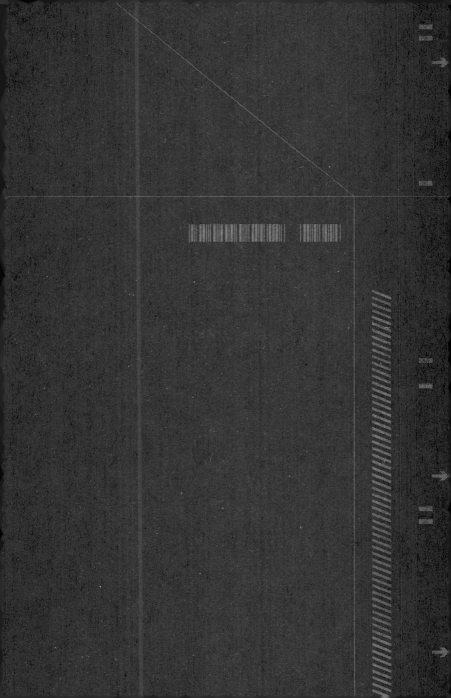

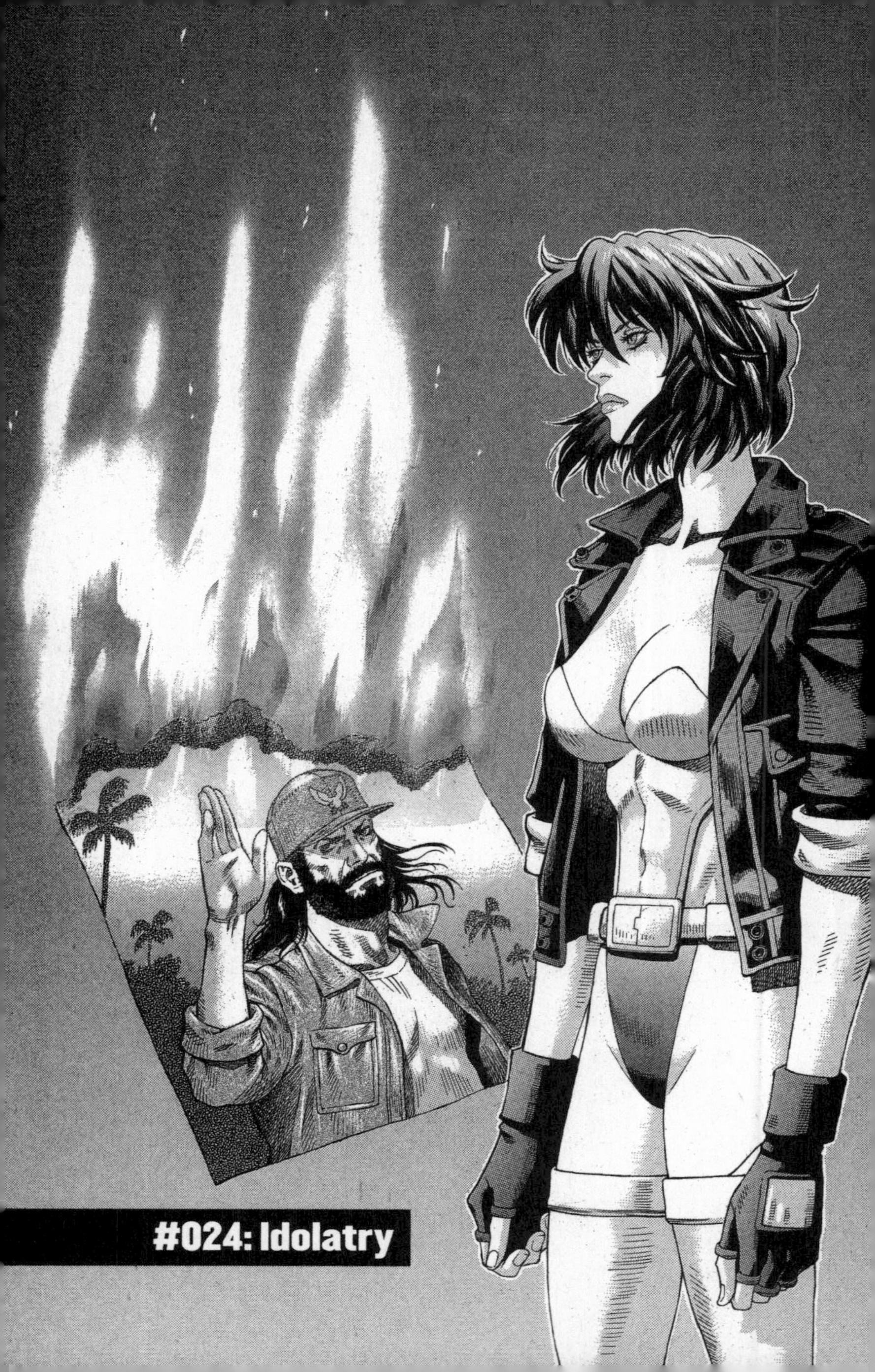

## #024: Idolatry

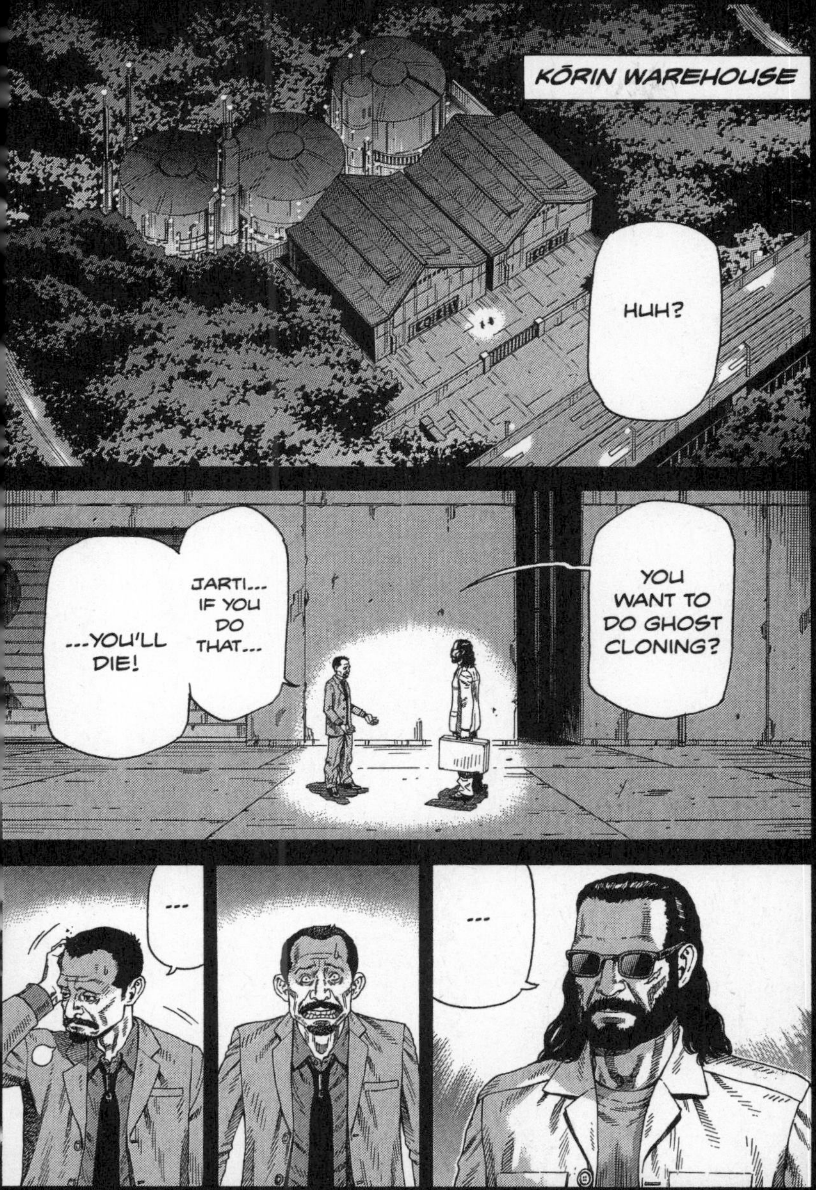
KŌRIN WAREHOUSE
HUH?
YOU WANT TO DO GHOST CLONING?
JARTI... IF YOU DO THAT...
...YOU'LL DIE!
...
...

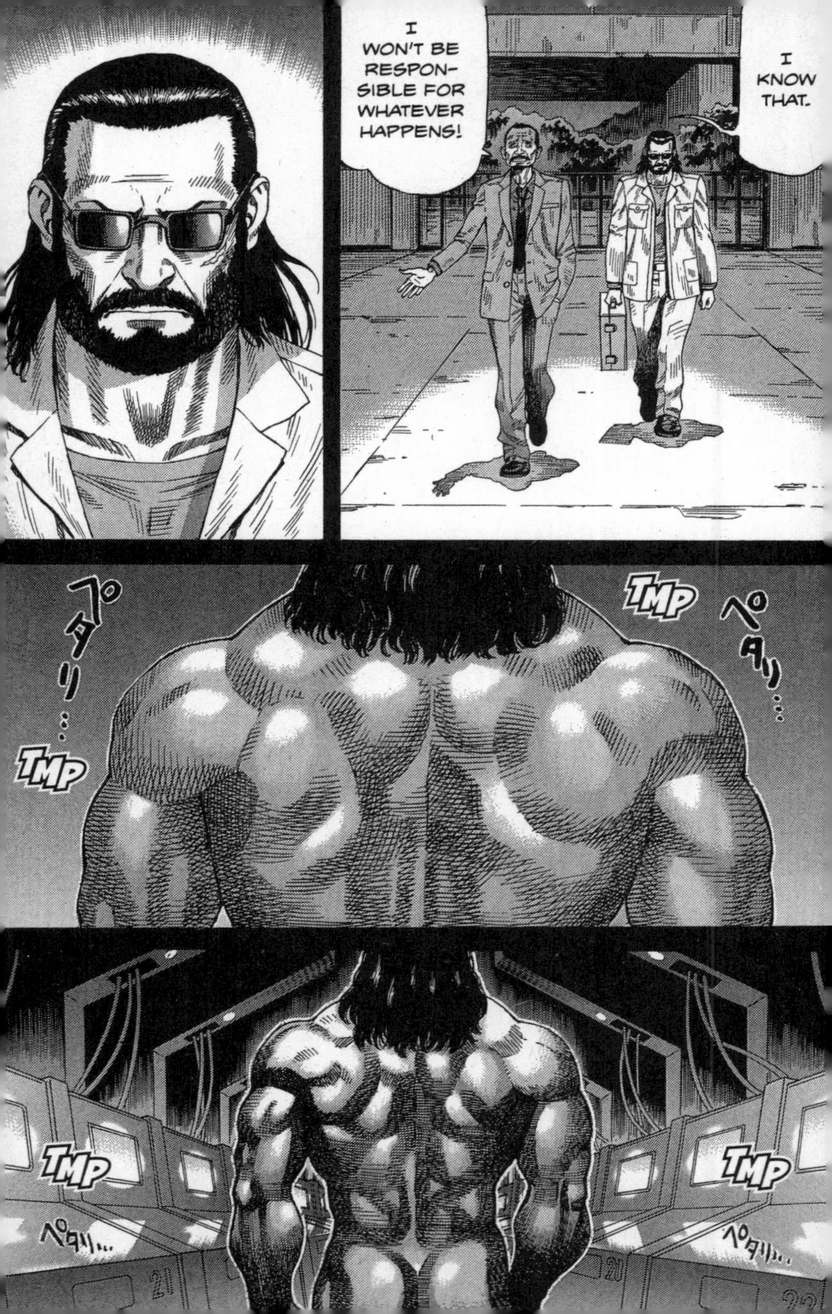
I WON'T BE RESPONSIBLE FOR WHATEVER HAPPENS!
I KNOW THAT.
TMP
ペタリ…
ペタリ…
TMP
TMP
ペタリ…
TMP
ペタリ…

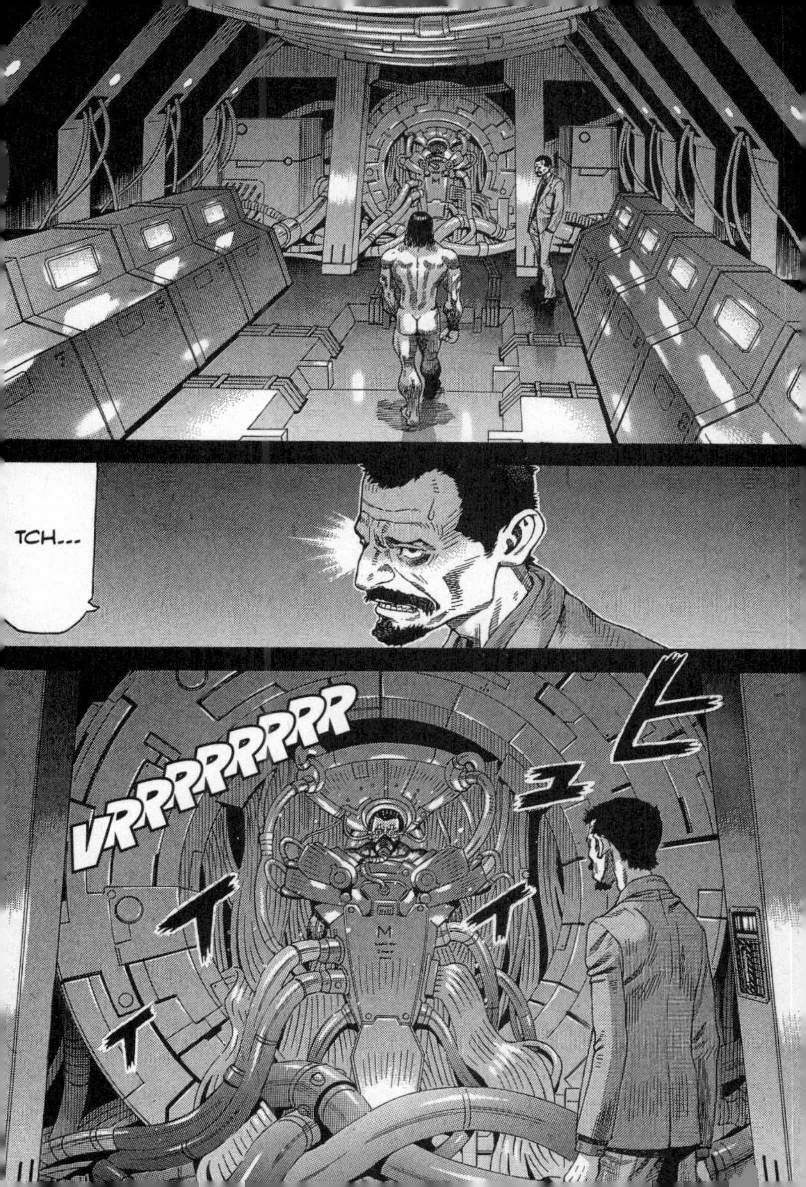
TCH...
VRRRRRRRR

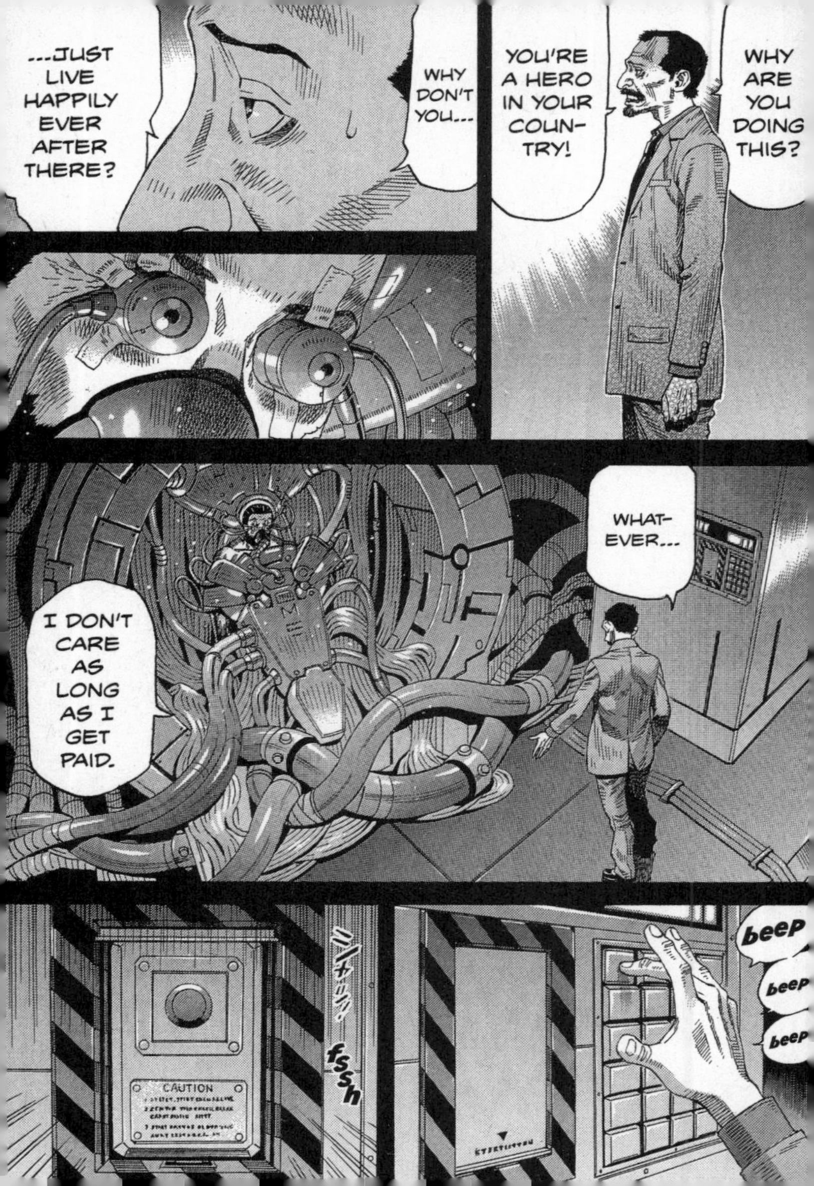
WHY ARE YOU DOING THIS?
YOU'RE A HERO IN YOUR COUN-TRY!
WHY DON'T YOU...
...JUST LIVE HAPPILY EVER AFTER THERE?
WHAT-EVER...
I DON'T CARE AS LONG AS I GET PAID.
beep
beep
beep
fssh
CAUTION

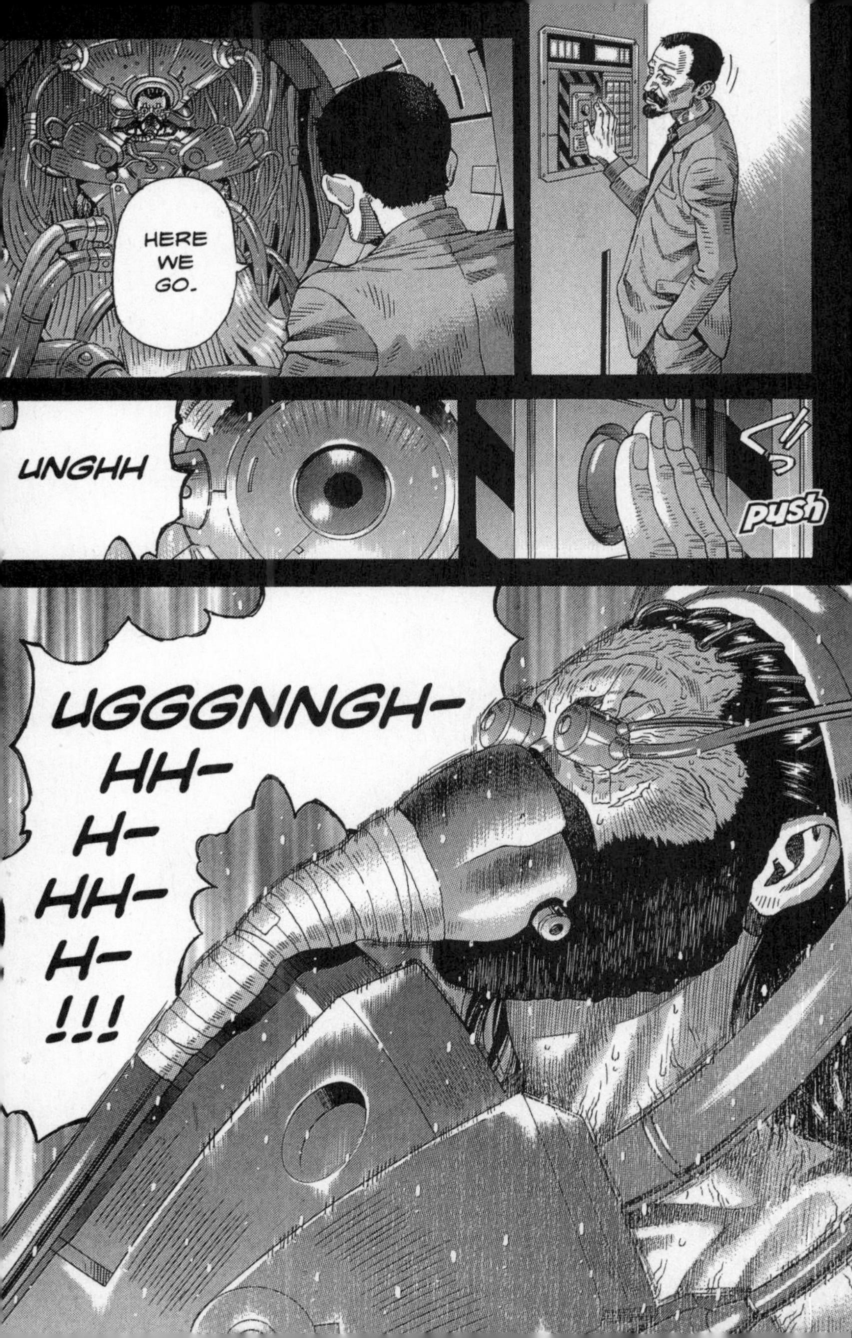
HERE WE GO.
push
UNGHH
UGGGNNGH-HH-H-HH-H-!!!

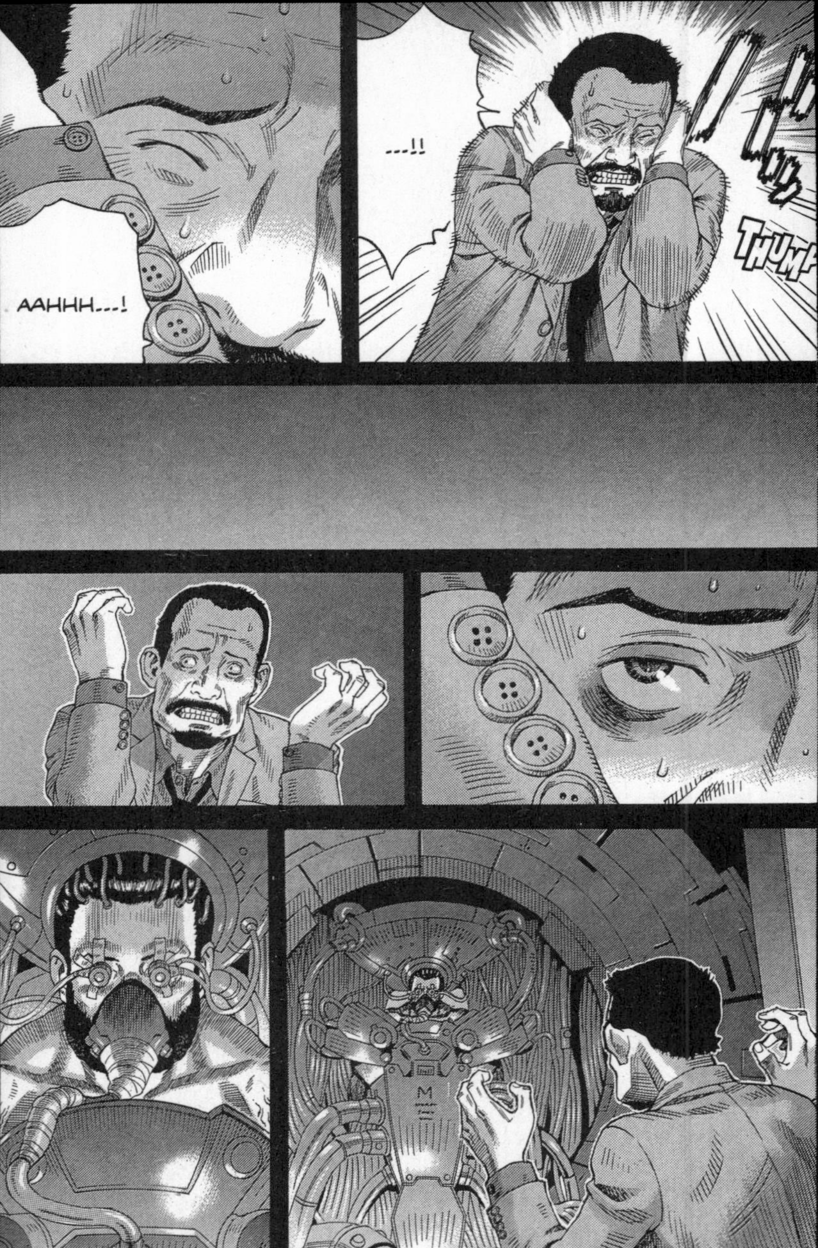
THUMP
---!!
AAHHH---!

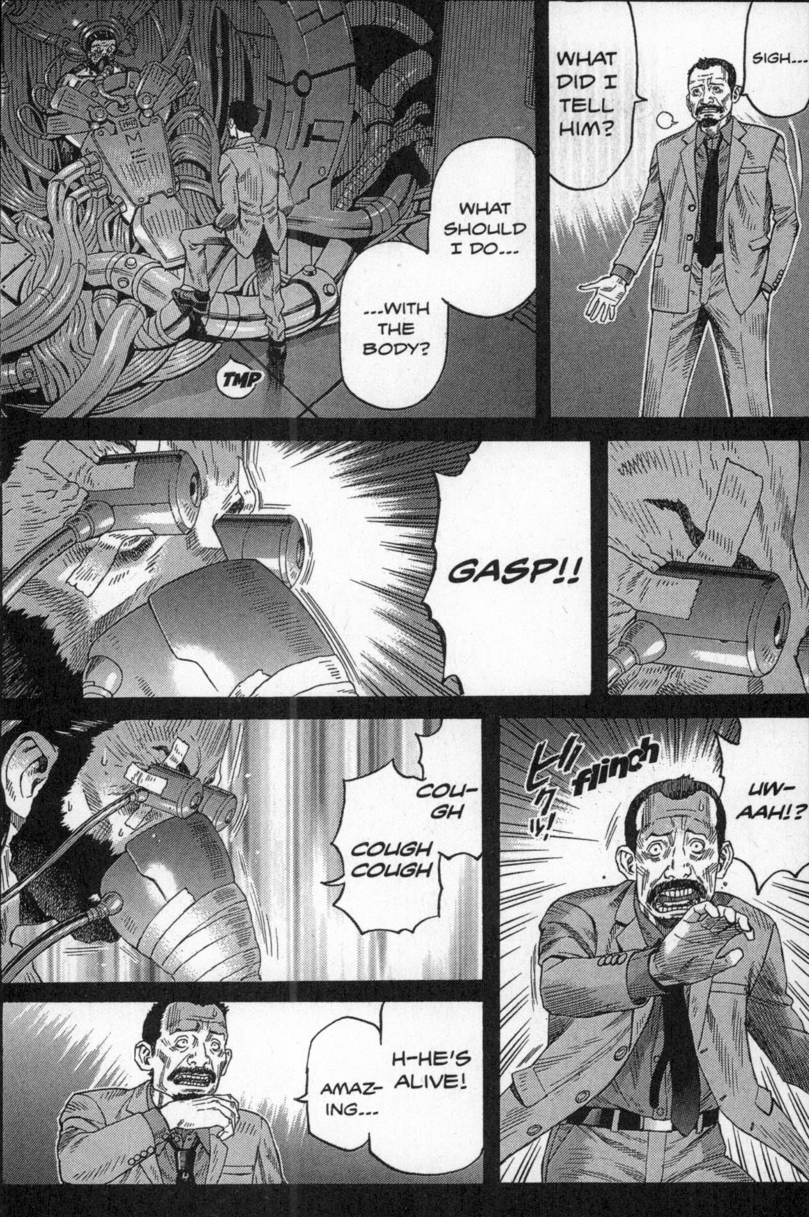
SIGH...
WHAT DID I TELL HIM?
WHAT SHOULD I DO...
...WITH THE BODY?
TMP
GASP!!
COUGH-GH
COUGH COUGH
ビクッ!
flinch
UW-AAH!?
H-HE'S ALIVE!
AMAZ-ING...

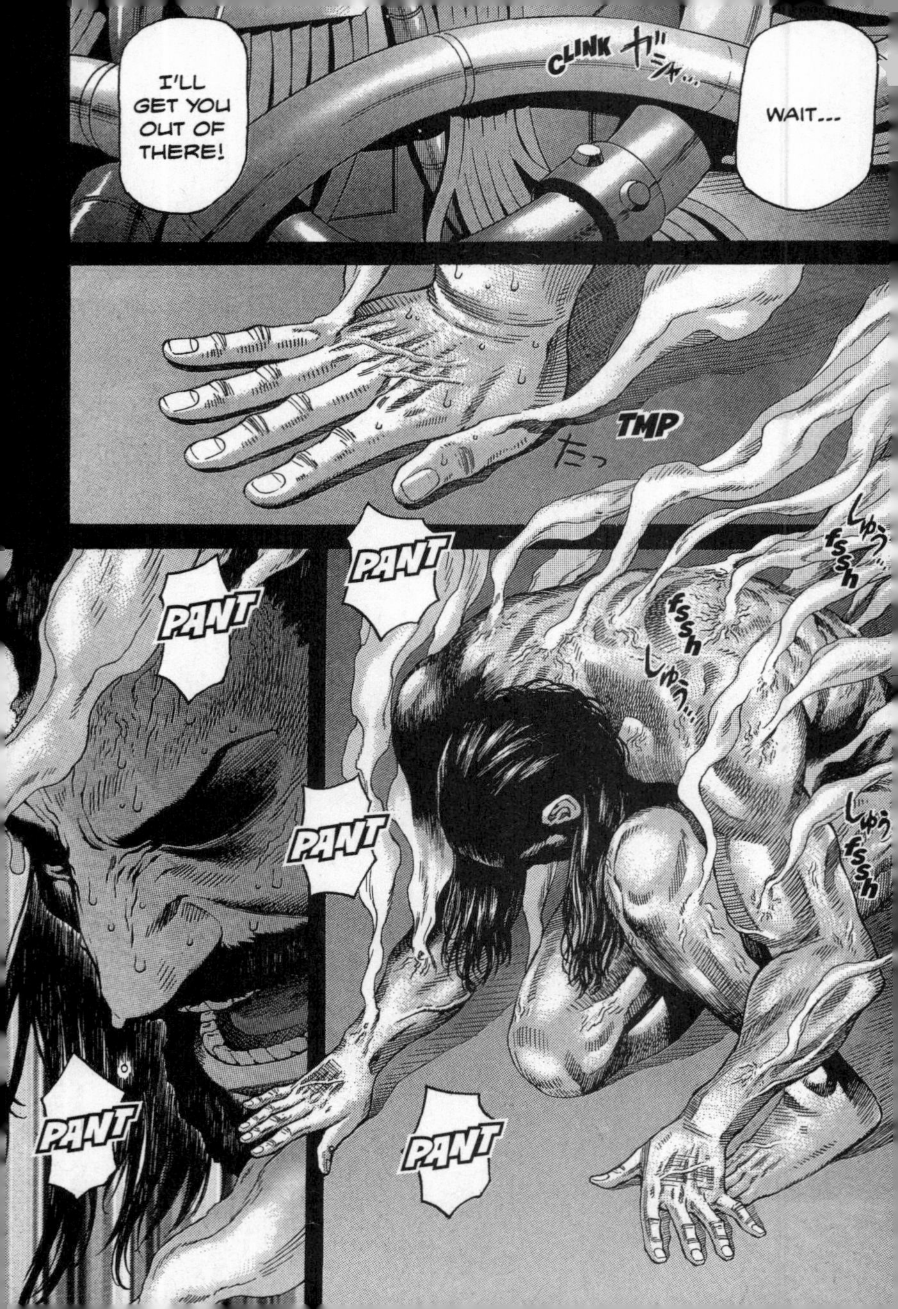
WAIT...
CLINK ガシャ...
I'LL GET YOU OUT OF THERE!
TMP
たっ
PANT
しゅう fsssh
fsssh しゅう...
しゅう fsssh
PANT
PANT
PANT
PANT

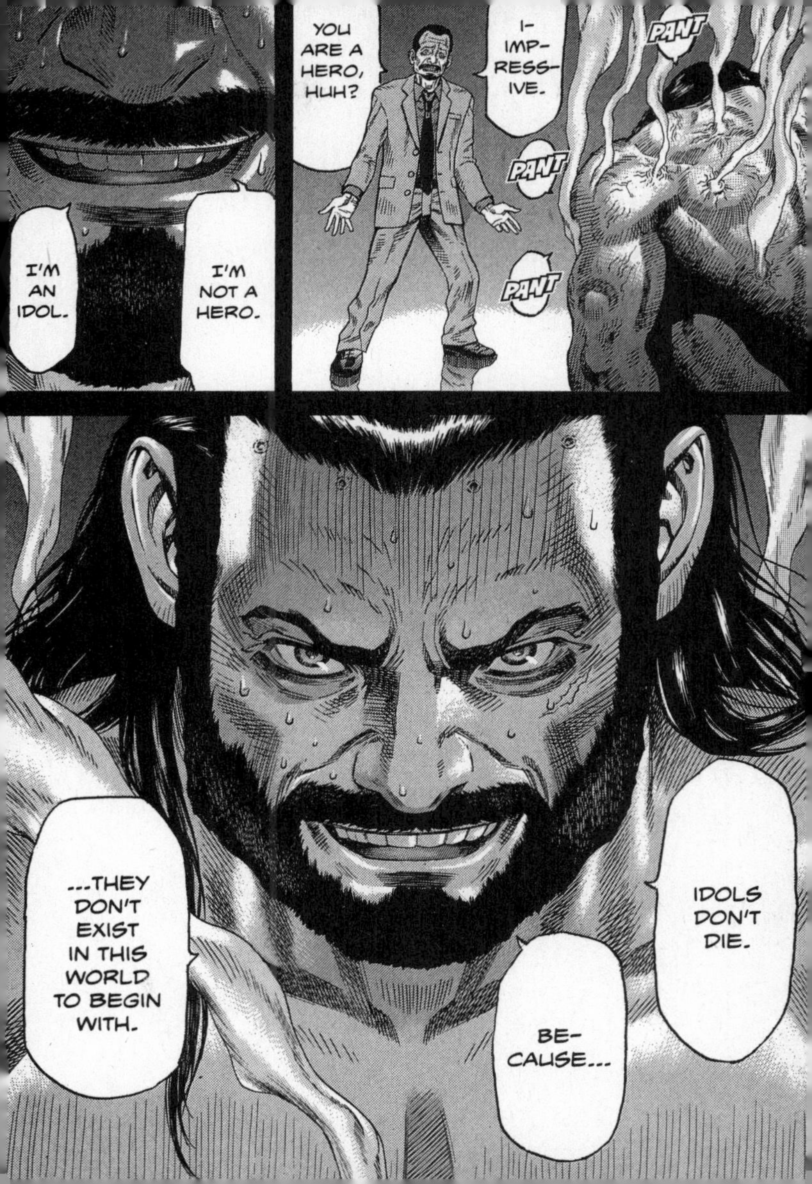
PANT
I-IMP-RESS-IVE.
YOU ARE A HERO, HUH?
PANT
PANT
I'M NOT A HERO.
I'M AN IDOL.
IDOLS DON'T DIE.
BE-CAUSE...
...THEY DON'T EXIST IN THIS WORLD TO BEGIN WITH.

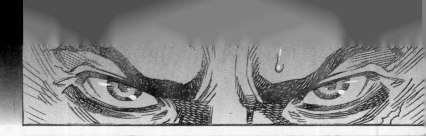

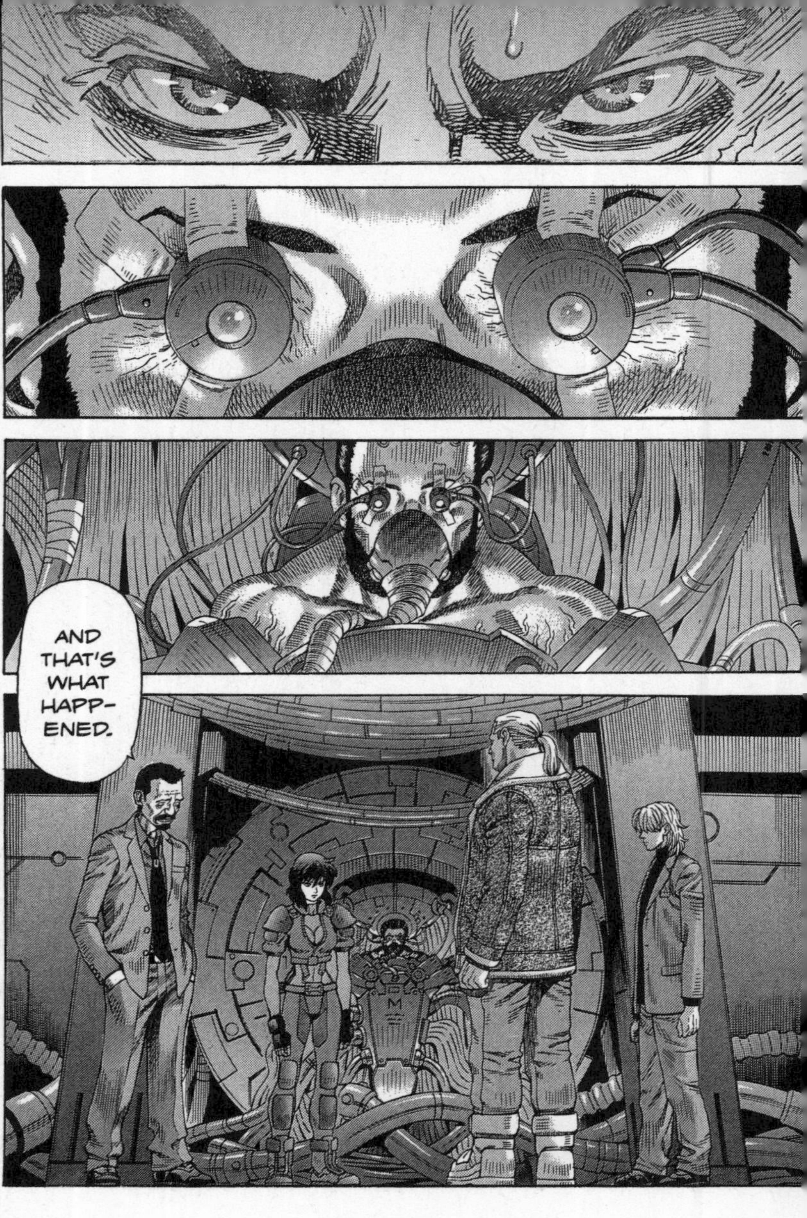
AND THAT'S WHAT HAPP- ENED.

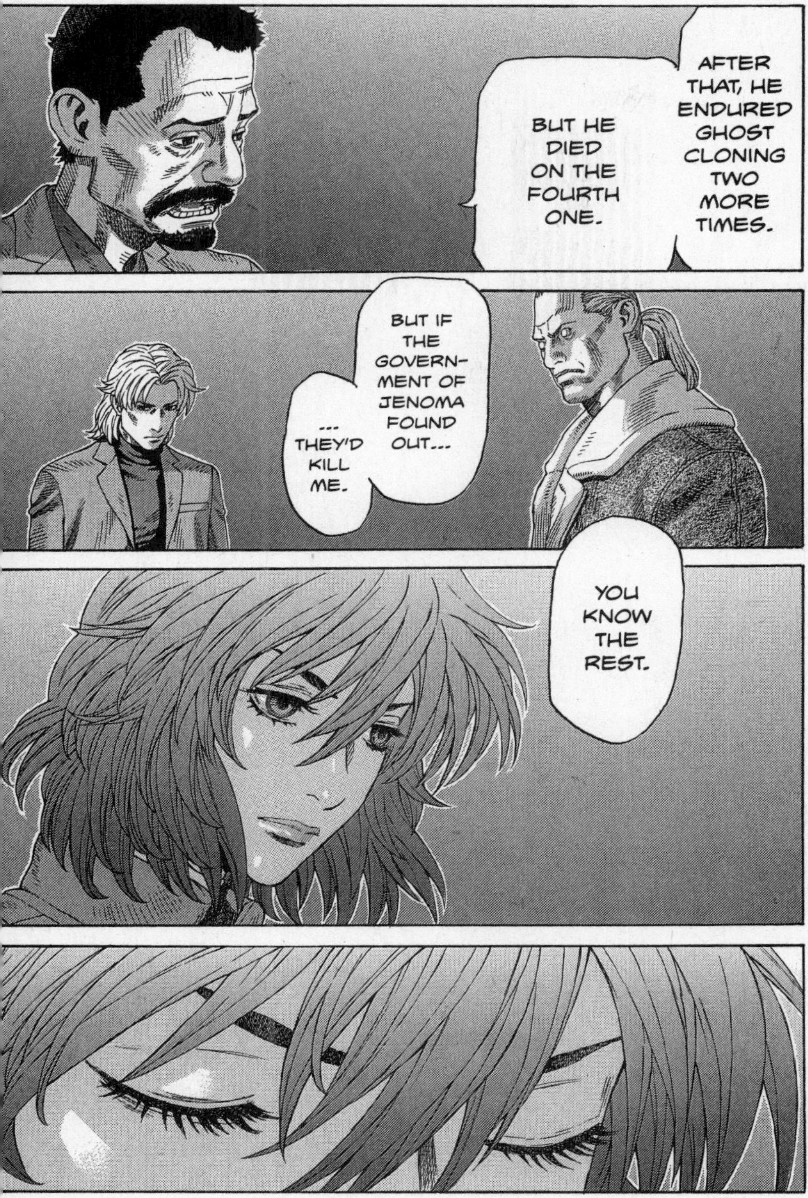
AFTER THAT, HE ENDURED GHOST CLONING TWO MORE TIMES.
BUT HE DIED ON THE FOURTH ONE.
BUT IF THE GOVERN-MENT OF JENOMA FOUND OUT...
...THEY'D KILL ME.
YOU KNOW THE REST.

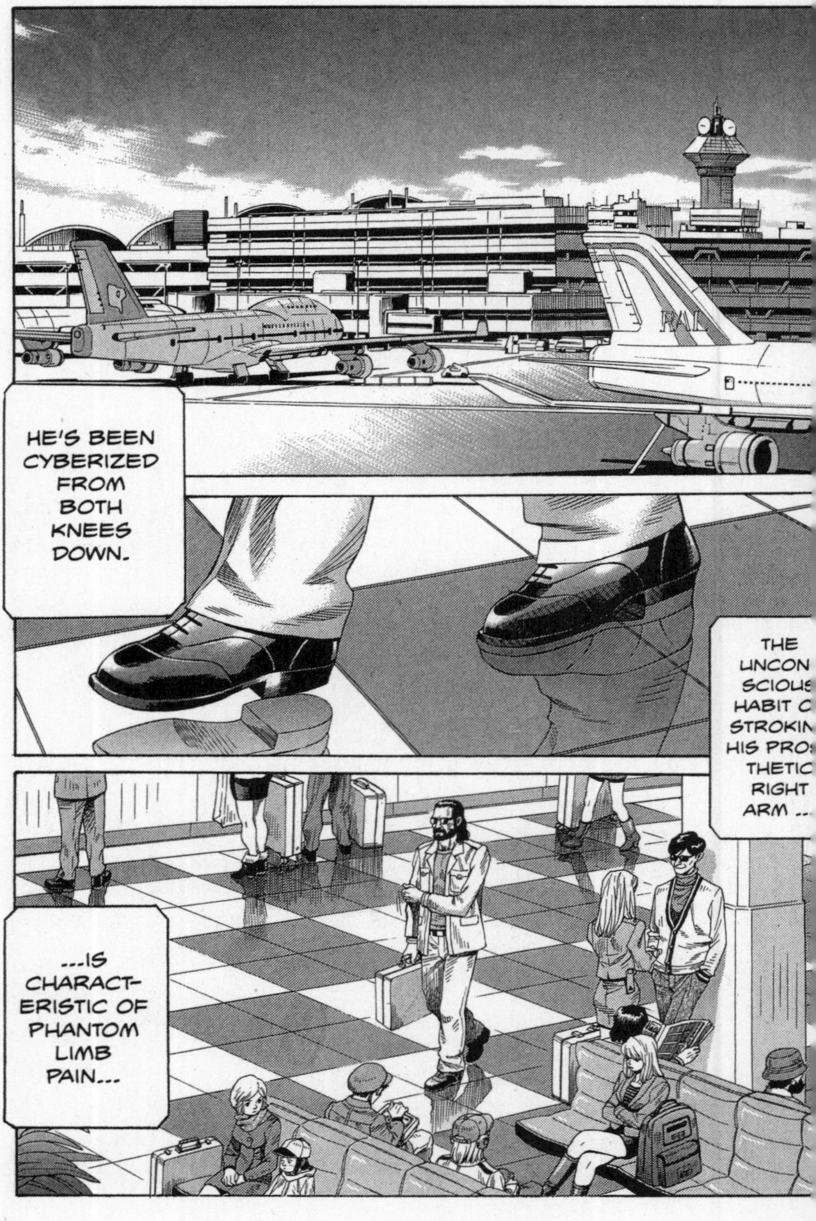
HE'S BEEN CYBERIZED FROM BOTH KNEES DOWN.
THE UNCON SCIOUS HABIT O STROKIN HIS PROS THETIC RIGHT ARM ...
...IS CHARACT-ERISTIC OF PHANTOM LIMB PAIN...

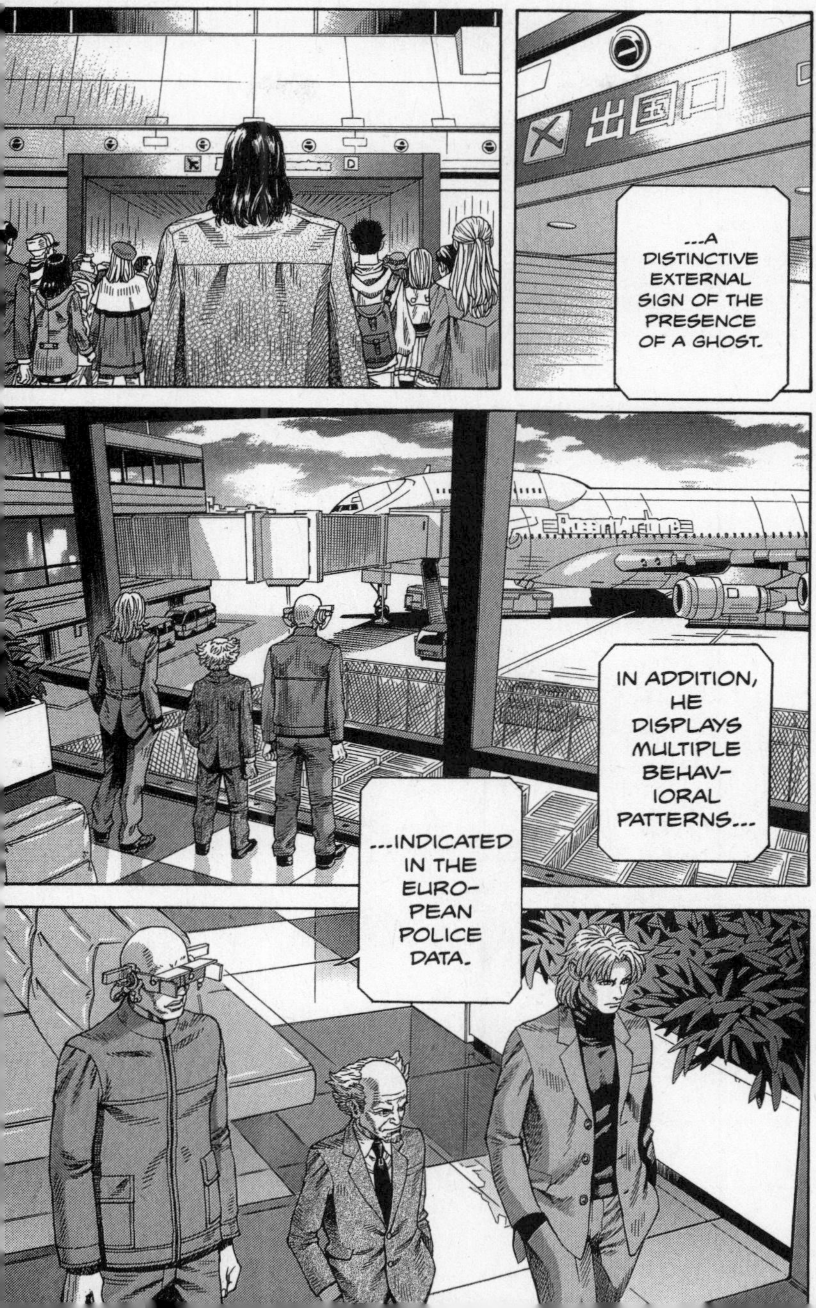
出国口
...A DISTINCTIVE EXTERNAL SIGN OF THE PRESENCE OF A GHOST.
IN ADDITION, HE DISPLAYS MULTIPLE BEHAV-IORAL PATTERNS...
...INDICATED IN THE EURO-PEAN POLICE DATA.

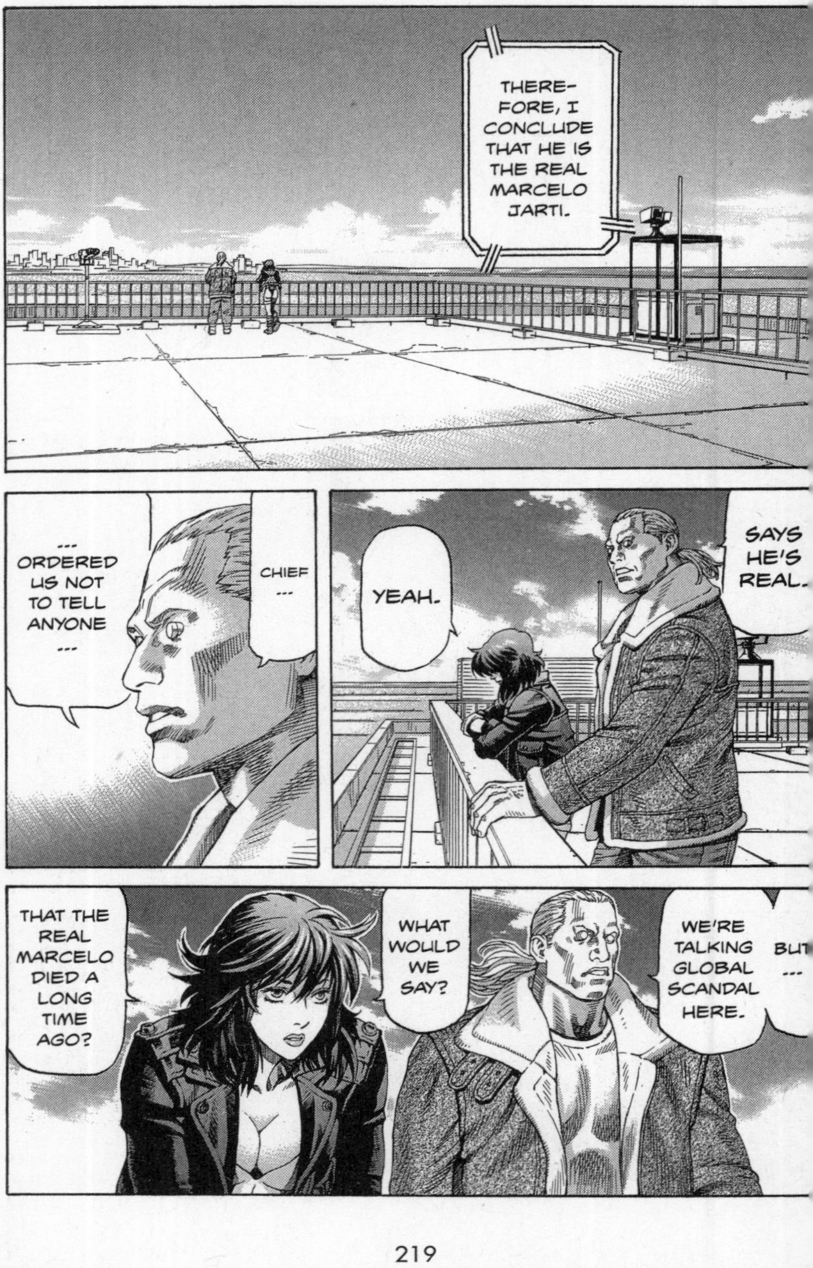
THERE-FORE, I CONCLUDE THAT HE IS THE REAL MARCELO JARTI.
SAYS HE'S REAL.
YEAH.
CHIEF ---
--- ORDERED US NOT TO TELL ANYONE ---
BUT ---
WE'RE TALKING GLOBAL SCANDAL HERE.
WHAT WOULD WE SAY?
THAT THE REAL MARCELO DIED A LONG TIME AGO?

ONLY ONES WHO'D BE HAPPY ARE THE DELTA FORCES AND THE SAS.

--- YEAH.

heh

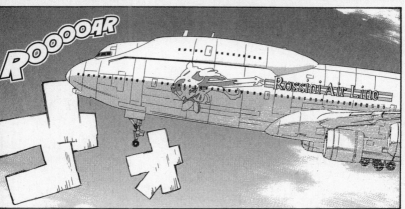

ROOOOAR

Rossini Air Line

HE SURVIVED GHOST CLONING THREE TIMES.

MUST BE ROUGH BEING A HERO.

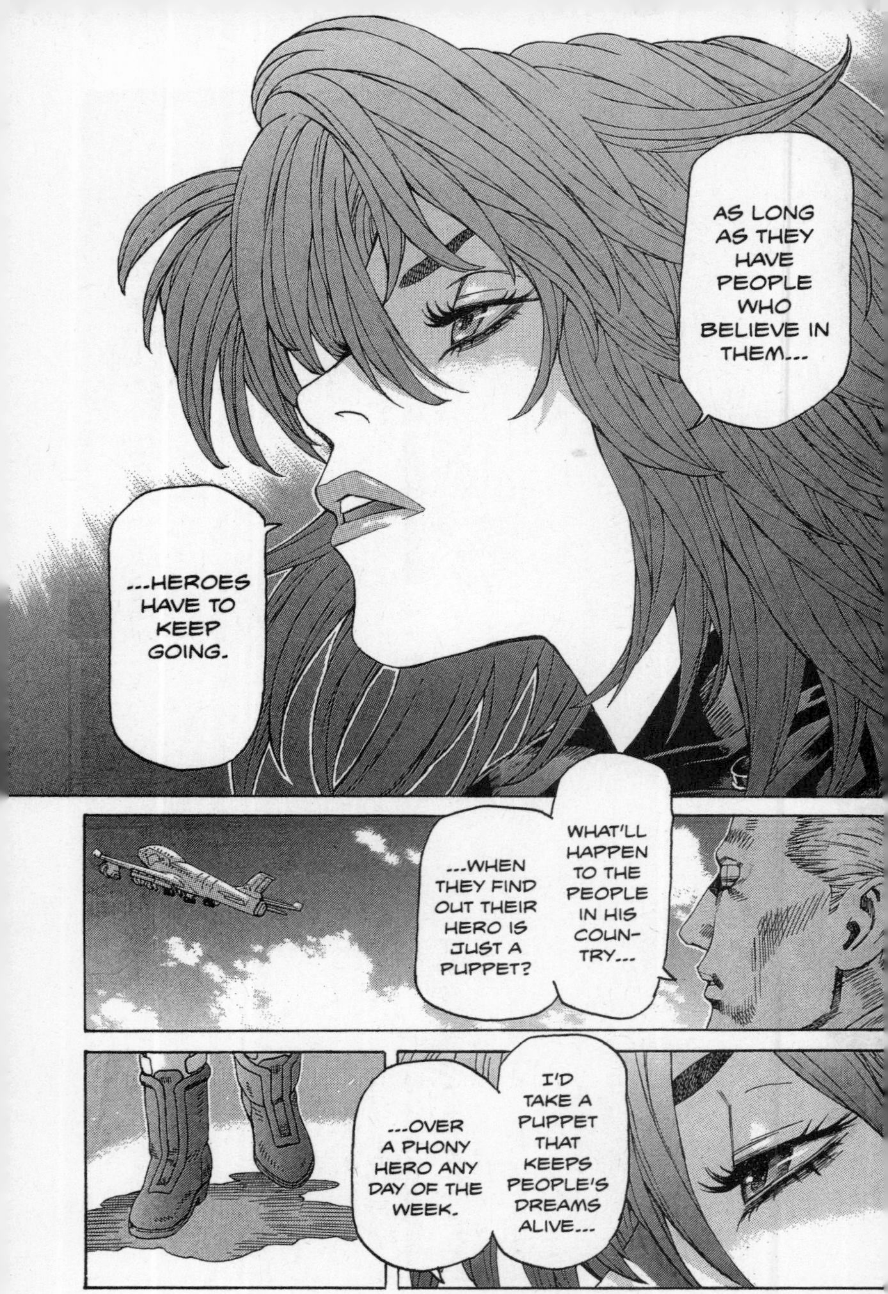
AS LONG AS THEY HAVE PEOPLE WHO BELIEVE IN THEM...
...HEROES HAVE TO KEEP GOING.
WHAT'LL HAPPEN TO THE PEOPLE IN HIS COUN-TRY...
...WHEN THEY FIND OUT THEIR HERO IS JUST A PUPPET?
I'D TAKE A PUPPET THAT KEEPS PEOPLE'S DREAMS ALIVE...
...OVER A PHONY HERO ANY DAY OF THE WEEK.

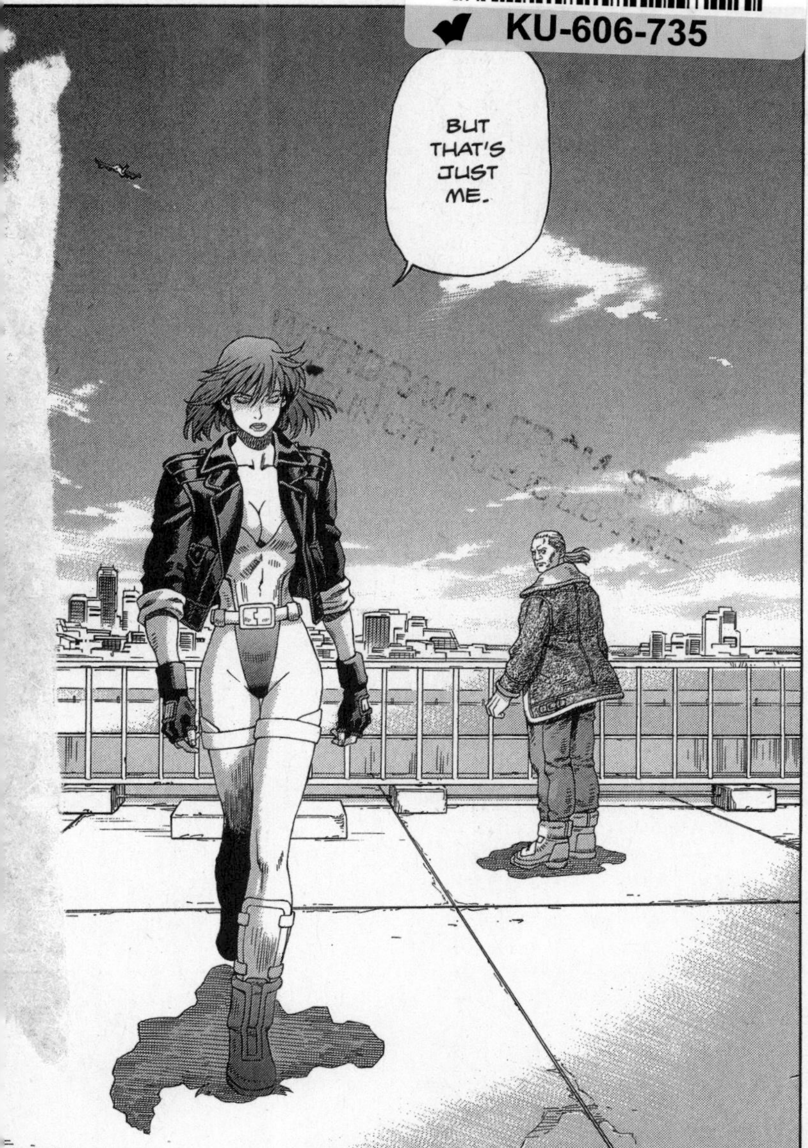
BUT THAT'S JUST ME.

Episode 3: IDOLATER END